Corporate Social Responsibility, Accountability and Governance

Global Perspectives

Corporate Social Responsibility, Accountability and Governance

GLOBAL PERSPECTIVES

EDITED BY ISTEMI DEMIRAG

Greenleaf
PUBLISHING

2 0 0 5

© 2005 Greenleaf Publishing Ltd

Published by Greenleaf Publishing Limited
Aizlewood's Mill
Nursery Street
Sheffield S3 8GG
UK
www.greenleaf-publishing.com

Printed on paper made from at least 75% post-consumer waste
using TCF and ECF bleaching.
Printed in Great Britain by William Clowes Ltd, Beccles, Suffolk.
Cover by LaliAbril.com.

British Library Cataloguing in Publication Data:
    A catalogue record for this book is available from the British Library.

ISBN 187471956X

Contents

Part 4: Corporate governance and its implications for regulators and civil society 247

**Part 5: Multinational companies and their implications for the new governance
structures, regulators and civil society** 313

Acknowledgements

I would like to express my sincere thanks to everyone who has contributed to this book. In particular, I am indebted to all the contributors who have not only given encouragement but who also acted as referees for some of the submissions to this book. I am also grateful to my colleagues at Queen's University Belfast and especially to the Head of the School of Management and Economics, Mr Jim Bradley, and Professor John Gardner, Dean of the Faculty of Legal, Social and Educational Sciences, for giving me generous sabbatical study leave, which enabled me to complete this book. I am also indebted to Professors Noel Hyndman and Donal McKillop, for their unfailing support and encouragement throughout this project. My thanks go to Mr Iqbal Khadaroo, who has not only helped the administration of this project and kept a watchful eye on the entire process of editing it, but also significantly contributed to three of the chapters in this book.

I have immensely benefited from my links with those at the Institute of Governance, Public Policy and Social Research at Queen's University Belfast. I am grateful for the opportunity given to me as board member of the institute to develop the ideas central to this work. In particular I would like to thank the head of the Institute, Professor Elizabeth Meehan, Deputy Director, John Barry, and also Professor Melvin Dubnick and Dr Justin O'Brien. They have each provided generous help and support for the project and advised on political science perspectives. I have appreciated their council and encouragement.

Finally, I am also grateful to Greenleaf Publishing, and in particular to John Stuart and Dean Bargh for their willingness to commission me to edit this book, and for the technical and design support during the last two years.

Istemi Demirag
June 2004

Preface

This book explores recent global developments in the field of corporate social responsibility, accountability and governance within the context of the emerging relationships between the state regulators, corporations and civil society. The perspectives and the case studies included in the book cover contemporary real issues from the United Kingdom, the United States, Canada, Germany, Sweden, Finland, the Netherlands, Brazil, Mexico, Russia and the Central Asian countries. The global perspective adopted here reflects and builds on urgent calls from public- and private-sector policy-makers as well as academics to develop better governance and accountability in business, social responsibility, sustainable development and in ethics.

This book is divided into five parts. In Part 1, the complex concepts of responsibility, accountability and governance are discussed, and in particular the presumed relationships between the state, the market and civil society in improving accountability and governance are explored and critiqued. Part 2 consists of chapters relating to corporate social responsibility and stakeholder theory. Part 3 is concerned with empirical studies covering governance structures, networking and corporate social responsibility. Part 4 includes chapters on corporate governance and its implications for regulators and civil society. Part 5 consists of chapters dealing with multinational companies and how their form impacts on national governance regimes, and a summary is provided with emerging international patterns of accountability and governance structures. Some comments are also made concerning the current state of research and recommendations for further scholarly directions traced.

Foreword

The 'business case' for corporate social responsibility, which suggests that socially and environmentally aware companies can expect to reap financial rewards, is seemingly gaining widespread acceptance within the business community. This is particularly apparent in the ever-increasing number of prominent companies parading their social, ethical and environmental credentials by producing, paper or web-based, social and environmental, or sustainability, reports. In so doing, reporting companies claim, they are demonstrating a clear commitment to transparency and accountability to their key stakeholder groups. However, in the prevailing voluntaristic, business case-centred climate within which such initiatives are taking place, little thought appears to have gone into the question as to how stakeholders, other than the capital provider group, can actually use corporate disclosures offered in order to hold management accountable for the social and environmental consequences of their actions. While much corporate rhetoric abounds concerning notions of stakeholder dialogue and engagement, rigorous analysis of the governance implications of their claimed commitment to the principles of corporate social responsibility is largely conspicuous by its absence.

It is the 'missing link' between CSR (and associated reporting initiatives) and governance mechanisms that are capable of embracing true stakeholder accountability that this edited volume seeks to explore. A wide range of case studies, drawing on experiences of both public- and private-sector initiatives in Europe, the United States, Canada, South America and Asia, offer insightful analysis of the complex relationships between the state, the market and civil society in the development of CSR, accountability and sustainable development. A common feature of a number of these case studies lies in the emphasis placed on stakeholder network and partnership approaches in order to ensure that sustainable development may be conceptualised as something more than the 'business as usual' approach to which so many corporations appear to be wedded. However, quite rightly in this writer's opinion, a number of contributors are also at pains to emphasise that such networks and partnerships do not in themselves preclude the need for government regulation in appropriate circumstances. The essential point here is that without some countervailing power being offered to the ever-growing corporate domination of the new globalised economy little can be achieved in terms of introducing meaningful social and environmental accountability as 'other voices' continue to be ignored.

A further particularly noteworthy feature of the book lies in the multidisciplinary perspective employed in order to analyse the political, social, economic, technological, legal and organisational shaping of CSR. The complexities underpinning the concept are thereby clearly drawn out and the gross over-simplifications inherent in the prevailing consultancy-driven, business-case literature painfully exposed. Above all, the book offers a sound, practically and theoretically informed contribution to public policy debate.

Professor David L. Owen
International Centre for Corporate Social Responsibility
Nottingham University Business School

Introduction

RESPONSIBILITY, ACCOUNTABILITY AND GOVERNANCE: THE PRESUMED CONNECTIONS WITH THE STATE, THE MARKET AND CIVIL SOCIETY AND AN OVERVIEW

Istemi Demirag

Queen's University Belfast, UK

The recent collapse of major American companies and the financial scandals that followed have been a major cause for concern in a vast number of studies recently undertaken on accountability, governance and regulations. Moreover, the issues of sustainable development, social corporate accountability and responsibility, and public-sector reforms have also been at the top of governments' agendas in the past decade or more. There have been growing calls from regulators, civil society and academics alike to ensure that good governance, greater accountability and ethical norms are embedded into corporations' codes of practice. The major failures in regulatory mechanisms or markets have also contributed to major environmental disasters (Bhopal; Union Carbide Corporation 1984) and scandals over child labour exploitation (Nike in Indonesia) by multinational companies in developing countries. These failures gave rise to the need to explore alternative forms of governance and regulations worldwide. The contributors to this book have come together in an attempt to highlight some of these issues from a global perspective, to provide a better understanding of them, and to make some tentative suggestions towards their solutions.

This book assesses the usefulness and robustness of some of the relevant concepts and theory, and, by the use of international case studies, illustrates some of the difficulties faced in implementing the theory in practice. This book also helps by 'grounding' some of these concepts and theories. It tests their conceptual soundness on a case-by-case basis in the search for developing more useful theories in the fields of governance, accountability, social responsibility, ethics and regulation.

We define 'corporate social responsibility' as corporate attitudes and responsibilities to society for social, ethical and environmental issues, including sustainable developments. Gray *et al.* (1995) define social reporting as the process of communicating the social and environmental consequences of organisations' economic actions to particular interest groups within society and to society at large. The concepts of accountability and responsibility are often used interchangeably in the accounting literature and very little definitional agreement exists (Lindkvist and Llewellyn 2003). Accountability is frequently associated with the execution of responsibilities and being answerable for them (Alexander 1996). The US Government Accounting Standards Board defines accountability as 'being obliged to explain one's actions, to justify what has been done' (GASB 1987: 21). Stewart (1984), Romzek and Dubnick (1987), and Sinclair (1995) have grouped accountability into various forms, which include: communal, contractual, legal, managerial, organisational, professional, personal, political and public. The forms of accountability differ in terms of dealing with the questions of 'to whom' the accountor is accountable (e.g. Mayston 1993), and 'for what' (Pallot 1992, 2003; Coy and Pratt 1998; Broadbent and Laughlin 2003). Jordan and Tuijl (2000) distinguish accountability from responsibility on grounds that the latter is a normative concept and that accountability has formal obligations embedded within its definition. Bovens (1998: 30-31) regards accountability as a form of responsibility that meets two criteria: blameworthiness and choice on the part of the individual being held to account. In contrast, Dubnick (1998) regards responsibility as a subtype of a more general concept of accountability. Unless there is some special purpose, we will use accountability and responsibility interchangeably throughout this book.

As we will see below, management of companies for sustainable development or social corporate accountability cannot rely only on 'good governance' or 'state regulations'. There is a growing literature emphasising the significance of a number of evolutionary networks between markets, states and civil societies, through a learning process and communication with stakeholders, in search for better governance mechanisms (Demirag et al. 2000). Developing relationships between businesses, states and civil society is not only a dynamic but also a complex process (Clark and Demirag 2002; Demirag and Solomon 2003). Moreover, the exact nature of the mechanism(s) involved is contingent rather than preset. The assumed relationship between governance systems and socially responsible behaviour or sustainable investments by corporations is problematic at best. For example, the modernisation by governments and various New Public Management reforms have been adopted in a variety of jurisdictions on the assumption that such changes would result in greater transparency, social responsibility, democracy and ethical behaviour in both private and public sectors (Demirag et al. 2004). Dubnick (2002), however, argues that accountability-based reforms have been used 'promiscuously' as a panacea for problems of governance without recourse to empirically grounded and tested theory. It would seem that not only are the concepts of governance and accountability very complex and problematic but their presumed relationships with corporate social responsibility, sustainable development and other socially desirable objectives may be questionable.

Contributors to this volume have also argued, as we will see in the following review, that accountability and governance structures may provide useful complementary mechanisms to influence behaviour and performance of companies—while not suggesting that better governance can be a surrogate for government regulations.

The following sections provide a short summary of the chapters included in the book.

In Part 1 (Emerging governance structures, risks and networking), Bertels and Vredenburg explore the deficiencies associated with the concept of management in the context of corporate social responsibility, based on traditional organisational structures in governance literature. Highlighting the fact that governance is a much more complex phenomenon than management, they seek to broaden the notion of governance by considering the implications of informal structures developed among various stakeholders. They argue that governance, in its broader context, includes 'the various structures, processes, systems and cultures through which an organisation sets out its objectives, processes, implements its objectives and monitors its performance'.

Referring to the earlier work by Garcia and Vredenburg (2003) and Vredenburg and Westley (2002), they point out that, when multiple stakeholders are involved in decision-making, often with different objectives and interests, it is important to understand the complex web of interdependency, inter-organisational and inter-sectoral collaboration needed to achieve both singular and common purposes. Citing Gray's (1985, 1989) seminal work on facilitating collaboration between organisations and multi-party situations, they outline three sequential phases of inter-organisational domain development: problem setting, direction setting and structuring.

In order to gain wider support for their assertion of the need to increase the boundaries of governance in public-sector issues, Bertels and Vredenburg examine three case studies of water supply systems in Canada, involving a municipal department, a public–private partnership and a municipally owned corporation. The case studies cover a range of organisational structures. In each case, no overarching organisation was able to influence or control the whole domain, and domain-based collaborative governance mechanisms have supported the formal structures. They conclude that, for the domain-based governance to work effectively, each participant must participate in the problem definition process, acknowledge their dependence on the other actors and participate in the formation of a shared vision of the conceptual boundaries. In addition, trust must be earned from the other participants before the benefits of domain-based collaborative governance can be realised.

Meyer draws our attention to some general problems of network regulation. These include the evolution of networks, which may challenge the balance needed for successful co-operation; the interpersonal relationships between the negotiators that may lead to clique building and estrangement from organisation members; and the fact that networks may not be the most efficient modes of decision-making in comparison with 'market' or 'hierarchy' modes. Meyer argues that 'good' governance in multi-actor policy networks requires adequate communication tools within and between organisations, to ensure co-ordination towards the common goal of 'good' decisions. The communicative process between the board and members in civil-society organisations needs to develop policies to deal with social responsibilities and secure social integration by representing the interests of their target groups. Meyer points out that our understanding of this process is hampered by a lack of research. Based on his evaluation of environmental communication within the communication structure of 30 federal associations in Germany, he presents his initial findings on this issue with the important caveat that his empirical evidence needs to be supported by further studies.

Turcotte and Gendron explore the collaboration of multi-stakeholders (corporations, civil society and government) in the context of deregulation and sustainable development. They point out that multi-stakeholder partnerships bring together many perspectives, but can be seen as conflict resolution mechanisms as well as sites of learning and innovation as advocated by Driscoll (1996) and Logsdon (1991). They then argue that multiple stakeholder collaborative processes (MCPs) can be seen as an alternative governance system to those regulated by the state or market forces. They point out that the rise of new social movements have transformed the institutional political process. While voluntary initiatives and self-regulation are increasingly seen as a means of achieving consensus among multi-stakeholders, these approaches have also received much criticism. It has been argued that voluntary initiatives have had little impact and are preferred by companies who fail to implement regulations on environment. The result is complacency and inertia.

In view of this controversy, the authors set out to investigate the role of MCPs through two case studies: the 3R Round Table on waste management and the ARET initiative regarding toxic substances. They conclude that in both limitations arose in the reaching of consensus on specific action plans. They argue that, when controversial subjects are raised, consensus is often possible on general principles as participants may block the collaborative process by imposing their own views and voting against the proposals. Turcotte and Gendron, however, point out that MCPs can provide guidance for future actions and decisions and, far from excluding or replacing traditional regulatory activities, they can be seen as contributing to the legitimacy of the regulatory processes. They also provide the opportunity for the expression of diverse and possibly divergent perspectives, bringing in novel ideas and contributing to a change in business practices in the long term.

Lüth, Schäfers and Helmchen examine the role of regulation in global markets involving a multifaceted web of relationships. In this context, they examine normative and descriptive views of the relationships between regulators, corporations and civil society. The advantages of regulation include reputation as a responsible actor, being able to influence the regulation process, less criticism from NGOs and the benefits of the regulation itself (Dyllick 1989). The authors recommend that companies build capacities within, develop new lobbying strategies, implement incentives for change, define the operational and strategic boundaries of their responsibilities, and revise membership policies of industry cartels. They conclude by questioning the concept of 'sustainable governance framework' and recommend that new governance mechanisms such as stakeholder dialogues, facilitated discourses, joint fact finding and mediation processes be introduced.

Demirag, Dubnick and Khadaroo argue that most previous studies on Private Finance Initiatives (PFIs) have considered accountability and value for money (VFM) only at the initial planning and development stages. They argue that little attention has been given to post-construction of capital infrastructures.[1] In order to develop such a framework, the authors first review the relevant literature. They point out that risk may be incorporated at the discount rate, but it is often added to the public-sector comparator (PSC) in order to bring in an element of risk, which PFI contracts presumably pass on to the private partner. The extent of risk that actually passes on after the completion of the construction project is also problematic.

The authors argue that no attempt has been made to link the relevant types of accountability and VFM at the various stages of the PFI processes. They identify five main stages for the PFI: initiation set-up, implementation, internal monitoring and external monitoring. The respective forms of accountability are then identified and

---

1   For example, see Broadbent et al. 2003a, 2003b and Shaoul 2004. See also Grimsey and Lewis 2004.

VFM drivers appropriate to each forms of accountability identified. The authors recommend that further research is needed to examine the extent to which PFIs are meeting the VFM objectives identified at the pre-contract stages and the stakeholders involved in the implementation and monitoring processes.

Quigley explores the Civil Aviation Authority (CAA)'s role in the Y2K operation together with industry, the media, the government and various international partners. In seeking answers to the question of how effective the UK aviation industry's risk management plans were for handling the Y2K issue, Quigley uses Hood *et al.*'s (2001) analytical regime-based framework at the meso level. The framework employs three different perspectives to explore risk regulation. The market failure perspective justifies government intervention because markets cannot effectively manage the risk. This seems feasible given the industry's high dependency on technology with complex and interdependent systems. The opinion responsive perspective posits that risk regulation is a response to the preferences of civil society. In particular, the public and media salience of the issue and the uniformity of the opinions to explore this perspective is relevant here. Finally, the interests perspective considers the role of private- or public-interest groups in shaping the manner in which risk is regulated in the industry. This hypothesis argues that regulatory activity reflects the interplay between organisational interests. In this context Quigley refers to Wilson (1980) and points out that client politics and other interest groups theory may play a significant role in the way the risk is managed.

Quigley concludes that Hood *et al.*'s 2001 framework is useful but has several major limitations. There are numerous factors that can simultaneously influence government policy-making as well as the problems of identifying public opinion. Despite these drawbacks, he argues that the model helps illuminate a discussion about risk regulation and bring out different aspects of the key institutions, ideas and players active in the regulatory space leading to a richer analytical treatment of complex, multi-dimensional problems that exists between supra-state, state, industry and civil society.

In Part 2 (Corporate social responsibility and stakeholder theory) Byerly reviews recent relevant literature on corporate social responsibility theory and articulates the concept by considering the relevance of a number of recent key developments and issues including globalisation, power, social contract, leadership, the new evolutionary economics and the common good (Boggs 2000; Carroll 1991; Carroll 1999; Davis 1960). The role of corporations in networks of other social corporate activities as partners and leaders are also examined (Daly and Cobb 1994; Gilpin 2000). Byerly highlights the emergence of interdisciplinary theory and real-world examples of corporations recognising a new social contract stemming from the need for global leadership and action, acknowledging the necessity of partnership, mutual engagement, responsibility and commitment to achieve the future goals of all in partnership with governments and communities.

Armstrong provides an interesting background to theoretical frameworks that could be explored in studying governance mechanisms. Drawing on clans and transaction costs (Ouchi 1980), institutional isomorphism (DiMaggio and Powell 1983), agency theory (Jensen and Meckling 1976), occupational communities (Van Maanen and Barley 1984) and resource dependence (Pfeffer and Salancik 1978), he addresses stakeholder partnership issues and makes several propositions in order to develop a more robust framework in the study of governance issues. He argues that stakeholder partnership may create a clan form of transaction mediation that can offer a greater level of discipline in performance by sharing complementary resources, sharing expertise and knowledge, improving reputations of participants and improving corporate governance. This can lead to superior performance to what could be achieved through market or regulatory approaches alone. Armstrong suggests that, if the occupation of business executives were to become more professionalised, we might expect that CEOs would develop a shared set of performance standards for ethical and social behaviour and that they would enforce these standards within their professional clan. There are of course difficulties with these suggestions. Decisions in organisation are often influenced by variety of actors and interest groups. Moreover, in the recent corporate governance failures, such as Enron and WorldCom, the most prominent actors involved were accountants and lawyers, who have highly professionalised occupations.

Dempsey posits that effective co-operation between business corporations, civil society and public sector (government) can only be achieved if there are well-understood ethical standards, which are underpinned by shared community values. Where there are multi-stakeholders involved in issues dealing with environmental and social responsibility, it is important that ethical standards are well understood by all concerned. Dempsey, however, points out that it is no longer enough to show support for agendas supporting corporate responsibility, socially responsible investment, or environmental accountability. There is now a pressing need for more direct action than simply reporting on these issues. Direct engagement on issues, activities and performance indicators that are most material to all the internal and external stakeholders is needed. In addition to responsibilities expected from corporations, civil societies must also act in more transparent and accountable manner. Dempsey concludes that true stakeholder engagement requires mutual accountability in all three sectors (private, public and civil society) in order to build effective, sustainable partnerships that are economically, environmentally and socially viable.

In Part 3 (Empirical studies on emerging governance structures and corporate social responsibility) Bleischwitz, Andersen and Latsch are concerned with the governance structure for sustainable development. They argue that 'network governance of collective learning process' is an appropriate structure for sustainable development. Having outlined the main reasons for the failure of markets and governments, the authors refer to political science, new institutional economics and evolutionary economics, which depart from the models of rational choice; that is, they do not rely on the assumption of fully rational behaviour with perfect information. In addition to the role of the collective processes outlined above, the governance of sustainability also requires innovation-inducing regulation where the government acts as buffer for the societal problems by bringing together heterogeneous actors and solving specific problems (Bleischwitz 2003). They point out that governments often provide incentives for eco-efficient services and the ministries receive support from established interest groups. To illustrate the usefulness of their governance approach to sustainability development Bleischwitz, Andersen and Latsch, referring to Johnson and Jacobson (2002), give examples of the development of the wind turbine industries in Sweden, the Netherlands and Germany. They point out that the perceptions of private and public actors in these emerging industries were crucial in the successful development of technologies, knowledge generation and product markets. The case also shows the co-evolutionary relationship between state, firms and societal actors in the development of sustainable markets and the consequences of failure by one party.

Munkelien, Goyer and Fratczak argue that economists have become involved in CSR by introducing the concept of the triple bottom line. This concept includes three important spheres of sustainability for successful businesses: namely, the economic, environmental and social spheres. Using non-financial reports as surrogate to triple-bottom-line reports or sustainability reports, the authors posit that CSR can be assessed by the use of these reports in Scandinavian countries.

The authors report that, even though the Scandinavian countries endorsed the Global Compact, very few have signed it. Most companies expected more direct guidance from their respective governments for their responsibility in CSR. Finland, however, shows some exceptions in the field of CSR. Although Finnish companies do not require triple-bottom-line reporting, such reporting is more common in Finland than in other Scandinavian countries. The Swedish government appears to have the most active CSR approach compared to other Scandinavian countries, but still only a few Swedish corporations use triple-bottom-line reporting. The authors acknowledge that the reasons for these divergent CSR practices found among the companies operating from four Scandinavian countries have not been explored; they indicate that Scandinavian governments have been very influential in channelling the activities of corporations in the field of CSR.

Durán and Thompson focus on Protected Areas (PAs), areas of land or sea, managed through legislation or other means, and especially dedicated to the protection and maintenance of biological diversity and natural and associated cultural resources (IUCN 1994). They discuss the major factors influencing the governance of PAs and the approaches that Mexican and Canadian PAs are following in order to enhance governance and management effectiveness. Based on ten case studies carried out in Mexico and Canada, they show the need to improve governance and management among all the stakeholders (governments and corporations) as well as PAs at local, regional and international levels. The authors argue that PAs by themselves can do little to improve governance if there is no co-ordination between other actors and stakeholders. The key issues, which need to be tackled, include drafting policies and setting rules to govern economic activity that pay attention to social, economic and environmental needs. Referring to work by Kaufmann and Kraay (2003), and Werlin (2003), they conclude that inadequate governance raises questions about PAs' ability to deal effectively with natural resources and to get foreign funds

Based on their case studies, Durán and Thompson point out that the downsizing and privatisation, financing, land tenure and law enforcements are the most pressing problems facing PA's in Canada and Mexico. They recommend that the adoption of environmental management systems (EMSs), and other types of certification mechanisms, can help PA's improve their management and governance. However, this would need to be done by establishing sound working relationships with stakeholders on surrounding lands, and demonstrating PAs' contribution to the quality of life, both nationally and internationally.

Betit explores the transition of ownership to employees in a US company. The company was formed to manufacture hardwood and plywood reels for steel and wire cable in 1951. However, the transition of ownership started in 1996 and the chapter draws from conversations, interviews and meeting notes over a seven-year period with the owners, Vice President, Human Resources Director and the employee-owners of the company. The case study serves to illustrate the point that global businesses are becoming more interconnected, interdependent, interactive and pervasive.

Betit argues that, in her case-study company, employee governance is both a source and recipient to change. Betit explores information sharing, participation, the decision-making and allocation of resources, and distribution of wealth in her case-study company. Accountability to internal and external communities is also examined. She concludes that, despite financial difficulties facing it, the company continued its 100% employee-ownership and governance, as well as maintaining relationships within the group, and to their communities even though falling sales made it more difficult to be responsive.

Puppim de Oliveira examines the role of civil-society actors in providing information and facilitating environmental policies based on the work of Anderson and Leal (1992) and Brinkerhoff (1996). Using a case study of the state's federation of industries in Rio de Janeiro (FIRJAN), he illustrates how an NGO can facilitate, manage and eliminate solid waste by providing technical advice and mediating among buyers and sellers of solid material. Puppim de Oliveira concludes that economic mechanisms can be effectively used for waste management and this can cost much less than direct regulation.

In Part 4 (Corporate governance and its implications for regulators and civil society), Šević examines two main models of corporate governance: the Anglo-American and the continental European. He notes that the liberal American model of regulation is becoming more socially responsible while the European and non-liberal Japanese models are trying to achieve the efficiency benchmark set by the American model (Demirag 1998). The author then describes the main characteristics of both systems, adding that Americans had traditionally more regulation but this realisation came as a surprise in the 1970s when they recognised that their systems were more regulated than those in Europe. The response was a large scale of deregulation with the consequent financial disasters such as the Enron debacle and the Californian energy crisis. Referring to the work of Puri and Brook (2002), and Jensen (2001), he suggests that a modified stakeholder model offers greater opportunities to deal with the inherent weaknesses of each system, taking into account the wider range of stakeholders. Šević also sees some role for 'regulation by litigation' as a last resort.

Demirag and O'Brien examine the changing regulation of US financial markets following the recent collapse of major US companies and the financial scandals that surfaced afterwards. The recent organisational and regulatory changes surrounding the Securities and Exchange Commission (SEC) and the New York Stock Exchange (NYSE) are examined as case studies in the chapter. The state's (in)ability to control these institutions after a period of deregulation is also explored.

Demirag and O'Brien adapt the Streeck and Schmitter (1985) framework (SS) in their study of US financial regulation. The authors conclude that the relationships between the state, the market and the organised interest groups need to be more explicitly explored, if it is going to capture the dynamic power relationships between these groups, using a more robust theoretical framework than the SS model of social order can provide (Demirag 1995). The chapter then calls for further research using complementary theoretical frameworks and paradigms on the subject. Demirag and O'Brien also argue that the limits of government's ability to deal with the failures in the financial markets also raises the pertinent question of the effectiveness of legislation, without the need to re-evaluate the underlying mechanisms and systems of regulation. The issues identified in this chapter certainly call for further research in financial regulation within the context of globalisation.

Samaha, using a framework derived from the theories of complex adaptive systems (CASs) explores the dynamics of social systems undergoing dramatic change. The deregulation of the electric utility market in the USA have had mixed results—success in some areas and catastrophe in others such as the Enron debacle. Samaha posits that neither the regulators nor the major utilities understood how deregulation has affected them, as the high risks were the results of definable design flaws in the regulatory system. She argues that the California energy crisis has indicated that markets by themselves do not work and there is a real role for government regulation.

Schmidt and Bondarenko critically examine the validity of the relevant theoretical propositions for the understanding of the existing control mechanisms in place for controlling corruption in the post-Soviet Russia. Drawing on the conventional models of human rights norms, in particular the 'spiral model' of Keck and Sikkink (1998a, 1998b), and Risse *et al.* (1999), they highlight the contributions of the conventional norm transfer models to corruption studies.

They conclude that the likelihood of successful norm diffusion into domestic systems may be overstated and the process of norm diffusion in corruption is more difficult and different from that found in human rights literature. Moreover, the role of NGOs in this process may be overstated with often counter-accusations being made to their Western counterparts for the financial scandals and corruption cases in their own countries—a situation that is more unlikely in the case of human rights violations. Another major difficulty of the conventional models of norms diffusion is that it is difficult to distinguish which domestic changes are induced by transnational networks and which are part of the of the systematic transformation.

Schmidt and Bondarenko posit that the effects of recent attempts to democratise and privatise Soviet society have also created new opportunities for different forms of corruption. The authors finish their chapter by stating that corruption and transformation are complex issues involving all levels and sectors of society. They recommend more research in the conventional theoretical models of transnational norm transfer.

In Part 5 (Multinational companies and their implications for the new governance structures, regulators and civil society) Bastmeijer and Verschuuren explore the role of law, government regulation, multinational companies and NGOs in addressing various transboundary sustainability issues. The issues that could be considered as part of the sustainability debate include prevention of adverse environmental impact, safeguarding human rights, racial discrimination and ensuring good working conditions and protection of child labour. They argue that relationships between governments, multinational companies and NGOs are changing. The authors posit that, under the command-and-control approach, attention was given to norm setting by governments through legislation where NGOs tried to influence the substance of legislation through their relationships with government. Bastmeijer and Verschuuren conclude that governments have to find a way to work with multiple stakeholders but legislation is still needed to support this development. In order to ensure that there is no free-rider issue and that it is easy to enforce legislation and developed norms, governments need to codify the norms that have been agreed on by companies and NGOs. They argue that market incentives and pressure by local communities are also important factors in the performance of corporations towards their environmental responsibilities.

Bryane Michael examines the impact of globalisation on the development of international corporate responsibility (ICR), in particular the role of multinational companies in engaging ICR partnerships with international governments and international NGOs. Michael suggests that international government organisations such as the World Bank have several roles to play in ICR engagement. The Bank can act as a 'clearing-house' of corporate social responsibility, advocate or watchdog assessing company regulation and auditing; provide consulting services in developing countries taking equity or debt positions in the companies they advise; and can tie country lending to national implementation and compliance with ICR programmes.

Given the range of options outlined for government organisations, MNCs and international NGOs, Michael develops a model to bring out the possible effective strategic interactions. He concludes that his model helps to identify areas where the three key actors involved might under-provide ICR activity due to the strategic nature of their interaction, or may fail to balance economies of scale in ICR provision with local needs.

In the final chapter Demirag, Barry and Khadaroo provide concluding remarks on emerging governance structures and practices. The chapter highlights the important international trends emerging in corporate social responsibility and sustainable development. It reflects and builds on some of the important findings of the contributors to this volume as well as the authors' current research in this area.

References

Alexander, J. (1996) 'Spirited Dialogue: Michael Harmon's Responsibility as Paradox', *Public Administration Review* 56.6: 593-96.

Anderson, T.A., and D.R. Leal (1992) 'Free Market Versus Political Environmentalism', *Harvard Journal of Law and Public Policy* 15.2: 297-310.

Bleischwitz, R. (2003) 'Cognitive and Institutional Perspectives of Eco-Efficiency: The Case of Waste', *Ecological Economics* 46: 453-67.

Boggs, C. (2000) *The End of Politics: Corporate Power and the Decline of the Public Sphere* (New York: The Guilford Press).

Bovens, M. (1998) *The Quest for Responsibility: Accountability and Citizenship in Complex Organisations* (Cambridge, UK: Cambridge University Press).

Brinkerhoff, D.W. (1996) 'Coordination Issues in Policy Implementation Networks: An Illustration from Madagascar's Environmental Action Plan', *World Development* 24.9: 1,497-510.

Broadbent, J., and R. Laughlin (2003) 'Control and Legitimation in Government Accountability Processes: The Private Finance Initiative in the UK', *Critical Perspectives on Accounting* 14.1–2: 23-48.

——, J. Gill and R. Laughlin (2003a) 'Private Finance Initiative: The PFI in the National Health Service A Risky Venture?', *International Accountant* 20 (September 2003): 36-37.

——, —— and —— (2003b) 'Evaluating the Private Finance Initiative in the National Health Service in the UK', *Accounting, Auditing and Accountability Journal* 16.3: 422-45.

Carroll, A.B. (1991) 'The Pyramid of Social Responsibility: Toward the Moral Management of Organizational Stakeholders', *Business Horizons* 34: 39-48.

—— (1999) 'Corporate Social Responsibility', *Business and Society* 38.3: 268-95.

Clark, W., and I. Demirag (2002) 'Enron: The Failure of Corporate Governance', *Journal of Corporate Citizenship* 8 (Winter 2002): 105-22.

Coy, D., and M. Pratt (1998) 'An Insight into Accountability and Politics in Universities: A Case Study', *Accounting, Auditing and Accountability Journal* 11.5: 540-61.

Daly, H.B., and J.B. Cobb (1994) *For the Common Good* (Boston, MA: Beacon Press).

Davis, K. (1960) 'Can Business Afford to Ignore Social Responsibility?', *California Management Review* 2.2: 70-76.

Demirag, I. (1995) 'Social Order of the Accounting Profession in Turkey: The State, the Market and the Community', in C. Balim, E. Kalaycioglu, C. Karatas, G. Winrow and F. Yasamee (eds.), *Turkey: Political, Social and Economic Challenges in the 1990s* (Leiden, Netherlands: Brill): 256-75.

—— (ed.) (1998) *Corporate Governance, Accountability and Pressures to Perform: An International Study* (Studies in Managerial and Financial Accounting series, Volume 8; Greenwich, CT: JAI Press).

—— and J. Solomon (2003) 'Developments in International Corporate Governance and the Impact of Recent Events', *Corporate Governance: An International Review* 11.1: 1-7.

——, S. Sudarsanam and M. Wright (2000) 'Corporate Governance: Overview and Research Design', *The British Accounting Review* 32 (December 2000): 341-54.

——, M. Dubnick and I. Khadaroo (2004) 'Exploring the Relationship between Accountability and Performance in the UK's Private Finance Initiative (PFI)', paper presented at the *Corporate Governance Conference*, Institute of Governance, Public Policy and Social Research, Queen's University Belfast, 20–21 September 2004.

DiMaggio, P., and W.W. Powell (1983) 'The Iron Cage Revisited: Institutional Isomorphism and Collective Rationality in Organisational Fields', *American Sociological Review* 48: 147-60.

Driscoll, C. (1996) 'Fostering Constructive Conflict Management in a Multistakeholder Context: The Case of the Forest Roundtable on Sustainable Development', *International Journal of Conflict Management* 7.2: 156-72.

Dubnick, M.J. (1998) 'Clarifying Accountability: An Ethical Theory Framework', in N.P.C. Sampford and C.-A. Bois (eds.), *Public Sector Ethics: Finding and Implementing Values* (Leichhardt, NSW: The Federation Press/Routledge).

—— (2002) 'Seeking Salvation for Accountability', paper presented at *American Political Science Association*, Boston, MA, 29 August–1 September 2002.

Dyllick, T. (1989) *Management der Umweltbeziehungen: Öffentliche Auseinandersetzungen als Herausforderungen* (Wiesbaden, Germany: Gabler).

Garcia, P., and H. Vredenburg (2003) 'Building Corporate Citizenship Through Strategic Bridging in the Oil and Gas Industry in Latin America', *Journal of Corporate Citizenship* 10 (Summer 2003): 37-49.

GASB (Government Accounting Standards Board) (1987) 'Concepts Statement no. 1: Objectives of Financial Reporting, Official Releases', *Journal of Accountancy* 164.3: 196-205.

Gray, B. (1985) 'Conditions Facilitating Inter-Organizational Collaboration', *Human Relations* 38.10: 911-36.

—— (1989) *Collaborating: Finding Common Ground for Multiparty Problems* (San Francisco, CA: Jossey-Bass).

——, R. Kouhy and S. Lavers (1995) 'Corporate Social and Environmental Reporting: A Review of the Literature and a Longitudinal Study of UK Disclosure', *Accounting, Auditing and Accountability Journal* 8.2: 47-77.

Grimsey, D., and M.K. Lewis (2004) 'The Governance of Contractual Relationships in Public–Private Partnerships', *Journal of Corporate Citizenship* 15 (Autumn 2004): 91-109.

Hood, C., H. Rothstein and R. Baldwin (2001) *The Government of Risk: Understanding Risk Regulation Regimes* (Oxford, UK: Oxford University Press).

IUCN (The World Conservation Union) (1994) *Guidelines for Protected Area Management Categories. Part II. The Management Categories* (Cambridge, UK: IUCN Publications Service Unit).

Jensen, M.C. (2001) 'Value Maximization, Stakeholder Theory, and the Corporate Objective Function', *Journal of Applied Corporate Finance* 14.3: 8-21.

—— and W. Meckling (1976) 'Theory of the Firm: Managerial Behaviour, Agency Costs and Ownership Structure, *Journal of Financial Economics* 3: 305-60.

Johnson, A., and S. Jacobson (2002) *The Emergence of a Growth Industry: A Comparative Analysis of the German, Dutch and Swedish Wind Turbine Industries* (Mimeo; Göteborg, Sweden: Department of Industrial Dynamics, Chalmers University of Technology).

Jordan, L., and V. Tuijl (2000) 'Political Responsibility in Transnational NGO Advocacy', *World Development* 28.12: 2,051-65.

Keck, M.E., and K. Sikkink (1998a) *Activists beyond Borders: Advocacy Networks in International Politics* (Ithaca, NY/London: Cornell University Press).

—— and —— (1998b) 'Transnational Activist Networks in the Movement Society', in D.S. Meyer and S. Tarrow (eds.), *The Social Movement Society: Contentious Politics for a New Century* (Lanham, MD: Rowman & Littlefield).

Kaufmann, D., and A. Kraay (2003) *Governance and Growth: Causality Which Way? Evidence for the World in Brief* (World Bank Group Working papers and Articles; Washington, DC: World Bank).

Lindkvist, L., and S. Llewellyn (2003) 'Accountability, Responsibility and Organization', *Scandinavian Journal of Management* 19.2: 251-73.

Logsdon, J.M. (1991) 'Interests and Independence in the Formation of Social Problem-Solving Collaborations', *Journal of Applied Behavioural Science* 27.1: 23-37.

Mayston, D. (1993) 'Principals, Agents and the Economics of Accountability in the New Public Sector', *Accounting, Auditing and Accountability Journal* 6.3: 68-96.

Ouchi, W.G. (1980) 'Markets, Bureaucracies, and Clans', *Administrative Science Quarterly* 25: 129-41.

Pallot, J. (1992), 'Elements of a Theoretical Framework for Public Sector Accounting', *Accounting, Auditing and Accountability Journal* 5.1: 38-59.

—— (2003), 'A Wider Accountability? The Audit Office and New Zealand's Bureaucratic Revolution', *Critical Perspectives on Accounting* 14.1–2: 133-55.

Pfeffer, J., and G.R. Salancik (1978) *The External Control of Organisations: A Resource Dependence Perspective* (New York: Harper & Row).

Puri, P., and T. Brook (2002) 'Employees as Corporate Stakeholders', *Journal of Corporate Citizenship* 8 (Winter 2002): 49-61.

Risse, T., S.C. Ropp and K. Sikkink (eds.) (1999) *The Power of Human Rights. International Norms and Domestic Change* (Cambridge, UK: Cambridge University Press).

Romzek, B.S., and M.J. Dubnick (1987) 'Accountability in the Public Sector: Lessons from the Challenger Tragedy', *Public Administration Review* 47.3: 227-38.

Shaoul, J. (2004) 'A Critical Appraisal of the Private Finance Initiative: Selecting a Financial Method or Allocating Economic Wealth?', *Critical Perspectives on Accounting* 16.4: 441-71.

Sinclair, A. (1995) 'The Chameleon of Accountability: Forms and Discourses', *Accounting, Organisations and Society* 20.2–3: 219-37.

Stewart, J. (1984) 'The Role of Information in Public Accountability', in A.G. Hopwood and C.R. Tomkins (eds.), *Issues in Public Sector Accounting* (Oxford, UK: Philip Allan).

Streeck, W., and P. Schmitter (1985) 'Community, Market, State and Associations?', in W. Streeck and P. Schmitter (eds.), *Private Interest Government* (London: Sage).

Union Carbide Corporation (1984) *Bhopal*, available at www.bhopal.com/facts.htm.

Van Maanen, J., and S.R. Barley (1984) 'Occupational Communities: Culture and Control in Organisations', in B.M. Staw and L.L. Cummings (eds.), *Research in Organisational Behaviour* 6: 287-366 (Greenwich, CT: JAI Press).

Vredenburg, H., and F. Westley (2002) 'Sustainable Development Leadership in Three Contexts: Managing for Global Competitiveness', *Journal of Business Administration,* Special Issue, 'Bringing Business on Board: Sustainable Development and the B-school Curriculum': 239-59.

Werlin, H.H. (2003) 'Poor Nations, Rich Nations: A Theory of Governance', *Public Administration Review* 63.3: 329-42.

Wilson, J. (1980) *The Politics of Regulation* (New York: Basic Books).

Part 1
Emerging governance structures, risks and networking

1

Broadening the notion of governance from the organisation to the domain
A STUDY OF MUNICIPAL WATER SYSTEMS IN CANADA

Stephanie Bertels and Harrie Vredenburg*
University of Calgary, Canada

The last two decades have seen a global increase in the involvement of the private sector in the provision of services traditionally provided by governments. Efforts to deliver more with less have motivated governments to seek out new sources of financing and to consider the creation of partnerships involving the public, private and not-for-profit sectors (Lowndes and Skelcher 1998). Public–private partnerships have been proposed to tackle a range of public goods such as healthcare delivery, water delivery, education, telecommunications and transportation services. Not surprisingly, the global dialogue that surrounds the movement towards increased private-sector involvement has become greatly polarised. Proponents of the involvement of the private sector propose that governments need to 'steer rather than row'—a phrase popularised by the advocates of New Public Management (Osbourne and Gaebler 1992). Thus, rather than operating institutions, governments should establish the framework within which private companies can perform this function. On the other side of the debate, opponents of the involvement of the private sector fear a loss of control over precious public goods (Barlow and Clarke 2002). They fear that, in the quest to increase efficiency, private firms may ignore social objectives, such as keeping the cost of water and power affordable, or providing a service in poor areas.

Recent concerns over the ineffectiveness of private-sector governance (Clark and Demirag 2002; Sims and Brinkmann 2003) have served to accentuate public concerns

* The authors acknowledge financial support received from the Social Sciences and Humanities Research Council of Canada and the Enbridge Environmental Case Study Grant Program at the Haskayne School of Business. We also thank the case-study participants for their time and input into this project. Finally, we thank the anonymous reviewers and the editor for their helpful comments.

about transparency and accountability in the provision of public goods. While there is a widespread appetite for reinforcing governance practices, we argue that traditional management theory offers limited guidance for the rapidly evolving models under which public, private and not-for-profit sectors co-operate in the provision of public services. We build on a literature that views issues such as resource management, water supply, third-world development, climate change, biodiversity conservation and sustainable development as domain problems best addressed through inter-organisational and inter-sectoral collaboration (Emery and Trist 1965; McCann 1983; Trist 1983; Gray 1985, 1989; Westley and Vredenburg 1991, 1997; Sharma *et al.* 1994; Vredenburg and Westley 2002; Garcia and Vredenburg 2003; Hall and Vredenburg 2003). We examine three case studies of Canadian municipal water systems with dramatically different formal organisational structures. Yet, despite differing formal structures, similar informal collaborative structures have evolved in all three cases to overcome the challenges of operating in a multifaceted domain. We maintain that traditional notions of governance that focus on organisational structure are insufficient to explain the appearance of these informal structures. In response, we assert that traditional views of governance in terms of markets and hierarchies must be broadened to include notions of domain-based collaborative governance in order to address problem domains that require the participation of multiple parties.

1.1 Water supply: an example of a domain-based approach

Concerns about the transparency and accountability of public–private partnerships are particularly acute in the water sector, where failures in governance can have tragic consequences. Water is one of the many 'public goods' traditionally provided by governments around the world. Yet, amid a global crisis of ageing water infrastructure insufficient to meet the needs of the world's swelling population, governments are increasingly contemplating including the private sector in the provision of what has typically been considered a public good. As a result, over the last two decades, the global water industry has entered a period of unprecedented growth and transformation (Finger and Allouche 2002). This growth has been driven by the forces of globalisation and fuelled by a much broader process of market liberalisation (McFetridge 1997).

In Canada, several recent episodes of water-borne illness have led to a heated debate regarding the appropriate governance model (or models) for ensuring the safety of municipal water supply. In May 2000, in Walkerton, a small farming community in Ontario, seven people died and more than 2,300 became ill from an outbreak of *Escherichia coli* O157:H7 in the town's water supply (O'Connor 2002a). Eleven months later, an estimated 5,800–7,100 people from areas in and around North Battleford, Saskatchewan, became ill with enteric disease caused by the presence of the parasite *Cryptosporidium* in their water supply (Laing 2002). The public inquiries into these tragedies highlighted the need for more transparency and accountability, including better oversight by regulators and the need for more investment in water supply infrastructure. Like in other countries, many municipalities in Canada are facing ageing infrastructure and are struggling to supply the necessary capital and expertise to revamp and modernise their water systems. In response to the Walkerton and North Battleford tragedies, Canadian municipalities have been reviewing the governance structures of their water systems and examining the relationships between the people that operate these systems and the government agencies that oversee them.

Regardless of how well a drinking water system is operated, unexpected incidents may still occur. Thus, a degree of redundancy is often necessary to guard against the failure of any one safeguard. Experts in water supply agree that what is needed is a multi-level risk management approach to protecting water supply—termed a 'multi-barrier approach' in the water industry (Federal-Provincial-Territorial Committee on Drinking Water 2002). The report of the inquiry into the Walkerton tragedy explains that 'every step in the chain, from water supply through treatment to distribution, needs careful selection, design, and implementation, so that the combination of steps provides the best defense against calamity when things go wrong' (O'Connor 2002b: 72). A multi-barrier approach looks at all the components of a drinking water system and identifies the safeguards needed to provide a sound management plan from source to tap. Different systems will have different critical components and the specific tools or actions chosen as safeguards will vary accordingly, but the premise is the same: a multi-barrier approach recognises the interrelationship of health and environmental issues. It encourages collaboration between efforts aimed at protecting health and those aimed at protecting the environment.

If a multi-level risk management approach to water supply is to be successful, different levels and agencies of government, citizens' groups and perhaps even private companies all need to work together to evaluate the needs of the system and ensure the right safeguards are in place. Traditional hierarchical governance methods are frequently unsuccessful in these situations. Attempts by individual organisations to solve problems that affect multiple parties are often unco-ordinated and can even cause unanticipated problems for other stakeholders. According to Emery and Trist (1965), these difficulties often stem from a failure to conceptualise problems and organise the solutions at the **domain** level. These authors introduced the notion of **turbulent environments**, where problems are characterised by uncertainty and consist of complex and unclear boundaries. In these environments, individual organisations cannot be expected to be able to adapt through their own independent actions. Emery and Trist (1965) assert that these types of situation demand some overall form of organisation that is essentially different from the hierarchically structured forms to which we are accustomed. They argue that co-operation among organisations is imperative to control environmental turbulence in any given domain.

Trist (1983) uses the notion of a 'problem domain' to describe issues that are too extensive and multifaceted to be addressed by any one organisation. The policy environment often consists of a group of independent government departments, individuals and private agencies that interact with each other only over questions of resource allocation and disagreements over funding. In this kind of environment, the inter-organisational domain is a more appropriate unit of analysis than the organisation because the policy system is dynamic and will expand or contract with changes in the definition of the problem. Simply stated, organisations may come and go, but the problem will persist.

1.2 The need for domain-based collaboration

When multiple stakeholders are connected through a complex web of interdependencies, inter-organisational and inter-sectoral collaboration is required to achieve both singular and common purposes (Trist 1983; Gray 1985; Westley and Vredenburg 1991, 1997; Sharma *et al.* 1994; Lowndes and Skelcher 1998; Vredenburg and Westley 2002; Garcia and Vredenburg 2003). According to Gray, 'collaboration is a process through which parties who see different aspects of a problem can constructively explore their differences and search for solutions that go beyond their own limited vision of what is possible' (1989: 5). 'Since each stakeholder can apprehend only a portion of the problem, by pooling perceptions, greater understanding of the context can be achieved' (Gray 1985: 916).

Adopting a process view, Gray found that the effective initiation and maintenance of collaboration at the domain level is dependent on the achievement of several conditions at appropriate phases in the collaboration process. The process of domain-based collaboration has been described by several authors (McCann 1983; Trist 1983; Gray 1985, 1989). In Trist's (1983) language, the various stakeholders need to develop a shared appreciation of the domain problem and establish an acceptable identity for the domain that directs the path forward. After the domain is defined, the boundaries of the domain are shaped by choosing which organisations are to be included and excluded. Eventually, an internal structure evolves as stakeholders secure common ground and accept each other's differences.

Gray (1989) outlines three sequential phases of inter-organisational domain development: problem setting, direction setting and structuring. The first phase, problem setting, is largely concerned with identifying the problem and determining the identity of legitimate stakeholders. Gray notes, 'unless some consensus is reached about who has a legitimate stake in an issue and exactly what the joint issue is, further attempts at collaboration will be thwarted' (1985: 917). As the problem becomes better defined, new stakeholders may emerge and others may become excluded. However, the successful identification of the problem relies on the participation of key stakeholders early in the process. Willingness to come to the table may be affected by the stakeholders' expectations about the possible outcomes and by their perception of the legitimacy of both the other stakeholders and the convener (Gray 1985). Collaboration begins once stakeholders begin to recognise their interdependence. The boundaries of the domain become defined through agreement on a common problem. These conditions need to be established before moving on to the direction-setting and structuring phases. If the problem-setting process is incomplete, the later processes will suffer and the result may be effective solutions to the wrong problems (McCann 1983).

The second stage, direction setting, seeks a common vision of the ends that are to be achieved by the process and preliminary agreement on the means of action. This phase further explores the coincidence in values among stakeholders (Gray 1985). Adjustments may need to be made in an attempt to balance the power among stakeholders (Westley and Vredenburg 1991). At this stage, stakeholders must also understand the role the larger environment plays in shaping the range of possible solutions (McCann 1983). As described by Gray (1989), the last stage, structuring, is largely functional and assures the viability of the collaboration. It concerns how the agreed-upon ends will become institutionalised. Agreements must be reached regarding the degree of ongoing interdependence, who will undertake the functional roles and how the relationships will be regulated between the various stakeholders (McCann 1983).

An acceptance of the need for collaborative action naturally leads to the discussion of stakeholders. Freeman's (1984) seminal stakeholder model is conceptualised as a wheel with the organisation as the hub and with stakeholders at the end of each spoke. These spokes represent the bi-directional relationships between the organisation and each of its stakeholders. But in this model, relationships are each treated independently and are generally viewed from the point of view of the organisation. We feel it is necessary to make a distinction between Freeman's organisation-centric view of stakeholder relations and the domain-based view of stakeholder collaboration. As shown in Figure 1.1, in domain-based collaboration there is no assumption of a central organisation. Instead, all stakeholders are assumed to participate in shaping solutions to the problem domain.

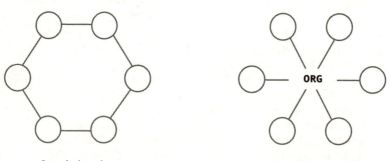

Domain-based   Organisation-centric

FIGURE 1.1 Domain-based and organisation-centric stakeholder collaboration

1.3 Expanding traditional views of governance

Once a distinction is made between domain-based and organisation-centric collaboration, we see that governance is not solely an organisational issue. When there is no longer a single entity with control, the notion of formal control becomes much less relevant. Furthermore, discussions of governance have almost exclusively explored corporate governance, narrowly defined in terms of a relationship between management, the board of directors and shareholders. We argue that governance, in its broadest sense, includes the various structures, processes, systems and cultures through which an organisation sets out its objectives, implements its objectives and monitors its performance. We propose that the notion of governance needs to be expanded beyond the organisation to include the problem domain. Interestingly, recent reviews of the field of corporate governance in special issues of both the *Academy of Management Review*

(Daily *et al.* 2003) and *The Journal of Corporate Citizenship* (Zadek and McIntosh 2002) support broadening of the scope of theoretical investigations into governance and accountability. In particular, Zadek and McIntosh (2002) note that businesses will be under increasing pressure to develop governance mechanisms that will enable them to make complex decisions that take into account the interests of a diverse group of stakeholders.

At issue, then, is what type of governance is best suited to the provision of public goods such as water. The study of organisational control has been strongly influenced by two theories that find their foundation in the rational models of economics: agency theory (Jensen and Meckling 1976; Eisenhardt 1989a) and transaction cost economics (Williamson 1975, 1985). Both of these theories assume that economic actors behave rationally and seek to maximise their own self-interest above all else (Eisenhardt 1989a). Several authors question the assumptions made in these formal control theories about individualistic motivations resulting in principal–agent interest divergence. The rational choice assumptions understate the influence of trust or of a sense of duty or fairness, which are both at odds with the assumption of self-interest. Formal theories of control do not consider how an agent's concern for the well-being of another person might limit the pursuit of their own self-interest (Wilson 1989; DiIulio 1994; Doucouliagos 1994; Davis *et al.* 1997).

In his development of transaction cost theory, Williamson (1975) framed governance as a choice between two ideal types at opposite ends of a continuum: 'markets' based on a price mechanism and 'hierarchies' based on authority. At the inter-organisational level, the continuum of formal mechanisms from markets to hierarchies struggles at the end-points. In many inter-organisational collaborations there is no overarching organisation with legitimate authority. When there is no longer a single entity with authority, pure hierarchy is no longer an option. Furthermore, as uncertainty and complexity increase, the expected cost to construct and enforce appropriate contracts also increases. This uncertainty leads to incomplete contracting because the contractual obligations of each party cannot be unambiguously specified for every possible situation (Park 1996). Under these conditions, market contracting can become prohibitively expensive.

As our cases will demonstrate, Williamson's dichotomy does not necessarily outline the full range of possible governance choices. Several authors assert that there is a third mode of governance that can be differentiated from the more traditional modes of hierarchy and markets. These three modes of governance are thought to be brought about by the three mechanisms of price, authority and trust, respectively (Bradach and Eccles 1989). Different authors refer to these three contrasting modes of governance as: markets, bureaucracies and clans (Ouchi 1980); market-based, command-and-control and voluntarist (Karp and Gaulding 1995); market, hierarchy and network (Lowndes and Skelcher 1998); market, unilateral and bilateral (Heide 1994); and market, hierarchical and collaborative (Phillips *et al.* 2000). What we will refer to as the domain-based collaborative mode of governance is essentially a normative process in which the organisations within a domain come to adopt the norms of a larger system through an initiation or socialisation process. This socialisation serves to produce goal alignment and reduce the traditional agency costs of incentives and monitoring. According to Heide (1994: 74), 'deviance or opportunism is dealt with in a proactive fashion; members use self control based on their internalised values'. It is important to note that, although we make reference to these three forms of governance as ideal types, in practice relationships are rarely governed exclusively by one form or another. Often these types serve as building blocks for the creation of complex structures of control (Bradach and Eccles 1989).

1.4 Formal and informal mechanisms of control

The three modes of governance outlined above are often divided into two separate classes based on their use of formal or informal mechanisms. Markets and hierarchies are seen to rely primarily on formal mechanisms, while the collaborative form of governance is seen to rely on informal social structures (Falkenberg and Herremans 1995; Dyer and Singh 1998). Informal systems are founded on common values and beliefs and attempt to eliminate goal divergence through socialisation. Thus, collaborative governance works best in an atmosphere of trust, mutual benefit and reciprocity (Karp and Gaulding 1995; Lowndes and Skelcher 1998).

Formal systems have been shown to lack the scope and flexibility required to deal with intractable domain problems because organisations can never specify a set of written rules that will cover all possible contingencies (Falkenberg and Herremans 1995). In contrast, collaborative governance is said to encourage experimentation and variety, which makes it desirable under conditions of ambiguity (Ouchi 1979). As a result, under conditions of uncertainty, informal social controls have been found to supplement and even replace formal mechanisms of control (Ouchi 1980; Granovetter 1985; Falkenberg and Herremans 1995; Karp and Gaulding 1995). Lowndes and Skelcher (1998) conclude that sustained inter-organisational collaboration is reliant on the underlying presence of informal collaborative governance regardless of which of the two formal structures predominates.

1.5 The cases

In this study, we explore the governance of municipal water systems in Canada. Water supply is but one of many types of public good where one overarching organisation is not capable of directing the entire problem domain. The successful application of a multi-level risk management approach to water supply will require that different levels and agencies of government, citizens' groups and, in some cases, private companies work together to evaluate the needs of their system and ensure that the right safeguards are in place. In Canada, the responsibility for water safety falls under provincial jurisdiction. The provincial ministries of environment generally have responsibility for source protection and, in most provinces, the regulation and monitoring of water treatment facilities. The provincial ministries of health are generally responsible for ensuring that there are appropriate sampling plans and for dealing with incidents of adverse water quality, which may include calling boil water advisories. It is the municipalities that are generally responsible for water treatment, sampling, distribution, and system and infrastructure maintenance. Some municipalities may share this responsibility with neighbouring municipalities, regional governments and not-for-profit agencies or, in some cases, the private sector.

Until recently, the traditional formal governance structure for the delivery of drinking water in Canada has been publicly owned and operated water utilities. Owing to increasing financial pressures and ageing water infrastructure, Canadian municipalities have been considering other options including the creation of municipally owned corporations and partnerships between the public and private sectors. Some Canadian municipalities have already experimented with public–private partnerships in the form of operations and maintenance contracts or, as in one case, a design–build–operate contract for a water treatment facility. But public–private partnerships for water supply seem to be losing favour with a sceptical Canadian public (Brubaker 2003). To explore a spectrum of current governance choices for the delivery of drinking water services, three case studies were conducted in Canadian municipalities using an inductive case-based approach (Glaser and Strauss 1967; Eisenhardt 1989b; Yin 2003). Interviews using open-ended questions were conducted with the management and employees of each water utility, elected representatives, key contacts at regulatory agencies and, where applicable, with the private companies with whom these municipalities contract for water treatment services. In total, 34 interviews averaging from 60 to 90 minutes were conducted across Canada between May and August 2003. The three cases presented below were selected to explore the range of formal governance structures currently employed in the delivery of municipal drinking water in Canada. They have been selected from three different provinces across Canada and include a municipally owned corporation, a municipal department and a public–private partnership. The formal structures of each municipality are depicted in Figure 1.2.

1.5.1 The municipally owned corporation: the case of EPCOR in Edmonton, Alberta

The water supply for the City of Edmonton, Alberta, is currently provided by EPCOR Water Services, a municipally owned corporation whose sole shareholder is the City of Edmonton. In preparation for the deregulation of Alberta's power industry, Edmonton Power, the City's power utility, was incorporated as a separate organisation at arm's length from the City in 1995. The City of Edmonton's Water Branch was similarly incorporated as Aqualta in 1996, and Edmonton Power, Aqualta and Eltec (a provider of non-regulated electrical and other commercial services) came together under the new corporate umbrella of EPCOR in 1996. The company is governed by an independent board of directors with the City of Edmonton as its sole shareholder. In 1999, all of the EPCOR utility businesses were unified under the EPCOR brand, while the company was reorganised into distinct subsidiaries; the water branch took the name of EPCOR Water Services.

In 1983, prior to incorporation, while water was still provided municipally, the City of Edmonton experienced a major outbreak of giardiasis (an intestinal illness) which affected more than 800 people. The outbreak, coupled with tea-coloured, foul-smelling tap-water caused by heavy spring run-offs, spurred a shift in focus for the senior management in the City's water branch from water quantity to water quality. The

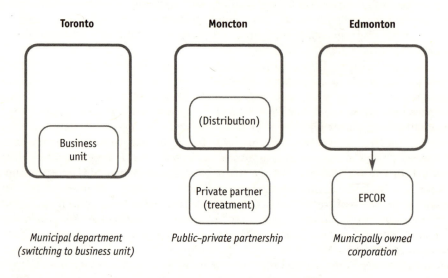

FIGURE 1.2 Range of formal governance structures for water supply

organisation undertook a significant shift in culture to a focus on quality assurance and transparency. But, while the culture was beginning to change within the organisation, there were still few links to the regulators that were meant to monitor the system.

It took an incident in another community to initiate a change in the relationship between the regulators and the operators of the system. In the spring of 1993, an estimated 403,000 people in Milwaukee, Wisconsin, suffered from a water-borne outbreak of intestinal illness. At the time, water quality standards and the testing of patients for *Cryptosporidium* all across North America would not have been adequate to detect this outbreak. Back in Edmonton, the lead drinking water inspector from the health department (Capital Health) and the quality assurance manager for the City's water supply became apprehensive about the potential for a similar outbreak in Edmonton. They were concerned that the existing system was ill equipped to deal with this new threat to water quality. With no overarching organisation with responsibility for dealing with the problem, these two individuals recognised the need to build a more open, trusting relationship between their two organisations with the shared goal of ensuring public safety. Their efforts towards increased monitoring revealed the presence of *Giardia* and *Cryptosporidium* cysts in the city's treated water during the spring run-off. A boil water warning was issued for persons with compromised immune systems, and the danger passed without any outbreak. Concerned that, in retrospect, the boil water advisory may have been unnecessary, both Capital Health and EPCOR saw the need to bring all of the key players together to formalise their boil water advisory protocol:

> The levels of *Giardia* were very low; it wasn't really a health concern, but the medical health officer told the media that those who were immunocompromised should boil their water. When the media got hold of it, it was presented as a boil water advisory. When we looked back on the incident, we realised

we had a communication problem. We decided it was time to sit down and develop a formal protocol so that everyone understands where everyone else is coming from. It helped because it let the water treatment plant know what we were expecting from them and vice versa. As a result, now we have constant communication. Most important is that the front-line workers [from the different organisations] now work together and understand our respective roles (interview, health inspector).

The development of a boil water advisory protocol served as a catalyst to strengthen the relationships between the Ministry of Environment, EPCOR and Public Health and helped to clarify the competences and weaknesses of each party. As a result of the success of the project, the parties saw value in continuing to meet on a regular basis. The resulting drinking water technical advisory committee now meets twice a year and includes participation by representatives from EPCOR, Public Health, the Ministry of Environment, the drainage branch of the City of Edmonton and research professors from the University of Alberta. The committee serves as a forum for ongoing discussions around water quality. All parties described the current relationship as strong and open and Edmonton's water and sewage treatment facilities are now among the most stringently regulated in Canada. The informal collaboration has enabled a level of trust and transparency that had not been achieved through formal governance mechanisms alone. One of the senior managers describes the change:

For instance, we'll have a problem in the plant and it will go to bypass; so there's not really a problem out in the system. But, as part of our process, we'll let them [the regulators] know that this happened and what we're doing to fix it—just so that they know. Our worst fear is that something happens and nobody reported it (interview, plant manager).

EPCOR's unique formal governance structure, set up as a separate corporation, has allowed it to expand beyond the City of Edmonton's borders. EPCOR Water Services has built its reputation slowly, initially by working with small communities in Alberta, to the point where EPCOR now provides water and distribution management to almost 1 million people in 45 communities across Western Canada. Its emphasis on being a leader means that EPCOR has received wide acceptance and is considered an expert in water supply. As a result, other municipalities in Canada have considered adopting EPCOR's unique formal governance structure. But, while EPCOR's switch in formal structure to a municipally owned corporation has been credited with providing the political independence and resources needed to invest in leading-edge technologies, it is the informal domain-based collaboration between the regulators and the operators of the system that is credited with upholding the focus on water quality and transparency. As we shall see in the next two cases, informal domain-based collaborative governance appears to be developing to overcome the lack of an overarching organisation capable of directing the domain, regardless of the formal governance structure.

1.5.2 The traditional model of the municipal department: the case of Toronto, Ontario

The majority of municipal water systems in Canada are structured as departments or divisions of the municipal administrative structure. The newly unified City of Toronto was selected as an example of this type of formal governance. In 1998, seven munici-palities in the Greater Toronto Area were amalgamated into a single city. As a result of the swift pace of amalgamation, there have been several iterations to the city's gover-nance structure and, nearly six years later, the governance model is still evolving. Prior to amalgamation, each municipality had its own water services branch. Post-amal-gamation, the production and distribution of potable water across the new city became the responsibility of the Water and Wastewater Division of Toronto's Works and Emer-gency Services Department.

In November 2002, the City of Toronto launched a review of governance options for water and waste-water services to address the need for renewed investment in infra-structure and to respond to new regulations being developed by the province. It was felt that, under the existing structure, the Water and Wastewater Division's ability to effectively manage its needs were limited by its current reporting relationship to the political structure, the approval process for rates and funding, internal charge-backs for corporate services and the need for concentrated political attention on water and waste-water issues (Toronto Works and Emergency Services 2002). The study reviewed three governance options: keeping the division within the city's administrative struc-ture; creating a municipal service board; or establishing a municipally owned corpora-tion (like EPCOR).

The study recommended that the City create a municipal service board. However, the board concept was met with public outcry and protests. The plan was seen as an unwanted move towards privatisation, partly based on comments by one city council-lor that the City was attempting to gain efficiencies and 'fend off privatisation'. In response, the city council voted to retain control of the waterworks and passed a motion against privatising water operations in the City of Toronto. In place of the municipal service board model, a special council committee was created to oversee Toronto's water and waste-water systems. Under the current plan, the Water and Wastewater Services Division will become a 'business unit' within the Works and Emer-gency Services Department. It would be allowed to operate with a greater degree of delegated financial and operational authority, have negotiated service-level agree-ments for all centrally provided services, and operate under administrative policies and procedures tailored to service the needs of the division.

While perhaps resolving some of the financial issues that the department faced within the City's administrative structure, the proposed changes in the formal gover-nance structure have not resolved the need for more co-ordinated action at the domain level. Prior to amalgamation, there was limited contact between the Ministry of Envi-ronment, Public Health and the Water and Wastewater Services Division. As noted in the Walkerton Inquiry report (O'Connor 2002b), the Ministry of Environment in Ontario was severely understaffed in the late 1990s prior to the Walkerton outbreak. In response to the Walkerton tragedy, the Ministry of Health drafted a province-wide Boil Water Advisory Protocol and the Ministry of Environment began to develop new drink-ing water regulations. Toronto's Water and Wastewater Services Division viewed the Ontario government's move towards compliance and authority-based regulator–oper-ator relationships as a step in the wrong direction and interpreted the response as a knee-jerk reaction to the recommendations of the Walkerton Inquiry. In response, Toronto's Water Division is attempting to counter the move towards prescriptive com-pliance by being more proactive in its communications with its regulators. In particular, it has been trying to reach out to the two ministries by offering its experience and technical expertise. Concerned that there was a lack of effective stakeholder consultation, Toronto's Water Division began meeting with its regulators to make its concerns known. In a similar manner to Edmonton, the last few years have seen the development of a water quality advisory committee, which meets quarterly and includes representatives from the Water Division, Public Health and the Ministry of Environment. Attendance varies and the participants describe the overall structure as 'informal and still developing'. But the Water Division is optimistic:

> Since we lit a fire there's been more of a recognition [by the regulators] that there are a lot of resources out there in the utilities. I think we've broken down a bit of that ivory tower . . . We've had some dealings with them recently that have been frustrating. But I think we have broken through (interview, quality assurance manager in the water division).

The parties involved see the development of this informal domain-based collaboration as a mechanism to increase communication and to build much-needed trust. To date, the regulators appear to be buying into the process:

> When the owners of the system were developing their adverse incident notification protocols, they allowed us to have input and they consulted with us. So they were not just doing it on their own; they were bringing us in and bringing other agencies in . . . as a result, the development of a water advisory group is something that we are looking at tightening up and having on a more regular basis (interview, public health officer).

1.5.3 Canada's first public–private partnership for water supply: the case of Moncton, New Brunswick

Like Edmonton, Moncton, New Brunswick, has what is considered to be a unique (and sometimes contentious) formal governance structure. Moncton is involved with USF Canada in a public–private partnership for water treatment services. For years, residents of Moncton and the neighbouring communities of Riverview and Dieppe endured turbid, discoloured tap-water with a host of taste and odour issues. When New Brunswick's Clean Water Act was enacted in 1995, its new requirements for sampling shone a spotlight on Moncton's problems. Unacceptable water quality led to repeated summer boil water orders including a month-long boil water order in July 1997 when levels of coliform bacteria (including faecal coliforms) were detected in the system. At the time, the relationship between the regulators and the municipality was quite adversarial. Things began to change during the boil water advisory of 1997, when a committee was struck to conduct a system-wide assessment and to develop a plan for the remediation of the system. All the key stakeholders were at the table including representatives from the three communities, the Ministry of Environment and Public Health. The Water Advisory Committee (WAC) served as a forum to exchange information quickly and efficiently and allowed its participants to gain a better idea of one another's knowledge and limitations. As the manager of water supply explains:

> Our relationship with our regulators has improved tremendously. Previously we hardly knew who the regulator was. We didn't know who to deal with. We

> didn't have regular meetings. They came down here in 1997 and sat in the
> boardroom downstairs and read us the riot act . . . Since then, we now meet
> regularly; we know the people. They turned from an adversary to an ally
> (interview, acting manager of water supply).

The water system assessment led Moncton's Department of Engineering and Public
Works to recommend the construction of a water treatment plant. At first, the department developed a traditional user-pay model of how to get there. However, with other
financial pressures competing for limited resources, the three cities decided to apply for
government assistance. While all three communities agreed that they needed a water
treatment plant, none of them listed it as a priority on their infrastructure programme
applications. Unable to secure provincial or federal funding to build a new water treatment plant, the City of Moncton began to explore a public–private partnership. The
City saw the potential to realise cost savings by optimising the design process and
decided to use a design–build–operate contract, surmising that, if the private company
had to operate the plant for 20 years, it shouldn't be cutting corners on its construction.
In May 1998, after competitive bidding from nine firms, the city signed an agreement
with US Filter (owned by water giant Vivendi) to finance, design, build and operate a
water treatment plant for 20 years. The company is responsible for producing water
that meets the Canadian drinking water quality guidelines while the City maintains
overall responsibility and control for the water system. During the system assessment
and during the construction of the new treatment plant, the Water Advisory Committee was seen as a necessary vehicle to promote open communication between the key
stakeholders and, as a result, it has continued to meet quarterly and is considered a
very important mechanism for managing the system. With the opening of the treatment plant, the plant manager also participates in the committee.

This final case reveals that the solution to Moncton's water problems was not to be
found in the selection of an appropriate formal governance mechanism for its water
system, but rather in the acknowledgment of the need to treat the problem as a domain
issue. As in the previous cases, a crisis served to reveal the absence of any overarching
organisation capable of managing the domain. Instead, the key stakeholders had to
step forward and develop a domain-based collaborative mechanism capable of governing the situation.

1.6 Discussion

Water supply is one of several areas where continued constraint on public resources has
motivated governments to experiment with the provision of public goods through the
creation of partnerships involving the public, private and not-for-profit sectors. Owing
to its need for multi-level risk management, it is also an area where one overarching
organisation does not exist that is capable of directing and co-ordinating the actions of
all the other organisations involved in the execution of the domain. The three case
studies presented above make use of a range of formal governance structures: a municipally owned corporation, a municipal department and a public–private partnership.
Yet, regardless of the differences in formal structure, in each case no overarching

organisation was capable of influencing the whole domain and the formal structures have proved insufficient to address the domain issues. In each case, domain-based collaborative governance mechanisms have evolved to supplement the formal structures.

As noted in the cases, trust takes on greater importance because decision-making now involves groups rather than individuals and includes a more diverse set of individuals (Rousseau *et al.* 1998; Dekker 2004). In the cases studied here, trust was built through domain-based efforts at collaboration. Phillips *et al.* (2000) explain that collaboration can be used to negotiate roles and responsibilities in a context where no legitimate authority sufficient to manage the situation is recognised. Thus, in the context of building a multi-barrier approach to water supply, there is a need to involve multiple agencies precisely because there is no overarching organisation that is capable of addressing the whole problem domain. In contrast, creating a new overarching organisation may simply limit the perspectives represented and thus limit the potential solutions. Domain problems inherently require a variety of perspectives (Westley and Vredenburg 1997). This was found to be the case in our study, in which participants in each of the Water Advisory Committees spoke of a need to 'revitalise the process' by including new players, such as the fire chief or staff from the waste-water services department, in order to keep the issues fresh and solicit new points of view.

Is the solution to the governance of problem domains, such as water supply, to mandate collaboration? In the right context, collaborative governance can be extremely efficient because it reduces the need for the monitoring requirements or incentives required by more formal governance structures (Phillips *et al.* 2000). However, successful collaborative governance relies on the development of common beliefs and norms through socialisation. Thus, mandating collaboration will not necessarily produce the desired outcomes. Effective collaboration requires that each stakeholder in the domain must acknowledge its dependence on the other actors and participate in the formation of a shared vision of the boundaries of the problem (Gray 1989; Westley and Vredenburg 1997). When one stakeholder does not actively participate in the problem definition process, it can disrupt the collaborative effort. For instance, in Moncton, the members of the water advisory committee expressed concerns about the arrival of a new plant manager and the need to re-establish a trusting relationship with this new agent. In addition, the regulators commented that a long-term view towards water supply benefits from consistency in staffing and expressed concerns that the private operator seemed to have too much staff changeover. It seems, then, that participants in the domain must earn the trust of the other participants before the benefits of domain-based collaborative governance can be realised. It seems the lesson for the governance of public–private partnerships is that the private-sector participants in the domain will need to prove themselves and demonstrate their commitment to solving the domain problem above any commitment to corporate profits.

1.7 Conclusions

Water supply is but one of several areas in which efforts to deliver more with less have motivated governments to experiment with the provision of public goods through the creation of partnerships involving the public, private and not-for-profit sectors. The cases in this study were selected to explore the range of formal governance structures currently employed in the delivery of municipal drinking water in Canada. Despite the differences in formal structure, in each of the cases, no overarching organisation was able to influence the whole domain, and the formal organisational governance structures have been unable to address the domain-based issues. In each case, it was domain-based collaborative governance mechanisms that evolved to supplement the formal organisational governance structures. The delivery of municipal water supply is just one example of a situation in which examining governance from a domain perspective may prove more insightful than the traditional organisation-centric views of governance as a choice between markets and hierarchies.

This chapter contributes to the literature on the governance of multi-sector partnerships in two ways. First, it acknowledges that there is often a need for a domain approach when multiple stakeholders are connected through a complex web of interdependencies and no overarching organisation exists to control the domain. Second, it broadens the traditional management concept of governance from a focus on organisational structure to include domain-based notions of governance. In particular, domain-based stakeholder collaboration can serve as a form of governance, which may have particular relevance to the delivery of public goods such as water. More research needs to be done to determine under which conditions domain-based collaborative governance may prove a successful alternative or supplement to traditional, more formal forms of governance such as markets and hierarchies.

References

Barlow, M., and T. Clarke (2002) *Blue Gold: The Battle against Corporate Theft of the World's Water* (Toronto: Stoddart).

Bradach, J.L., and R.G. Eccles (1989) 'Price, Authority and Trust: From Ideal Types to Plural Forms', *Annual Review of Sociology* 15: 97-118.

Brubaker, E. (2003) 'Private Water Runs Dry', *The National Post*, 30 July 2003: FP15.

Clark, W.W., and I. Demirag (2002) 'Enron: The Failure of Corporate Governance', *Journal of Corporate Citizenship* 8 (Winter 2002): 105-22.

Daily, C.M., D.R. Dalton and A.A. Canella (2003) 'Corporate Governance: Decades of Dialogue and Data', *Academy of Management Review* 28.3: 371-82.

Davis, J.H., F.D. Schoorman and L. Donaldson (1997) 'Toward a Stewardship Theory of Management', *Academy of Management Review* 22.1: 20-47.

Dekker, H.C. (2004) 'Control of Inter-Organizational Relationships: Evidence on Appropriation Concerns and Coordination Requirements', *Accounting, Organizations and Society* 29: 27-49.

DiIulio, J.J., Jr (1994) 'Principled Agents: The Cultural Bases of Behavior in a Federal Government Bureaucracy', *Journal of Public Administration Research and Theory* 4.3: 277-318.

Doucouliagos, C. (1994) 'A Note on the Evolution of *Homo Economicus*', *Journal of Economic Issues* 28.3: 877-83.

Dyer, J.H., and H. Singh (1998) 'The Relational View: Cooperative Strategy and Sources of Interorganizational Competitive Advantage', *Academy of Management Review* 23.4: 660-79.

Eisenhardt, K.M. (1989a) 'Agency Theory: An Assessment and Review', *Academy of Management Review* 14.1: 57-74.

—— (1989b) 'Building Theories from Case Study Research', *Academy of Management Review* 14.4: 532-50.

Emery, F.E., and E.L. Trist (1965) 'The Causal Texture of Organizational Environments', *Human Relations* 18: 21-32.

Falkenberg, L., and I. Herremans (1995) 'Ethical Behaviours in Organizations: Directed by the Formal or Informal Systems?', *Journal of Business Ethics* 14.2: 133-43.

Federal-Provincial-Territorial Committee on Drinking Water (2002) *From Source to Tap: The Multi-Barrier Approach to Safe Drinking Water* (Ottawa: Canadian Council of Ministers of the Environment).

Finger, M., and J. Allouche (2002) *Water Privatisation: Trans-national Corporations and the Re-regulation of the Water Industry* (New York: Spon Press).

Freeman, E.R. (1984) *Strategic Management: A Stakeholder Approach* (Boston, MA: Pitman).

Garcia, P., and H. Vredenburg (2003) 'Building Corporate Citizenship through Strategic Bridging in the Oil and Gas Industry in Latin America', *Journal of Corporate Citizenship* 10 (Summer 2003): 37-49.

Glaser, B., and A. Strauss (1967) *The Discovery of Grounded Theory: Strategies for Qualitative Research* (Hawthorne, NY: Aldine de Gruyter).

Granovetter, M. (1985) 'Economic Action and Social Structure: The Problem of Embeddedness', *American Journal of Sociology* 91.3: 481-510.

Gray, B. (1985) 'Conditions Facilitating Interorganizational Collaboration', *Human Relations* 38.10: 911-36.

—— (1989) *Collaborating: Finding Common Ground for Multiparty Problems* (San Francisco: Jossey-Bass).

Hall, J., and H. Vredenburg (2003) 'The Challenges of Sustainable Development Innovation', *MIT Sloan Management Review* 45.1: 61-68.

Heide, J.B. (1994) 'Interorganizational Governance in Marketing Channels', *Journal of Marketing* 58 (January 1994): 71-85.

Jensen, M.C., and W.H. Meckling (1976) 'Theory of the Firm: Managerial Behavior, Agency Costs, and Ownership Structure', *Journal of Financial Economics* 11: 5-50.

Karp, D.R., and C.L. Gaulding (1995) 'Motivational Underpinnings of Command-and-Control, Market-Based, and Voluntarist Environmental Policies', *Human Relations* 48.5: 439-65.

Laing, R.D. (2002) *Report of the Commission of Inquiry into Matters Related to the Safety of Public Drinking Water in the City of North Battleford, Saskatchewan* (North Battleford, Saskatchewan: Queen's Printer).

Lowndes, V., and C. Skelcher (1998) 'The Dynamics of Multi-organizational Partnerships: An Analysis of Changing Modes of Governance', *Public Administration* 76: 313-33.

McCann, J.E. (1983) 'Design Guidelines for Social Problem-Solving Interventions', *Journal of Applied Behavioral Science* 19: 177-89.

McFetridge, D.G. (1997) *The Economics of Privatization* (Benefactor's Lecture; Toronto: C.D. Howe Institute).

O'Connor, D.R. (2002a) *Part One Report of the Walkerton Inquiry: The Events of May 2000 and Related Issues* (Toronto: Ministry of the Attorney General, Queen's Printer for Ontario).

—— (2002b) *Part Two Report of the Walkerton Inquiry: A Strategy For Safe Drinking Water* (Toronto: Ministry of the Attorney General, Queen's Printer for Ontario).

Osbourne, D., and T. Gaebler (1992) *Reinventing Government: How the Entrepreneurial Spirit is Transforming the Public Sector* (Reading, MA: Addison-Wesley).

Ouchi, W.G. (1979) 'A Conceptual Framework for the Design of Organizational Control Mechanisms', *Management Science* 25.9: 833-48.

—— (1980) 'Markets, Bureaucracies and Clans', *Administrative Science Quarterly* 25.1: 129-41.

Park, S.H. (1996) 'Managing an Interorganizational Network: A Framework of the Institutional Mechanism for Network Control', *Organization Studies* 17.5: 795-824.

Phillips, N., T.B. Lawrence and C. Hardy (2000) 'Inter-organizational Collaboration and the Dynamics of Institutional Fields', *Journal of Management Studies* 37.1: 23-43.

Rousseau, D.M., S.B. Sitkin, R.S. Burt and C. Camerer (1998) 'Not So Different After All: A Cross-Discipline View of Trust', *Academy of Management Review* 23.3: 393-404.

Sharma, S., H. Vredenburg and F. Westley (1994) 'Strategic Bridging: A Role for the Multinational Corporation in Third World Development', *Journal of Applied Behavioral Science* 30.4: 458-76.

Sims, R.R., and J. Brinkmann (2003) 'Enron Ethics (or: Culture Matters More Than Codes)', *Journal of Business Ethics* 45.3: 243-56.

Toronto Works and Emergency Services (2002) *Water and Wastewater Services Annual Report 2002* (Toronto: City of Toronto).

Trist, E. (1983) 'Referent Organizations and the Development of Inter-Organizational Domains', *Human Relations* 36.3: 269-84.

Vredenburg, H., and F. Westley (2002) 'Sustainable Development Leadership in Three Contexts: Managing for Global Competitiveness', *Journal of Business Administration* (Special Issue: 'Bringing Business on Board: Sustainable Development and the B-School Curriculum'): 239-59.

Westley, F., and H. Vredenburg (1991) 'Strategic Bridging: The Collaboration between Environmentalists and Business in the Marketing of Green Products', *Journal of Applied Behavioral Science* 27.1: 65-90.

—— and —— (1997) 'Interorganizational Collaboration and the Preservation of Global Biodiversity', *Organization Science* 8.4: 381-403.

Williamson, O.E. (1975) *Markets and Hierarchies. Analysis and Antitrust Implications: A Study in the Economics of Internal Organization* (New York: The Free Press).

—— (1985) *The Economic Institutions of Capitalism: Firms, Markets, Relational Contracting* (New York: The Free Press).

Wilson, J.Q. (1989) *Bureaucracy: What Government Agencies Do and Why They Do It* (New York: Basic Books).

Yin, R.K. (2003) *Case Study Research: Design and Methods* (Thousand Oaks, CA: Sage).

Zadek, S., and M. McIntosh (2002) 'Introduction', *Journal of Corporate Citizenship* 8 (Winter 2002; Special Issue: 'Corporate Transparency, Accountability and Governance'): 16-21.

2

Regulation, responsibility and representation
CHALLENGES FOR INTRA-ORGANISATIONAL COMMUNICATION

Wolfgang Meyer
Saarland University, Germany

Every discussion about **good governance** assumes the commonly shared opinion that performance of governance is nowadays more or less imperfect. Scientific debates are primarily directed at the institutional structure of the political system and its ability to support the production of appropriate solutions for societal problems (Pierre 2000). According to the declining influence of national governments as a result of economic globalisation (Steger 2003), multi-actor policy networks, including public authorities (government, political parties, administration, etc.) and private actors (commercial enterprises, non-profit organisations, interest groups, etc.), are supposed to be a promising alternative for future decision-making at different levels of the political system (transnational, national, regional, etc.) in modern democratic states.

The participation of non-state organisations in political decision-making is far from new: apart from various forms of 'lobbying', political institutions in some countries are giving civil-society actors the freedom to decide on well-defined aspects of their own affairs. However, the problem-solving capability of self-regulating systems, such as the German system of *Tarifautonomie* (for an overview, see Streeck and Rehder 2003), is at least questionable and there is still no evidence that governance of multi-actor policy networks is, per se, superior to regular forms of political government.

This chapter discusses one important factor that may hinder improvement in governance through multi-actor policy networks. Direct participation in political decision processes will provide new challenges to the communications capacity of corporate actors from civil society, and interest organisations in particular. The central assumption here is that the vast majority of today's non-governmental organisations will not be able to manage these additional communications tasks within their existing communications structures and routines. As a result, multi-actor policy networks may even increase the inequality of participation opportunities, and, therefore, decrease the legitimacy of network decisions.

This chapter develops this argument in four steps. First, Section 2.1 outlines the increasing demand for communication to support collective action in multi-actor policy networks (compared with other co-ordination mechanisms). Hence, good governance in multi-actor policy networks requires adequate communication tools within and between organisations to ensure co-ordination towards the common goal of 'good' decisions.

As one of the main linkages between government and the political system, social responsibility must be redefined for civil-society actors. Participation in decision-making means taking responsibility for its impacts on 'the people' in general and cannot be reduced to the particular interests of the organisation's members. Therefore, balancing the requests for social responsibility (due to co-operation with other organisations in policy networks) and for members' accountability (due to the relationship between board and membership within organisations) is a task for **top-down communication**, the process of informing members about the development of negotiations and the reasons why delegates should accept common solutions. This aspect is discussed further in Section 2.2.

Representation of member interests within the network is the main task of civil-society organisations: their delegates have to speak for 'the members'. In order to ensure correct representation, democratic structures of opinion-building and internal clarification have to be implemented, leading the communication flow from members to negotiators. Hence, **bottom-up communication** is required in order to aggregate individual opinion into a collectively agreed position and to transfer it through delegates into the network negotiations. Further details on this issue can be found in Section 2.3.

Section 2.4 discusses recent communication capabilities of interest organisations to manage the tasks of top-down and bottom-up communication in policy-forming processes within multi-actor policy networks. According to the results of our own evaluation studies on the implementation of environmental communication within the communications infrastructure of about 30 federal associations in Germany (Meyer *et al.* 2002), we can make some assumptions that may serve as a starting point for more systematic research on this topic. Although the empirical evidence is still weak, some recommendations for measures accompanying the implementation of multi-actor policy networks can be offered and are presented in the concluding section.

2.1 Regulation in networks: co-ordination between independent corporate actors

The decision-making capability of national governments is challenged from two sides. As Hanf and O'Toole (1992: 166) mentioned, 'modern governance is characterised by decision systems in which territorial and functional differentiation desegregate effective problem-solving capacity into a collection of sub-systems of actors with specialised tasks and limited competence and resources'. Therefore, differentiation as an outcome of modernisation increases the demand for co-ordination between state and non-state organisations within the national framework (Mayntz 1994).

Supplementing this intra-national development is the globalisation process with its increasing number of transnational linkages in the economic as well as in the political sphere, confronting the steering ability of centralised national governments from an international perspective (Prakash and Hart 2001). Hence, globalisation, as another outcome of modernisation, increases the requirement for co-ordination between national organisations—concerning both state and non-state actors—on a transnational policy level (Beck 1999).

Co-ordination between formally independent corporate actors, at both the national and international level of policy-making is, therefore, becoming increasingly important for problem-solving. Traditional mechanisms to match individual behaviour for collective action—**market** and **hierarchy**—reach their limits and give way to new hybrid forms of co-ordination subsumed under the term **network** (Powell 1990). Therefore, multi-actor policy networks are assumed to be the solution to today's governance problems and come into the focus of scientific research.[1] For a consensual, minimal definition, Börzel (1997: 1) suggested the understanding of a policy network

> as a set of relatively stable relationships which are of non-hierarchical and interdependent nature linking a variety of actors, who share common interests with regard to a policy and who exchange resources to pursue these shared interests acknowledging that co-operation is the best way to achieve common goals.

As participants in such inter-organisational co-operations, several different state organisations (national and local government, legislative and administration, federal and regional agencies, etc.) and non-state organisations (multinational, small and medium-sized enterprises [SMEs], non-profit organisations, interest groups and associations, etc.) have been recognised in empirical analysis on various policy fields at the local, regional, national and international level of policy-making.[2]

Overcoming the serious problems of horizontal self-co-ordination is the most important objective for multi-actor policy networks. Collective action of corporate actors to produce collective goods is always challenged by egoistic behaviour and bargaining dilemmas that have to be regulated by sufficient institutions and measures (Olson 2000; Heckelman and Olson 2003). Therefore, 'networks' are primarily structural modes to solve these co-ordination problems. In general, four key elements of 'network regulation' can be identified:

- **Trust.** Trust in the reliability of each member to act in a co-operative way is needed to ensure collective action (Knill 2000: 119ff.). In the case of corporate actors, fair contribution to the common tasks means the guarantee of intra-organisational decisions corresponding with collective targets and agreements.

---

1   Compare Marin and Mayntz 1991; Jordan and Schubert 1992; Börzel 1997; Rhodes 1997; Marsh 1998; Koob 1999; Knill 2000; Dinter 2001.

2   E.g. from a comparative perspective on health policy, see Banting and Corbett 2002; for public policy in the United Kingdom, see Richards and Smith 2002.

- **Durability.** To produce trust, to avoid cheating and to overcome 'prisoner dilemma' situations, continuous (or, as a minimum, repeated) interaction between the same actors is necessary.[3] Therefore, networks have to be stable constellations of actors at least to a certain extent and over a recognisable time period.

- **Strategic dependency.** Continuous interaction between formally independent and voluntary participating actors leads to 'strategic dependency' (Streeck and Schmitter 1996: 137ff.) due to shared production of collective goods. Therefore, the scope of action for each actor in every decision situation is reduced to co-operative alternatives because egoistic behaviour risks future support of partners.

- **Institutionalisation.** Rules are, nevertheless, needed to stabilise the bargaining process in networks, especially to balance power disparities between members (Bachmann 2000: 108ff.) and to protect network products against external takeover. Thus an institutional framework regulating the modalities of participation, the process of decision-making, the distribution of commonly produced benefits and the possibility of access to and exit from networks have to be developed (Mayntz and Scharpf 1995: 19ff.).

Although a great variety of co-ordination types between formally independent actors can be subsumed under the category 'network', some general problems of this regulation type can be identified (Meyer and Baltes 2004):

- **Evolution of networks.** The relationship between stability and change in networks is unclear from both theoretical and empirical perspectives. On the one hand, networks need to be stabilised to ensure the development of trust between participants. As a result, network members, as well as formal and informal rules of interaction, have to remain more or less constant over time, because any change would challenge the balance needed for successful co-operation. On the other hand, to protect the network from both internal and external takeovers, an institutionalisation process with ongoing changes of rules and agreements is necessary. Furthermore, the modernisation process requires the possibility to include new actors. Networks as modes of regulation seem to be fragile constructions, tending towards bureaucratic closure (hierarchy) or dispersal of co-operation (market). However, the evolution of networks and the opportunities for governing networks successfully over time are coming more and more into the focus of network research (Sydow and Windeler 2000).

- **Negative side-effects.** Political science literature emphasises the deterministic forces challenging the functionality of the existing political system (Sørensen 2002), and most authors understand multi-actor policy networks as an opportunity for greater participation of civil society and increasing problem-solving capacity. Nevertheless, multi-actor policy networks may also pro-

---

3　On the considerations of game theory, see Ordeshook 2003; especially on the importance of repeated interaction, see Axelrod 1984.

duce negative side-effects that may follow—in the worst case—the 'iron law of oligarchy' (Michels 1987). Due to the extensive communicational activities between delegates in multi-actor policy networks, the interpersonal relationship between the negotiators may lead to 'clique building' and estrangement from the organisational members they represent. The absence of a democratic control mechanism and a lack of transparency of bargaining processes within the group may strengthen this problem. Moreover, even if delegates stay loyal to their electorate, the members of their organisation may mistrust them and expect such oligarchic tendencies.

- **Inefficiency.** Despite the question as to whether multi-actor policy networks are effective modes for decision-making and problem-solving, they are certainly not very efficient compared to market and hierarchy. While competition in the market proved to be an effective *and* efficient way to co-ordinate exchanges of goods and services, bureaucratic rationality in hierarchies offers an optimised way to handle routine tasks quickly (assuring a minimum of communication and co-ordination expenses) and productively (assuring the involvement of exactly those actors needed to produce a collective good). Compared to these co-ordination modes, a network is rather inefficient because of the amount of informal and non-task-related communication necessary for the production of *trust*.

The extended need for communication to co-ordinate action of formally independent actors is not only mentioned in the literature concerning network regulation, but can also be found in small-group research on decision-making and problem-solving (Ostrom 1990). In decision situations, communication increases the benefit of co-operation through the possibility of identifying the intentions of others and decreases the costs of co-operation through the possibility to address one's own intention to others (Bohnet 1997). Thus 'good' governance needs a high degree of communication in the bargaining process. Moreover, not only the *quantity* but also the *quality* of interaction is important. Some recent studies show, for example, the importance of decision styles (e.g. Sweet *et al.* 2003) and information processing (e.g. Brauner and Scholl 2000) for decision-making and problem-solving. Therefore, one can expect an enormous expenditure on communication in multi-actor policy networks—especially if they should be able to produce political decisions.

From the perspective of corporate actors involved in multi-actor policy networks, the communications task is not only limited to interaction with other participating organisations. It also has effects on intra-organisational communication processes to a certain extent. Each organisation develops structures and routines to communicate and it is not probable that participation in multi-actor policy networks automatically leads to a radical change in these communication modes. Hence, non-state actors do not build up their communication modes for direct participation in political decision-making and this might create problems. Therefore, two selected examples for possible internal communication problems, concerning top-down communication (responsibility) and bottom-up communication (representation) in civil-society organisations, will be briefly described in the next two sections.

2.2 Responsibility and 'top-down' communication

One of the most important questions within governance discussions in political science is how should non-state actors be included into the policy-forming process. Moreover, the problem can be focused on the extent to which non-state actors should be involved in decision-making: are decisions on policies still in the hands of government (leaving non-state organisations as only a consulting voice preliminary to decisions), or are these decisions the outcomes of bargaining processes between government and civil society, offering all participants voting-rights (however weighted)?

In the first case, there would be no change to the usual practice that can be observed since the installation of democratic political systems. On one hand, non-state organisations are engaging in lobby work with the objective of influencing government policy in the direction of their members' interests—most associations and pressure groups see this as one of their main objectives (Meyer 2002). On the other hand, governments are forming consultant expert groups and commissions including members of non-state organisations to use their expertise and to win the support of their members for policy decisions. The formal and informal constitutions of several democratic nation states—including Germany (Reutter 2001) and the UK (Baggott 1995)—accept the right of civil-society organisations to bring their interests into the policy-forming process and define how to do so.

Therefore, only the direct involvement of non-state organisations in decision-making, giving them the right to vote and commit themselves to take on social responsibility for these shared decisions, will make a difference to the actual practice and might open the opportunity for improvement. It is a characteristic of the democratic system that political leaders are accountable for their decisions to their electorate. This is also true for most civil-society organisations to the extent that they are democratically organised: the board of a non-state organisation is accountable to its members who have the right to (re)elect their leaders in a way described by the articles and statutes of the organisation. The difference between government and non-state organisations is easy to consider: while government leaders are accountable to 'the people', leaders of non-state organisations are dependent on the particular interests of 'members'. The dilemma for civil-society actors in political decision-making is connected with intra-organisational conflicts between social and member responsibility. If delegates from non-state organisations agree with a common network decision that provokes the members of their organisation, they may be held responsible for this behaviour and be voted out at the next election. If they try to push the opinion of their organisation through the network decision process, they risk a breakdown of bargaining and might be blamed (more or less publicly) for their 'blockade policy'.

The only possible way to fight this dilemma is communication from negotiators to members, which should mention the following aspects:

- **Transparency of decision process.** If the constraints of the bargaining process are revealed, members might understand the opportunities for their delegates and will be enabled to judge fairly on the way they acted in this situation. However, it is important to assure the credibility of this information and to show the rationality of the delegates' decision having the collective advantages of members in mind. In other words, top-down communication is required to (re)produce *trust* in delegates' behaviour among members.

- **Internal marketing.** Another kind of top-down communication is needed to assure the support of bargaining strategies developed by delegates and to mobilise members to push these strategies through. In contrast to the transparency goal that is directed at cognitive and rational perspectives, internal marketing appeals to the emotional side and tries to (re)produce *identification* as the basis for negotiations used by the organisation's delegates.

- **Adoption of social responsibility.** The delegates who are involved in political decision-making and have to take social responsibility need to, at least partially, transfer this burden to their electors. Therefore, top-down communication (re)produces *responsibility* for the public good.

This last consideration in particular is strongly related to the shift from 'consulting' to 'deciding' in multi-actor policy networks. Communication to (re)produce trust in delegates and identification with their positions is necessary for any organisation that is involved in bargaining processes with other organisations (provided that it has democratic internal structures). Participation in multi-actor policy networks may probably increase the problems associated with these communication processes. However, the new challenge for top-down communication in non-state organisations is the transfer of 'social responsibility' to their members.

By reviewing scientific literature on 'social responsibility', one has to state that there is a remarkable lack of empirical research into civil-society organisations. While a lot of material can be found on the question of how social responsibility can be included in corporate governance processes within commercial enterprises, mainly multinational firms (OECD 2001; Bryane 2003), these aspects are rarely mentioned for non-profit interest organisations (for an exception, see Take 2002). Unlike business with its economic self-interest, organisations engaged in human rights, environmental protection, peacekeeping, social work and so on, seem to be *a priori* qualified for social responsibility. Moreover, such civil-society organisations are even developing social responsibility within a society and are able to mobilise people for goals that are poorly represented by market forces or political decisions (Marschall 2002).

Nevertheless, social responsibility within interest organisations is strongly limited to the organisation's goals and cannot be seen as a comprehensive effort. The organisation's activities are directed towards some well-defined area of policy and they only represent the particular interests of their members in this specific area. They have to separate this interest from others and protect it against other particular interests represented by other civil-society organisations. In other words, an interest organisation is an 'advocate of social responsibility' that is limited to one specific policy arena.

Therefore, civil-society organisations that are advocates of social responsibility in a particular field face specific problems when it comes to addressing other aspects of social responsibility. While government's 'social responsibility' refers to the balance of all kinds of interests in political decisions, civil-society organisations try to strengthen the weight of their members' partial interest. For commercial enterprises, these interests are focused on the economic system and an expansion of 'corporate social responsibility' to embrace other aspects (e.g. the ecological system) seems to be possible if they are not contrary to economic objectives (although most recent empirical work emphasises the importance of intra-organisational communication processes and the lack of communication capabilities in most enterprises for this objective; Brentel *et al.* 2003). In contrast, interest organisations are primarily active in the political system and their members are engaged for specific objectives in a limited policy area. Therefore, the expansion of 'social responsibility' beyond these political borders means to embrace (or at least to accept) competing political interests and top-down communication must signal the need for compromises. The difficulties for managing top-down communication increase if delegates of an organisation are directly involved in decision-making: competing interests will make it difficult to reach a solution that will satisfy members. Particularly for interest organisations this aspect may become essential as will be outlined in the following chapter on the representation function of multi-actor policy network members.

2.3 Representation and bottom-up communication

Representation of the electorate, offering each member the same right and opportunity to get his or her interests represented by delegates within the political system, is one of the most important democratic principles (Dahl 1998). In most democratic countries, representation is a right but not a duty for citizens: participating in elections (or other institutionalised ways to express one's political opinion) is a voluntary decision for each member of the electorate. Insofar as the total number of delegates is independent of the election turnout, only the distribution of delegates and not the quantity of votes determines the political decisions in parliament. The active participation of citizens is not a precondition for government and parliament to make political decisions.

By contrast, interest organisations are highly dependent on the active and passive support of their members. Their primary task is the aggregation of individual interests on a specific topic and the transfer of this common position to the political system. With only a few exceptions, people join these organisations voluntarily because they support the political objectives. The freedom to participate in interest organisations is limited only by the rules of the organisation, to guarantee a homogenous selection of members with common interests and to prevent external takeovers by people with competing interests. These collectively defined selection criteria form the group of 'clients', while individual decisions within this group finally build the group of 'sponsors' and/or 'members' of an interest organisation.

From an individual perspective, the decision of 'clients' to become 'sponsors' and/or 'members' follows their own objectives. Since they spend their limited resources (time and money), they are evaluating the practice of the organisation critically according to their individual interests. If the organisation fails this test, they have the opportunity to leave the organisation (exit) or to fight for its realisation within the organisation (voice). At any rate, the 'loyalty' of voluntary members of an organisation is not given but has to be (re)produced all the time (Hirschman 1970).

As a result of voluntary membership, interest organisations have to organise bottom-up communication in special ways:

- **Finding topics.** To increase support (and in most cases political influence), interest organisations have to address issues perceived as relevant not only by their members but also by clients still outside the organisation. By observing the interests of clients, interest organisations have to find new issues that are of certain relevance and to integrate them in their political strategies. In other words, bottom-up communication is necessary to (re)produce *topics* for their activities that can mobilise clients and increase political influence.

- **Need-oriented services.** Besides political issues, organisations have to offer attractive services to their members as incentives for bringing personal resources into the organisation. Such incentives have to correspond with the needs of members and must be perceived as comparative advantages of membership. Therefore, some information on the needs of members is necessary and bottom-up communication is an important tool to (re)produce *benefits* for members.

- **Representation of interests.** As mentioned above, interest organisations have to aggregate personal interests of members to a common position that will be publicly represented by the board. This process of internal opinion-building is primarily a task of bottom-up communication that has to inform the board about different positions and to support the exchange of arguments between various parts of the organisation. Hence, bottom-up communication is the key tool to (re)produce *representation* of members' will within organisations.

Participation in multi-actor policy networks with the aim of decision-making and problem-solving may create some positive effects (e.g. the increasing opportunities to influence political decisions may be recognised by clients as a new incentive) and negative effects (e.g. the organisation may be made responsible for mismanagement) on these issues of bottom-up communication. In particular, the representation task will be challenged: while the ongoing disintegration process destabilises existing political institutions (Fuchs 1999), a new institution such as a multi-actor policy network will transfer the attempt to integrate 'the people' into political decision-making from political parties to civil-society organisations (primarily to interest organisations). Therefore, the burden of *social integration* will be largely delegated to interest organisations and the increasing heterogeneity of opinions within 'clients' will make this effort more difficult. The direct inclusion of interest organisations into political decision-making and problem-solving increases the demand for representative opinion-building within the organisation. A professional communication management is needed to ensure equal opportunities and rights for representation.

The next section highlights the current abilities of interest organisations to handle communication processes and the problems that may occur in view of the new demands associated with their participation in multi-actor policy networks.

2.4 Communications capabilities in interest organisations

The ability of interest organisations to meet the rising demands of top-down and bottom-up communication associated with participation in multi-actor policy networks has not yet been the focus of scientific research. While a systematic analysis is still missing, some results from our own evaluation studies on the implementation of environmental communication within the communications infrastructure of about 30 federal associations in Germany should be mentioned here instead (Meyer *et al.* 2002).

Although these interest organisations are very different in size, organisational structure and sphere of political activities, some generalised remarks on their communications infrastructure can be made:

- **Decentralised structures.** Most associations are strongly decentralised organisations and concentrate their resources in sub-units on the regional level. National offices are quite small with restrictions in personnel and budget. Their primary tasks are: co-ordination of the activities of, more or less, independently acting sub-units and lobby work. The activities of central units are regarded with suspicion by the sub-units and centralised direction and control (even during communication processes) are widely disputed or even rejected.

- **Internal heterogeneity.** Due to historical development and the resulting regional distribution of the membership, sub-units are strongly distinguished by their relative strength and influence within the organisation. The disparities do not—in most cases—reflect the regional distribution of clients. In some cases, single sub-units even dominate the policy of the association.

- **Production-oriented communication management.** Communications management in associations is strongly oriented towards the quality of the production process, neglecting the importance of professional feedback systems. In most cases, the central units have the task of controlling the information production process while the sub-units organise the transmission of this information. Sometimes sub-units refuse to report the success or failure of this process to the central unit. Measures to monitor the use of information by members are rarely implemented. Therefore, only partial knowledge (belonging to active feedback or informal reflections on the 'mood' within membership) can be used for improvement of information quality by communications management.

- **Aggregation of interests.** Institutions for aggregating members' opinions and representing their interests are implemented in all associations, according to national laws. Nevertheless, in some organisations tendencies towards oligarchy can be found. Virtually all associations have only very limited professional staff resources and most work has to be done by members in a voluntary capacity. Therefore, the availability of these 'activists' is another important source for unequal distribution of capabilities between sub-units. Moreover, the voluntary and merely durable input of 'activists' shapes the (self-)perception of organisations and may divide them from the perspective of the 'silent majority'. Associations lack the professional communication tools required to counterbalance this development through the systematic collection of representative data.

Faced with the new task of participation in multi-actor policy networks, most organisations may be able to do this on a local or regional level. For professional communication management on the national or international level, the existing infrastructure seems insufficient in many cases. Bottom-up communication in particular is largely handled on an informal and not very professional basis. Consequently top-down communication lacks valid 'feedback' information, which is indispensable for quality management. The transfer of social responsibility in top-down communication, including (at least implicitly) the willingness to compromise with external and competing interests, seems to be nearly impossible in an environment characterised by huge inequalities between rival sub-divisions. Hidden internal conflicts may come to light if the political consequences of an organisation's common position increase. Obviously, such a development will also have consequences for the aggregation of interests produced by bottom-up communication. Moreover, the existing communications structures are yet not transparent (even for the national board), the available resources for communications management are poor and the acceptance of an extension of centralised structures—necessary for professional communications management—is low.

Of course, the results presented are limited to the German case and the sample of associations is not representative (although some very important collective actors are included). The situation in other countries may be different as it is between various types of interest organisations. Nevertheless, one should be sceptical about the general ability of interest organisations to contribute to good governance when being involved actively in political decision-making.

2.5 Conclusion

This chapter has tried to show some of the most important relations between inter-organisational co-ordination in multi-actor policy networks and intra-organisational communication concerning interest organisations. Insofar as multi-actor policy networks are a response to the declining problem-solving ability of national governments, a direct involvement in decision-making of civil-society organisations (and not only a consulting voice) is necessary. In contrast to other co-ordination mechanisms, networks are unstable constellations that need a lot of communication activities between their members to assure sound performance. These efforts are not only limited to inter-organisational communication but also have some consequences for intra-organisational communication processes. From the perspective of interest organisations, direct involvement in political decision-making means increasing social responsibility that has to be transferred from delegates to organisation members through top-down communication. Furthermore, a demand for better representation of client interests, ensuring social integration, has to be stated. This challenges bottom-up communication to aggregate personal interests into a communicable common position of the organisation, which will be the basis for network negotiations.

The main purpose of this chapter has been to demonstrate that interest organisations and their intra-organisational communication structures are affected in a specific way by their integration into political decision-making. Two main reasons for the peculiarity of interest-organisations were stressed: the voluntary nature of membership and the need to disassociate their own positions from competing political interests. Both of these factors make constructive involvement in network negotiations more difficult for interest organisations than for state authorities or commercial enterprises. It has been argued that only professional communications management can counterbalance the related problems.

The central assumption, the limited ability of interest organisations to handle the additional communications tasks associated with participation in multi-actor policy networks, was stated and described in some findings from one of our evaluation researches. The main reasons for these limitations were identified in the lack of professional communication structures and the strongly decentralised nature of most interest organisations. Nevertheless, if interest organisations are not able to solve their internal communicational problems, this will also affect the problem-solving capability of the policy networks in which they are involved.

Some recommendations for measures that should accompany the implementation of multi-actor policy networks can be derived from the empirical material that has been presented:

- **Strengthening central units.** If non-state actors should be involved in national decision-making, they require well-equipped central units. Non-profit organisations that are highly dependent on voluntary work are especially short of the necessary resources for active participation in multi-actor policy networks. Given that all delegates within the political system are paid for carrying out their mandate, interest organisations (though not the individual delegates) should also get some remuneration for their participation to build up an adequate internal information system.

- **Support for communications management.** Professional communications management must be supported at the national level as a condition for active participation in decision-making. This is necessary not only to counterbalance the inequality between commercial enterprises and civil-society organisations but also to ensure democratic representation within the organisational structure. Free professional consultation services should be offered, to improve the quality of communications management.

- **Controlling opinion-building.** Political institutions for controlling the intra-organisational processes of opinion-building must be implemented in order to avoid oligarchic tendencies. These control instances must be independent from the network and its members.

These recommendations should be seen only as 'first hints' that definitely need to be backed by more systematic analysis on the relation between governance structure and internal communications within civil-society actors. Such research is highly necessary to ensure important and valuable input from non-governmental organisations on good governance.

References

Axelrod, R. (1984) *The Evolution of Co-operation* (New York: Basic Books).

Bachmann, R. (2000) 'Die Koordination und Steuerung interorganisationaler Netzwerkbeziehungen über Vertrauen und Macht', in J. Sydow and A. Windeler (eds.), *Steuerung von Netzwerken: Konzepte und Praktiken* (Opladen/Wiesbaden, Germany: Westdeutscher Verlag): 107-25.

Baggott, R. (1995) *Pressure Groups Today* (Manchester, UK/New York: Manchester University Press).

Banting, K.G., and S. Corbett (eds.) (2002) *Health Policy and Federalism: A Comparative Perspective on Multi-Level Governance* (Montreal: McGill University Press).

Beck, U. (1999) *The Reinvention of Politics: Rethinking Modernity in the Global Social Order* (Cambridge, UK: Polity Press).

Bohnet, I. (1997) *Kooperation und Kommunikation: Eine ökonomische Analyse individueller Entscheidungen* (Tübingen, Germany: Mohr).

Börzel, T.A. (1997) 'What's so Special about Policy Networks? An Exploration of the Concept and its Usefulness in Studying European Governance', *European Integration Online Papers* 1.016; eiop.or.at/eiop/texte/1997-016a.htm, accessed 29 June 2005.

Brauner, E., and W. Scholl (eds.) (2000) 'Information Processing in Groups', *Group Processes and Intergroup Relation* 3 (Special Issue): 115-217.

Brentel, H., H. Klemisch and H. Rohn (eds.) (2003) *Lernendes Unternehmen: Konzepte und Instrumente für eine zukunftsfähige Unternehmens- und Organisationsentwicklung* (Wiesbaden, Germany: Westdeutscher Verlag).

Dahl, R.A. (1998) *On Democracy* (New Haven, CT/London: Yale University Press).

Dinter, S. (2001) *Netzwerke: Eine Organisationsform moderner Gesellschaften?* (Marburg, Germany: Tectum).

Fuchs, D. (1999) 'Soziale Integration und politische Institutionen in modernen Gesellschaften', in J. Friedrich and W. Jagodzinski (eds.), *Soziale Integration* (Sonderheft 39 der Kölner Zeitschrift für Soziologie und Sozialpsychologie; Opladen, Germany: Westdeutscher Verlag): 147-78.

Hanf, K., and L.J. O'Toole Jr (1992) 'Revisiting Old Friends: Networks, Implementation Structures and the Management of Inter-organisational Relations', in G. Jordan and K. Schubert (eds.), 'Policy Networks', *European Journal of Political Research* 21.1–2 (Special Issue): 163-80.

Heckelman, J.C., and M. Olson (eds.) (2003) *Collective Choice: Essays in Honor of Mancur Olson* (Berlin/Heidelberg, Germany: Springer).

Hirschman, A.O. (1970) *Exit, Voice and Loyalty: Responses to Decline in Firms, Organizations, and States* (Cambridge, MA: Harvard University Press).

Jordan, G., and K. Schubert (eds.) (1992) 'Policy Networks', *European Journal of Political Research* 21 (Special Issue): 1-12.

Knill, C. (2000) 'Policy-Netzwerke: Analytisches Konzept und Erscheinungsform moderner Politiksteuerung', in J. Weyer (ed.), *Soziale Netzwerke: Konzepte und Methoden der sozialwissenschaftlichen Netzwerkforschung* (Munich/Vienna: Oldenbourg): 111-34.

Koob, D. (1999) *Gesellschaftliche Steuerung: Selbstorganisation und Netzwerke in der modernen Politikfeldanalyse* (Marburg, Germany: Tectum).

Marin, B., and R. Mayntz (eds.) (1991) *Policy Network: Empirical Evidence and Theoretical Considerations* (Frankfurt/New York: Campus).

Marschall, M. (2002) 'Legitimacy and Effectiveness: Civil Society Organizations Role in Good Governance', *Poverty Reduction Strategies Forum* 29 October–1 November 2002, Baden, Austria (www.strategy-spb.ru/Koi-8/Proekt/Int_progr5/legitimacy_and_effectiveness.htm, accessed 29 June 2005).

Marsh, D. (1998) *Comparing Policy Networks* (Maidenhead, UK: Open University Press).

Mayntz, R. (1994) *Modernization and the Logic of Interorganizational Networks* (Working Paper No. 4; Cologne: Max-Planck-Institut für Gesellschaftsforschung [MPIfG]).

—— and F.W. Scharpf (1995) 'Steuerung und Selbstorganisation in staatsnahen Sektoren', in R. Mayntz and F.W. Scharpf (eds.), *Gesellschaftliche Selbstregelung und politische Steuerung* (Frankfurt/New York: Campus): 9-38.

Meyer, W. (2002) 'Regulating Environmental Action of Non-governmental Actors: The Impact of Communication Support Programmes in Germany', in F. Biermann, R. Brohm and K. Dingwerth (eds.), *Global Environmental Change and the Nation State: Proceedings of the 2001 Berlin Conference on the Human Dimensions of Global Environmental Change* (PIK-Report No. 80; Potsdam, Germany: Potsdam Institute for Climate Impact Research, www.glogov.de/upload/public%20files/pdf/publications/bc%20proceedings/bc2001/pik_report_80.pdf): 360-70.

—— and K. Baltes (2004) 'Network Failures: How realistic is durable co-operation in global governance?', in K. Jacob, M. Binder and A. Wieczorek (eds.), *Governance for Industrial Transformation: Proceedings of the 2003 Berlin Conference on the Human Dimensions of Global Environmental Change* (Berlin: Environmental Policy Centre, www.glogov.org/upload/public%20files/pdf/publications/bc%20proceedings/bc2003/2003%20Proceedings.pdf): 31-51.

——, K.-P. Jacoby and R. Stockmann (2002) *Evaluation der Umweltberatungsprojekte des Bundesumweltministeriums und des Umweltbundesamtes: Nachhaltige Wirkungen der Förderung von Bundesverbänden* (Texte 02-36; a short version in German and English can be downloaded from www.ceval.de as CEVAL-Working paper no. 7; Berlin: Umweltbundesamt [UBA]).

Michael, B. (2003) 'Corporate Social Responsibility in International Development: An Overview and Critique', *Corporate Social Responsibility and Environmental Management* 10.3: 115-28.

Michels, R. (1987) 'Die oligarchischen Tendenzen der Gesellschaft: Ein Beitrag zum Problem der Demokratie [1908]', in R. Michels, *Masse, Führer, Intellektuelle: Politisch-soziologische Aufsätze 1906–1933* (Frankfurt/New York: Campus): 133-81.

OECD (Organisation for Economic Co-operation and Development) (ed.) (2001) *Corporate Social Responsibility: Partners for Progress* (Paris: OECD).

Olson, M. (2000) *The Logic of Collective Action: Public Goods and the Theory of Groups* (Cambridge, MA: Harvard University Press [1965]).

Ordeshook, P.C. (2003) *Game Theory and Political Theory: An Introduction* (Boston, MA: Birkhauser).

Ostrom, E. (1990) *Governing the Commons: The Evolution of Institutions for Collective Action* (Cambridge, UK: Cambridge University Press).

Pierre, J. (ed.) (2000) *Debating Governance: Authority, Steering, and Democracy* (Oxford, UK: Oxford University Press).

Powell, W.W. (1990) 'Neither Market nor Hierarchy: Network Forms of Organization', *Research in Organizational Behaviour* 12: 295-336.

Prakash, A., and J.A. Hart (eds.) (2001) *Globalization and Governance* (London/New York: Routledge).

Reutter, W. (2001) 'Verbände zwischen Pluralismus, Korporatismus und Lobbyismus', in W. Reutter and P. Rütters (eds.), *Verbände und Verbandssysteme in Westeuropa* (Opladen, Germany: Leske & Budrich): 75-101.

Rhodes, R.A.W. (1997) *Understanding Governance: Policy Networks, Governance, Reflexivity and Accountability* (Maidenhead, UK: Open University Press).

Richards, D., and M.J. Smith (2002) *Governance and Public Policy in the United Kingdom* (Oxford, UK: Oxford University Press).

Sørensen, E. (2002) 'Democratic Theory and Network Governance', paper presented at workshop no. 12, 'Demokrati og administrative reform i norden', at the NOPSA-Conference 2002 in Ålborg (www.socsci.auc.dk/institut2/nopsa/arbejdsgruppe12/eva.pdf, accessed 29 June 2005).

Steger, M.B. (2003) *Globalization: A Very Short Introduction* (Oxford, UK: Oxford University Press).

Streeck, W., and B. Rehder (2003) *Der Flächentarifvertrag: Krise, Stabilität und Wandel* (Working Paper 03/6; Cologne: Max-Planck-Institut für Gesellschaftsforschung [MPIfG]).

—— and P.C. Schmitter (1996) 'Gemeinschaft, Markt, Staat—und Verbände?', in P. Kenis and V. Schneider (eds.), *Organisation und Netzwerk: Institutionelle Steuerung in Wirtschaft und Politik* (Frankfurt/New York: Campus): 123-64.

Sweet, S., N. Roome and P. Sweet (2003) 'Corporate Environmental Management and Sustainable Enterprise: The Influence of Information Processing and Decision Styles', *Business Strategy and the Environment* 12: 265-77.

Sydow, J., and A. Windeler (2000) 'Steuerung von und in Netzwerken: Perspektiven, Konzepte, vor allem aber offene Fragen', in J. Sydow and A. Windeler (eds.), *Steuerung von Netzwerken. Konzepte und Praktiken* (Opladen/Wiesbaden, Germany: Westdeutscher Verlag): 1-25.

Take, I. (2002) *NGOs im Wandel: Von der Graswurzel auf das diplomatische Parkett* (Wiesbaden, Germany: Westdeutscher Verlag).

3

Multi-stakeholder collaborative processes, regulation and governance
TWO CANADIAN CASE STUDIES

*Marie-France Turcotte and Corinne Gendron**
Université du Québec à Montréal (UQÀM), Canada

In 1987, the UN-commissioned Brundtland Report invited governments to help promote sustainable development and environmental protection by supporting local voluntary initiatives and the early resolution of related disputes. It set the tone for the decade(s) to come. In the spirit of its own Deliberative Meetings, it suggested 'that public and private organizations and NGOs . . . establish special panels or rosters of experts with experience in various forms of dispute settlement and special competence' (WCED 1987). Recommendations from the Earth Summit in 1992 followed suit, calling for more partnerships, multi-stakeholder forums, negotiations and direct collaborative planning between concerned parties. These positions were later echoed by numerous academics.[1]

Since then a number of initiatives involving multi-stakeholder collaborative processes (MCPs) have brought together a host of social actors to reconcile the complex and competing interests of deregulation and sustainable development. Many have laid the groundwork for project and policy proposals and have been instrumental in drafting effective sector-specific regulatory measures. Over the years MCPs have taken many different forms, but all typically include representatives from industry, civil society and government organisations.

A variety of promises were brought to the table in this new wave of social initiatives, which were alternately described as 'conflict-resolution mechanisms',[2] and 'sites of

*   We would like to thank the FCAR (Fonds pour la Formation de Chercheurs et d'Aide à la Recherche, Québec) Young Researchers Programme and the SSHRC-INE for their support in funding the research on which this chapter is based.
1   See Barouch 1989; Kellman 1992; Callon 1993; French 1995; Hoffman *et al.* 1999; Long and Arnold 1995; Porter and Salvesen 1995; Healey 1997; Roome 1998.
2   See Gray 1985, 1989; Gray and Wood 1991; Wood and Gray 1991; Logsdon 1991; Waddock 1989.

learning and innovation',[3] where wide-ranging perspectives could interface within a framework of constructive confrontation (Brown 1991). MCPs were even viewed as alternative systems of government, or as co-ordination mechanisms whose activities could take place outside of the spheres of market and state.

The partnerships that have been forged between environmentalist NGOs and businesses through MCPs mark a fundamental paradigm shift in approaches to environmental issues, and are the index of a noteworthy change in the governance of business. In 1999, Hoffman *et al.*'s study of the chemical industry demonstrated how, within the past four decades, environmentalists have become part of the institutional context of the industry. As the traditional, state-monitored, regulatory process progressively frees itself from a representative approach, the concept of consultation has been expanded to embrace versatile modes of participation from diverse combinations of stakeholders. Deregulation and the rise of new social movements have reconfigured the institutional political process (Melluci 1983; Eder 1993) and thus our systems of governance (Cashore 2002). Eder (1993) stresses that the concept of public space has been utterly transformed through the efforts of these new movements, whose action-oriented institutional logic favours adapted forms of self-organisation over hierarchical formalities involving the government. According to Waddell (2003), multi-stakeholder initiatives such as the Global Action Networks constitute a fundamental departure from a world in which the government used to hold the key to arbitration (a Government World), toward a new division of power among stakeholders (a Governance World).

In the 1990s, a flurry of multi-stakeholder collaborative initiatives took place in Canada (Turcotte 2003) and the United States (Irwin and Stansbury 2004) within the context of progressive deregulation that had begun a decade earlier (Chevalier 1987). Many hypothesised that by using a consensus decision-making process to develop voluntary initiatives and self-regulation, MCPs were more effective and better adapted to sector-specific realities than regulation imposed by the state (see Tietenberg 1985; Stavins 1989; Pearce *et al.* 1989; Doern 1990). However, others feared that voluntary initiatives would have little impact (Davies and Mazurek 1996); that they would attract self-interested polluters (Lenox and Nash 2003); that the dialogue approach of these multi-stakeholder partnerships could lead to complacency (Poncelet 2001); that such partnerships were poor substitutes for state control; and that they would ultimately reveal themselves to be factors of inertia (Newton and Hart 1997) rather than catalysts for a better system of governance.

Beyond this controversy, we would contend that MCPs are not inherently exclusive of, nor designed to replace, traditional regulatory mechanisms. By the same token, we would also submit that they can act as complementary systems of governance. For the most part, the effectiveness of MCPs is contingent on their access to traditional regulatory mechanisms, such as government incentives and legislation. We will present two case analyses of MCPs held in Canada to illustrate these points: the '3R Round Table' and the 'ARET' initiatives.

3   See Pasquero 1991; Turcotte and Pasquero 2001; Roome 1998; Driscoll 1995, 1996.

3.1 Case 1: the 3R Round Table on waste management

In 1994, the regional municipality of a large Canadian city formed a round table on waste management.[4] Waste management was a growing concern and several proposed solutions, including incinerators and new landfill sites, had provoked major controversies. It was in this context that the regional municipality invited 20 organisations, representing industry, unions, environmental activists, citizens' groups, scientists and government organisations, to participate in a multi-stakeholder collaborative process (MCP). The 3R Round Table initiative was launched to make consensus-based decisions regarding a regional plan for waste management that were consistent with a philosophy of sustainable development and the three-Rs principle: reduce, re-use and recycle.

The 3R Round Table MCP was chaired by a qualified, well-known, facilitator who had previously presided over a number of public hearings on the environment. The process consisted of several meetings during which participants set out operational guidelines for discussions, shared their concerns regarding waste management and agreed to produce a final report that would serve as a policy guideline for the municipal authorities, who were to draft a comprehensive waste management plan. Widely divergent viewpoints were apparent from the start and reflected the disparate expectations of the 3R Round Table participants regarding the mandate and objectives of the MCP.

The meetings of the 3R initiative provided each participant with the opportunity to present his or her assessments and solutions, with the final round of deliberations being devoted to formulating various waste management options. During the closing stages of the process, the facilitator wrote up a final report, which provided a summary of the 3R Round Table's consensus decisions. The report was circulated among the participants to obtain their individual approval before publication, but it was not formally endorsed by the organisations that the participants represented. Turcotte and Pasquero (2001) examined the results of this MCP's activities to assess consensus, learning and the resolution of problems. In their final analysis, they conclude that some gains were made with regard to consensus. Participants were united in their endorsement of the 3R principle (reduce, re-use and recycle). However, major differences came to light when the MCP attempted to formulate concrete implementation measures. Environmental groups held that the 3R action plan should make waste reduction the top priority, whereas industry and government organisations contended that recycling programmes were easier to implement.

In the end, members of the 3R Round Table did reach an agreement on general principles. When questioned on the specifics of the 3R report, Round Table respondents stated that it was the result of a consensus. Consensus around identifying priorities for an action plan was reached, including an education and awareness-raising campaign on the 3Rs, the need for more environmental regulation and the necessity of managing hazardous waste. However, no consensus was reached on 'details', such as where the 3R campaign was to obtain financing, which segments of society it should target, and what type of regulations might be most appropriate, based on the Round Table's expressed concerns. On a practical level, the members of the 3R Round Table did not agree on precise definitions of the subject matter. For example, there were three definitions of the word 'reduction' in the report, and participants disputed the meaning of

4   Based on Turcotte 1997 and Turcotte and Pasquero 2001.

both the '50% waste reduction' objective and its timetable. Similarly, no consensus was reached as to what discarded products ought to be re-used, to whom re-use operations might be entrusted, or how such operations might take place.

The 3R Round Table was a venue for learning (Turcotte 1997; Turcotte and Pasquero 2001) and a substantial quantity of information was exchanged between participants. As they strove to resolve various problems, original ideas emerged and even some new vocabulary was developed. For example, their deliberations produced the paradoxical, but useful, expression 'safe hazardous waste' (SHW) in reference to discarded products (such as batteries and paint) that could be re-used or recycled. When not properly processed, toxic SHW trace elements can be found in the earth, water and air, causing serious damage to the environment and often endangering the health of many species, including humans. Processing SHW as hazardous waste is not only costly but can also introduce subsidiary environmental problems. The 3R Round Table therefore made a valuable contribution in creating the SHW concept and promoting the re-use or recycling of partially used cans of paint and spent batteries. Further, during the MCP's deliberations, some organisations recognised the opportunity for creating new markets for safe hazardous waste and, subsequent to the 3R initiative, proceeded to implement SHW re-use or recycling programmes.

3.2 Case 2: the ARET toxic substance initiative

The Accelerated Reduction/Elimination of Toxics (ARET) Renewal Programme was a voluntary initiative established in the early 1990s by the federal government of Canada in response to a proposal from representatives of industrial and environmental groups.[5] The goal of the programme was to eliminate 30 persistent, toxic and bio-accumulative substances, and to reduce the production of 87 other toxic substances through a co-operative initiative designed to deliver results more expediently and efficiently than regulatory measures would do on their own. The programme was supported by a Stakeholders' Committee that brought together representatives from industry, associations of health professionals, governments, unions, and environmental and native groups. Its purpose was threefold:

- To establish criteria for toxicity
- To draw up a list of target substances based on these criteria
- To propose ways in which industry could manage its toxic emissions

Two years after its inception, this MCP had identified and classified approximately 100 toxic substances, several of which were listed as target priorities. But when the time came to define the means by which to reduce or eliminate the targeted substances, major dissensions caused the NGOs and union organisations to withdraw from the programme.

---

5 Based on Turcotte and Ali's analysis (2002).

In their case analysis of this MCP, Turcotte and Ali (2002) note that establishing criteria for toxicity and drawing up the list of priority toxic substances were seen as major achievements by all ARET participants, but, when faced with defining a *modus operandi*, the MCP reached a breaking point. On one hand, so far as the NGOs were concerned, the purpose of the ARET Renewal Programme was to eliminate toxic substances for which there were no 'safe emission levels'. On the other hand, representatives from industry held that the purpose of the programme was to reduce the presence of these substances in the environment according to their 'relative levels of risk'. In fact, the scope of the programme was not precisely staked out from the start, and, since its focus was later restricted to external emissions rather than including emissions in the workplace, union groups (who were already questioning the relevance of the MCP's objectives) eventually lost interest in the process.

Overall, the most notable dissensions within the ARET initiative concerned the role of government and the MCP's 'coercive' potential. In one camp, non-governmental organisations and unions wanted to see coercive legislation passed to eliminate the most hazardous substances, based on the information provided by ARET. This camp felt that the general malaise that prevailed in the MCP deliberations was generated by the 'passive' attitude of the federal regulatory authority involved—an attitude that (in their opinion) showed a 'lack of leadership' at Environment Canada. In the other camp, the remaining participants viewed their involvement in ARET as a voluntary effort that did not imply adopting any mandatory action plan for their respective organisations. Notwithstanding their arm's-length relationship with regard to the process, many representatives from industry insisted that the MCP had introduced a 'free ride' problem, in that they found they were being solicited to take action while their competitors were not bound in any way to participate in reaching ARET's objectives.

The ARET programme carried on despite the departure of the NGOs. In 2001, the remaining participants tabled a final report, revealing the noteworthy achievements of the MCP: some 300 factories and 169 organisations had submitted plans within the framework of the programme, resulting in an average reduction of 67% in toxic emissions among participating businesses—a tangible environmental gain. However, it is worth noting that participants from the industry side confided that the principal motivating factor in achieving this objective was the advent of new provincial and federal regulations on effluent waste.

Despite its positive points, participants in ARET conceded that the departure of the NGOs had created an ideological vacuum and the programme's reputation had suffered for it. VanNijnatten (1998) notes that the presence of the NGOs in ARET was pivotal to establishing a legitimate multi-stakeholder collaborative process. Indeed, according to the industry members in ARET, the NGOs played a fundamental role in securing public credibility for the initiative.

3.3 MCPs as complementary governance mechanisms

What are we to conclude from the 3R and ARET initiatives? Did these MCPs act as governance mechanisms and as plausible substitutes for government-imposed regulatory approaches? It can be said that both cases demonstrated the limitations of MCP consensus decision-making in formulating specific action plans. While the 3R Round Table consensus report showed that the MCP initiative had produced a variety of valuable concepts, no unanimous decisions were reached regarding how these disparate notions might be implemented. Similarly, the ARET initiative failed to reach a consensus in defining its fundamental objectives (i.e. eliminating versus reducing toxins)—a major shortcoming and a sizeable bone of contention for the NGOs and union organisations, which withdrew from the consensus decision-making process.

In weighing the relative merits of multi-stakeholder collaborative processes as open exercises in consensus decision-making, we maintain that MCPs offer remarkable flexibility as voluntarily defined public spaces—but flexibility always comes at a price. For one thing, by guaranteeing inclusive participation in a deliberative forum, MCPs confer an implicit right to veto decisions on all participants, any one of whom may block the process at any time by attempting to 'win' his or her respective point. As a result, when controversial subjects are raised, it often happens that consensus can only be reached on general principles. Hence, although preserving a measure of ambiguity makes it easier to run MCPs, it can also greatly restrict both their scope and moral authority.

In addition, we can say that, when it comes to achieving substantive, legally binding objectives in the areas of sustainable development and environmental protection, MCPs are not practical substitutes for state authority. This point was clearly illustrated in the ARET case, in which government regulations were key in achieving emission reductions. Nevertheless, the dialogue within the ARET process inculcated major changes within the cultural framework of polluting industries. Or, as the institutionalists might put it (Scott 1995), the ARET MCP inspired normative changes that were instrumental in supporting regulatory coercion.

Likewise, in the 3R Round Table case, deliberations spawned cognitive changes (i.e. learning and new mind-sets) and set the stage for concrete action (e.g. some companies began to recycle or re-use 'safe hazardous waste'). The 3R MCP very clearly offered the advantage of including a broad spectrum of social actors—an invaluable asset in resolving complex problems. Certainly, in this heated context, even a consensus on general principles proved to be a useful tool in orienting action (Turcotte and Pasquero 2001). The ideas raised during deliberations were later disseminated through various networks and eventually implemented by businesses and social entrepreneurs in a market-oriented perspective.

The MCPs offered a forum for constructive confrontation. Participants in both of our cases had an opportunity to increase their understanding of the issues at hand, propose potential solutions, and develop new and original ideas. It is equally true that neither MCP acted as a substitute for government regulation. However, and most significantly, they did act as salient complementary instruments for civil society in a broader perspective of governance. Davies and Mazurek (1996) caution that such voluntary initiatives have little impact when they are unsupported by legislation, but input from stakeholders provides the government with valuable leverage to persuade businesses to adopt specific voluntary measures or to formulate key legislation. Lenox and Nash (2003) have also found that voluntary programmes lead to self-regulation only when sanctions for malfeasance are explicitly attached to programmes. These findings, along with our own observations, lead us to conclude that society is well and truly bound to replenish its arsenal of coercive resources to protect the common good.

Involving civil society in deliberative processes to define the common good is a long-standing political tradition (Offe 1997). But, while MCPs are often associated with the idea of consensus, social conflicts are not likely to melt away in the first round. Indeed, the cases we examined proved to be veritable microcosms of the dynamics currently at work in our society. As such, the oft-times trying antagonisms encountered during (and in reaction to) MCPs should not be viewed as obstacles but rather as opportunities to revisit, construct and revise our conception of the common good within an ongoing process of social production (Touraine 1969).

References

Barouch, G. (1989) *La décision en miettes: Systèmes de pensée et d'action à l'oeuvre dans la gestion des milieux naturels* (Paris: Édition l'Harmattan).

Brown, L.D. (1991) 'Bridging Relations and Sustainable Development', *Human Relations* 44.8.

Callon, M. (1993) 'Comment décider en situation d'ignorance', in M. Beaud, C. Beaud and M.L. Bouguerra (eds.), *L'État de l'environnement dans le monde* (Paris: Éditions La Découverte): 294-96.

Cashore, B. (2002) 'Legitimacy and the Privatization of Environmental Governance: How Non-State Market-Driven (NSMD) Governance Systems Gain Rule-Making Authority', *Governance: An International Journal of Policy, Administration, and Institutions* 15.4: 503-29.

Davies, T., and J. Mazurek (1996) 'Industry Incentives for Environmental Improvement: Evaluation of US Federal Initiatives', prepared for the *Global Environmental Management Initiative*, Washington, DC.

Doern, G.G. (1990) *The Environmental Imperative: Market Approaches to the Greening of Canada* (Toronto: CD Howe Institute).

Driscoll, C. (1995) 'Diversity, Dialogue, and Learning: The Case of the Forest Round Table on Sustainable Development (doctoral dissertation; Queen's University Kingston, Canada).

—— (1996) 'Fostering Constructive Conflict Management in a Multistakeholder Context: The Case of the Forest Roundtable on Sustainable Development', *International Journal of Conflict Management* 72: 156-72.

Eder, K. (1993) *The Institutionalization of Social Movement: Towards a New Theoretical Problematic in Social-Movement Analysis?* (Working Paper; Florence: European University Institute, October 1993).

Environment Canada (1999) *Consultation Paper on the Future of ARET* (Ottawa: Environment Canada).

French, H.F. (1995) 'Partnership for the Planet: An Environmental Agenda for the United Nations', *Worldwatch Paper* 126.

Gray, B. (1985) 'Conditions Facilitating Inter-Organizational Collaboration', *Human Relations* 38.10: 911-36.

—— (1989) *Collaborating: Finding Common Ground for Multiparty Problems* (San Francisco: Jossey Bass).

—— and D.J. Wood (1991) 'Collaborative Alliances: Moving from Practice to Theory', *Journal of Applied Behavioral Science* 27.1: 3-22.

Healey, P. (1997) *Collaborative Planning: Shaping Places in Fragmented Societies* (Basingstoke, UK: Macmillan).

Hoffman, A.J., J.J. Gillespie, D.A. Moore and K.A. Wade-Benzoni (1999) 'A Mixed-Motive Perspective on the Economics versus Environment Debate', *The American Behavioral Scientist* 42.8: 1,254-76.

Irwin, R.A., and J. Stansbury (2004) 'Citizen Participation in Decision Making: Is it Worth the Effort?', *Public Administration Review* 4.1: 55-65.

Kellman, S. (1992) 'Adversary and Co-operationist Institutions for Conflict Resolution in Public Policy-making', *Journal of Policy Analysis and Management* 11.2: 178-206.

Lenox, M.J., and J. Nash (2003) 'Industry Self-regulation and Adverse Selection: A Comparison across Four Trade Association Programs', *Business Strategy and the Environment* 12: 343-56.

Logsdon, J.M. (1991) 'Interests and Interdependence in the Formation of Social Problem-Solving Collaborations', *Journal of Applied Behavioral Science* 271: 23-37.

Long, F.J., and M.B. Arnold (1995) *The Power of Environmental Partnerships* (Orlando, FL: Harcourt Brace).

Melucci, A. (1983) 'Mouvements sociaux, mouvements post-politiques', *Revue internationale d'action communautaire* 10.50: 13-30.

Newton, T., and J. Hart (1997) 'Green Business: Technicist Kitsch?', *Journal ofr Management Studies* 34: 75-98.

Offe, C. (1997) *Les démocraties modernes à l'épreuve* (Paris/Montreal: L'Harmattan).

Pasquero, J. (1991) 'Supraorganizational Collaboration: The Canadian Environmental Experiment', *Journal of Applied Behavioral Science* 27.1: 38-64.

Pearce, D., A. Markandya and E.B. Barbier (1989) 'Princes and Incentives for Environmental Improvement', in D. Pearce, A. Markandya and E.B. Barbier (eds.), *Blueprint for a Green Economy* (London: Earthscan Publications).

Poncelet, E.C. (2001) 'A Kiss Here and a Kiss There: Conflict and Collaboration in Environmental Partnerships', *Environmental Management* 27.1: 13-25.

Porter, D.R., and D.A. Salvesen (1995) *Collaborative Planning for Wetlands and Wildlife* (Washington, DC: Island Press).

Roome, N.J. (1998) 'Introduction: Sustainable Development and the Industrial Firm', in N.J. Roome (ed.), *Sustainability Strategies for Industry* (Washington, DC: Island Press): 1-23.

Scott, W. Richards (1995) *Institutions and Organizations* (Thousand Oaks, CA: Sage).

Stavins, R.N. (1989) 'Clean Profits: Using Economic Incentives to Protect the Environment', *Policy Review* 48: 58-63.

Tietenberg, T.H. (1985) *Emission Trading: An Exercise in Reforming Pollution Policy* (Washington, DC: Resources for the Future).

Touraine, A. (1969) *La société post-industrielle: Naissance d'une société* (Paris: Denoël).

Turcotte, M.-F. (1997) *La prise de décision par consensus: Un cas en environnement* (Paris: L'Harmattan).

—— (2003) 'Les apprentissages des comités multipartites', proceedings from the *Forum sur les Comités de concertation en environnement et en santé environnementale: Nouvelle gouvernance?*, Montreal, Canada, 30–31 October 2003.

—— and B. Ali (2002) 'Lessons from a Broken Partnership: The Case of ARET', in T. Bruijn and A. Tukker (eds.), *Partnership and Leadership: Building Alliances for a Sustainable Future* (Dordrecht, Netherlands: Kluwer Academic Publisher): 237-50.

—— and J. Pasquero (2001) 'The Paradox of Multistakeholder Collaborative Roundtables', *Journal of Applied Behavioral Science* 37.4 (December 2001): 447-67.

VanNijnatten, D. (1998) 'The Day the NGOs Walked Out: Accelerated Reduction/Elimination of Toxics Multistakeholder Process and Lack of Support from Non-governmental Organizations', *Alternative Journal* 24.2.

Waddell, S. (2003) 'Global Action Networks: A Global Intervention Helping Business Make Globalization Work for All', *Journal of Corporate Citizenship* 12 (Winter 2003): 27-42.

Waddock, S.A. (1989) 'Understanding Social Partnership, An Evolutionary Model of Partnership Organizations', *Administration and Society* 21.1: 78-100.

WCED (World Commission on Environment and Development) (1987) *Our Common Future: Report of the World Commission on Environment and Development* ('The Brundtland Report'; Oxford, UK: Oxford University Press): Section 90, 269.

Wood, D.J., and B. Gray (1991) 'Toward a Comprehensive Theory of Collaboration', *Journal of Applied Behavioral Science* 27.2: 139-62.

4
Levels of new governance from a corporate perspective

Arved Lüth, Stefan Schäfers and Constanze J. Helmchen

IFOK Institute for Organisational Communication, Germany

The end of the Cold War was a catalyst for the overhaul of the state system as agreed in the Peace of Westphalia of 1648: former absolutes—the territorially fixed state and its singular authority in governing this territory and representing it to the outside—have given way to a multitude of actors, 'a shift away from the state—up, down, and sideways—to supra-state, sub-state, and above all, non-state actors. These new players have multiple allegiances and global reach' (Slaughter 1997: 1).

Within this multifaceted web of relationships, regulatory frameworks are expected to help all actors to manoeuvre and organise their increasingly interconnected, if not interdependent, dealings: it is not only companies that are dependent on efficient regulation to act, calculate risks and monitor their operations. Policy-makers are given less time and less relevant information decide on issues they cannot really oversee. Coping with the density of interdependent facts and identifying the best possible solution, policy-makers draw on the expertise and knowledge of companies, NGOs and other non-state actors. German corporate actors, for a long time, have in fact been actively participating in shaping, rather than merely being affected by, regulatory frameworks. This situation changed slightly in the 1990s, probably due mainly to two reasons: first, a major part of relevant decisions are now made at EU level and, second, the private sector, as well as international and indeed the EU institutions being heavily criticised as being promoters of a (to say the least) 'unfair' globalisation.

Globalisation and the growing complexity of issues leave a broad footprint even on a company's governance structure: approximately 60,000 transnational corporations (TNCs), 40,000 NGOs and 300 international organisations produce a complexity that simply cannot be represented in organisational charts. The integration of transnational governance structures with the organisation and strategic behaviour of individual companies highlights institutional problems. These are said to arise partly due to a lack of international regulatory authorities with the jurisdiction and impact to implement and monitor rules at an international level. The lack of regulation, and indeed lack of global governance, leads to TNCs having to act under highly uncertain circumstances: they are expected to monitor social and environmental standards, corruption or child labour, all of which vary widely worldwide causing transaction insecurities (Homann and

Gerecke 1999: 453). However, companies are not only *affected* by regulations or the lack of governance; they have both the potential and the responsibility to *effect* proper regulation themselves—an argument not least underlined by the well-known fact that approximately 50 out of the 100 largest economic units worldwide are TNCs next to national economies (see McIntosh *et al.* 1998; Gabel and Bruner 2003).

'The complexities of globalisation have led to calls for a global institutional response' (Nye 2001). A worldwide regulatory structure, however, is not feasible and not to be expected. Furthermore, governments need years to regulate new markets and products due to a substantial time-lag between detecting the need and the initiation or alteration of a specific regulation. Understanding the necessity to structure markets and societal spheres in general in a swift reaction to changed realities, companies increasingly see the importance of new models of governance and their role as part of the policy-making system.

One of the key aspects in the globalisation game is the growing complexity of modern societies: global corporations develop new products, change and promote manufacturing, distribution and lifestyle patterns, and thereby have an impact on worldwide market structures and societies themselves. How do regulatory frameworks respond to that challenge? The first step, visible already in some instances, for national and international policy-makers and regulators is the integration of experts from different disciplines and various affected non-state actors, including corporate actors, in the formulation of adequate regulations and the identification of new governance structures. A next step will be the institutionalisation of such forms of governance: 'New de-centralised forms of market regulation may [under certain circumstances] be more effective and more democratic in increasing their access to mechanisms of public accountability in widely dispersed global contexts' (Bohman 1999: 512).

The following identifies some examples of how companies are already dealing with their new role as policy-makers within models of **new governance** on a domestic scale.[1] Founded on an institutional economics perspective, incentive structures and interest conflicts are clarified and possible alternatives for better governance are developed. Offering the experience of some best-practice cases at different levels of corporate involvement in regulatory frameworks, the chapter delineates concluding recommendations.

4.1 Different levels of regulation

There are several levels of regulation and, accordingly, different spheres in which companies take a role in the regulatory process.

- Regulation at the *institutional level*: rules or ordinances that apply for all actors in a society and thus regulate and simplify the interaction of the members of the society (see Homann and Suchanek 2000: 207). These rules are

---

1   See Kaul *et al.* 2002 and Witte *et al.* 2003 for a discussion of the changing role of various actors in transnational and global governance.

created and implemented by governments at different levels (e.g. the European, national and local level). Corporate involvement at this level of the regulation process often means that companies initiate regulation, influence the outcome of an ongoing regulatory process or try to stop a certain regulation. Traditionally, these activities are specified as lobbyism.

- *Industry-specific* regulation is initiated by companies and their organisations in order to address industry-specific problems. These regulations are often created as collective self-restrictions and are retained outside the state legal system. Governments are thus ordinarily involved neither in the creation, nor in implementing, nor monitoring such regulations.

- Individual *corporate regulation* aims at issues that are neither regulated by market forces, that is to say aspects outside the realm of a company's core business, nor otherwise by regulations maintained at one of the other two levels— in other words, institutional or sector-wide regulations. These internal rules address environmental and social matters or corruption on an individual basis as part of corporate governance. Examples for regulations at company level are code of conducts or individual self-restrictions (Suchanek 2001: 116-19).

The level of action—and of regulation—is determined by the issue that is tackled. Following the principle of subsidiarity companies start to solve problems individually before stepping onto the next higher level of regulatory involvement. The presentation of the different levels of corporate regulation (see Fig. 4.1) illustrates that, within the scope and focus of this chapter, the term **regulation** shall be understood in a broad sense. Not merely written laws at the international, national or regional level but also standards, ordinances, internal rules or self-restrictions are subsumed as part of this idiom.

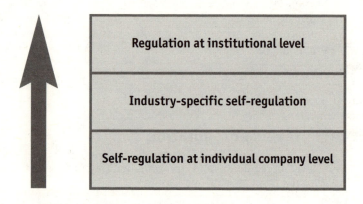

FIGURE 4.1 Corporate regulation at different levels

The following elucidates how companies are already acting as part of policy-making structures and presents relevant examples following these three levels of corporate regulation: corporate regulation at institutional level, industry-specific self-regulation and self-regulation at individual company level.

4.2 Corporate regulatory involvement

4.2.1 Corporate regulation at institutional level

Regarding corporate involvement at institutional-level policy-making, two aspects are important to realise and thus will be elaborated:

- First, by influencing regulation processes at the institutional level ('lobbyism') companies can have an important impact on the design of regulatory frameworks and thereby on determining the inherent public benefits

- Second, in order to gain public approval of these lobbyist activities, that is to say to counter the negative image of the lobbyist profession, transparency and openness are needed. Otherwise corporate involvement in regulatory processes is easily regarded as clandestine activities to the detriment of public health, safety and welfare

The role of 'lobbyism' in today's society

Corporate involvement at institutional level regulation is often equated with lobbyism, a 'dirty' business in which companies try to influence policy-makers in order to gain improper advantages over competitors. This public attitude comes from a long list of scandals and political affairs, such as the Elf Aquitaine affair in East Germany, which fuel the opinion that lobbyism is merely corruption by another name.

Being principally excluded from the information channels between policy-makers and lobbyists, public suspicion is understandable. However, most lobbyists are probably misjudged: lobbyists in fact have an important role in regulation processes. They supply policy-makers with important information in order to create efficient institutional solutions (Wicke 2000). Moreover, they act under competitive conditions since in any given argument one side is countered by a lobbyist from the opposing side. With different interests and opinions these opposing lobbyists will thus deliver different information, whichever furthers their respective cause. Thus, the sum total of information supplied makes for a very heterogeneous, diverse set of facts from all interested stakeholder groups and would thereby enable the policy-maker to find the solution with the largest benefit to all (McChesney 1991). Unfortunately parliamentarians—unlike civil servants in a ministry—often lack the necessary relevant knowledge to judge the information in order to take a fact-based, well-informed decision. That is where a second factor comes in: the trustworthiness of and even personal ties to certain lobbyists.

Policy-makers, on the other hand, have (at least theoretically) a strong incentive to identify a solution to a regulatory problem that benefits as many stakeholders as possible to a maximum degree—that is to say, with the highest overall public benefit. Policy-makers should have to prove that they have used the decreasing public resources to generate the highest possible public benefit. Regarding the *relation* between policy-makers and lobbyists, theoretically both have an incentive to operate with accurate information in order not to jeopardise their relationship and constructive mutual dependency (Wicke 2000; Breton 1996: 29). At least at this level—so the institutional economics perspective of the lobby-system argues—lobbyism sets incentives to both lobbyists and policy-makers to act in the interests of society.

Regarding the extent of regulation by policy-makers *vis-à-vis* the more flexible approach to market forces, it is useful to take a glance at the development of European-level regulatory activities. After realising that 'relying on a strategy based totally on harmonisation would be over-regulatory, would take a long time to implement and could stifle innovation',[2] 'total harmonisation' yielded to 'optional' and 'minimum' harmonisation and the principle of 'mutual recognition'.[3]

Considered in terms of this chapter's focus on regulatory frameworks and their design, this development in the last four decades shows the move from 'ex-ante, top-down harmonization imposed by public authorities' to 'ex-post, bottom-up harmonization' (Majone 1999: 314). The latter and present system takes into account much more seriously market mechanisms and utilises non-binding standards, certificates and self-regulating mechanisms in striving for full market integration in the European Union, and in order to allow for local idiosyncrasies and adequate room for innovation.

However, of course there have been many cases where both lobbyists' incentives and the appeal of self-regulation are sidelined by the pursuit of more immediate or larger gains. In many cases competition has been an excuse for secretly trying to acquire the maximum of government subsidies or for disguising an unsustainable or unsafe business as long as possible. To counter these experiences, the information exchange between lobbyists and policy-makers has to become more transparent in order to gain public trust and approval. Integrating and involving the most relevant stakeholders in an open dialogue process is not only something that is done by policy-makers; moreover, it does also makes sense in theory.[4]

Open dialogue processes *can* lead to problem-specific results and to regulations with a far higher public approval rate: with the right process design and thorough preparatory actors, and interest mapping, a dialogue or mediation process can manage to integrate all important stakeholders and thus allow them to voice both anxieties and suggestions; if constructive transparency and openness are thus warranted, instruments of

2   Commission of the European Communities 1985, as quoted in Majone 1999: 313.
3   Based on the reasoning that the basic *aims* of national regulations are generally the same, such as the protection of human health and the environment; the *specific methods* to achieve these ends may differ among the European Member States.
4   Ideally, one may argue for the inclusion of 'all' stakeholders. However, identifying the right actors to represent all relevant interests often determines whether anything can be achieved at all. The selection of these individual participants to a process may be determined by characteristics such as the degree of personal concern, clout and attitude towards constructive dialogue. See the extensive literature on dialogue and mediation process design, as listed, e.g., in Meister and Helmchen 2003.

dialogue and mediation can indeed create and foster an atmosphere of trust and credibility enabling decision-makers to discuss options much more candidly and determine more inclusively the best solution.[5]

4.2.2 In practice

One example of such a transparent regulation process is the mediation and dialogue process in the context of an extension of the airport of Frankfurt-Main in Germany. In the late 1990s primarily Lufthansa but also the airport operator, FRAPORT AG, as well as the state of Hesse, demanded the building of a new runway for the airport in order to increase the number of landings and passengers, respectively, and to reinforce the airport's standing as one of the most important worldwide. In contrast to the economic interests of these actors, residents and environmental groups took a different position. Due to growing noise exposure the residents of the Rhein–Main region tried—and are still trying—to prevent the extension. Environmental groups fear the loss of a large forest area. In order to prevent a situation similar to the one 20 years ago, which escalated in a confrontation that lasted several years (and climaxed in the death of two policemen), the state of Hesse began a mediation process to identify a general agreement between all stakeholders in 2000. The process was organised as a participative, regional preparation of the official negotiation process at institutional level.

IFOK as an independent institute was asked to organise and give advice to the three mediators in the process. After convincing Deutsche Lufthansa and FRAPORT AG of the necessity of the process, they participated with most of the other important stakeholders (local and regional policy-makers, companies and NGOs) in the mediation. Within the process all stakeholders voiced their opinion and found a compromise that was accepted by most of the participants. Central results include the approval of the new the runway in conjunction with a ban on night flights, the optimisation of flight traffic in the air and on the ground, as well as an anti-noise pact and the regional dialogue forum to continuously monitor and support the mediation results. This mediation and dialogue process and especially the practice of *joint fact finding* during the process led not only to a higher acceptance of the decision[6] but also to a 'better' decision because not only specialised experts but also local knowledge was utilised. The companies involved were one equal part of the decision process. Although the two companies acted in their own interest during the mediation process, they accepted the necessity of a mediation process.

Another example of corporate regulation at institutional level is the Initiative für Beschäftigung (IfB; Initiative for Employment) which was founded by German companies in co-operation with IFOK to face the problem of high unemployment and social tensions. The idea of the IfB is to assemble companies and unions to find innovative solutions for more employment. At the local level companies and unions initiate, conduct and finance pilot projects, which were presented at a project fare in 2000. In addition, the IfB identifies restrictions and problems caused by existing regulations that dis-

---

5   A recent study by IFOK (Meister and Helmchen 2003) shows that this prospective gain in trust, credibility and legitimacy of decisions is a primary incentive for both public administration and companies to enter into stakeholder dialogue and mediation processes.

6   See Ewen 2003: 77-79 and also www.dialogforum-flughafen.de (in German only).

able the creation of jobs, such as in their 'Berliner Botschaften' ('Messages from Berlin'). Moreover, alternatives to overcome these problems were proposed, many of which have been adopted in the reform of the German job market. Meanwhile, the idea of influencing the institutional framework conditions through the experiences of local projects became increasingly important to the IfB. Consequently, different topical working groups are continuously discussing detected institutional problems and try to influence politics by proposing better regulations.[7]

4.2.3 Industry-specific regulation

In contrast to corporate involvement in regulatory procedures at the institutional level, industry-specific regulation creates rules within a specific industry: these are sets of collective self-restriction to solve industry-specific problems and address issues that are regulated by neither legislative measures on the institutional level nor by market forces. In other words, they are binding not in a legal sense but only within a specific industry by virtue of a company's voluntary engagement or possibly an industrial association's conditions. However, experience has shown that, once an industry-specific regulation is established, well received and good experiences gained, industry-specific regulations may become regulations at the institutional administrative level, rendering it a binding law for all (Meister and Banthien 1998: 92).

The regulation process is usually organised by the relevant industrial association drawing on individual companies. To initiate and conclude such an industry-wide regulation process can be motivated by the aim either:

- To avert a public intervention on a legal or quasi-legal level (prevention) or

- To reduce the insecurities and risks for all involved companies caused by the lack of appropriate regulations (reaction)

Furthermore, in seeking a regulation appropriate to reach these objectives and have substantial impact, there are four premises to be considered:

- The regulation must be beneficial for all involved companies.

- The regulation needs an integrated efficient and credible sanctioning system in case companies act against the regulation.

- The regulation should not annul socially beneficial competition between companies (Suchanek 2001: 117-18).

- In order to achieve public acceptance, all important stakeholders should be involved in discussing and drafting the regulation.

4.2.4 In practice

Some 30 years ago the German chemical industry realised that self-regulation on environmental issues was needed. This was mainly a response to the pressure of early envi-

---

7   See the German website www.initiative-fuer-beschaeftigung.de.

ronmental NGOs and policy-makers. After a set of self-restrictions the German chemical industry endorsed and joined the **Responsible Care initiative** which was launched in 1985 by the Canadian chemical industry: the members of the initiative commit themselves to the protection of the environment, product liability, industrial safety and healthcare for employees, transport safety and stakeholder dialogue. While the overall outcome of the Responsible Care initiative is widely valued by many stakeholders, some problematic areas remain (Meister and Banthien 1998: 100-101). Critics say that the question of monitoring and evaluation and the implementation of the precautionary principle were never really successfully debated. After the start of the European Chemicals Policy proceedings[8] corporations became hesitant to demonstrate too much voluntary activity in the field.

One of the most successful—very focused—voluntary initiatives with less direct impact on health and safety appears to be the **Global Reporting Initiative**, initially launched by CERES, a US coalition of environmental, investor, and advocacy groups working together for a sustainable future, and UNEP (the United Nations Environment Programme), now acting as an independent body. The milestone of producing a set of guidelines for triple-bottom-line reporting was accomplished; the overall aim, however, remains: to make sustainability reporting mainstream—in other words, to ensure that, apart from financial reporting, and the relatively widely practised environmental reporting, *sustainability* reporting becomes the norm offering extensive information also of a company's dealings with its employees, surrounding neighbourhood and wider community, including distant suppliers and customers.

Other high-profile initiatives are less focused and according to observers do not seem to have a clear-cut goal at the moment: the **World Business Council for Sustainable Development,** German business network **econsense** and even the **Global Compact** have difficulties in demonstrating added value apart from promoting their own label.[9] Individually all members demonstrate some activity, but critics ask for results such as industry-specific or even cross-industry initiatives which would make use of these joint forces for sustainable development and offer some form of accountability.

4.2.5 Corporate regulation at company level

Regulation at company level means corporate self-regulation without the participation of other actors (neither policy-makers nor competitors in the same industrial sector): these may be either intra-organisational rules or regulations that determine the relationship with external stakeholders. These rules could be interpreted as the individual self-commitment of a company, such as activities within a company's corporate social responsibility programme or corporate codes of conduct. Corporate self-regulation should be understood as the first stage of regulation; only if self-regulation fails to solve problems will the next step up the regulation hierarchy be taken (industry-wide action or institutional-level regulation).

---

8 europa.eu.int/comm/environment/chemicals
9 See the extensive discussions on these forums' value and legitimacy in connection with the World Summit on Sustainable Development (WSSD) in Johannesburg in September 2002 (www.johannesburg.org).

In this case—unlike collective industry-wide self-commitments—no competition-neutral rules are created to which all competitors are committed. Thus individual corporate regulation may cause competitive disadvantages for specific companies as self-commitment often implicates the loss of (mainly short-term) returns. Are there any incentives for companies to commit themselves to self-restrictions? Where are the advantages of such behaviour? Generally speaking, self-restrictions can lead to several advantages with a long-term impact: first of all, self-commitment improves the reputation of a company. Empirical research has proven that reputation and trust have a positive impact on the intensity of co-operation, the costs of interaction and customer demand, and therefore are important determinants of economic success (Suchanek 2001: 113). Moreover, self-committed companies tend to have a better relationship with NGOs[10] and policy-makers opening new channels of communication: affecting the institutional level of regulation, a company may thus prevent or influence new institutional and binding regulations; it also may establish a communication relationship with critical voices on the NGO scene and civil society which prevents costly and lengthy protest activities or even legal cases (Meister and Helmchen 2003). Without the expectation of these long-term benefits, there is no likelihood of companies implementing self-regulation.

4.2.6 In practice

An example may be drawn from a global corporation that has long-standing experience in integrating sustainability into core business processes: BASF, the world's largest chemical company. BASF's stance on sustainability and corporate responsibility is clear in that they are practised for the sake of business and long-term profits. 'CSR and sustainable development must be integrated into corporate business processes otherwise it will not work'.[11] BASF has developed a global code of conduct for labour standards and internal social performance assessments. There are several incentives for the corporation to do this: to avoid business risks and reputation risks and to retain a motivated workforce.[12]

There are numerous examples of European corporations that choose to directly communicate with the general public or engage critical citizens and NGOs in a dialogue to identify appropriate solutions to questions and problems arising from the production site and or usage of the companies' products.[13] In fact, environmental mediation and dialogue should be considered as two extremes of a spectrum of instruments that help both corporations, civil society and public authorities to complement traditional regulatory processes: dialogue processes, on the one hand, such as continuous communication with neighbours and critics, can successfully pre-empt complaints to public reg-

---

10   See Tuxworth and Sommer 2003, specifically on 'challenge partnerships' between companies and NGOs.

11   Dr Lothar Meinzer, Director of BASF's Sustainability Centre at the IFOK Brussels Seminar, 'New Governance: Business and Society as Policy-Makers', 18 June 2003 (unpublished presentation).

12   See Pearce et al. 2002 for an in-depth exploration of why companies engage in sustainable development policies.

13   See Meister and Helmchen 2003 for an extensive list of examples of dialogue and mediation processes at industrial sites and around infrastructure projects.

ulators and thereby anticipate possible problems early on; mediation, on the other hand, is the appropriate instrument to address conflicts that have already escalated and search for sustainable resolution options.

4.3 Prerequisites and problems

Handling this set of new roles companies need to develop competence and credibility—to match the rising expectations and their lack of legitimacy as a policy-maker. Companies need to understand the workings and politics of multi-level, multi-interest regulatory frameworks. In order to enjoy trust and credibility, business also needs to demonstrate that it represents (and does not merely amplify) society's demands.

The most challenging of the three levels, no doubt, is that of industry-specific regulation. It is here that companies can come together in a relatively new sphere of regulation-setting which was traditionally determined by policy-makers or left to the individual goodwill of each company. In order to create efficient regulation at industry level, however, companies and their associations need the competence to:

- Detect problems that need regulation

- Determine the adequate level of regulation

- Initiate a regulation process with the participation of all important actors

- Organise and appropriately facilitate a regulation process (Meister and Banthien 1998: 93-94)

- Establish credibility as 'honest' actors with clear interests but no hidden agenda

- Demonstrate the sincerity of the commitment by avoiding window-dressing activities; and thus

- Demonstrate their legitimacy to act as a policy-maker

The core challenge of individual corporate regulations is to handle the disadvantage of self-restricting one's activities and thus incurring a loss in revenue while a competitor does not, but instead benefits from collective regulation. This classical free-rider problem is the reason for the relatively limited commitment of companies in corporate regulation. In fact, only if the advantages, such as those described above, clearly outweigh the costs of self-regulation will a company decide to go ahead (Olson 1965). These advantages are the reputation of being a responsible actor, influencing the regulation process in the company's interests (as described only in a very limited framework), less criticism or attacks from NGOs and, instead, a constructive dialogue with NGOs—and of course the benefits of the regulation itself (which are also benefits for the investing company) (Dyllick 1989: 143).

4.4 Recommendations

In considering the development towards a system of sustainable governance through establishing multi-actor, interactive 'learning regulatory frameworks' including the participation of companies, the following points should be noted:

- **Build capacities within the corporation.** Companies are, in fact, already part of the regulatory process and realise that this inclusion is part of their new set of responsibilities in a changed world of multiple actors and alliances. In order to respond to this new responsibility companies need to understand their new task and build up competences accordingly.

- **Develop new lobbying strategies.** Current business lobbying strategies in many cases aim in an 'unsustainable' direction: short-term benefits and opposing any form of additional legislation. We would not ask for less lobbying against regulation but more lobbying for better regulation. A revisiting of corporate lobbying activities to assess their mid-term consequences would thus be beneficial. To improve the quality of the regulatory framework and international regimes, reservations against transparent and direct communication processes should, instead, aim at the inclusion of more diverse stakeholders in corporate lobbying.

- **Implement incentives for change.** Within companies' internal regulation processes a similar case is true: to achieve ownership for sustainability and corporate governance issues companies should develop and implement incentive schemes for their personnel. For example, as long as the anti-corruption guideline does not pay off (while premiums are paid for sales) the guideline will not be effective.

- **Define boundaries.** Companies are advised to define the limits of their responsibility and activities within the regulation process and openly communicate them. Thereby, they can avoid unrealistic expectations as well as exaggerated fears from the public.

- **Revise membership policies.** The way forward points towards a co-operative style of corporate policy: instead of acting as individual corporations the power of new networks and campaigns should be used to design regulatory frameworks that foster sustainable development. If existing networks fail to deliver what they promised and were intended for, companies should not hesitate to leave. National or international networks are often event-driven membership organisations lacking the stamina to influence framework conditions in long-run.

Expanding the main focus of this chapter, here are three recommendations in which NGOs and national governments should be specifically involved:

- **Bridge governance gaps.** Together with NGOs companies should help to identify areas where a multi-sectoral approach could successfully bridge a lack of governance.

- **Join forces of sustainability councils.** Together with national governments' sustainability councils (such as the German 'Rat für Nachhaltige Entwicklung'), companies should build a work stream to find out how a more sustainable international framework might be established and who would be necessary to achieve this.

- **Use more effective methods in international policy-making.** Having worked in an international organisation or in international politics people are often somewhat frustrated: it seems that progress is achieved only by significant events or through the mediation of an outstanding personality. There are, however, not enough outstanding personalities in international politics to solve all the problems that need to be solved. In these processes of international bargaining and diplomacy there is—as the former UN ambassador Andrew Young put it—a distinct lack of result orientation whereas the amount of 'protocol' seems to force many parties to use bilateral agreements which are more effective but lacking in transparency. If the basis for sustainable and learning frameworks is seen in multilateralism—and in the view of many authors there is no alternative in terms of legitimacy—new 'open' methods of policy-making, public participation and stakeholder dialogue are needed. Many of these methods are already there—they just have to compete against 'old boys' networks and politicians' personal magic box for successful political leadership.

In our view, there is chiefly one big issue to resolve: what does a sustainable global governance framework look like? To deliberate this question in detail is beyond the scope of this chapter. However, instead of attempting to translate the nation-state model to a globalised regulatory regime with a centralised mandated authority, Bohman, for example, argues, new multi-actor decentralised forms of market regulation can be envisaged. In fact, 'cosmopolitan democracy [functions by] dispersing control horizontally and thereby distributing influence more widely and creating locations for the free and equal exercise of political freedom'.[14] Concretely speaking, this will include mechanisms of *new governance*—such as stakeholder dialogues, facilitated discourses, joint fact-finding, mediation processes and in may cases a result-driven 'workshop approach'. Ideally, such a framework would continually improve and develop towards a global learning framework, which sets the right incentives and enables governments, business and civil society alike to strive for mutually advantageous—'sustainable'—solutions.

---

14 While Bohman (1999) focuses specifically on global civil society exerting influence on regulations and monitoring agreements on a variety of issues that are 'enforced by the power of international publicity', this chapter argues that to a certain extent and under certain circumstances corporate actors, too, can play a significant and useful role in structuring regulatory frameworks.

References

Bohman, J. (1999) 'International Regimes and Democratic Governance: Political Equality and Influence in Global Institutions', *International Affairs* 75.3: 499-513.

Breton, A. (1996) *Competitive Governments: An Economic Theory of Politics and Public Finance* (Cambridge, UK: Cambridge University Press).

Dyllick, T. (1989) *Management der Umweltbeziehungen: Öffentliche Auseinandersetzungen als Herausforderungen* (Wiesbaden, Germany: Gabler).

Ewen, C. (2003) 'Anatomie der Konfliktregelung: Das Mediationsverfahren zur Zukunft des Frankfurter Flughafens', in J.-D. Wörner (ed.), *Das Beispiel Frankfurt Flughafen: Mediation und Dialog als institutionelle Chance* (Dettelbach, Germany: Röll): 55-80.

Gabel, M., and H. Bruner (2003) *Global Inc.: An Atlas of the Multinational Corporation* (New York: The New Press).

Homann, K., and U. Gerecke (1999) 'Ethik der Globalisierung: Zur Rolle der multinationalen Unternehmen bei der Etablierung moralischer Standards', in M. Kutschker (ed.), *Perspektiven der internationalen Wirtschaft* (Wiesbaden, Germany: Gabler).

Homann, K., and A. Suchanek (2000) *Ökonomik: eine Einführung* (Tübingen, Germany: Mohr Siebeck).

Kaul, I., K. Le Goulvenn and M. Schnupf (eds.) (2002) *Global Public Goods Financing: New Tools for New Challenges* (New York: UNDP Office of Development Studies).

Majone, G. (1999) 'Regulation in Comparative Perspective', *Journal of Comparative Policy Analysis: Research and Practice* 1.3: 309-24.

McIntosh, M., D. Leipziger, K. Jones and G. Coleman (1998) *Corporate Citizenship: Successful Strategies for Responsible Companies* (London: Financial Times Professional).

Meister, H.-P., and H. Banthien (1998) 'The Role of International Industry Associations in the Development and Implementation of Corporate Ethics: The Case of the Chemical Industry and Responsible Care', in B.-N. Kumar and H. Steinmann (eds.), *Ethics in International Management* (Berlin: de Gruyter): 112-21.

—— and C. Helmchen (2003) 'Dialogue and Mediation on Environmental Issues in Europe: Experiences, Success Factors and Perspectives' (Brussels: Study on behalf of the European Commission, Directorate General for Environment).

Nye, J. (2001) 'Globalization's Democratic Deficit: How to Make Internal Institutions More Accountable', *Foreign Affairs* 80.4.

Olson, M. (1965) *The Logic of Collective Action: Public Goods and the Theory of Groups* (Cambridge, MA: Harvard University Press).

Pearce, B., P. Roche and N. Chater (2002) *Sustainability Pays* (London: Forum for the Future/Centre for Sustainable Investment).

Slaughter, A. (1997) 'The Real New World Order', *Foreign Affairs* 76.5.

Suchanek, A. (2001) *Ökonomische Ethik* (Tübingen, Germany: Mohr Siebeck).

Tuxworth, B., and F. Sommer (2003) *Fair Exchange: Measuring the Impact of Not-for-Profit Partnerships* (London: Forum for the Future).

Wicke, K. (2000) *Interessengruppen in der Demokratie* (diplomarbeit; Katholische Universität Eichstätt).

Witte, J.M., C. Streck and T. Benner (2003) *Progress or Peril: Partnerships and Networks in Global Environmental Governance* (Washington, DC/Berlin: Global Public Policy Institute, GPPi).

5

A framework for examining accountability and value for money in the UK's Private Finance Initiative

Istemi Demirag, Melvin Dubnick and M. Iqbal Khadaroo

Queen's University Belfast, UK

Over the last decade, public–private partnerships (PPPs) have gained momentum across the globe for delivering public services (Olson *et al.* 1998; English and Guthrie 2003; Newberry and Pallot 2003). In the UK, one form of PPP, which has been the subject of much debate and controversy, is the Private Finance Initiative (PFI) (Broadbent and Laughlin 1999, 2003a, 2003b).

Accountability is a complex concept which has many alternative definitions as we will discuss later in this chapter. For the purpose of this chapter, we define accountability in its wider sense as the management of expectations of various stakeholders, often with diverse and conflicting objectives. It is seen as both ethical (Dubnick 1998) and helpful for improving performance (Barberis 1998; Cavalluzzo and Ittner 2004). Value-for-money (VFM) decisions are taken as surrogate for performance in PFI and are thus assumed to be a function of accountability. More and better accountability is therefore expected to yield improved VFM decisions (assuming resources input remains the same) in PFI. This assumed view is problematic and has received only scant attention in the extant literature (see Demirag *et al.* 2003). The purpose of this chapter, therefore, is to develop a framework for better understanding the interaction between accountability and VFM at the various stages of the PFI processes.

There is seemingly a consensus for a greater degree of accountability (Mayston 1999; Cavalluzzo and Ittner 2004). However, the questions of what constitutes accountability, what form or shape it takes, and to whom accountability should be addressed, require further clarification (Gray and Jenkins 1993; Sinclair 1995; Schedler 1999; Mulgan 2000). It is these lacunae in the literature that this chapter addresses.

The PFI literature has mostly examined accountability issues (Mayston 1999; Ball *et al.* 2001; Broadbent and Laughlin 2003a; Edwards and Shaoul 2003a, 2003b; Newberry and Pallot 2003; Baker 2003) and value-for-money (VFM) issues (Froud and Shaoul 2001; Kirk and Wall 2001, 2002; Heald 2003; English and Guthrie 2003; Broadbent *et al.* 2003a; Shaoul 2004; Edwards and Shaoul 2004), often dealing with them as they arise and in an ad hoc manner. While most of these studies examined these concepts in health, education, roads and information technology at the contract negotiation stage, few explored PFI as a long-term staged process.

This chapter is organised as follows. Section 5.1 situates PFI in the context of New Public Management (NPM) reforms, explains the meaning of and the government's justification for PFI. The following sections explore the accountability and VFM literature on PFI and propose a framework for examining the types of accountability and their VFM implications at the various stages of the PFI project. Section 5.5 provides some conclusions and directions for further research.

5.1 New Public Management reforms and the UK's Private Finance Initiative

Over the last two decades, the UK's public sector has been swept by various waves of modernisation programmes aimed at increasing efficiency, transparency and accountability (Humphrey *et al.* 1993; Broadbent and Laughlin, 2004).[1] These reforms, commonly known as the 'New Public Management' took various forms (Broadbent and Guthrie 1992; Hood 1995).

The Finance Management Initiative was introduced in 1982 (HM Government 1982) to improve the efficiency and effectiveness of the public sector through delegation of responsibility and measuring performance (Gray and Jenkins 1993). The Next Steps Initiative was introduced in 1988 (Efficiency Unit 1988, 1991) to improve managerial and political accountability in the public sector by making public-sector chief executives directly accountable to ministers for the results and performance of their departments (Hyndman and Eden 2002). The aim of the Comprehensive Spending Review (HM Treasury 1998) and Resource Accounting and Resource Budgeting reforms (HM Treasury 2001) were to improve transparency and accountability through better management of finances and accounting for taxpayers' money (Talbot 2001; Mellett 2002).

The push to adopt the private sector 'contracting approach' to public-sector service provision can be traced back to Compulsory Competitive Tendering (Parliament 1980), Best Value (DETR 1998) and more recently PFI (HM Treasury 1997) (for further analysis of the issues raised in these documents, see Broadbent and Laughlin 1999, 2003a, 2003b; Maile and Hoggett 2001; Midwinter 2001). PFI was officially introduced in 1992 by Chancellor Norman Lamont under John Major's Conservative government (House of Commons 1992) and was later embraced by Tony Blair's Labour government when it came to power in May 1997. It refers to the provision of public services such as schools, hospitals, roads, prisons and defence through a private-sector consortium, which builds and operates the required asset, the public sector purchasing its output, in

---

1   The role of government in providing finance for the infrastructure of public services has been increasingly questioned by a number of authors under the UK government's modernisation agenda (Broadbent and Laughlin 2004). This has broken down the traditional boundaries between the public and private sectors.

exchange for a stream of revenue payments over the contract period (HM Treasury 1997). It is one form of public–private partnership (PPP). The latter is an umbrella term that refers to the various forms of co-operation and collaboration between the private and public sector, including: design, build, finance and operate (DBFO); build, own, operate and transfer (BOOT); build, operate and transfer (BOT); and PFI (Schaeffer and Loveridge 2002).

Despite this broad vision for PFI, more myopic perspectives have dominated its translation into actual policy. This is most evident in the UK Treasury's formal justification for PFI, which focused on the VFM at the point of design and procurement. For the government, PFI provides better VFM than traditional procurement. Thus, VFM may be achieved by leveraging private-sector expertise and creativity in PFI projects, the transfer of appropriate risk to the private sector, and through better scope for innovation by the private-sector contractors. The budget report (HM Treasury 2003a: 271) highlighted these justifications for PFI as follows:

> In addition to requiring capital investment to be undertaken by the private sector, the ability of the private sector partner to be innovative and manage risks appropriately allocated to it can result in a specified level of service at a price that represents value for money . . . The Government is committed to developing PFI and other partnership arrangements with the private sector to further enhance the delivery of public services and to ensure the delivery of a higher sustainable level of public sector investment. The Government wants to exploit all commercial potential and spare capacity in public sector assets through a sensible balance of risk and reward.

The PFI policy has been challenged primarily because of differences in values and ethos between the public and private sector and the wider implications of the role of the private sector in the provision of welfare services (Broadbent and Laughlin 2003b). PFI is attractive to a government facing pressure to increase investment in infrastructure on the one hand and reduce public debt on the other (Mayston 1999; English and Guthrie 2003). It enables the provision of public services without the need for immediate or direct capital outlay (Grimsey and Lewis 2002; Newberry and Pallot 2003). In addition, it enables the government to avoid the 'the political costs of raising taxes' (Baker 2003: 447).

This short-sighted view of VFM shapes and drives PFI programmes and impacts accountability. As we see in the review of the literature that follows, it also wreaks havoc with the analysis of PFI.

5.2 Accountability in PFI

Accountability is a complex, abstract and elusive concept (Sinclair 1995). It may be defined as 'an obligation to present an account of and answer for the execution of responsibilities to those who entrusted those responsibilities' (Gray and Jenkins 1993: 55). Accountability itself takes various forms including communal, contractual, managerial and parliamentary (Stewart 1984; Sinclair 1995; Laughlin 1996). The communal accountability process involves meeting stakeholders' needs through consultation and seeking their involvement in the decision-making process. The contractual accountability process involves entering into a legally binding agreement over standards of performance by laying them down in writing and in specific enforceable terms. It involves the creation of liabilities and obligation to comply through the judicial process (Dubnick 1998). Managerial accountability is the process of making 'those with delegated authority answerable for producing outputs or the use of resources to achieve certain ends' (Sinclair 1995: 222). These relate to internal structures that are set up to implement, monitor and evaluate programmes. Parliamentary accountability is the process of holding government executives to account for the policies they have pursued. In the UK, the National Audit Office (NAO) and the Audit Commission conduct VFM investigations and report their findings to the Public Accounts Committee. The latter acts on these reports by calling on public-sector executives to account for their (in)action in cases where they have failed to achieve VFM.

Mayston (1999: 349) criticises PFI on grounds of poor communal and managerial accountability processes at the contract negotiation stage, and suggests that the PFI 'process is unlikely to increase efficiency and accountability' in the NHS. The reasons given include: lack of freedom of public-sector managers to choose between PFI and traditional procurement; secrecy and lack of accountability; high tender costs; and the costs of risks transfer which are recouped from the public sector. Ball *et al.* (2001) argue that PFI externalises costs to the future generation of taxpayers and that the rates of return to equity holders are high because of high risk and high bidding costs which are charged back to the public sector. They also argue that the private sector lacks innovative behaviour in the case of school PFI projects.

Broadbent and Laughlin (2003a) argue that governments are in a uniquely powerful position to dictate NPM reform actions, and parliamentary institutions such as the NAO and Audit Commission act as important vehicles to legitimise their PFI policies. The accountability process here is a political rather than a managerial one.

Newberry and Pallot (2003) argue that, in the case of New Zealand, PFI provides the government with 'a means of escape' from tight constraints imposed by fiscal targets and from public and parliamentary scrutiny. They argue that PFI commitments, which are excluded from public-sector liabilities and estimates and in the process are not reported to parliament, burden future generations of taxpayers and commit future governments. In this respect, they advocate public-sector accounting reform to enable the achievement of fiscal responsibility and transparency objectives. English and Guthrie (2003) and Mayston (1999) reached similar conclusions about PFI activities in the Australian and UK public sectors, respectively.

Baker (2003) suggests that the Enron business model, which has been facilitated by deregulation in the US electricity and gas industries, is a PPP involving the private sector supplying public utilities. He argues that Enron was a business failure as well as an accounting failure and that the government and accounting standard-setters need to reconsider their contribution to the Enron scandal and their roles in allowing certain (PFI) practices to become legitimate activities. Currently, various regulatory reforms such as the introduction of the Sarbanes–Oxley Act 2002 and tighter non-consolidation rules have been introduced in the wake of the Enron collapse to regulate accounting for special-purpose companies (SPCs).

Edwards and Shaoul (2003a) argue that it is doubtful whether, in the case of school PFI projects, communal accountability processes are able to meet the needs of the school stakeholders and deliver VFM particularly where there is a conflict of interests among the stakeholders. They argue that the Pimlico School PFI failed because of the opposition by school governors who raised concerns about the VFM case, lack of information on the costs and nature of the facilities provided.

Edwards and Shaoul (2003b: 397) examined two failed information technology PPPs on an *ex post* basis to highlight the problems that arose as a result of failure of contractual and managerial accountability processes. The authors showed that PPP contracts did not transfer risks in the way that was expected primarily because they were hard to enforce, provisions for compensation were inadequate, and it was difficult for the public sector to 'walk away' because of the statutory nature of the services. They found that the public agencies and the public at large, and not the private contractors, bore the management risks and costs of failure. In this context Broadbent *et al.* (2003b) argue that, in practice, PFI contracts are relationships based on grounds that if the contract is invoked the working relationship may be compromised.

It can be inferred from the accountability literature on PFI that communal, contractual, managerial and parliamentary accountability processes are important to obtain VFM in PFI. These accountability processes are not distinct but are related and feed into one another. The public sector is ultimately accountable to public service consumers and taxpayers. This implies that contractual, managerial and parliamentary accountability processes need to feed back to the communal accountability process. But there is also a need for the actors to address and work within the parameters of authority and objectives set forth by the legislation, and thus to connect to parliamentary accountability. The means for accomplishing this are manifest in the contractual and managerial accountability mechanisms that emerge in the PFI process. Table 5.1 shows the various ways in which current studies of PFI have examined accountability issues related to these interconnected accountability systems found in different PFI contexts.

5.3 VFM in PFI

The Green Book (HM Treasury 2003b) and 'Partnerships for Prosperity' (HM Treasury 1997) provide guidance on PFI appraisal and 'how' VFM is achieved through PFI contracting. But, as noted, the narrow perspective assumed by the Treasury does not adequately define 'what' is meant by VFM and 'for whom' VFM is to be achieved. This is a theme reflected in the academic literature on VFM (see e.g. Mayston 1999; Shaoul 2004). As we will discuss below, the government has put procedures in place to ensure that only projects that are capable of delivering VFM over their lifetimes will be approved.

Implied in VFM is the existence of—and need for—a standard by which to guide and assess PFI-related decisions and actions. Many researchers view VFM as an 'investigation' to determine how resources have been utilised. Glynn (1985) and Jacobs (1998) define VFM as an 'examination' to determine whether an organisation is performing economically, efficiently and effectively in its use of resources, operations, procedures and pursuit of objectives (Jacobs 1998). According to Glynn (1985: 29), economy is 'acquiring resources of an appropriate quality for the minimum cost'. Efficiency is about

Publication	Study	Research method
Mayston 1999	Identifies a number of areas for concern over PFI contracting in the NHS	Case study
Ball *et al.* 2001	Debate VFM and the generational accountability of school PFI contracts	Case study
Broadbent and Laughlin 2003a	Examine the process of control and 'legitimation' in the public sector by using the example of the UK's PFI	Literature review
Newberry and Pallot 2003	Examine government financial management accountability processes in New Zealand that encourage PPP	Literature review
Baker 2003	Examines the unintended consequences of deregulation on PPP activities by examining Enron	Case study
Edwards and Shaoul 2003a	Explore the PFI appraisal process and the reasons why the Pimlico School PFI failed to reach financial close	Case study and interviews
Edwards and Shaoul 2003b	Examine some of the problems that the public sector faces when PFI contracts fail	Case study and interviews

TABLE 5.1 PFI accountability studies

ensuring that maximum output is obtained from a given amount of resources devoted or, conversely, that a minimum level of resources is devoted to a given level of output (Glynn 1985). Effectiveness is about ensuring 'that the output from any given activity is achieving the desired results' (Glynn 1985). Although the economy aspects of VFM are relatively easy to quantify, assessing policy efficiency and effectiveness is more difficult. This is primarily because of the difficulties involved in measuring output (to assess efficiency) and outcome (to assess effectiveness).

With its focus narrowed on design and procurement issues, the Treasury's VFM publications on PFI mostly consider the narrow 'economy' dimension of VFM at the expense of other non-quantifiable ideals. For example, the Treasury (1997: para. 3.10) states that 'value for money will need to be demonstrated by comparison of private sector PFI bids with a detailed public-sector comparator (PSC)'. The PSC (also known as the reference project) is the 'purportedly neutral benchmark' of the most efficient form of public-sector delivery (English and Guthrie 2003: 504). *The Green Book* (HM Treasury 2003b) explains that the PSC is a discounted cash flow analysis of the costs to the public sector of providing the public service. Risks transferred to the private sector are added to these costs to obtain the 'risk-adjusted PSC' which is then compared with PFI bids. The difference is called VFM.

Accordingly, the NAO's VFM auditing 'analytical framework' and VFM reports are wholly dedicated to 'examining PFI projects as they are agreed between the public sector clients and the private sector suppliers' at the contract negotiation stage (NAO 1999: 1). Shaoul (2004: 8) concurs by stating that the NAO's VFM audit has 'for a variety of conceptual reasons focussed on economy rather efficiency and effectiveness'. Shaoul (2004) further argues that the VFM appraisal considers public-sector costs rather than wider societal issues and that the VFM benefits of PFI compared with traditional procurement, in the NHS, are marginal and subjective.

The bias of the myopic focus on the design and procurement stages of the PFI is most evident in the accounting procedures established for VFM. The central concerns of the accounting mechanisms are over certain types of risk and how they are allocated between the government and the PFI contractor. From the Treasury's perspective (HM Treasury 1997: 11), there are seven types of risk involved in PFI contracting: design and construction risks; commissioning and operating risks; demand (or usage) risks; residual value risks; technology and obsolescence risks; regulation (including taxation and planning permission) risks; and project financing risks. According to the Treasury, VFM is achieved through the optimal allocation of these risks between the public and private partners (HM Treasury 1997).[2] However, for the purpose of PFI accounting, not all PFI risks are relevant. According to Financial Reporting Standard (FRS) 5 (ASB 1998), a party has to account for the underlying PFI assets in its financial statements if it bears the risks and benefits of the assets. The UK's Accounting Standards Board (ASB) places more emphasis on demand risks and residual value risks in determining which party owns the underlying PFI assets. Construction risks, which are relevant for VFM analysis, are not relevant for PFI accounting on the grounds that they crystallise before the PFI asset is built.

Kirk and Wall (2002) argue that because the government is keen to keep PFI off the public sector's balance sheet it would pass on risk to the private sector, which might not represent VFM. In this respect, the authors question whether the ASB's rule may have reduced VFM for PFI schemes. Kirk and Wall (2001) further argue that, although both the Treasury and the ASB might agree on PFI accounting principles, the implication of the related properties remaining off the public sector's balance sheet might mean that the objective of providing VFM to the public may not be achieved. Heald (2003) concurs by stating that PFI accounting and VFM analysis should not be concerned with the risk transferred to or shared with the private sector but with total risks and the amount of risk borne by the public sector. Nevertheless, the author argues that academic researchers cannot gain access to PFI information for a comprehensive analysis of accounting and VFM. In this respect, Broadbent *et al.* (2003a) state that this assessment should be left to parliamentary institutions as they have better access to PFI information.

Froud and Shaoul (2001) argue that the risks transfer process at the contract appraisal stage is subjective because it is difficult to identify, allocate and value risks. This problem is compounded by the fact that it is hard to assess the extent to which risks have really been transferred to private-sector contractors who use special purpose companies to limit their liabilities. The authors found that there is inadequate explanation of the methodology used for assessing and valuing risks in NHS PFI contracts.

English and Guthrie (2003) highlight the importance of parliamentary scrutiny by public-sector auditors to achieve VFM. They argue that PFI outcome depends on public

---

2 Two recent studies (see Flyvbjerg *et al.* 2002 and Mott MacDonald 2002) show that traditional procurement suffers from cost overruns and delays in relation to PFI contracts, provided that budgets for these contracts are set realistically. In this respect, Grimsey and Lewis (2004) argue that PFI may provide better VFM by reducing these costs and delays through better project management. However, Edwards and Shaoul (2004) found that the public sector paid a higher premium to ensure that road PFI contracts were built to budget and on time.

policy parameters issued by PFI regulators and their implementation at the micro organisational level through interactions with PFI stakeholders. In particular, they argue that the Australian government is using PFI because of its commitment to adopt NPM reforms and the desire to reduce public debts. In addition to the PSC, the public interest test (PIT), which involves assessing the 'positive (or negative) environmental consequences' of PFI policies, is used to achieve VFM at the contract negotiation stage (English and Guthrie 2003: 504). The authors posit that, at the micro organisational level, governments are not as successful as private-sector consortia at identifying and shifting risk and hence at achieving VFM. Nevertheless, they argue that *ex post* monitoring mechanisms such as parliamentary scrutiny are important for achieving VFM.

Broadbent *et al.* (2003a) also argue that monitoring of PFI projects over their lifetime (usually 25–30 years, depending on negotiation) is an important mechanism for achieving VFM. They criticise PFI on the grounds that little thought has been given to the design of post-project evaluation systems of PFI contracts and their operation. In this respect, they propose an evaluation framework, which would draw from pre-PFI implementation VFM financial and non-financial appraisal considerations to provide 'pointers' for relevant factors to be considered for evaluation. They argue that this system should primarily be the responsibility of the NAO and Audit Commission who have an important 'control and legitimation' role to play (Broadbent and Laughlin 2003a).

Surveys of public- and private-sector managers conducted by Pricewaterhouse-Coopers (1999), ACCA (2002) and Ernst & Young (2002) also reveal that VFM and risk transfer processes are subjective and that PFI may not be having a beneficial effect on public services. The PricewaterhouseCoopers (1999) survey of 140 senior decision-makers revealed that 74% of private-sector managers and 84% of public-sector managers believe that PFI enables the public sector to procure services that they would otherwise have to do without. Only 13% of private-sector managers and 35% of public-sector managers believe that the PFI procurement is carried out efficiently; 14% of private-sector managers and 23% of public-sector managers believe that the government has the necessary skills to procure and manage projects well; and only 24% of private-sector managers and 47% of public-sector managers believe that the public sector is capable of writing output specifications to achieve VFM.

ACCA (2002) conducted a survey of 200 of its members in the public sector. According to the survey, 42% did not think PFI is beneficial to public services; 57% did not believe that PFI provides VFM; 57% agreed that, because PFI is now the only procurement route, public organisations are prevented from achieving VFM; 58% did not believe that PFI schemes are all objectively tested for VFM; 28% strongly disagree that PFI enables public-sector organisations to benefit from private-sector expertise; 39% would not opt for private-sector involvement in future, if they were able to choose freely between PFI and traditional procurement; and 48% would not advise other organisations to use the PFI route.

Ernst & Young (2002) conducted a survey of 26 public-sector CEOs in the NHS who had procured buildings and services through PFI. According to the survey, 88% had their facilities delivered according to plan; over 50% believed that there is either no or limited knowledge sharing in PFI; over 70% perceived the relationship between themselves and the PFI provider as being average or better; only 57% of respondents believed the current output specifications, performance regimes and monitoring systems are manageable; over 85% stated that response from the public has been positive; 70%

stated that the response from clinical and non-clinical staff has been positive; 85% believed that PFI is flexible in terms of variations mechanisms.

As indicated in Table 5.2, the PFI literature has mostly focused on examining VFM at the contract negotiation stage (PricewaterhouseCoopers 1999; Mayston 1999; Froud and Shaoul 2001; ACCA 2002; Shaoul 2004). Accordingly, these studies have criticised the financial appraisal of VFM, including the uncertainty involved in predicting future cash flows, the subjectivity involved in risks transfer processes and the discount rate used in the appraisal. English and Guthrie (2003) and Broadbent *et al.* (2003a) highlight the importance of investigations carried out by parliamentary institutions to achieve VFM. Edwards and Shaoul (2004) examined the *ex post facto* VFM and accountability issues in the context of roads PFI contracts, which they argue are underresearched. Nevertheless, we argue that most of these studies have failed to consider VFM as a long-term process and have not explored the importance of the various types of accountability and their VFM implications. In addition, the implications of postimplementation VFM monitoring by public-sector managers, contractors, users and other stakeholders seem to have been ignored by PFI researchers.

Publication	Study	Research method
Pricewaterhouse-Coopers 1999	Survey of public- and private-sector managers to assess their perceptions about VFM in PFI	Survey
Froud and Shaoul 2001	Examine the process of VFM appraisal in the NHS at the contract negotiation stage, mostly through a critique of the Treasury's *Green Book*	Case study
Kirk and Wall 2001	Examine accounting for PFI and the VFM implications for PFI assets remaining off the public sector's balance sheet	Analysis of comments to the ASB
Kirk and Wall 2002	Question whether the ASB's PFI accounting rule has reduced the scheme's VFM	Case studies
ACCA 2002	Survey of ACCA members in the public sector to assess their perceptions about VFM in PFI	Survey
Ernst & Young 2002	Survey of public-sector CEOs in the NHS to examine their VFM perceptions of the NHS buildings and services provided under PFI	Survey
Heald 2003	Examines the interaction between VFM and accounting for PFI	Literature review
English and Guthrie 2003	Examine the macro-economic justification for PFI and its implementation at the organisational level	Literature review
Broadbent *et al.* 2003a	Propose a framework for evaluating PFI for VFM in the NHS	Case studies and interviews
Shaoul 2004	Criticises the *ex ante* VFM appraisal of PFI contracts	Case study
Edwards and Shaoul 2004	Examine accountability and VFM on an *ex post facto* basis in the context of roads PFI contracts in the UK	Case study

TABLE 5.2 PFI VFM studies

5.4 Towards an understanding of the linkages between types of accountability and VFM in PFI

The analysis above shows that many studies have examined and raised numerous accountability and VFM issues at specific stages of the PFI process. The Treasury's guidance on PFI also places much emphasis on the early implementation and set-up stages at the expense of the post-implementation stages (see Appendix). No attempt has been made to link the relevant types of accountability and VFM at the various stages of the PFI processes. We have attempted to conduct such an analysis by identifying five stages of the PFI process and the VFM drivers and the forms of accountability relevant to the various stages. This is illustrated in Table 5.3.

PFI stage	Description of the stage	Forms of accountability	Value-for-money (VFM) drivers
1. Initiation	Treasury guidance steps 1–3 (see Appendix)	Communal	Consensus that PFI is cheaper than the PSC
2. Set-up	Treasury guidance steps 4–13 (see Appendix)	Contractual	Fulfilment
3. Implementation	Treasury guidance step 14 (see Appendix)	Managerial	Efficiency and effectiveness
4. Internal monitoring	Progress of PFI contracts is monitored through operational review meetings with public-sector project managers, private-sector facilities managers and users of the service	Managerial	Efficiency and effectiveness
5. External monitoring	PFI contracts are assessed for VFM by the NAO and Audit Commission and findings are reported to parliament, representing public interest	Parliamentary	Policy goal achievement

TABLE 5.3 Accountability, VFM and the PFI processes

PFI procurement is initiated through an assessment of business objectives, needs and constraints including that of affordability. An outline business case (OBC), specifying the output requirements, is prepared by the public-sector agency in consultation with PFI stakeholders. It involves assessing the costs and benefits of the various options including do nothing, do minimum, traditional procurement (PSC) and PFI. The accountability relationship at this stage is mostly communal as it involves stakeholders specifying 'what' services are required to satisfy their needs. The objective of this stage is to reach consensus among stakeholders that PFI or the traditional procurement alternative represents better VFM.

The set-up stage involves the creation of a project board and project team. The project board has the power to make decisions and is usually made up of senior members from the public-sector procuring agency (for example, the CEO and project manager) and representatives from the government department providing the funding. On the other hand, the project team is responsible for taking the project forward, negotiating with the PFI contractors and ensuring that service requirements, as specified by the various stakeholders in the previous stage, are incorporated into PFI contracts. It usually comprises a project manager, representatives from the user community, consultants and members with technical expertise. The accountability relationship at this stage is mostly contractual as it involves putting performance standards in writing. The VFM drivers at this stage involve fulfilment of the needs of the public-sector stakeholders.

Once contractual terms and conditions are agreed, contracts are signed and implemented. This involves construction and delivery of the PFI assets and provision of services by the private-sector contractor. The accountability relationship is mostly managerial; it involves checking that the PFI assets and services are delivered efficiently and effectively according to terms stipulated in the contracts. The VFM drivers involve assessing the suitability of PFI services in meeting the objectives and needs identified at the initiation stage.

The progress of PFI projects is monitored internally by the public-sector procuring agency through monthly operational review meetings and quarterly strategic review meetings. The accountability relationship at this stage is mostly managerial. Operational review meetings involve project managers, the PFI facilities manager and users, who would monitor services, change orders, complaints and maintenance issues among others. This would form the basis for paying contractors' monthly unitary payments. Quarterly meetings involve senior representatives from the public-sector and the private-sector service providers to discuss current progress and future strategic directions of PFI. At this stage, user satisfaction surveys may be carried out to assess the efficiency and effectiveness of PFI in meeting their needs.

External monitoring of PFI contracts is carried out by parliamentary institutions such as the NAO and Audit Commission. They mainly examine PFI contracts, as agreed between the public-sector and private-sector service provider and the delivery of PFI services according to terms contractually agreed. Their reports are tabled in the Public Accounts Committee and are generally available to the public. The VFM drivers at this stage relate to examining whether PFIs are achieving policy goals and whether they have applied in the public interest.

The above five-staged process may be used as a generic framework for further investigating the stakeholders involved, their accountability perceptions and VFM expectations from the PFI process. However, given the nature of PFI, VFM is necessarily a long-term and dynamic process which needs to be assessed over the life of the contract. In this respect, VFM is contingent on accommodating the changing expectations of stakeholders and would be based on a continuous assessment of how PFI is meeting stakeholders' needs over time.

5.5 Summary and conclusions

The objective of this chapter was to evaluate the accountability and VFM literature on PFI and to examine the relationships between these concepts. In this respect, we have proposed a five-staged framework for further researching and understanding the accountability relationships and the VFM drivers relevant at the various stages.

We argue that most PFI studies have examined the initiation and set-up stages where PFI contracts are being negotiated and very few studies have explored the accountability and VFM issues arising at the important implementation and monitoring stages. Moreover, these studies have not examined PFI as comprising various interrelated stages with different types of accountability and VFM driver.

Communal and contractual forms of accountability seem to be more dominant at the initiation and set-up stages of the PFI process. The first stage involves reaching consensus among the various stakeholders about the best procurement option to meet their expectations and needs. Service requirements are then incorporated into detailed contracts which are expected to fulfil those needs. These pre-contract stages which, in most cases, last for up to three years, have important implications for the duration of the PFI contract.

Managerial and parliamentary forms of accountability are required to ensure that PFI objectives are met. Implementation and internal monitoring processes feed back to the more specific PFI stakeholders whereas external monitoring processes feed back to the general public. Further research at these stages might involve examining the extent to which the PFI meets the VFM objectives identified at the pre-contract stages. In addition, the accountability perceptions and VFM expectations of the diverse stakeholders involved in the implementation and monitoring process may be examined.

Appendix: the PFI procurement process

Steps	Description
1. Establish business needs	Procurement proceeds only after a rigorous examination of business objectives, needs and constraints including that of affordability.
2. Appraise options	The cost and benefits of the various options including do nothing, do minimum, traditional procurement and PFI are examined.
3. Prepare an outline business case (OBC) and a reference project	An OBC, supporting the case for investment and for the PFI approach, based on the options appraisal, is prepared. It specifies the output specification rather than 'how' the service is to be delivered. A reference project, usually a public-sector comparator (PSC), is prepared for benchmarking purposes.
4. Create a project team and project board	A procurement team, led by a full-time project manager, and a project steering board to which it reports and which can take decisions, are appointed. The project team needs to include people with the relevant skills required in the PFI negotiation process and users.
5. Decide tactics	This involves deciding how much information to request at the pre-qualification, when to seek fully costed proposals and when to select a preferred bidder.
6. Invite expressions of interest; publish *Official Journal of European Community (OJEC)* notice	Advertisement includes explanation of the project, indication of the information required for any assessment of the potential supplier's economic and financial standing and technical capacity, and the criteria for award.
7. Pre-qualify bidders	The general competence of the interested suppliers is assessed. Proposals for the particular project are not covered.
8. Shortlist bidders	Bidders are shortlisted based on specific competence (e.g. risks management). Bidders not taken forward are informed and debriefed quickly on why they were not selected.
9. Refine the appraisal	The OBC and any PSC are further refined in the light of new information. The affordability and funding arrangements are reaffirmed.
10. Invitation to negotiate (ITN)	The ITN specifies the services required in output terms; the constraints on the project scope; the proposed contractual terms (lengths and payment mechanism); the criteria for evaluation of bids and the scope for variant bids (such as variations on proposed contracts duration, risk allocation).
11. Receipt and evaluation of bids	Bids received are evaluated in accordance with the principles and criteria set out in the ITN document. From the best and final offers received, the preferred bidder is then chosen.
12. Selection of the preferred bidder and the final evaluation	The preferred bidder is selected and the PFI proposition is retested against the key VFM and affordability criteria. Risks transferred to the private sector under PFI are costed and added to the PSC. The expected accounting treatment of the contract is reconfirmed with the client's auditors.
13. Contract award and financial close	Once the contract is signed and a contract award notice placed in the *OJEC*, the contract is implemented.
14. Contract management	New processes, systems and management systems are put in place.

Source: Adapted from HM Treasury 1997, 1999

References

ACCA (Association of Chartered Certified Accountants) (2002) 'ACCA Members' Survey: Do PFI Schemes Provide Value for Money?', www.acca.co.uk/news, 30 January 2004.

ASB (Accounting Standards Board) (1998) *Amendment to FRS5 Reporting the Substance of Transactions: Private Finance Initiative and Similar Contracts* (London: HMSO).

Baker, R. (2003) 'Investigating Enron as a Public Private Partnership', *Accounting, Auditing and Accountability Journal* 16.3: 446-66.

Ball, R., M. Heafey and D. King (2001) 'Private Finance Initiative: A Good Deal for the Public Purse or a Drain on Future Generations?', *Policy and Politics* 29.1: 95-108.

Barberis, P. (1998) 'The New Public Management and a New Accountability', *Public Administration* 76.3: 451-70.

Broadbent, J., and J. Guthrie (1992) 'Changes in the Public Sector: A Review of Recent "Alternative" Accounting Research', *Accounting, Auditing and Accountability Journal* 5.2: 3-31.

—— and R. Laughlin (1999) 'The Private Finance Initiative: Clarification of a Future Research Agenda', *Financial Accountability and Management* 15.2: 95-114.

—— and —— (2003a) 'Control and Legitimation in Government Accountability Processes: The Private Finance Initiative in the UK', *Critical Perspectives on Accounting* 14.1–2: 23-48.

—— and —— (2003b) 'Public Private Partnerships: An Introduction', *Accounting, Auditing and Accountability Journal* 16.3: 332-41.

—— and —— (2004) 'The Role of PFI in the UK Government's Modernisations Agenda', *British Accounting Association Conference Proceedings 2004*, University of York, UK, 14–16 April 2004.

——, J. Gill and R. Laughlin (2003a) 'Evaluating the Private Finance Initiative in the National Health Service in the UK', *Accounting, Auditing and Accountability Journal* 16.3: 422-45.

——, —— and —— (2003b) 'The Development of Contracting in the Context of Infrastructure Investment in the UK: The Case of the Private Finance Initiative in the National Health Service', *International Public Management Journal* 6.2: 173-98.

Cavalluzzo, K.S., and C.D. Ittner (2004) 'Implementing Performance Measurement Innovations: Evidence from Government', *Accounting, Organizations and Society* 29.3: 243-67.

Demirag, I., M.J. Dubnick and M.I. Khadaroo (2003) 'Exploring the Relationships between Accountability and Performance in the UK's Private Finance Initiative (PFI)', *British Accounting Association Special Interest Group in Corporate Governance Conference Proceedings 2003*, University of Liverpool, UK, 12–13 December 2004.

DETR (UK Department of the Environment, Transport and the Regions) (1998) 'Modern Local Government: In Touch with the People', Command Paper, Cm 4014, www.odpm.gov.uk, 30 November 2003.

Dubnick, M. (1998) 'Clarifying Accountability: An Ethical Theory Framework', in C. Sampford and N. Preston (eds.), *Public Sector Ethics: Finding and Implementing Values* (London: Routledge).

Edwards, P., and J. Shaoul (2003a) 'Controlling the PFI Process in Schools: A Case Study of the Pimlico Project', *Policy and Politics* 31.3: 371-85.

—— and —— (2003b) 'Partnerships: For Better, For Worse?', *Accounting, Auditing and Accountability Journal* 16.3: 397-421.

—— and —— (2004) 'Highway Robbery? The UK Experience with Private Finance in Roads', *British Accounting Association Conference Proceedings 2004*, University of York, UK, 14–16 April 2004

Efficiency Unit (1988) *Improving Management in Government: The Next Steps* (London: HMSO).

—— (1991) *Making the Most of Next Steps: The Management of Ministers' Department and their Executive Agencies* (London: HMSO).

English, L.M., and J. Guthrie (2003) 'Driving Privately Financed Projects in Australia: What Makes Them Tick?', *Accounting, Auditing and Accountability Journal* 16.3: 493-511.

Ernst & Young (2002) *Project Finance: Progress and Prospects. Healthcare PFI: A Survey* (London: Ernst & Young, October 2002).

Flyvbjerg, B., M.S. Holm and S. Buhl (2002) 'Underestimating Costs in Public Works Projects: Error or Lie?', *Journal of the American Planning Association* 68.3: 279-95.

Froud, J., and J. Shaoul (2001) 'Appraising and Evaluating PFI for NHS Hospitals', *Financial Account-ability and Management* 17.3: 247-70.

Glynn, J.J. (1985) *Value for Money Auditing in the Public Sector* (London: Prentice Hall).

Gray, A.G., and W.I. Jenkins (1993) 'Codes of Accountability in the New Public Sector', *Accounting, Auditing and Accountability Journal* 6.3: 52-67.

Grimsey, D., and M. Lewis (2002) 'Accounting for Public Private Partnerships', *Accounting Forum* 26.3: 245-70.

—— and M.K. Lewis (2004) 'The Governance of Contractual Relationships in Public–Private Partner-ships', *Journal of Corporate Citizenship* 15 (Autumn 2004): 91-109.

Heald, D. (2003) 'Value for Money Tests and Accounting Treatment in PFI Schemes', *Accounting, Audit-ing and Accountability Journal* 16.3: 342-71.

HM Government (1982) *Efficiency and Effectiveness in the Civil Service* (Cmnd 8616; London: HMSO).

HM Treasury (1997) 'Partnerships for Prosperity', Treasury Taskforce guidance, www.ogc.gov.uk, 29 January 2004.

—— (1998) *Public Services for the Future: Modernisation, Reform, Accountability. Comprehensive Spend-ing Review: Public Service Agreements 1999–2002* (Cmnd 4181; London: HMSO).

—— (1999) *Step-by-Step Guide to the PFI Procurement Process* (London: HMSO).

—— (2001) *Managing Resources: Full Implementation of Resource Accounting and Budgeting* (London: HMSO).

—— (2003a) 'Maintaining Macroeconomic Stability', in *Budget Report 2003: Building a Britain of Eco-nomic Strength and Social Justice* (London: HMSO): 19-44.

—— (2003b) *The Green Book: Appraisal and Evaluation in Central Government* (London: HMSO).

Hood, C. (1995) 'The New Public Management in the 1980s: Variations on a Theme', *Accounting, Orga-nizations and Society* 20.2–3: 93-109.

House of Commons (1992) *Hansard Debates* 213 column 998, 12, November 1992.

Humphrey, C.G., P. Miller and R.W. Scapens (1993) 'Accountability and Accountable Management in the UK Public Sector', *Accounting, Auditing and Accountability Journal* 6.3: 7-29.

Hyndman, N., and R. Eden (2002) 'Executive Agencies, Performance Targets and External Reporting', *Public Money and Management* 22.3: 17-24.

Jacobs, K. (1998) 'Value for Money Auditing in New Zealand: Competing for Control in the Public Sec-tor', *British Accounting Review* 30.3: 343-60.

Kirk, R.J., and A.P. Wall (2001) 'Substance, Form and PFI Contracts', *Public Money and Management* 21.3: 41-46.

—— and —— (2002) 'The Private Finance Initiative: Has the Accounting Standards Board reduced the scheme's value for money?', *Public Management Review* 4.4: 529-47.

Laughlin, R. (1996) 'Principals and Higher Principals: Accounting for Accountability in the Caring Pro-fession', in R. Munro and J. Mouritsen (eds.), *Accountability: Power, Ethos and the Technologies of Managing* (London: International Thomson Business Press).

Maile, S., and P. Hoggett (2001) 'Best Value and the Politics of Pragmatism', *Policy and Politics* 29.4: 509-19.

Mayston, D. (1999) 'The Private Finance Initiative in the National Health Service: An Unhealthy Devel-opment in New Public Management?', *Financial Accountability and Management* 15.3–4: 249-74.

Mellett, H. (2002) 'The Consequences and Causes of Resource Accounting', *Critical Perspectives on Accounting* 13.2: 231-54.

Midwinter, A. (2001) 'New Labour and the Modernisation of British Local Government: A Critique', *Financial Accountability and Management* 17.4: 311-20.

Mott MacDonald (2002) *Review of Large Public Procurement in the UK* (London: HM Treasury).

Mulgan, R. (2000) 'Accountability: An Ever-expanding Concept?', *Public Administration* 78.3: 555-73.

NAO (National Audit Office) (1999) *Examining the Value for Money of Deals under the Private Finance Ini-tiative* (HC 739; London: HMSO).

Newberry, S., and J. Pallot (2003) 'Fiscal (Ir)Responsibility: Privileging PPPs in New Zealand', *Account-ing, Auditing and Accountability Journal* 16.3: 467-92.

Olson, O., J. Guthrie and C. Humphrey (1998) 'International Experiences with New Public Financial Management Reforms: New World? Small World? Better World?', in O. Olson, J. Guthrie and C. Humphrey (eds.), *Global Warning: Debating International Developments in New Public Financial Management* (Oslo: Cappelen Akademisk Forlag).

Parliament (1980) *Local Government Planning and Land Act 1980* (London: HMSO).

PricewaterhouseCoopers (1999) 'Attitudes to the Private Finance Initiative: A Survey of Senior Decision Makers', www.pwcglobal.com/uk/eng/ins-sol/survey-rep/pfi.html, 30 November 2003.

Schaeffer, P., and S. Loveridge (2002) 'Toward an Understanding of Types of Public–Private Cooperation', *Public Performance and Management Review* 26.2: 169-89.

Schedler, A. (1999) 'Conceptualizing Accountability', in A. Schedler, L.J. Diamond and M.F. Plattner (eds.), *The Self-restraining State: Power and Accountability in New Democracies* (Boulder, CO: Lynne Rienner Publishers).

Shaoul, J. (2004) 'A Critical Appraisal of the Private Finance Initiative: Selecting a Financial Method or Allocating Economic Wealth?', *Critical Perspectives on Accounting* (forthcoming).

Sinclair, A. (1995) 'The Chameleon of Accountability: Forms and Discourses', *Accounting, Organizations and Society* 20.2–3: 219-37.

Stewart, J. (1984) 'The Role of Information in Public Accountability', in A.G. Hopwood and C.R. Tomkins (eds.), *Issues in Public Sector Accounting* (Oxford, UK: Philip Allan).

Talbot, C. (2001) 'UK Public Services and Management (1979–2000): Evolution or Revolution?', *International Journal of Public Sector Management* 14.4: 281-303.

6

Risk regulation regimes in aviation
WERE THE CHIPS EVER REALLY DOWN IN THE UK'S MANAGEMENT OF Y2K?

*Kevin Quigley**

Queen's University Belfast, UK

> The most doom and gloom predictions foresee planes tumbling from the sky
> (House of Commons Library 1998)

Aviation disaster was one of the most feared consequences of the Millennium Bug (Y2K).[1] The example epitomised the potential seriousness of Y2K to the public, the government and the aviation industry. In response to the perceived risks the government and the Civil Aviation Authority (CAA) co-ordinated a vast Y2K operation, reflecting the far-reaching and interdependent nature of the industry.

In the end, no planes tumbled from the sky. But did that mean that the UK government's Y2K operation had regulated the risk effectively? For the purposes of this chapter I use Hood, Rothstein and Baldwin's (2001) meso-level, regime-based analytical framework to compare and contrast three different government programmes devised to regulate the risk associated with Y2K in the aviation industry—the CAA's *Safety* programme; the government's *National Infrastructure Forum* (NIF); and the CAA's *Business as Usual* programme.

Hood *et al.*'s framework uses three hypotheses to explain risk regulation. The first, the Market Failure Hypothesis, examines the government's intervention as a necessary

* I would like to thank my academic supervisors, Rick Wilford and George Philip, as well as John Quigley, Sara Quigley, Istemi Demirag and the anonymous referee, all of whom commented on earlier drafts of this chapter. In addition, I wish to thank the staff at the CAA for meeting with me to discuss their Y2K operation, providing me with documentary evidence of the operation and for commenting on an earlier draft of this chapter.

1 Y2K, or 'the Millennium Bug', referred to the fact that, in computer programmes created in the 1960s onwards, most year entries had been programmed in two-digit shorthand: 1965, for instance, was entered as '65'. As the year 2000 approached, anxiety grew that systems would be unable to distinguish between 20th-century entries and 21st-century entries (would '01' be treated as 1901 or 2001?). Such ambiguity, it was feared, would result in systems producing unreliable information or failing altogether.

one given the technical nature of the risk and the inability of the market to manage the risk effectively without such intervention. The second, the Opinion Responsive Hypothesis, examines the extent to which risk regulation responds to the preferences of civil society. The third, the Interests Hypothesis, examines the role of organised groups in shaping the manner in which a risk is regulated in the industry.

Hood *et al.*'s framework is a comparative tool. This chapter is part of a larger comparative project that is considering how government agencies that depend highly on technology manage the risks associated with their technology. The Millennium Bug is the chief case study. (See the Appendix for additional notes.) By comparing three government and regulator responses to Y2K within aviation, this chapter seeks to examine variety in government responses to risk.

Ultimately, the aviation risk regulation regime's reaction to Y2K can be attributed to a safety-conscious industry, the obscure nature of the Y2K bug and a complex technological environment. But the framework helps to illustrate that the UK aviation industry's response to Y2K dwarfed that which the technical nature of the bug required. Indeed, the reaction can also be attributed to a highly centralised risk management plan devised at the political centre, which was influenced by parliamentary institutions, the technology industry, media pressure and the government's anxiety over public perception. Ultimately, the CAA's 'Business as Usual' commitment was a compromise between safety concerns, managing public perception and working within that which the major players in the industry could deliver.

6.1 Risk regulation regimes

Hood *et al.* argue that the recent literature on risk and its management has sought to explain trends from a macroscopic or world historical perspective (e.g. Beck 1992; Majone 1994). Yet this broad-brush, macro-level approach has failed to explain risk regulation variety across policy fields and geographic locations, despite emerging evidence that such variety exists (e.g. Cheit 1990; Shrader-Frechette 1991; Breyer 1993; HSE 1996, 1998; HM Treasury 1996).

In their recent study of risk regulation in the UK, Hood *et al.* deploy the 'regime literature'[2] by way of exploring variety in the different policy areas[3] (2001: 5). Using this diverse literature as their springboard, they define regimes thus: 'the complex of institutional geography, rules, practice and animating ideas that are associated with the regulation of a particular risk or hazard' (2001: 9). This broad definition allows for flex-

2   See e.g. in international relations, Krasner 1983; in public policy, see Elkin 1986; Dowding 1996; Bryant *et al.* 1993; in systems theory, see Beer 1966; Teubner 1987; Brans and Rossbach 1997; in institutional analysis, see Stringer 1967; Rhodes and Marsh 1992; Heclo 1978; Dowding 1995; for policy instruments, see Hood 1983; Ogus 1994; for interest groups, see Wilson 1980; for cultural theory, see Adams 1995; Schwartz and Thompson 1990; Thompson *et al.* 1990.

3   (1) Attacks by dangerous dogs outside the home; (2) lung cancer caused by radon gas at home; (3) and at the workplace; (4) cancer caused by benzene from vehicle exhaust; (5) and at the workplace; (6) attacks on children by paedophiles; (7) injuries and deaths from vehicles on local roads; (8) health from pesticides in food; (9) and in water (Hood *et al.* 2001: 37).

ibility as Hood *et al.* read across various policy contexts while drawing together a variety of institutional perspectives in order to understand what shapes risk regulation.

Hood *et al.* hypothesise that within these regimes context shapes the manner in which risk is regulated. 'Regime context' refers to the backdrop of regulation. There are three elements that Hood *et al.* use to explore 'context'—the technical nature of the risk; the public's and media's opinions about the risk; and the way power and influence are concentrated in organised groups in the regime. These three elements are commonly employed explanations in the public policy literature and can be related, to some extent, to a normative theory of regulation as well as a positive one (Hood *et al.* 2001: 61). Figure 6.1 illustrates the competing pressures that shape risk regulation regimes.

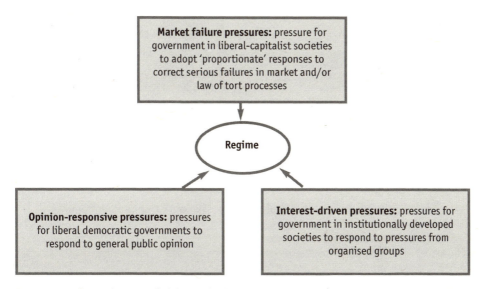

FIGURE 6.1 Three shapers of risk regulation regimes

Hood *et al.* derive three sub-hypotheses, each linked to a competing pressure, to determine the extent to which each pressure explains the policy settings, the configuration of state and other organisations directly engaged in regulating the risk, and the attitudes, beliefs and operating conventions of the regulators, or what they call 'risk regulation content' (2001: 21). In short, risk regulation content considers the size, structure and style of risk regulation within the regime.

Each of the three critical elements in 'risk regulation regime content' (i.e. size, structure, style) is characterised further through the three elements of a cybernetic control system: information gathering; standard setting and behaviour modification. In this sense, control means the ability to keep the state of a system within some preferred subset of all its possible states. If any of the three components are absent, a system is not under control in a cybernetic sense (Hood *et al.* 2001: 23-25). They note in their research that risk regulation has tended to focus on standard setting. But to consider risk regulation in only that light is limiting because it does not explore the full spectrum of regulatory activity. Indeed, the three components are interdependent. Therefore, in addition to referring to the style, structure and size of the regulatory regime, they refer to the regulatory regime's ability and willingness to gather information, set standards and modify behaviour by way of keeping the regime under control. Table 6.1 summarises the approach, with the three sub-hypotheses in parentheses.

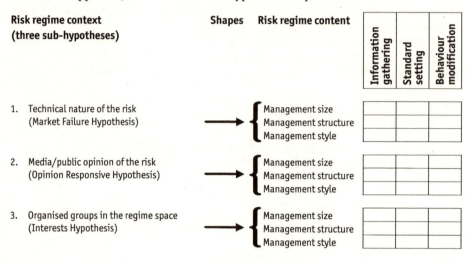

Risk regime context (three sub-hypotheses)	Shapes	Risk regime content	Information gathering	Standard setting	Behaviour modification
1. Technical nature of the risk (Market Failure Hypothesis)	→	Management size Management structure Management style			
2. Media/public opinion of the risk (Opinion Responsive Hypothesis)	→	Management size Management structure Management style			
3. Organised groups in the regime space (Interests Hypothesis)	→	Management size Management structure Management style			

TABLE 6.1 Hood, Rothstein and Baldwin's (2001) risk regulation regime framework

6.2 Regime content: size, structure and style of the response to Y2K in aviation

This part of the chapter briefly summarises the three government programmes in terms of the key elements of risk regulation regime content—size, structure and style.

The **size** of the government's regulatory ambition with respect to Y2K emerged over time. After some initial awareness raising and information gathering on the nature of the bug in 1996 and 1997 (see, for example, DTI 1996) in May 1998, Number 10 Downing Street and the Cabinet Office proposed an ambitious strategy across the public services: 'to ensure no material disruption to essential public services as a result of the Millennium Bug' (HMSO 2000: 67). Originally the CAA approached Y2K as it did any other safety issue (CAA 1998). The CAA's early approach, referred to in briefing material as the *Safety* programme, aimed to take reasonable steps to ensure that the mitigation of Y2K-related risk was carried out in a co-ordinated fashion and to acceptably safe standards. By way of reply to the government's call for 'no material disruption to service', the CAA started a voluntary programme within the aviation industry in which the industry promised 'business as usual', and emphasised the need to maintain a high level of safety.

Structurally, between 1996 and mid-1998, the government added committees and teams to co-ordinate action on the bug right across the national infrastructure. MISC4, with the support of Action 2000, was established 'to co-ordinate action on the Millennium Bug across public and private sectors' (Blair 1998: 7; NAO 1999b: 11). Existing under the aegis of Action 2000 was the National Infrastructure Forum (NIF). The NIF, which became the primary forum for meeting the government's promise of no material disruption to service, consisted of some 250 organisations from 25 sectors, private, public and regulated, that delivered essential services in the UK according to a study conducted by Ernst & Young for Cabinet Office (Ernst & Young 1998; NAO 1999a: 12). At Cabinet Office, the Year 2000 Team co-ordinated activity and chased progress across government and the Media Communications Unit (MCU) co-ordinated communications and media events (Cm 4703 2000: 32; Blair 1998: 7). Finally, though not strictly part of government, it bears noting that the Science and Technology Committee and the Public Accounts Committee held several hearings and published numerous reports on Y2K, which clearly fed into the government's Y2K process.

At the CAA, the *Safety* programme followed standard structural reporting mechanisms, chiefly safety audits of the industry carried out by the CAA. *Business as Usual*, on the other hand, requested that the top 15 players in the industry collaborate to ensure that the industry worked as normal over the millennium period (CAA 1999a). As part of the programme, the CAA contracted AEA Technology Consulting to conduct independent surveys of the participants. These results were then fed up to the NIF. There were also numerous international bodies with whom the CAA liaised. (Fig. 6.2 depicts the Y2K-related regulatory space in the UK aviation industry.)

Formally the government promised a **style** of transparency and vigilance. The prime minister committed the government to openness during the process and promised ministerial commitment. Thus, the government started delivering regular statements to the House of Commons on the government's progress on the Y2K issue, based on regular, detailed departmental submissions to Cabinet Office. At NIF meetings, heads of organisations and sectors collectively were expected to commit themselves publicly to Y2K compliance, and some variation of 'no material disruption to service'. Action 2000 enforced a traffic light marking system to indicate sector-level progress towards Y2K compliance (i.e. Blue;[4] Yellow; Red). The government and the NAO published sector-level results quarterly in 1999 (January, April, July, October).

The CAA's **style** was a mixture of compliance statements and more informal, negotiated sector-wide summaries with the big industry players. After issuing information on Y2K to the industry in 1997 and 1998, in January 1999 the CAA began assessing the industry's readiness. As part of the *Safety* programme the CAA expected Y2K compliance statements from all of the 1,880 organisations that it regulated. It also conducted audits of approximately 8–10% of the organisations. If organisations did not produce Y2K compliance statements, then their inaction was followed up with letters and phone calls from the CAA. If organisations failed to demonstrate Y2K compliance, then the CAA had the power to withdraw, suspend or limit licences, though ultimately the CAA deemed it was unnecessary to enact these powers, deciding the few who had not produced com-

4   Green was not used because Action 2000 felt that a 100% guarantee could not be issued.

pliance statements represented negligible risk. As part of the *Business as Usual* programme AEA Technology reviewed questionnaires, conducted site visits and developed short assessments in consultation with the participant organisations that were based on Action 2000 definitions of readiness. Blue/Yellow/Red sector-wide results were then published based on the results of the *Business as Usual* programme, which fed into the government's NIF reporting requirements. The *Business as Usual* programme was voluntary and the reports were sector-wide; they were not company-specific.

6.2.1 Y2K results in the aviation industry

As part of the *Business as Usual* programme, National Air Traffic Service (NATS) airports and airlines were declared 'business as usual' (i.e. 100% blue light) by 21 April 1999, 12 July 1999 and 20 October 1999, respectively (see CAA 1999a, 1999b, 1999c; NATS 1999b). Under the *Safety* programme the CAA concluded that, of the 1,880 organisations it regulated, there was a question mark concerning Y2K compliance hanging over about 20 companies, most often because they failed to produce compliance certificates. In any event, the CAA did not consider the compliance of these particular companies to be a matter of public safety. In late 1999 the Department of the Environment, Transport and the Regions (DETR) declared that UK airlines could offer regular service if they wished. No significant Y2K-related failures in the UK aviation industry were reported on or around 1 January 2000.

6.3 Regime context

This part of the chapter uses Hood *et al.*'s three sub-hypotheses to explore the context from which the Y2K regulatory response emerged and to determine the extent to which each of the three government programmes can be explained by these hypotheses.

6.3.1 Market Failure Hypothesis

According to the Market Failure Hypothesis, regulatory regime content reflects the inherent nature of each risk, and specifically the extent to which it is feasible for markets, including insurance or the law of tort, to operate as regulators of risk. Regulatory size and regime structure reflect the scale of the risks (Hood *et al.* 2001: 70). If the government's response to Y2K aligned with this hypothesis, we would expect to see a strong emphasis on information gathering across the industry but particularly among those with fewer resources: namely, small to medium-sized enterprises (SMEs). Once the information was gathered and the risk was determined to be relatively low with respect to health and safety-critical systems (as we shall see), we would expect to see a less formal approach, which emphasised the potential disruption to business and administration. Contrary to what this hypothesis would predict, however, the government's reaction to Y2K grew over time: it focused progressively on organisations that did not require the pressure of the CAA.

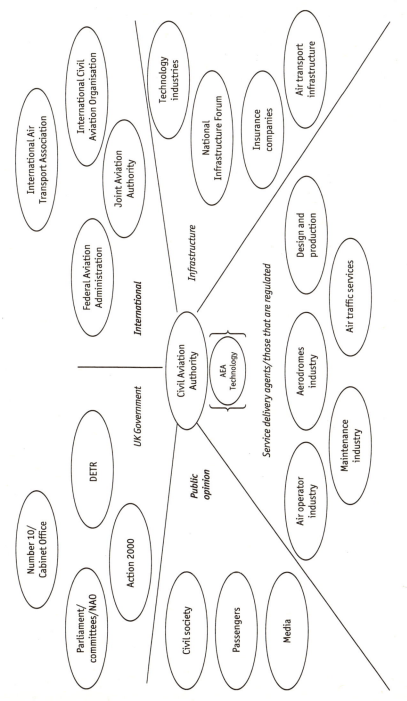

The five categories are not mutually exclusive

FIGURE 6.2 The Y2K-related regulatory space in UK aviation

Y2K was an obscure problem for both government and industry. Date-functionality is built into many systems but, because these systems were not always well documented and systems were perceived to be highly interdependent, trying to identify Y2K-related problems was like finding a match in a haystack on a very hot day. At the outset, the uncertainty and the perceived consequences were high.

Both industry and government knew they were dealing with a complex technological environment. Space, however, prevents a full discussion of the complexity of Y2K in technological terms in the aviation industry. The following examples are meant to be illustrative. Air traffic control is an extremely complex system that dwarfs almost all other Y2K operations. NATS's three air traffic control centres manage 5,000 flights passing through UK airspace as well as over the North Atlantic every 24 hours (NATS 1999b). NATS bespoke systems are extremely large and complex. Its Y2K operation involved examining 700 operational air traffic control and 170 non-operational systems (NATS 1999a).

The technology in the private aviation industry was also complex. Embedded chips contain programmed instructions running via processor chips. These chips are similar to stand-alone computers buried inside other equipment. A typical 747, for instance, can contain as many as 16,000 embedded chips. Moreover, on the ground, proliferation of systems underpinned the industry: finances, bookings, payments, staffing schedules, baggage handling, pilot licensing, seat assignment, security and access, parking, communications, monitoring of runways, train links and so on (GAO 1998). The American airline Delta, for instance, said that, of its 600 systems at its headquarters in Atlanta, almost half were considered mission-critical (Hodson 1998: 6).

The interdependent nature of the economy also made the problem more complex. Most organisations would not give a view on continuity of service without similar assurances from their suppliers (e.g. gas, electricity, water supply, etc.). Hence, much of the problem (and its solution) went beyond the control of one industry and its regulator. This problem was further exacerbated in the aviation industry because 75% of UK travel is international, and therefore international co-operation became critical to the solution.

The industry could not opt out of risk exposure. There was no specific Y2K legislation in the UK.[5] In any event, legal recourse was not considered a practical option by many. Barclays Bank noted, 'relying on legal remedies to address the problem is illusory' (Science and Technology Standing Committee 1997/98: 7). The risks associated with waiting until after 1 January 2000, to demonstrate systems failure, particularly in the aviation industry, were not considered acceptable. Similarly, the *Financial Times* reported that given the high degree of uncertainty insurance companies were threatening to withdraw coverage for flights over the New Year's period (Nairn 1998).

Given this pressure, therefore, there were considerable market incentives in place to motivate the industry to determine its exposure to risk. Passengers, and hence the industry, have a low tolerance for aviation-related risk.[6] It is perhaps not surprising to learn that the industry was leading the assault on Y2K. The CAA learned of Y2K concerns

---

5   CCTA (1997) (the government's agency that advises on IT procurement and management) recommended that organisations should move quickly to arbitration in the event of legal disputes.

6   See Slovic 1992 for a discussion of psychometrics; see CAA 2002: ch.1, p. 6 for evidence of the UK's aviation safety record.

from the industry in 1996. The major players within the aviation industry committed considerable time and effort to ensure Y2K compliance in advance of the new millennium. The Air Transport Association (ATA) estimated that internationally, airlines spent US$2.3 billion on Y2K. BA, for example, the largest service provider in the UK, spent £100 million and had 200 people check 3,000 systems, 50 million lines of computer code, 40,000 PCs and printers and 800 applications (Bray 1999). The larger players did not do this massive check at the insistence of the CAA but rather because they recognised the potential seriousness of the problem.

Despite the perceived complexity of the Y2K problem, as more information about the bug was gathered, Y2K specialists in the aviation industry learned that the technical nature of the risk was overstated. With respect to embedded chips, for instance, Finkelstein points out that 'only a tiny portion of [embedded] systems have a clock at all and a very small subset of these use absolute as distinct from relative time' (2000: 2). The two leading airline manufacturers, Airbus and Boeing, agreed that jets were largely problem-free (Bray 1999). In its testing of 747s, for instance, Boeing reported that only four embedded chips were found with any date and time functionality (out of a possible 16,000), none of which were in any safety-critical systems (Hodson 1998: 6). Similarly, critical air traffic control systems work in real time and are therefore not date-dependent. By late 1998, the CAA, the Federal Aviation Administration (FAA) and American Airlines all noted publicly that while there may be some risk of operational disruption there was virtually no risk to people's health and safety (Hodson 1998: 6; House Committee on Transportation and Infrastructure Hearing 1998). In short, planes were never going to fall from the sky.

From the standpoint of this hypothesis, Number 10's National Infrastructure Forum (NIF) and the CAA's *Business as Usual* programme seem a little late and misplaced. While the NIF did allow for Y2K-related communication across sectors, by the time Number 10 and Cabinet Office established the NIF in late 1998 the major players in the aviation industry had gathered sufficient information to conclude that the problem was under control, particularly with respect to health and safety systems. Although the *Safety* programme audited only 8–10% of organisations, the top 15 companies were certain to be among them. In any case, judging by outcome it was the SMEs with older, less sophisticated systems and with fewer resources whose behaviour required modifying by way of a firm reminder from government regulators.[7] These smaller operators were not part of the *Business as Usual* programme but were included in the *Safety* programme. While the *Safety* programme may have lacked flexibility with its compliance statements, which allowed the CAA to place all the responsibility on the industry and potentially avoid blame itself, the Market Failure Hypothesis seems more aligned with the *Safety* programme than with the other two programmes.

In sum, government action on Y2K only partly reflects the technical nature of the risk. Because there was considerable uncertainty concerning the risk in 1997/1998, the Market Failure Hypothesis would anticipate government pressure on information gathering and co-ordination, particularly among SMEs, who were difficult to reach and persuade of the potential consequences of the Y2K threat. The *Safety* programme comes closest to meeting this criterion. As the CAA's and industry's awareness grew about the

---

7 See e.g. the approximately 20 smaller organisations that failed to produce Y2K compliance certificates to the CAA.

extent to which the risk had been overstated in the early days, however, we would expect to see a reduction in government activity. Instead we see the government's intervention growing, with the creation of the NIF and the CAA's related *Business as Usual* programme. Moreover, these programmes were disproportionately focused on the major players in the industry, who seemed to be less at risk. Table 6.2 compares the three programmes against the expected Market Failure response. The right column scores the extent to which the size, structure and style of each programme is aligned with expected outcome as per the Market Failure Hypothesis. The mark out of a possible three is offered as a high-level guide. It is not an exact measure.

	Size	Structure	Style	Alignment (✓)
Expected outcome	Medium-sized strategy, focused on raising awareness, particularly among SMEs	Industry-wide but decentralised and sensitive to SMEs	Less formal; awareness raising and information gathering; focus on obscurity of the problem; adverse business impacts and value of reliable systems inventory	
Safety programme **(CAA)**	✓	✓	✓/✗ Bottom-line compliance statements of complex problems offered blame-avoidance opportunity for regulator	**2.5/3**
National Infrastructure Forum—No Material Disruption	✗ High-cost strategy for low-probability event	✓/✗ Allowed for information sharing and reassurances across-sectors but not sufficiently focused on SMEs; too centralised, standardised for complex problem	✗ High, inflexible standard for complex, low-probability event; not sufficiently focused on SMEs	**0.5/3**
Business as Usual **programme (CAA)**	✗ High-cost strategy for low-probability event; little threat to safety	✗ Insufficiently focused on SMEs	✓ Given the players, CAA was right to be less formal	**1/3**

Legend ✓ = alignment ✗ = mismatch

TABLE 6.2 **Observed responses in three programmes compared with the expected outcome according to the Market Failure Hypothesis**

6.3.2 Opinion Responsive Hypothesis

The Opinion Responsive Hypothesis suggests that public attitudes shape regulatory regime content. That is, risk regulation is the way it is because that is how those affected by the risks want it to be. Hood *et al.* look to public and media salience of the issue and uniformity of opinion to explore this hypothesis (2001: 90). If the government's response aligned with this hypothesis, we would expect to see the government engaged in strategies to determine what public opinion was. Assuming a certain volatility in public opinion and acknowledging that even low-level anxiety could easily grow into high anxiety should there be Y2K-related failures in the national infrastructure, we would also expect to see a strong emphasis on high standards and modifying non-compliant behaviour. The NIF meets these criteria, as does the *Business as Usual* programme, though the latter only does to a lesser degree. The *Safety* programme's standard and enforcement, on the other hand, seem too prone to slippage for this hypothesis.

The government notes in its Y2K postmortem that the media often ran worst-case scenario stories and tended not to cover the work the government was doing to mitigate the risk.[8] By way of reply to this problem, as noted, Cabinet Office began to co-ordinate communications through the Media Communications Unit (MCU). The NIF, including *Business as Usual*, helped in this regard because it demonstrated (in a public form) critical sectors progressively moving towards Y2K compliance.

Figure 6.3 and Table 6.3 represent the total number of articles on Y2K in the selected newspapers between 1 January 1997 and 31 December 2000. The numbers in brackets indicate the total number of those articles that refer to aviation. (See the Appendix for notes on methodology.)

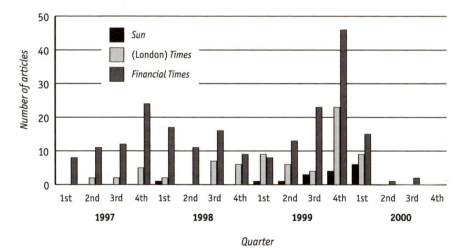

Note: the counts exclude letters to the editor

FIGURE 6.3 Number of Y2K-related articles in selected print media (chart)

---

8   Noted in Cm 4703: 29-39, as well as during several interviews.

	1997				1998				1999				2000				
	1st	2nd	3rd	4th	1st	2nd	3rd	4th	1st	2nd	3rd	4th	1st	2nd	3rd	4th	Total
Sun	0	0	0	0	1	0	0	0	1	1	3	4	6	0	0	0	**16**
(London) Times	0	2	2	5	2 (2)	0	7	6 (1)	9	6 (2)	4 (1)	23 (2)	9	0	0	0	**75**
Financial Times	8	11	12	24	17	11	16 (1)	9 (4)	8 (1)	13	23 (2)	46 (6)	15	1	2	0	**216**

The number of articles that refer to aviation in particular are indicated in brackets.

TABLE 6.3 Number of Y2K-related articles in selected print media (table)

Any coverage of a computer bug is unusual and in that sense Y2K coverage is exceptional. Nevertheless, the government's criticism that the media covered the Y2K story in an overly negative and exaggerated way has some important limitations that are worth noting. First, not all papers covered the story to the same degree. *The Times* covered the story considerably less than the *FT*; and the *Sun*, the most read and arguably the most alarmist newspaper in the UK, hardly covered the story at all.

Second, there was no shortage of sources from the IT industry (both 'cowboys' and CEOs from large organisations) as well as politicians who were prepared to supply the media with the exaggerated claims. It's not that the moderate voices were being edited out: there were not that many moderate voices. Government Y2K publications typically foreground the 'worst-case scenarios' and usually on page one.[9]

Third, a large communications machine at Cabinet Office can also have the effect of generating news—planning events, keeping the story in the public eye and in so doing keeping anxiety up. Certainly many Y2K co-ordinators at the operational level noted that the media coverage was exaggerated. But, at the same time, even the alarmist reporting seems to be quite consistent with the Cabinet Office and parliamentary outlook on Y2K. Indeed, most large organisations, both public and private, tended to report on how much they were doing—usually the bigger the better—rather than whether or not the bug was materialising in the manner in which some had predicted. Note, for instance, the description given by BA described in the Market Failure Hypothesis section of this chapter or the words of NATS's press release: 'NATS started work on the Year 2000 problem in Spring 1996 and has checked, and *where necessary corrected,* some 700 operational air traffic control and 170 non-operational systems (NATS 1999a; my emphasis).

Accepting these limitations, the media coverage of the bug was still intense and largely negative. The *FT* led the assault with 216 articles over the period in question. The *FT* is an opinion-leader, particularly in the City of London. The Y2K story appealed to the *FT*'s readership. Y2K was largely considered an IT/business problem, especially in

---

9   For examples see NAO 1997, 1998, 1999a, 1999b; the British House of Commons Library 1998; Science and Technology Standing Committee Report on Y2K 1997/1998.

1997. And indeed, particularly in this early period, the *FT*'s coverage seemed alarmist. The paper ran almost five times as many stories as *The Times* and adopted the term 'Millennium Bomb' for its coverage. (By 1999, for instance, it tended to use 'Y2K' or 'Millennium Bug'.) Interestingly, the *FT*'s relatively intense coverage in the last quarter of 1997 and the first two months of 1998 (38 articles in total) is followed by increased centralisation of the government's Y2K plan in March 1998, which led eventually to the introduction of the NIF. The point is not to argue that the *FT* drove the change; but the change does suggest an anxious environment existed at the end of 1997, and it forces the question of whether the *FT* helped to create it. Given the increased effort to co-ordinate communications at Cabinet Office on the subject, it seems reasonable at the very least to assume that the government was not immune to the pressures of the media, and particularly those of the *FT*. Although the *FT* changed tone somewhat by late 1998 and into 1999 regarding the UK, once it was clear that most large domestic organisations had a Y2K plan in place, it still tended to keep an anxious tone to much of its coverage by focusing on foreign governments who still seemed to be at risk. Many of the aviation-related stories in the third and fourth quarters of 1999, for instance, report on the questionable state of readiness of non-UK airlines and airports.

Although the government may have been persuaded by the *FT* to increase its Y2K co-ordination efforts, there are some (tenuous) indications that public opinion was not uniformly concerned about Y2K. In general, the vast majority of the public did little by way of planning for Y2K. Large populations participated in millennium celebrations seemingly without fear (Hamilton 2000). The Bank of England printed extra cash for the Christmas and New Year period, to satisfy a nervous market, but this proved unnecessary as demand for cash was no different from other Christmas and New Year periods (*Financial Times* 1999; Price 2000). Within air travel, the CAA notes that there was only a slight decrease in demand over the millennium period compared with previous New Year periods. Similarly, the NAO reported that anywhere from 25% of SMEs and 44% of small businesses had not taken the necessary steps to protect themselves against potential Y2K-related problems by mid to late 1999 (NAO 1999a).

In some respects, this hypothesis is constrained by the opaque nature of public opinion. First, while the government may have been organising a response for every possible outcome, the public may have become fatalists towards the end. That is, they felt they had little control over what was going to happen and therefore anticipation was pointless (Hood *et al.* 2001: 13). Second, they may have been at ease because of all the work the government did to ensure Y2K compliance. Third, public concern may have been latent. That is, while the public may not have been openly concerned about Y2K compliance, they may have become very concerned in a fairly short order had there been any problems. Fourth, public concern may have been selective. That is, just because one is not worried about the Y2K compliance of the local bank machine does not mean one is so *laissez-faire* about aviation safety.

The government did refer to polls taken on small businesses' Y2K compliance but the government seemed to use the numbers to gauge its success in *shaping* public opinion and the actions of businesses rather than to inform public policy[10] (Dunleavy 1991: 112; NAO 1997/1998).

10   In one interview at the CAA, the interviewee noted that he believed that Cabinet Office did some polling of anxiety levels regarding Y2K. He never saw them and I have never found them. The CAA did not conduct any polling.

Noting the caveats above but nevertheless accepting the *FT*, the NAO as well as several parliamentary committees as surrogates for just how negative public opinion could have become had there been any Y2K-related failures, the CAA's *Safety* programme did not seem sufficiently responsive: 90–92% of the industry was not audited; the programme's 'reasonable' standard was too low with too much discretion afforded to the CAA, particularly with respect to the SMEs; and public reporting and goals of transparency were not built into the process. The NIF with its promise of 'No Material Disruption' seems more aligned with the Opinion Responsive Hypothesis, with its high standard; with the actively engaged Number 10 as well as the involvement of parliament; and there was considerably more emphasis on transparency. The *Business as Usual* programme had some but not all of the latter characteristics. While the programme had a high standard and a third-party auditor for the audits, it was voluntary and the audit results were negotiated and agreed between the audited and the auditor.

In sum, the public and the media demand that the aviation industry maintain a high standard of safety, factually and perceptibly. The NIF emerged following a time of uniformly intense and negative media and parliamentary scrutiny. At this same time the aviation industry was starting to understand the Y2K problem better and get it under control. The NIF (and the *Business as Usual* programme by association) was a large-scale, economy-wide response to Y2K that would demonstrate in an open forum that all the critical services in the national infrastructure were moving towards Y2K compliance in a measurable way. It also allowed for some reassurances across sectors and countries. While the hypothesis leads to some important insights, it is constrained by methodological issues. Table 6.4 assumes a potentially anxious public and compares the three programmes against the expected outcome according to the Opinion Responsive Hypothesis.

6.3.3 Interests Hypothesis

The Interests Hypothesis argues that regulatory activity reflects the interplay and lobbying of organised interests. The concentration of interests is a critical feature in determining how risks are regulated (Hood *et al.* 2001: 112).

Given that 15 companies represent 80% of aviation travel in the UK, the industry could be described as *Client Politics* (Wilson 1980)—highly organised but one-sided lobby activity that results in stable capture. But the Y2K case seems to have changed the dynamics somewhat. There were several additional players, such as parliament, government, the media, companies from other key sectors of the economy and international regulators that were playing a much greater role and had a considerable stake in ensuring no hiccups during Y2K. The effect repositioned aviation somewhere between *Client Politics* and *Interest Group Politics*, in which organised lobby activity is high but contradictory, with compromise outcomes. This section considers the key players, including the IT industry, Number 10 and Cabinet Office, the CAA and the aviation industry by way of examining some of the compromise outcomes negotiated between them.

The IT/technology industries were the first groups to make noises about Y2K. Certainly, many technology service providers saw Y2K as an opportunity to generate revenue—overnight start-ups as well as the larger players, such as IBM, Unysis, Gartner and Cap Gemini (Nairn 1998). Representatives from these companies characterised the

	Size	Structure	Style	Alignment (✓)
Expected outcome	Large, vast	Centralised; focus on the entire industry, particularly on big players; includes parliament	Formal; low tolerance for slippage	
Safety programme (CAA)	✗ 'Reasonable standard' prone to slippage	✓/✗ Statements from everyone, but 90–92% of industry not audited	✗ Too much discretion; approx. 20 companies did not provide compliance statements	0.5/3
National Infrastructure Forum—No Material Disruption	✓	✓/✗ Not sufficiently focused on SMEs	✓	2.5/3
Business as Usual programme (CAA)	✓	✓/✗ Vast but not sufficiently focused on SMEs	✗ Too flexible; informal; negotiated audits; programme was voluntary	1.5/3

Legend   ✓ = alignment   ✗ = mismatch

TABLE 6.4 Observed responses in three programmes compared with the expected outcome according to the Opinion Responsive Hypothesis

issue to the press, to government officials and parliamentarians, among others (see for example Science and Technology Standing Committee 1997/98). But it would be incorrect to suggest it was only financial incentive that drove the Y2K story. Technology specialists were called on because they were the experts, and most of them agreed that the problem was real and could potentially have significant impacts.

Although the various technology industries did earn as a result of Y2K, the companies had anxieties of their own. On the one hand, they did not want to be seen as gouging the clients. On the other hand, as the custodians of the systems, the technology service providers felt they would be blamed if their clients' systems failed on 1 January 2000. Furthermore, if significant systems did fail, their clients might go out of business. Any of these scenarios—gouging, blaming or bankruptcy—could result in lost business post-1 January 2000, for the technology service providers.

Number 10 showed considerable interest in Y2K, almost from the first day of the new Labour Government. The government was able to mobilise top IT experts and channel considerable financial resources to ensure that the project was (more or less) completed before the (informal) 1 January 2000, deadline.[11] The commitment of the prime

11   The Year 2000 problem occurred because systems had to process four-digit year entries. Any system that forecasted had to process the year 2000 well before 1 January 2000. Nevertheless, most people referred to 1 January 2000 as the deadline.

minister was reinforced by MISC4, supplemented by quarterly, then monthly reporting requirements, which required detailed information about agency Y2K management. The regular reports, supplemented by NAO publications and parliamentary hearings, helped to put departments and agencies in the hot seat regularly. Similarly, 'No material disruption' minimised ambiguity by establishing a desired outcome by which departments and agencies could be more clearly judged. At the same time, it left a little wiggle room—'no *material* disruption to the *essential* services'—should there be any minor disruptions.

Given the high level of political interest at Number 10 the aviation industry had to participate in the NIF. Nevertheless, *Business as Usual* provides a useful insight to the compromises inherent in the process and the limitations to its effectiveness at the company-specific level. First, the results were reported at the sector level, and were not company-specific, which might have brought more market pressure to bear on individual organisations.[12] While legislation prevents the CAA from revealing company-specific information, Y2K was considered an unusual case and one that did produce exceptions. For instance, the government provided special status to AEA Technology to allow it to perform CAA functions. Nevertheless, Y2K company-specific information had the potential to create internal dissension within the sector. At a Public Accounts Committee hearing, one witness noted that in the finance sector some NIF organisations argued that failing companies should be named lest the reputation of the industry as a whole be damaged. And, indeed, when organisations in the sector threatened to name failing organisations, one such organisation argued that no one could prove negligence because nothing had yet failed (Committee on Public Accounts 1999: 2).

Second, despite the government publicly placing such importance on Y2K compliance and the desired target of 'no material disruption to service', *Business as Usual* was voluntary. One organisation was even able to withdraw from the programme. The organisation was undergoing a reorganisation of its company's reporting structure and it felt it could no longer meet the CAA's time-lines. The *Business as Usual* programme was therefore reduced to 14 from 15 (National Infrastructure Forum 1999: 113). This change had no impact, however, on the manner in which Y2K compliance was reported sector-wide. The sector was still declared fully compliant.

The Interests Hypothesis would anticipate a programme with a high standard, which emphasised good news stories, the role of the major players, and had considerable flexibility on the ground and offered financial incentives to become Y2K-compliant. The *Safety* programme seems most closely aligned with the Interests Hypothesis: it was sufficiently flexible in size and style, while it employed regular, industry-accepted reporting structures. The NIF, on the other hand, seems to deviate furthest from the hypothesis with the high standard and public profile. Ultimately, the *Business as Usual* programme seems to be a compromise between the other two programmes, with pressure being applied to industry through the high standard and the new third-party auditor while maintaining flexibility in participation and reporting.

In sum, a perceptibly high standard for Y2K compliance represented a confluence of interests for industry, the CAA, the government and various parliamentary institutions. These groups had a considerable stake in ensuring there were no or few Y2K-related hic-

12   Being Y2K-compliant was seen as an issue of competitive advantage. Many companies that were
     Y2K-compliant advertised the fact.

cups in the date changeover. The government and the CAA gathered detailed information on the bug and maintained a high standard throughout the run-up to Y2K, though the CAA's ability to enforce its high standard through the *Business as Usual* programme was constrained by the tenuous nature of voluntary, self-regulating relationships. Table 6.5 summarises this section.

	Size	Structure	Style	Alignment (✓)
Expected outcome	'Positive' goal to reassure customers; vast scope; some room for slippage	Focus on major players; industry-friendly committees; company-generated reports/assurances	Informal; flexible; information-sharing; no company-specific disclosure; emphasis on good news; room for slippage	
Safety programme **(CAA)**	✓ Sufficiently flexible	✓ Employs regular reporting relationship	✓/✗ Collegial environment between big players and regulator but bottom-line compliance statements provide insufficient flexibility	2.5/3
National Infrastructure Forum—No Material Disruption	✓/✗ Standard a little too high; but still some slippage allowed	✓	✗ High-public-profile reporting; high-level transparency for industry as a whole	1.5/3
Business as Usual **programme (CAA)**	✓/✗ High standard but good message to get behind	✓/✗ Don't want to be measured with SMEs—too many problems; anxiety with regards to external auditor	✓ Informal; flexible	2/3

Legend ✓ = alignment ✗ = mismatch

TABLE 6.5 **Observed responses in three programmes compared with the expected outcome according to the Interest Groups Hypothesis**

6.4 Conclusion

Hood *et al.*'s framework has limitations. The Opinion Responsive Hypothesis, for instance, seemed to be constrained by the fact that public opinion itself is a very elusive concept, often changing over time and place. Furthermore, the framework did not seem to allow for other potentially important aspects of context. For instance, while the Y2K programme was occurring at the CAA there were several other contentious aviation issues before parliament, such as NATS's privatisation and allegations of its mismanagement of a large software project (Leake 1998: 8). The politics of privatisation and NATS's history of IT management seem likely to influence the context affecting the management of Y2K, yet the framework did not easily allow for their inclusion.

There were other limitations to the framework. Notably, Hood *et al.* use the media extensively in the Opinion Responsive Hypothesis, yet, in the Y2K case, the media did not always seem to be an accurate barometer of public opinion. Rather, the media alone seemed more likely to be influencing government decisions (and possibly public opinion). As a consequence, the media could just as easily be treated in the Interests Hypothesis.

Nevertheless, the framework helps illuminate a discussion about risk regulation. Considering risk only at the macro level, where much of the present risk literature focuses, would miss important nuances in risk regulation. The 'risk society' would be drawn to an exercise such as the NIF—a broad, sweeping programme fighting a 'modern' risk across the entire national infrastructure. But it would fail to note the negotiated settlements that emerge between the high-level strategy at Number 10, and where the rubber hits the road in implementation (*Safety* programme and the *Business as Usual* programme). By way of summation, Table 6.6 synthesises the three 'Hypothesis Tables'. The summary table compares the key elements of the size, structure and style of the three key programmes—*Safety, No Material Disruption* and *Business as Usual*— against the expected outcome, according to each of the three hypotheses. The 'Alignment (✓) with expected outcome' sums each alignment by hypothesis. The sub-totals generate a ratio for each programme, and in so doing suggest the relative weight of each hypothesis in determining the manner in which the programme managed the risk. The bottom row of the table contains an overall total which demonstrates the relative weight of each hypothesis in determining the overall manner in which Y2K was managed by the aviation industry. The numbers should be used as a guide; they are not an exact measure.

In sum, the Interests Hypothesis was the most relevant hypothesis followed by the Opinion Responsive Hypothesis and then the Market Failure Hypothesis, in determining the size, structure and style of risk regulation in the aviation industry's Y2K story, though no one hypothesis dominated the management outright. Indeed, each of the hypotheses in isolation is predictive only about half of the time. More importantly, however, the summary Table 6.6 and Figure 6.4 highlight that different programmes were sensitive to different factors and audiences.

The *Safety* programme was aligned with the Market Failure Hypothesis and the Interests Hypothesis. This is perhaps not surprising. The role of the regulator is to fill a gap that regular market activity cannot or will not fill. As the Y2K story emerged, the CAA attempted to notify those it regulated to ensure they were aware of the problem and that they were fixing it. At the same time, the CAA enjoys a high-trust relationship with its bigger clients. CAA regulators comment that they try to create an environment in which the regulated companies can feel comfortable about bringing problems forward. This was the case with Y2K. The CAA employed the same practices that it always employs—information sharing, compliance statements and selected audits. This practice employed well-grounded routines, and reporting relationships, and had the accep-

	Regulatory control component	Market Failure Hypothesis	Opinion Responsive Hypothesis	Interest Groups Hypothesis
Expected outcome	Size	Medium-sized strategy, focused on raising awareness, particularly among SMEs	Large, vast	'Positive' goal to reassure customers; vast scope; some room for slippage
	Structure	Industry-wide but decentralised and sensitive to SMEs	Centralised; focus on the entire industry, particularly on big players	Focus on major players; industry-friendly committees; company-generated reports/assurances
	Style	Less formal; awareness raising and information gathering; focus on adverse business impacts and value of reliable systems inventory	Formal; low tolerance for slippage	Informal; flexible; information sharing; no company-specific disclosure; emphasis on good news; room for slippage
Programme	Regulatory control component	Market Failure Hypothesis	Opinion Responsive Hypothesis	Interest Groups Hypothesis
CAA Safety Programme (based on standard CAA practice)	Size	✓	✗ 'Reasonable standard' prone to slippage	✓ Sufficiently flexible
	Structure	✓	✓/✗ Statements from everyone, but 90–92% of industry not audited	✓ Employs regular reporting relationship
	Style	✓/✗ Bottom-line compliance statements of complex problems offers blame-shifting opportunity for regulator	✗ Too much discretion; approx. 20 companies did not provide compliance statements	✓/✗ Collegial environment between big players and regulator but bottom-line compliance statements provides insufficient flexibility
Alignment (✓) with expected outcome		2.5/3	0.5/3	2.5/3

Legend   ✓ = alignment   ✗ = mismatch

TABLE 6.6 Observed responses compared with expected responses according to the three hypotheses (continued over)

National Infrastructure Forum—No Material Disruption			
Size	✓/✗ High-cost strategy for low-probability event	✓	✓/✗ Standard a little too high; but still some slippage allowed — ✓
Structure	✓/✗ Allowed for information sharing and reassurances across sectors but not sufficiently focused on SMEs; too centralised; standardised for complex problem	✓/✗ Not sufficiently focused on SMEs	
Style	✗ Formal; too standardised	✓	✓/✗ High-public-profile reporting; high-level transparency for industry as a whole — ✓
Alignment (✓) with expected outcome	0.5/3	2.5/3	0.5/3
CAA Business as Usual			
Size	✗ High-cost strategy for low-probability event; little threat to safety	✓	✓/✗ High standard but good message to get behind — ✓
Structure	✗ Insufficiently focused on SMEs	✓/✗ Vast but insufficiently focused on SMEs	✓/✗ Don't want to be measured with SMEs—too many problems; anxiety with regards to external auditor
Style	✓	✓/✗ Too flexible; informal	✓ Informal; flexible
Alignment (✓) with expected outcome	1.0/3	1.5/3	2.0/3
Total	4.0/9	4.5/9	5.0/9

TABLE 6.6 (from previous page)

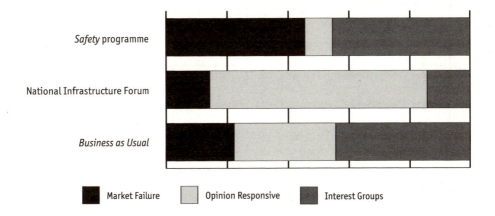

FIGURE 6.4 Y2K in the aviation industry: three hypotheses' influence on three government Y2K programmes

tance of the regulated community. At the same time, the approach left gaps as far as the Opinion Responsive Hypothesis was concerned, which became crucial in a high political and public-profile event. The professional discretion that the CAA enjoys left room for slippage and the regular routine was not sufficiently transparent.

Once Number 10 was convinced that Y2K was sufficiently serious, the 'No Material Disruption' target, an extremely high standard with an exceedingly wide scope, put considerable pressure on all regulators to become more actively involved in the Y2K programmes of those they regulate. Regulators and the regulated were now on the hot seat to develop a plan that could convince the government, parliament, the media and the public that systems would run smoothly over the millennium. This expectation was no small feat given the obscure and peculiar nature of the bug. Furthermore, the standardised reporting requirements established at Cabinet Office/Action 2000—standardised audit approaches, traffic light summary statements and high-public-profile reporting—left little room for subtlety. This approach seems less sensitive to the nuances of the market and industry dynamics in particular fields, and, therefore, deviates from the Market Failure Hypothesis and the Interests Hypothesis. The NIF, for instance, included all major players in the industry, but, as the CAA discovered, it was not the larger players that required the stick and carrot of the regulator—it was the SMEs who for various reasons presented a greater challenge.

The CAA's *Business as Usual* programme, by way of reply to the government's call for 'no material disruption' to service, shifted away from the Market Failure Hypothesis but only moved marginally away from the Interests Hypothesis. The *Business as Usual* programme seemed to do little by way of reducing the technical nature of the risk or complementing the activities of the market. Instead, the programme seems to be geared more towards communicating compliance, within the limits of that which the major players in the industry could deliver given the obscurity of the problem, the complexity of the technology and the limited time available. While the programme put new pressures on the major players with a new external auditor and high-public-profile reporting, there continued to be flexibility on the ground with respect to the audits, participation, continuity and disclosure. Hence, one might think of the *Business as Usual* programme as a compromise between, on the one hand, the major players in the industry, who were accustomed to the not-fully-transparent practices and procedures of the *Safety* programme and, on the other hand, Number 10 and Cabinet Office, who advocated a extremely high and standardised strategy (no material disruption) with a strong emphasis on transparency.

Y2K may seem like a rather mundane dress rehearsal in a post-9/11 environment. In fact, Y2K offers us an exceptional opportunity to examine how risk regulation regimes, which include industry, governments and regulators and the media, react in the face of uncertainty to a low-probability and high-consequence technological event with potential health, safety and economic consequences. Indeed, the current state of risk management has much in common with the period leading up to Y2K. What is important now is to focus on the study in retrospect and try to understand the strengths and weaknesses, opportunities and constraints that shaped the regulatory response and in so doing draw lessons to make present risk management more effective.

Appendix: methodology

This chapter is part of a larger comparative project that is considering how government agencies that are highly dependent on technology manage the risks associated with their technology. The Millennium Bug is the chief case study. For the purposes of the research project, Y2K allows us to test Hood *et al.*'s hypothesis that context shapes content. Unlike Hood *et al.*, however, who look at different types of risk, this research project considers (in some respects) the same risk across numerous fields and looks to determine which factors shaped management of the Y2K bug and whether or not there is variation across domains and countries.

The data concerning Y2K in this chapter come mostly from media clippings and primary and secondary UK government documents, including government department and agency Y2K files, National Audit Office (NAO) publications and documents from the British Parliamentary Library. I conducted 56 semi-structured interviews. Table 6.7 summarises the list of interviewees.

Within the field of aviation itself, the CAA provided me with internal Y2K briefing material and news releases, dated between 1998 and 2000. Staff at the CAA also commented on an early draft of this chapter.

For the media analysis in this chapter, I counted the headlines that appeared between 1 January 1997 and 31 December 2000 that included the term(s) 'Y2K', 'Millennium Bug', 'Millennium Bomb' and/or 'Year 2000 computer problem' in the three newspapers selected. From this total, I conducted a second search for articles that refer to 'CAA' or 'flights' within the body of the text in order to determine (approximately) how often these Y2K articles refer to aviation. I supplemented the searches with interviews with two senior IT/business journalists with over 30 years' reporting experience between them and who reported extensively on Y2K.

	US	UK
Federal Aviation Administration*/ Civil Aviation Authority	6	3
IT industry	5	1
IT journalists	1	1
Elected officials	1	1
Professional legislative staff	3	0
Executive Office of the President/ CITU	4	2
Staff from other agencies	11	17
Total	**31**	**25**

* Includes interviews with lead department

TABLE 6.7 Interviews to date

References

Adams, J. (1995) *Risk* (London: UCL).

Beck, U. (1992) *Risk Society* (London: Sage).

Beer, S. (1966) *Decision and Control* (New York: John Wiley).

Blair, T. (1998) 'Speech by the Right Honourable Tony Blair MP on The Millennium Bug to the Action 2000/Midland Bank Conference at the Barbican on Monday 30 March 1998', 10 Downing Street Press Notice obtained at the House of Commons Library.

Brans, M., and S. Rossbach (1997) 'The Autopoiesis of Administrative Systems: Niklas Luhmann on Public Administration and Public Policy', *Public Administration* 75: 417-39.

Bray, R. (1999) 'Guru gets airborne to bury millennium fears', *Financial Times*, 7 July 1999.

Breyer, S. (1982) *Regulation and its Reform* (Cambridge, MA: Harvard University Press).

—— (1993) *Breaking the Vicious Cycle* (Cambridge, MA: Harvard University Press).

Bryant, R., P. Hooper and C. Mann (1993) *Evaluating Policy Regimes: New Research in Empirical Macroeconomics* (Washington, DC: Brookings Institution).

CAA (Civil Aviation Authority) (1998) 'Year 2000', Memo to Aviation Industry, 8 July 1998.

—— (1999a) 'CAA Reports on Year 2000 Readiness', CAA News Release, 21 April 1999.

—— (1999b) 'UK Aviation Industry Now Ready for Year 2000', CAA News Release, 12 July 1999.

—— (1999c) 'UK Aviation Industry Now Ready for 2000', CAA News Release, 20 October 1999.

—— (2002) *Report and Accounts* (London: CAA).

CCTA (Central Computer and Telecommunications Agency) (1997) *Tackling the Year 2000: The Legal Implications* (London: HMSO).

Cheit, R. (1990) *Setting Safety Standards* (Berkeley, CA: University of California Press).

Cm 4703 (2000) *Modernising Government in Action: Realising the Benefits of Y2K* (London: HMSO).

Committee on Public Accounts (1999) *The Millennium Threat* (36th report; London: HMSO).

Dowding, K. (1995) 'Model or Metaphor? A Critical Review of the Policy Network Approach', *Political Studies* 43: 136-58.

—— (1996) *Power* (Buckingham, UK: Open University Press).

DTI (UK Department of Trade and Industry) (1996) 'Ian Taylor Welcomes Date Change 2000 Task Force', DTI Press Notice obtained from the House of Commons Library.

Dunleavy, P. (1991) *Democracy, Bureaucracy and Public Choice: Economic Explanations in Political Science* (London: Harvester).

Elkin, S. (1986) 'Regulation and Regime: A Comparative Analysis', *Journal of Public Policy* 6.1: 49-72.

Ernst & Young (1998) *Millennium Infrastructure Project*, Ernst & Young for Cabinet Office and obtained at the House of Commons Library.

Financial Times (1999) 'Millennium Bug', *Financial Times*, 7 June 1999.

Finkelstein, A. (2000) 'Y2K: A Retrospective View', obtained from www.cs.ucl.ac.uk/staff/ A.Finkelstein/archive.html, originally published in *Computing and Control Engineering Journal* 11.4 (August 2000): 156-59.

GAO (General Accounting Office) (1998) *FAA Systems: Serious Challenges Remain in Resolving Year 2000 and Computer Security Problems* (GAO/T-AIMD-98-251; Washington, DC: GAO).

Hamilton, A. (2000) 'Here's to the new Millennium', *The Times*, 1 January 2000.

Health and Safety Executive (1996) *Use of Risk Assessment with Government Departments* (report prepared by the Interdepartmental Liaison Group on Risk Assessment; London: Health and Safety Executive).

—— (1998) *Risk Assessment and Risk Management* (second report prepared by the Interdepartmental Liaison Group on Risk Assessment; London: Health and Safety Executive).

Heclo, H. (1978) 'Issue Networks and the Executive Establishment', in A. King (ed.), *The New American Political System* (Washington, DC: American Enterprise Institute).

HM Treasury (1996) *The Setting of Safety Standards: A Report by an Interdepartmental Group and External Advisers* (London: HM Treasury).

Hodson, M. (1998) 'Destination: Disaster', *The Times* (London) (Travel), 22 November 1998.

Hood, C. (1983) *The Tools of Government* (London: Macmillan).

——, H. Rothstein and R. Baldwin (2001) *The Government of Risk: Understanding Risk Regulation Regimes* (Oxford, UK: Oxford University Press).

House Committee on Transportation and Infrastructure Hearing (1998) 'Aviation and the Year 2000', Testimony of Jane F. Garvey, Federal Aviation Administrator, on 29 September 1998.

House of Commons Library (1998) *The Millennium Bug* (Research Paper 98/72; London: House of Commons Library).

Krasner, S. (ed.) (1983) *International Regimes* (Ithaca, NY: Cornell University Press).

Leake, J. (1998) 'Air chaos feared as new computer fails', *The Times*, 5 April 1998.

Majone, G. (1994) 'The Rise of the Regulatory State in Europe', *West European Politics* 17: 77-101.

Nairn, G. (1998) 'Flying into the Unknown', *Financial Times*, 2 December 1998.

National Audit Office (1997) *Managing the Millennium Threat* (London: HMSO).

—— (1998) *Managing the Millennium Threat II* (London: HMSO).

—— (1999a) *The Millennium Threat: 221 Days and Counting* (London: HMSO).

—— (1999b) *The Millennium Threat: Are We Ready?* (London: HMSO).

National Infrastructure Forum (1999) *National Infrastructure Assessment Programme: Final Report 1998–2000* (London: Action 2000, December 1999).

NATS (National Air Traffic Services) (1999a) 'NATS Declares Its Year 2000 Readiness', News Release, 29 March 1999.

—— (1999b) 'Business as Usual for NATS on Millennium Night', News Release, 20 December 1999.

Ogus, A. (1994) *Regulations: Legal Forms and Economic Theory* (Oxford, UK: Clarendon).

Price, C. (2000) 'Prophet of Doom Warns Worst is yet to Come', *Financial Times*, 1 January 2000.

Rhodes, R.A.W., and D. Marsh (1992) 'New Directions in the Study of Policy Networks', *European Journal of Political Research* 21: 181-205.

Schwartz, M., and M. Thompson (1990) *Divided We Stand* (Hemel Hempstead, UK: Harvester Wheatsheaf).

Science and Technology Committee (1997/98) *The Year 2000: Computer Compliance, Second Report to the House of Commons* (London: HMSO).

Shrader-Frechette, K. (1991) *Risk and Rationality* (Berkeley, CA: University of California).

Slovic, P. (1992) 'Perception of Risk: Reflections on the Psychometric Paradigm', in S. Krimsky and D. Golding (eds.), *Social Theories of Risk* (London: Praeger).

Stringer, J. (1967) 'Operational Research for Multi-Organizations', *Operational Research Quarterly* 18.2: 105-20.

Teubner, G. (1987) 'Juridification: Concepts, Aspects, Limits and Solutions', in G. Teubner, *Juridification in Social Spheres* (Berlin: de Gruyter).

Thompson, M., R. Ellis and A. Wildavsky (1990) *Cultural Theory* (Boulder, CO: Westview).

Wilson, J. (1980) *The Politics of Regulation* (New York: Basic Books).

Part 2
Corporate social responsibility and stakeholder theory

7
Seeking global solutions for the common good
A NEW WORLD ORDER AND CORPORATE SOCIAL RESPONSIBILITY

Robin T. Byerly

Appalachian State University, North Carolina, USA

> The corporation has, in fact, become both a method of property tenure and a means of organizing economic life. Grown to tremendous proportions, there may be said to have evolved a 'corporate system'—which has attracted to itself a combination of attributes and powers, and has attained a degree of prominence entitling it to be dealt with as a major social institution.
>
> *R. Edward Freeman* (1984)

> When one sits in the Hoop of the People, one must be responsible, because all of Creation is related, and the hurt of one is the hurt of all, and the honor of one is the honor of all, and whatever we do affects everything in the Universe.
> Lakota Instructions for Living passed down from White Buffalo Calf Woman.
>
> *Chief Arvol Looking Horse* (2001)

In a world that is rapidly being reordered as boundaries disappear through the proliferation of trade, the spread of a common economic system, astonishing new information and commercial exchange technologies, increased global interaction and cultural blending, we find ourselves increasingly dependent on each other. What affects one affects another, and so on. A new world order begets a world community that is increasingly interconnected and interdependent (Daly and Cobb 1994; Gelpi 1989; Hesselbein 1999).

Stakeholder concerns no longer tend to be specialised interests; they often reflect genuine human and environmental concerns that are shared by all. It has been suggested that the increasing scale of human activity and economic achievement has led to serious environmental crises and an industrial, competitive, materialistic society that is pronounced in its aggressiveness and its expectations of freedoms. Scientists, politicians and economists warn us of the seriousness of worldwide concerns and particularly those related to the environment, human rights and healthcare (Cairncross 1992; Gore 1992). Some have voiced a cry of anguish: are we destroying our own humanity and killing the planet (Daly and Cobb 1994)? Philosophers (Whitehead

1925), theologians (Pope John XXIII 1963) and economists (Daly and Cobb 1994) challenge us to recognise that something is wrong with present policies and approaches and to acknowledge the imperative that these concerns must be taken seriously. The call has been sounded by many—employees, investors, journalists, politicians, citizens—and the increasingly urgent plea is to find ways to ensure responsible behaviour on the part of businesses and a better establishment of trust (Beck 1998; Boggs 2000; Bryson and Cosby 1992; Hesselbein 1999).

Articulated here is an expanded concept of corporate social responsibility that is responsive to this new world order, to an increasingly global marketplace and society, and to a host of worldwide concerns. A remarkable emergence of interdisciplinary theory and real-world examples suggest that responsible corporations in today's world must first recognise a new social contract that stems from the need for global leadership and action; second, acknowledge the necessity of partnerships, mutual engagement, responsibility and commitment to achieve the future goals of all; and, third, embrace the growing opportunities for corporations to play significant leadership roles and to partner with governments and communities in seeking to serve the common good.

This argument is made in the following manner. First, a history of corporate social responsibility (CSR) theory is discussed with a focus on its evolution to the present day, which is then merged with a multidisciplinary perspective that draws from economics and international politics to enable a conceptual rendering of a broadened CSR perspective and new social contract. Next, several examples are cited to highlight some of the uniquely creative and responsible initiatives originating from business, industry and other societal groups. Based on the above, a number of suggestions are offered for building mutual engagement between corporations, stakeholders, governments, business partners and competitors that reflect a commitment to serve the common good.

7.1 Background and theory

Theory has evolved gradually regarding social concerns, society's expectations and corporate responsibility. Indeed, early management and economic theorists viewed the corporation as having a strong fiduciary responsibility to shareholders, but stopped short of considering any real obligation to other stakeholder groups (Friedman 1962; Teece 1984). The key issue of management was to generate above-average economic returns; social concerns were not considered a responsibility and tended to be relegated to government or other social institutions. Similar notions of free markets and the opportunities provided by capitalism continue to drive commerce, but current realities indicate that self-interested business behaviour is not benign and can even be quite harmful (Beck 1998; Singer 2001; Solomon 1999). Further, society is increasingly demanding additional measures of corporate responsibility beyond efficiency and profitability (Belasco 1999; Bryson and Crosby 1992; Christiansen 1989).

7.1.1 Corporate social responsibility and stakeholders

The evolution of CSR theory provides a sort of corporate social responsibility and performance paradigm that is, in its essence, a solid foundation for corporate social management and stakeholder engagement. The basic theoretical premise of CSR asserts that firms and managers have a duty beyond the classic fiduciary obligation to stockholders; they have a duty that extends also to stakeholders—groups and individuals that have a stake in or claim on the firm. Specifically, stakeholders are those who may be affected by the firm's actions. They may benefit or be harmed; their rights may be violated or respected by corporate actions (Carroll 1991; Freeman 1984). It has been argued from the inception of the CSR concept that the corporation's social responsibility is to attend to stakeholder rights and concerns and to take proactive, voluntary steps to avoid harm or wrongful consequences to those stakeholders (Bowen 1953; Carroll 1991; Freeman 1984; Walton 1967).

Thus, theory clearly suggests that corporations recognise a larger duty or obligation that springs from an awareness of stakeholders, how they might be impacted by corporate actions and their needs or concerns (Carroll 1991; Clarkson 1995; Donaldson and Preston 1995; Freeman 1984). Whether, how, and to what extent corporations feel obligated to respond may be determined by moral conviction, or the belief that their businesses can profit from such engagement or simply because the stakeholder is viewed to have its own power to influence the firm (Boatright 1994; Jawahar and McLaughlin 2001; Mitchell *et al.* 1997). On the other hand, stakeholders have often been identified as ends in themselves, forces to be reckoned with, in other words, valued entities with justifiable concerns and expectations (Brenner and Cochran 1991; Clarkson 1995; Jones 1995). Corporations can, and should, attribute legitimacy to their own impacted stakeholders and their claims.

While we acknowledge the legitimacy of many stakeholder claims, their justification for corporate engagement, however, is generally predicated on whether the stakeholder has the power to demand attention and, frequently, that power has not been enough. Indeed, some descriptive theory attempts to separate those claims, debate, argue and, in many ways, mitigate just whose claims get attention (Jawahar and McLaughlin 2001; Jones 1995; Mitchell *et al.* 1997). Nonetheless, in an increasingly global society characterised by interdependencies and interconnectedness, those claims begin to merge and many of those concerns affect us all (Beck 1998; Cairncross 1992; Deck 1999; Gore 1992).

7.2 Power

We can see that, in many ways, power has naturally accrued to corporations. It is reproduced and reinforced in a number of ways including society's perpetual rationalisation of the corporation's economic strength, its political influence on governments and its ability to commodify virtually every human activity (Boggs 2000). It has ownership and control of mass media, property and assets around the world. In recent times, corporations have grown almost beyond comprehension in size, assets, revenue generation, and both economic and societal influence. Freeman (1984) conceptualised the modern corporation as a powerful force of large proportion, with the means of organising economic life, and possessing significant attributes and powers to be dealt with as a major social institution.

But corporations did not always possess the prominence and dominance that they do now (Carroll 1991). Early social responsibility theorists took those limitations into account. They sought to define the social responsibilities of corporations by what they might reasonably be expected to assume, or by suggesting that social care extend only into a small sphere somewhat larger than their own profitability concerns (Bowen 1953). As the concept grew in acceptance by businesses, a broader notion emerged. Davis (1960) argued, with his 'Iron Law of Responsibility' that the social responsibilities of businesses need to be commensurate with their social power; further, he felt that to avoid social responsibility would lead to the gradual erosion of social power.

7.2.1 The social contract

Increasingly viewed as an institution of power, theorists began to recognise the need for good citizenship on the part of the corporation. McGuire (1963) suggested that the corporation take an interest in politics, in the welfare of the community, in education, in the well-being of its employees and the whole social world about it. Thus, the 'social contract' began to emerge and the view that businesses function by public consent. As so, they should subscribe to the basic purpose of serving society by assuming broader responsibilities, serving a wider range of human values and by contributing more to the quality of life than just supplying quantities of goods and services (Belasco 1999; Bowen 1953; Carroll 1991; Daly and Cobb 1994).

The sheer size and ownership of large corporations may suggest a positive duty as stakeholder theorists expect more from corporations than the law expects of individual property owners (Wijnburg 2000). This is reasonable because the law makes incorporation possible and, in a global market economy, extends the rights of individuals to collectively acquire more power than they would have otherwise. Further, the law usually asks for more responsibility where there is more power (Carroll 1991; Davis 1960).

7.2.2 Leadership

Surprisingly, at this time, the call for global leadership and a new paradigm of mutual responsibility and engagement has been sounded by a number of theorists from a variety of disciplines (Bernard 2000; Bryson and Crosby 1992; Costa 1998; Gilpin 2000; Hesselbein 1999). Frankly, however, while recognising the increasing power and influence of corporations, most theorists tend to seek solutions that would reduce or counteract that power. For example, Greider (1989) points to the failure of other institutions to adapt to current imperatives and revitalise themselves and he recognises corporate politics for its power to influence the political process. While he sees corporations as the main connective tissue linking people to their governments, he also warns of the danger if a new world order is built along the lines of massive economic (corporate) and political power. He appeals for an open public sphere, a thriving civic culture and a broad allocation of resources—in other words, a rebuilding of the building blocks of democratic politics.

Boggs (2000) links a lack of political leadership to corporate expansion, or colonisation, and points to the destructive effects of globalisation, or the global economy, contributing to environmental devastation, growing divisions between the rich and poor and others. He does note the power of modern corporations and portrays them as stronger than in the past, more ideologically self-conscious and increasingly global in scope and having a huge political influence. Still, he does not see corporate leadership as a solution and suggests that ethics will more often give way to more instrumental pursuits and remain subordinated to the standard criteria of control, efficiency and profits.

7.2.3 Economics

Economic theory builds on the rational propensity of individuals to act so as to optimise their own interests. Nonetheless, economists Daly and Cobb (1994) argue that if we work to avoid the destruction of community, our current ideas about market economics and capitalistic practice must be altered. They suggest a decentralisation of political and economic power with more worker ownership and participation in management, a subordination of economic goals to social goals that are democratically defined, and a fresh thinking about the possibilities of humane life in community. Such an approach is economically rational if we recognise that most of the problems faced by humanity today are interconnected and have a common source. If we can get away from national protectionism, and an over-reliance on traditional individualistic philosophies, then we can work together to build and empower communities to be self-sufficient and self-sustaining (Cairncross 1992; Christiansen 1989; Gelpi 1989; Gore 1992).

Support for such an approach has been garnered from important groups such as labour, businessmen, nationalists, the consciousness network and small groups with deep and knowledgeable concern for third-world developing countries (Daly and Cobb 1994; Gelpi 1989; Harmon and Toomey 1999; Solomon 1999). Admittedly, differences abound as to the leadership models prescribed, but all tend to recognise both the rising power and influence of corporations and the erosion of confidence in government. Further, all point to the need for leadership, the building of community and an economic, or political or CSR model that attempts to serve the common good.

7.3 A new world order and the common good

Stacer (1989) describes the hope of world citizens to find solutions for worldwide problems and urges that they do so by liberating themselves individually, resisting national individualism and responding to the call, not for a world state but for world citizenship. In his view, this will entail individual commitment and a worldwide social movement, and the building of a moral imperative that is not coercive but decidedly persuasive. Somerville and Mills (1999) ask the inevitable question: 'Who will provide leadership in the next century?' They argue that the growth of the global economy and the resulting interdependence of all nations serve to restrict the power of the nation-state and to enhance that of the business enterprise. They further note that world citizens are turning to business leaders as they look for answers to many social concerns.

Additionally, many predict a declining power of governments and point to a number of failings including: a depoliticised society where citizenship and individual participation has decayed, public discourse has drifted toward trivial concerns, and society has become acclimatised and accepting of common forms of domination (Boggs 2000; Gelpi 1989). Government and politics has further been described as being harmful to progressive social movements that have a vested interest in outcomes (Boggs 2000). The result is a lack of leadership, most particularly in regard to the worldwide problems cited above, at local, national and international levels.

If we are to honestly face this new world order, many suggest that we must enlarge stakeholder concerns to include the pursuit of goals that will serve the common good (Belasco 1999; Bryson and Crosby 1992; Christiansen 1989; Cragg 2000; Daly and Cobb 1994). Pope John XXIII defined the 'common good' as 'the sum total of conditions of social living, whereby men [sic] are enabled more fully and more readily to achieve their own perfection'. This definition can easily be extended in the present day to reflect 'the universal common good'. Pope John's advice then is most relevant today:

> All human beings, as they take an ever more active part in the public life of their own country, are showing increasing interest in the affairs of all peoples, and are becoming more consciously aware that they are living members of the whole human family (*Pacem in terris* [no. 125] 1963).

The new world order is characterised by pluralism and a need to build an inclusive, cohesive community. We have become, of necessity, full participants in the growing networked society and there is a call for engagement that we *all* must answer (Hesselbein 1999).

7.4 Creative social initiatives from business, industry and society

Adding further legitimacy to a broadened perspective on corporate social responsibility and the social contract are the increasing examples of caring business practice and response to global stakeholder issues, and the creative solutions being engineered by responsible corporations, both individually and in league with business and community partners. To cite a few examples, the Royal Dutch/Shell Group, the Chemical Manufacturers Association (CMA), and the Caux Round Table represent responsible corporate power at work through extraordinary leadership, stakeholder engagement and good citizenship at the firm, industry and international business alliance levels.

An 'awakening' sparked a transformation at the Shell Group to become a leader in global corporate citizenship. Its rebirth entailed a dramatic shift in the company's outlook and behaviour which included an allegiance to act on principle, balancing the firm's economic interests evenly with social and environmental interests, all geared toward sustainable development. In charting its new socially responsible direction, Shell built new principles and institutionalised change by initiating open communication and the building of relationships with stakeholders within and without the firm. While measuring both financial performance and social and environmental performance its intent is to engage the public in a 'two-way' conversation over profits and principles (Mirvis 2000).

Although the CMA is one of the oldest trade and industry associations in the United States, some of its principles and codes of conduct are relatively new. By establishing a voluntary code of conduct for participants in this industry called 'Responsible Care', those volunteering to participate accept the code's policies and rules of behaviour and subject themselves to regulation that includes monitoring and enforcement by the CMA (Prakash 2000). Such industry-level initiatives serve the common good by engaging citizens' groups in their development, minimising the adversarial nature of government intervention and legal action (somewhat distrusted by both corporations and citizens), and by providing firms greater flexibility to channel private interests toward achieving broader societal objectives in a manner from which all can benefit.

A number of international initiatives, alliances and treaties have sought to develop a set of universal principles to guide global business behaviour and to create some rules to which all parties involved can agree (e.g. US Department of Commerce Model Business Principles, Declarations of Human Rights or Labour Rights by the United Nations and International Labour Organisation, treaties established and endorsed following world summit meetings, etc.). To achieve a universal model of behaviour is a remarkable challenge given the myriad of players, each with its own self-interests and philosophies of what is acceptable behaviour in global commerce and what is not. Nonetheless, a success story is found in the efforts of the Caux Round Table, a group made up of international executives from large corporations who came together to fashion a voluntary set of business principles to which all could respect and uphold. These principles are based on the conviction that we can all live together and act for the common good. Created in 1992, many businesses around the world have voluntarily embraced these universal principles and others are continuing to do so (Caux Round Table 1994).

Clearly, the new corporate response appears to be more than just turning the public's concern for certain social issues to corporate advantage. Greater obligations created by interconnectedness and interdependencies warrant a positive and moral exercise of corporate power, a power that may fill the gap and answer the call by providing leadership that is attuned to worldwide stakeholder concerns, that legitimately seeks to lead through alliances with stakeholders and the pursuit of shared goals, and that recognises the power of stakeholders as community partners.

7.5 Corporate social responsibility and serving the common good

Simply stated, corporations have powers and attributes (Freeman 1984) that render them perhaps more capable than any other entity, government or otherwise, in the world. Further, corporations are proximate. They possess a near omnipresence as they exist and compete in literally every corner of the world and are, thus, close to stakeholders and their issues. In searching for leadership, corporations have come to be viewed as a last resort, as governments and nation-states are reduced in power, and as international organisations, treaties, meetings and trade agreements prove weak in their ability to deal with real issues (Boggs 2000; Bryant and Hodgkinson 1989; Gilpin 2000; Stacer 1989). It may well be that no individual or group is better empowered and capable to rise to this leadership challenge. Further, society's attention is increasingly fixed upon business, demanding more of it, and mandating more responsible behaviour (Beck 1998; Bryson and Crosby 1992).

How may corporations respond to the current call for leadership and better corporate social responsibility? What role should they play in the building of co-operative alliances to embrace and empower an inclusive and cohesive world community? And how can stakeholders come to accept corporate power and influence as a positive force that can truly serve the common good?

Leadership for the common good means sharing power; creating settings for mutual engagement and stakeholder assessment; reassessing old policies and programmes; openly engaging public debate, participation and collaboration; and reaching out beyond traditional organisational, even social and political, boundaries. Shared power requires corporations to do their part to build and empower communities to be self-sufficient and self-sustaining (Daly and Cobb 1994). National protectionism and staunch individualism will not adequately serve a world community. Gandhi was a great individual leader who united in a gentle, non-coercive way by respecting the differences of others, understanding, accepting and appreciating those differences. He taught us how to look at society as a gigantic machine made up of all kinds of parts—assembled properly they function efficiently and make the machine work. No part can function on its own, nor be discarded (Gandhi 1999). The leadership lesson Gandhi provided us is this: we must work in unison.

Our newly described social contract calls for mutual commitment and responsibility to meaningfully address issues that we all share in a connected and interdependent world community. A wide range of possibilities exist: several are suggested here. Corporations may better honour the new social contract, serve the common good and exercise wise use of their power by: first, looking internally and better regulating themselves; second, extending their outreach in new, more venturesome ways; third, partnering with governments, states and international agencies and initiatives; and, fourth, rising to the global challenge and need for leadership.

7.5.1 Corporations and self-regulation

Corporations can begin by looking inward. Legitimised power requires a consensus of values and the presence of trust. The time has come for more corporations to effectively build that trust through responsibility, integrity, corporate character and consistent responsible behaviour over time. This might be achieved in a number of ways. Many suggest that corporations redefine their roles within society and expand their thinking to recognise a larger purpose than simply serving their own narrowly defined interests (Bernard 2000; Gilpin 2000; Tavis 2000) and to set their own global values (Tavis 2000). Beck (1998) speaks of a cosmopolitan manifesto that represents global and local concerns, central human worries that are world problems with immediacy and criticality. Corporations, as world citizens, must make these concerns their own. Corporations can continue to build corporate character through leadership with integrity and values, walking the talk, establishing meaningful codes of ethics, making a solid commitment to change, focusing on two bottom lines—financial and social, controlling firm growth for the long haul and being exactly what they say they are—reporting performance honestly and eliminating the hype (Singer 2001).

Internally, corporations can forge new business models that more effectively align the variables that affect group behaviour, such as CEO, board of directors, strategies, culture (Costa 1998), and create new business structures that balance rules and individual discretion (Bryant and Hodgkinson 1989). More corporate leaders must develop leadership skills and build organisational incentives to harness the commitment of all within. And corporations can build public trust and partnership by serving as honest advocates—embracing, rather than ignoring, global concerns, educating others and leading the search for solutions.

7.5.2 Corporations and outreach activities

Increasingly, we see leading examples of corporate responsibility in firms that are looking beyond their own corporate boundaries, embracing society and making extraordinary initiatives that promote awareness and action on social issues. These can include corporate partnerships with competitors, other organisations, society and government to search for solutions to universal concerns. Corporations, through alliances and partnerships, can jointly work for progress and reform with the World Trade Organisation (WTO), the International Monetary Fund (IMF), the World Bank and the Business Roundtable. The Caux Business Roundtable and Newton (2000) propose that we universally accept the principles of *kyosei*, an environmental imperative to all to acknowledge, respect and foster 'community', which ultimately includes all human beings and takes in the entire living basis of human existence in determining values and honouring them.

The Social Venture Network was established in San Francisco in 1987 as a 'safe harbour' where social-activist entrepreneurs could meet to share best practices, commiserate and co-invest. At present, it is evolving into a broad-based advocacy organisation that is increasingly looking to make a powerful impact on society, increase its own public voice and become empowered to take principled action (Singer 2001). As a principled organisation, it provides wonderful guidance for all companies in today's highly charged, global marketplace. Those involved in social venture networks are responding to the call for social responsibility in the sense that it is not about them, nor even about their companies. It is about their mission, a mission that encompasses values, principles and environmental, local and global social concerns.

By working in unison so that all are better served, corporations can pioneer new checks, balances and regulation at firm and industry levels. They can participate and partner with Research Centres and Centres of Excellence, other businesses, politicians, economists and educators such as the University of Notre Dame Centre for Ethics and Religious Values in Business (Swenson 2000). As issues and concerns arise, corporations can no longer afford to wait for a crisis or government intervention; they must pay attention and heed new social movements. Additionally, perhaps recent corporate trends and growth strategies need to be resized and reigned in, as we witness numerous failings and abuses of large megamerger business entities. In the interests of a global society, Western firms need not dominate, but trim their sails and accept partnership of a more equitable nature in a world market (Gilpin 2000).

7.5.3 Corporations as partners

The global marketplace, while propelled by global production, lacks the stability that is made possible by an explicit political or authority structure. Nevertheless, it has been suggested that a transnational process of consensus formation does exist among official caretakers of the global economy, something that may be described by the French word *nébuleuse*, translated as the notion of 'governance without government' (Cox 2000). As states work together as agencies for bringing the global economy under better control, corporations can partner with states to develop and shape new structures of thought and political authority that are responsive to global concerns and that provide stability in the absence of global government.

New configurations are, even now, emerging with partnerships bridging public and private sectors, creative alliances being forged between governmental agencies and market parties (van Luijk 2000). Examples include the Caux Roundtable's 'Business Principles', the US Interfaith Centre on Corporate Responsibility's 'Principles for Global Corporate Responsibility', and the Coalition for Environmentally Responsible Economies (CERES) Principles. At the industry level, another example is the White House Apparel Industry Code of Conduct; finally, between nations we have consensus building through partnerships as evidenced in the European Community Charter, the Sullivan Principles and the Tutu Principles. All have the goals of achieving a clear frame of reference, a shift to affirmative goals, a record of responsible behaviour and a system that increases goodwill (Massie 2000). Restated, new partnerships foster new structures for new relationships perhaps, indeed, better positioned to serve the common good.

By partnering, corporations may work with labour unions to build a broader coalition of social forces and allow the public to be better educated. Corporations may work with governments to forge new treaties that may pave the way for global economic, labour and environmental concerns to be better addressed in the best interests of all and, in so doing, contribute to a more stable power structure by participating in American leadership with its 200-plus years of experience (Friedman 2000). Additionally, more and more businesses are responding to the European Union and heeding the restraints imposed by a cautionary European Commission that is mandating tougher standards for competitive and environmental behaviour (Mitchener 2002). Further, American government and businesses may learn from the capitalistic economies of Germany and Japan, nations that, while prospering with a Western economic system have, nonetheless, built in a number of safeguards for moral and ethical business responsibility.

Friedman (2000) suggests that pure market vision is inadequate; a globalised economy and society needs balance with appropriate social safety nets. In his view, a secure and stable globalised system requires an activist and generous American leadership, one that is undoubtedly most attainable through government, market and corporate partnership that is dedicated to serving more than its own personal interests.

7.5.4 Corporations as leaders

The Drucker Foundation asserts that leading ourselves and our organisations 'beyond the walls' is the first requirement for success in the years to come. The Chairman of the Board of Governors of the Drucker Foundation offers a new definition of leadership: 'the capacity of a human community—people living and working together—to bring forth new realities' (Hesselbein 1999: 78). As traditional walls are dissolving, not only must organisational leaders find new meaning for what they actually own and control; they also must deal with the problems and disasters that cannot be contained within other nations' or communities' boundaries. Further, this new leadership will draw on diverse areas (business, government, art, science and others) and it must involve interplay of corporations, individuals and communities (Senge 1999).

Corporations as leaders will build bridges; the corporation in a healthy society requires three sectors: public (government), private (business) and social (community) (Somerville and Mills 1999). All are interconnected and interdependent. As governments appear to be losing the ability to solve both domestic and international public issues, new models of leadership and co-operation can unleash the inventive, innovative power of individuals, social organisations and corporations (Helgeson 1999). Through a worldwide mobilisation, we can embrace the future and an inclusive, cohesive community.

7.6 Conclusion

Recent theorists appear to converge in their views on corporate social responsibility. All reflect near universal concern for moral processes and outcomes based on the idea that stakeholders have worth, and that we can share understandings and values (Jones and Wicks 1999; Shankman 1999; Wijnburg 2000). Many suggest that we are missing an adequate theory of the common good (Daly and Cobb 1994; Gelpi 1989). Further, most are coming to agree that in an increasingly interdependent society, individual good is not possible outside the context of common good. When couched in light of the current prominence and dominance of many modern corporations, as well as the extraordinary ethical failures of too many large corporations, a broadened perspective emerges. This newer argument challenges traditional economic views of the firm and calls for a new paradigm in which the interests of the firm are seen as an extension of the interests of a larger community, an efficient market is also a fair market, and corporations are regarded as much for social contribution as for economic power (Cragg 2000; Shankman 1999).

In the global community and marketplace, there is little of which any participant can say, 'This is mine alone' (Deck 1999). We are all—citizens, states, corporations—part of the whole, incredibly interconnected and truly interdependent. Social and economic reason suggests that we must all begin to converge in some of our goals and work to co-ordinate efforts. In the politics of the common good and the democratic process, everyone in the society ought to be able to share in an advancing quality of life (Christiansen 1989). The mutuality of commitment to the common good and shared responsibility mandate that corporations, governments and even individual stakeholders work to accept shared visions, and future hopes for all members of the global community.

The survival of all depends on our ability to recognise a new social contract, a heightened sense of responsibility and work in unison to serve the common good by attending to the needs and concerns of all. This responsibility extends to all, but the call is increasingly being sounded to businesses, the powerful engines of this new world order that have remarkable power, if properly used, to make a difference, pioneer solutions, strengthen stability and aid global development regarding human, labour and environmental concerns.

References

Beck, U. (1998) 'The Cosmopolitan Manifesto', *New Statesman* 124.4377: 28-30.

Belasco, J. (1999) 'Creating Success for Others', in F. Hesselbein, M. Goldsmith and I. Somerville (eds.), *Leading beyond the Walls* (San Francisco: Jossey-Bass): 189-98.

Bernard, M. (2000) 'Post-Fordism and Global Restructuring', in R. Stubbs and G.R.D. Underhill (eds.), *Political Economy and the Changing Global Order* (Ontario: Oxford University Press Canada): 152-62.

Boatright, J. (1994) 'What's so Special about Shareholders?', *Business Ethics Quarterly* 4: 393-408.

Boggs, C. (2000) *The End of Politics: Corporate Power and the Decline of the Public Sphere* (New York: The Guilford Press).

Bowen, H.R. (1953) *Social Responsibilities of the Businessman* (New York: Harper & Row).

Brenner, S.N., and P.L. Cochran (1991) 'The Stakeholder Theory of the Firm: Implications for Business and Society Theory and Research', in J.F. Mahon (ed.), *International Association for Business and Society: 1991 Proceedings*: 449-67.

Bryant, R.C., and E. Hodgkinson (1989) 'Problems of International Co-operation', in R. Cooper, B. Eichengreen, C. Henning, G. Holtham and R. Putnam (eds.), *Can Nations Agree?* (Washington, DC: The Brookings Institution): 1-11.

Bryson, J.M., and B.C. Crosby (1992) *Leadership for the Common Good* (San Francisco: Jossey-Bass).

Cairncross, F. (1992) *Costing the Earth: The Challenge for Governments, the Opportunities for Business* (Boston, MA: Harvard Business School Press).

Carroll, A.B. (1991) 'The Pyramid of Social Responsibility: Toward the Moral Management of Organizational Stakeholders', *Business Horizons* 34: 39-48.

Caux Round Table (1994) *Caux Principles for Business*, Minnesota Centre on Corporate Responsibility.

Chief Arvol Looking Horse (2001) *White Buffalo Teachings* (dreamkeepers.net).

Christiansen, D. (1989) 'The Common Good and the Politics of Self-interest: A Catholic Contribution to the Practice of Citizenship', in D.L. Gelpi (ed.), *Beyond Individualism* (Notre Dame, IN: University of Notre Dame Press): 54-86.

Clarkson, M. (1995) *A Risk Based Model of Stakeholder Theory* (Toronto: University of Toronto's Centre for Corporate Social Performance and Ethics).

Costa, J.D. (1998) *The Ethical Imperative* (Reading, MA: Addison-Wesley).

Cox, R.W. (2000) 'Political Economy and World Order: Problems of Power and Knowledge at the Turn of the Millennium', in R. Stubbs and G.R.D. Underhill (eds.), *Political Economy and the Changing Global Order* (Ontario: Oxford University Press Canada): 25-37.

Cragg, W. (2000). 'Human Rights and Business Ethics: Fashioning a New Social Contract', *Journal of Business Ethics* 27: 205-14.

Daly, H.E., and J.B. Cobb (1994) *For the Common Good* (Boston, MA: Beacon Press).

Davis, K. (1960) 'Can Business Afford to Ignore Social Responsibilities?', *California Management Review* 2 (Spring 1960): 70-76.

Deck, M.C. (1999) 'Stewards, Wastrels, or Thieves', *Business and Society* 38.1: 7-8.

Donaldson, T., and L.E. Preston (1995) 'The Stakeholder Theory of the Corporation: Concepts, Evidence, and Implications', *Academy of Management Review* 20.1: 65-91.

Freeman, R.E. (1984) *Strategic Management: A Stakeholder Approach* (Boston, MA: Pitman).

Friedman, M. (1962) *Capitalism and Freedom* (Chicago: University of Chicago Press).

Friedman, T.L. (2000) *The Lexus and the Olive Tree* (New York: Anchor Books).

Gandhi, A. (1999) 'The Four Principles of Leadership', in F. Hesselbein, M. Goldsmith and I. Somerville (eds.), *Leading Beyond the Walls* (San Francisco: Jossey-Bass): 217-26.

Gelpi, D.L. (1989) 'Conversion: Beyond the Impasses of Individualism', in D.L. Gelpi (ed.), *Beyond Individualism: Toward a Retrieval of Moral Discourse in America* (Notre Dame, IN: University of Notre Dame Press): 1-30.

Gilpin, R. (2000) *The Challenge of Global Capitalism* (Princeton, NJ: Princeton University Press).

Goldsmith, M., and C. Walt (1999) 'New Competencies for Tomorrow's Global Leader', in F. Hesselbein, M. Goldsmith and I. Somerville (eds.), *Leading beyond the Walls* (San Francisco: Jossey-Bass): 159-66.

Gore, A. (1992) *Earth in the Balance: Ecology and the Human Spirit* (Boston, MA: Houghton-Mifflin).

Greider, W. (1989) *The Trouble with Money* (Knoxville, TN: Whittle Direct Books).

Harmon, R., and M. Toomey (1999) 'Creating a Future We Wish to Inhabit', in F. Hesselbein, M. Goldsmith and I. Somerville (eds.), *Leading beyond the Walls* (San Francisco: Jossey-Bass): 251-60.

Helgeson, S. (1999) 'Dissolving Boundaries in the Era of Knowledge and Custom Work', in F. Hesselbein, M. Goldsmith and I. Somerville (eds.), *Leading Beyond the Walls* (San Francisco, CA: Jossey-Bass Publishers): 49-56.

Hesselbein, F. (1999) 'The Community Beyond the Walls', in F. Hesselbein, M. Goldsmith and I. Somerville (eds.), *Leading beyond the Walls* (San Francisco: Jossey-Bass): 1-17.

Jawahar, I.M., and G.L. McLaughlin (2001) 'Toward a Descriptive Stakeholder Theory: An Organizational Life Cycle Approach', *Academy of Management Review* 26.3: 397-414.

Jones, T.M. (1995) 'Instrumental Stakeholder Theory: A Synthesis of Ethics and Economics', *Academy of Management Review* 20: 404-37.

—— and A.C. Wicks (1999) 'Convergent Stakeholder Theory', *The Academy of Management Review* 24.2: 206-21.

Massie, R.K. (2000) 'Effective Codes of Conduct: Lessons from the Sullivan and CERES Principles', in O.F. Williams (ed.), *Global Codes of Conduct* (Notre Dame, IN: University of Notre Dame Press): 280-94.

McGuire, J.W. (1963) *Business and Society* (New York: McGraw-Hill).

Mirvis, P.H. (2000) 'Transformation at Shell: Commerce and Citizenship', *Business and Society Review* 105.1: 63-84.

Mitchell, R.K., B.R. Agle and D.J. Wood (1997) 'Toward a Theory of Stakeholder Identification and Salience: Defining the Principle of Who and What Really Counts', *Academy of Management Review* 22: 853-86.

Mitchener, B. (2002) 'Increasingly, Rules of Global Economy are set in Brussels', *Wall Street Journal*, 23 April 2002: A1.

Newton, L.H. (2000) 'Who Speaks for the Trees?: Considerations for any Transnational Code', in O.F. Williams (ed.), *Global Codes of Conduct* (Notre Dame, IN: University of Notre Dame Press): 267-79.

Pope John XXIII (1963) 'Pacem in terris', 125, *Encyclical of Pope John XXIII on Establishing Universal Peace in Truth, Justice, Charity and Liberty, Given at Rome and St Peter's on Holy Thursday, the Eleventh Day of April in the Year 1963*.

Prakash, A. (2000) 'Responsible Care: An Assessment', *Business and Society* 39.2: 183-209.

Senge, P. (1999) 'Leadership in Living Organizations', in F. Hesselbein, M. Goldsmith and I. Somerville (eds.), *Leading Beyond the Walls* (San Francisco: Jossey-Bass): 73-90.

Shankman, N.A. (1999) 'Reframing the Debate between Agency Theory and Stakeholder Theories of the Firm', *Journal of Business Ethics* 4.1 (May 1999): 319-34.

Singer, T. (2001) 'Can Business Still Save the World?', *Inc. Magazine*, 30 April 2001: 58-62.

Solomon, R.C. (1999) *A Better Way to Think About Business* (New York: Oxford University Press).

Somerville, I., and D.Q. Mills (1999) 'Leading in a Leaderless World', in F. Hesselbein, M. Goldsmith and I. Somerville (eds.), *Leading beyond the Walls* (San Francisco: Jossey Bass): 227-42.

Stacer, J.R. (1989) 'The Hope of a World Citizen: Beyond National Individualism', in D.L. Gelpi (ed.), *Beyond Individualism: Toward a Retrieval of Moral Discourse in America* (Notre Dame, IN: University of Notre Dame Press): 188-218.

Swenson, W. (2000) 'Raising the Ethics Bar in a Shrinking World', in O.F. Williams (ed.), *Global Codes of Conduct* (Notre Dame, IN: University of Notre Dame Press): 3-12.

Tavis, L.A. (2000) 'The Globalization Phenomenon and Multinational Corporate Developmental Responsibility', in O.F. Williams (ed.), *Global Codes of Conduct* (Notre Dame, IN: University of Notre Dame Press): 13-38.

Teece, D.J. (1984) 'Economic Analysis and Strategic Management', *California Management Review* 26.3: 87-110.

Van Luijk, H.J.L. (2000) 'In Search of Instruments: Business and Ethics Halfway', *Journal of Business Ethics* 27.1 (September 2000): 3-8.

Walton, C.C. (1967) *Corporate Social Responsibilities* (Belmont, CA: Wadsworth).

Whitehead, A.N. (1925) *Science and the Modern World* (New York: Macmillan).

Wijnburg, N.M. (2000) 'Normative Stakeholder Theory and Aristotle: The Link between Ethics and Politics', *Journal of Business Ethics* 25.4: 329-42.

8
Toward better governance
THE STAKEHOLDER PARTNERSHIP FRAMEWORK

Craig E. Armstrong
University of Texas at San Antonio, USA

> We've gone through a crisis of accountability that spanned many sectors; it was not merely Wall Street. It was government. It was not-for-profits. It was religious institutions. It was even the media. We have seen failures of governance that, to a certain extent, reflected a larger societal issue, a dislocation, a disjunction between people being put in positions of authority and their understanding of their fiduciary duties. Now, having gone through this series of scandals, I believe there has been a fundamental change that will last for some time
>
> Eliot Spitzer (*Business Week* 2003: 129)

Is there a universal governance system applicable to all corporations? The crisis of accountability described by New York State Attorney, General Spitzer, suggests that corporate governance structures systematically fail society. Among the many devastating impacts of this failure are the loss of public trust in the institutions whose mission it is to ensure sound governance and accountability, and the realisation that the market, management and regulatory systems established to support this mission were woefully inadequate. The challenges of achieving effective corporate governance have been a part of the business landscape since the 1930s, when legal and regulatory forces vested the majority of power in the hands of executives. This resulted in the creation of 'agency relationships' which involved business owners (principals) engaging another person, or persons (agents), to take actions on their behalf which involved the delegation of work and some decision-making authority (Jensen and Meckling 1976). Despite the contractual obligations accepted by executives in this relationship, the current governance crisis has illustrated how shareholders have been disenfranchised both by these executives and the boards of directors assigned to oversee their activities. The market and bureaucratic dynamics of corporate governance since the 1930s have provided ample examples of two main problems that can occur in agency relationships: first, the agency problem that arises when the goals of the principal and agent conflict and it is difficult, or expensive, for the principal to verify what the agent is actually doing; and, second, the problem of risk sharing that arises when the principal and agent have different attitudes toward risk (Eisenhardt 1989). The typical setting for analysis of these problems, such as structuring the agent's compensation to be congruent with the goals of the principal, has been the corporation. Jensen (2000) argues, however, that agency problems arising from conflicts of interest may be generalised to virtually all forms of co-operative activity among individuals. If agency problems can afflict all forms of social exchange, and if current market, management and regulatory forces are unable to prevent or mitigate them, then a new form of corporate governance is required that elevates the *legal contract* aspect of the agency relationship into a *social contract* that governs a stakeholder relationship. This chapter focuses on the social contract that must be achieved within the profession of CEO, and at the level of inter-organisational relations.

It is important to emphasise here that the challenges of achieving effective corporate governance have been a part of the business landscape since the 1930s. Since then, organisation scientists have developed theoretical frameworks related to corporate governance along the dimensions of: transaction costs (Ouchi 1980; Williamson 1975); institutional isomorphism (DiMaggio and Powell 1983); behaviour of agents (Jensen and Meckling 1976; Eisenhardt 1989); occupational communities (Van Maanen and Barley 1984); resource dependence (Pfeffer and Salancik 1978; Provan 1983); and stakeholder management (Freeman 1984). While these theoretical frameworks have found widespread acceptance in the literature of organisation science both theoretically and empirically, the practical aspects of these frameworks somehow escaped implementation by managers, regulators and other stakeholders in the governance of corporations. The current response to crises in corporate governance is far more grounded in our legal system because of this than in any form of a management system. This chapter seeks to contribute toward an improvement of a management system for corporate governance that addresses problems at the level of the CEO and the corporation, by incorporating the practical applications of long-accepted organisational theories into tangible actions. By doing so, it is hoped that we can come closer to a universal model for corporate governance that has eluded both practitioners and researchers since the 1930s.

8.1 Transaction costs and corporate governance

Co-operative action requires interdependence between individuals. This interdependence calls for a transaction or exchange in which each individual gives something of value and receives something of value in return. In a market relationship, the transaction takes place between the two parties and is mediated by a price mechanism in which the existence of a competitive market reassures both parties that the terms of the exchange are equitable. In a bureaucratic relationship, each party contributes labour to a corporate body that mediates the relationship by placing a value on each contribution and then compensating it fairly (Ouchi 1980). Market-based transactions can be judged as equitable based on the price mechanism of a competitive market, while bureaucracy-based transactions can be judged as equitable to the extent that a social agreement exists that gives the bureaucratic hierarchy the legitimate authority to provide this mediation (Ouchi 1980).

In both cases, the demand for equity gives rise to transaction costs whenever it becomes difficult to determine the value of goods or services. These costs come in the form of any activity that is performed to satisfy each party to an exchange that the value given and received is in accord with expectations (Ouchi 1980). In market transactions, for example, manufacturers may find it necessary to incur the cost of having their processes certified as meeting third-party quality standards. Or they might have to maintain their own laboratory to test the quality of raw materials provided by their suppliers before using them to manufacture their own products. In bureaucratic transactions within an organisation, the bureaucratic hierarchy provides a means for mitigating high market-based transaction costs with standardised employment agreements, working conditions and performance expectations, but the organisation must assume transaction costs to maintain its own bureaucratic hierarchy. Bureaucratic transactions also describe the exchanges that take place between organisations and the government agencies that regulate them. Both the regulated organisations and the regulating agencies incur bureaucratic costs to ensure the development of, and compliance with, appropriate performance standards.

In matters of corporate governance, the interdependent parties in these market and bureaucratic relationships can include corporations, government agencies, investment institutions, local communities, employees, suppliers, customers and other stakeholders. The transaction costs that are incurred by each of these parties for assuring that corporations meet some prescribed level of corporate governance standards, arise from the costs of developing the performance standards, implementing systems for monitoring performance, enforcing performance standards when a party does not fulfil its obligations, and participating in joint activities that lead to refinements and improvements in the governance standards that meet the needs of all stakeholders.

Recent dramatic examples of corporate governance systems failure strongly suggest that solutions for improved governance will not arise from more intensive forms of market and bureaucratic-based transactions. What may be more promising is a framework for corporate governance that places existing market and bureaucratic forms of transactions under a 'clan' form of organising (Ouchi 1980). The clan form of organising for corporate governance is a more promising approach for improving governance than alternatives that rely on increasing market transaction costs (e.g. adopting and implementing 'ISO-style' governance quality programmes) or bureaucratic costs (e.g. having to develop and comply with a greater number of potentially overly prescriptive regulations or increasing staffing levels of government enforcement agencies). This clan form of governance can be achieved by socialising and professionalising the managers who practice forms of corporate governance by establishing stakeholder partnerships to manage the process, and by exploiting the forms of institutional isomorphism that arise from the interactions of disparate stakeholders bonded by similar goals for corporate governance. Importantly, the clan form of transaction mediation becomes an inter-organisational relationship based on the normative requirements of reciprocity, legitimate authority, and common values and beliefs, offering a greater level of discipline in performance not achievable through the more explicit market and regulatory approaches. The clan form of transaction mediation also represents a governance mode that can reduce the costs of current market and bureaucratic controls, and improve their effectiveness.

Broadly stated, 'clans' are groups of people in occupational communities who consider themselves to be engaged in the same sort of work, whose identities are drawn from that work, and who share a common set of values, norms and perspectives (Van

Maanen and Barley 1984). A professional community that prescribes certain educational requirements for membership, and codifies these values, norms and perspectives as further requirements for members, reinforces a professional identity in the minds of both its members and outsiders, and legitimises any role of self-regulating that the community decides to pursue. In many cases, the shared values, norms and perspectives of a professional community become a 'code of honour' which must not be violated if a member hopes to remain in the community. At West Point, for example, cadets are expected to commit to 'a lifetime of honourable living' because their profession requires that trust becomes sacred and integrity becomes a requisite quality for each professional (US Military Academy 1998). West Point's code of honour becomes a *de facto* performance standard for ensuring that certain types of undesirable behaviour do not occur for the good of the organisation and the profession. In the case of West Point cadets, violation of the honour code can carry the ultimate punishment of expulsion from the professional clan of military officers. This code provides the military with a means of enforcing appropriate professional conduct that is far more cost-effective than any forms of market- or bureaucracy-based monitoring.

8.2 Socialising and professionalising managers

The path toward achieving a clan approach to organising starts with the steps of socialising and professionalising managers. Following Barnard (1968) and Mayo (1945), Ouchi (1980) notes that organisations are difficult to operate because their members do not share a selfless devotion to the same objectives. This aspect of modern organisations is a departure from Mayo's (1945) pre-industrial organisations in which apprentices were socialised into the objectives of both the craft and the organisation. As pre-industrial organisations transformed their mode of organising toward a bureaucracy-based model, traditional worker know-how, skills and selfless devotion were displaced by machines, procedures and an emphasis on technical progress over craft progress (Mayo 1945). The occupation of professional manager emerged to maintain bureaucratic structure and oversee technical progressions in service of the bureaucracy. The technical progress that occurs in bureaucratic forms of organisations causes periodic de-skilling of workers that requires continual innovation, adaptation and organisational learning. Thus, the 'craft' of bureaucratic organising incurs transaction costs associated with innovation, adaptation and worker learning to maintain competitiveness. At the beginning of the 21st century, our bureaucratic organisational forms are confronted with a 'free agent nation' (Pink 2001) in which uncertain organisational boundaries and employee loyalty provide few guarantees that organisations will realise returns on these costs. At the same time, business managers represent a group of professionals who have been trained in the craft of management with formal business school educations and corporate 'apprenticeships' that serve as a rite of passage to positions of greater responsibility, influence and compensation. The 'trade' of professional manager has emerged to mirror many of the aspects of the pre-industrial trades, without a clear unifying framework for socialisation of the profession and only a narrowly defined commitment to the organisation in terms of fiduciary duty.

Can the problems posed by high market and bureaucracy-based transaction costs, poor corporate governance track records and uncommitted workforces be fixed by 'socialising' business managers? Many business executives follow an educational and professional development path through business schools and management positions that mirrors the socialisation and professionalisation processes of lawyers and medical doctors. Despite similarities in professional socialisation and progression, the discipline of organisation management lacks a basic concept of professionalisation that underscores professions in law and medicine: the notion of self-regulation. The transfer of policy-making authority from government to an occupation through self-regulation is considered to be necessary in such professions because the special expertise and training that professionals possess makes others unable to evaluate performance or determine the best policies for such occupations (Hughes 1965). Thus, professionals in the legal and medical occupations assume a form of bureaucratic transaction costs posed by self-regulation, because these costs are far less than transaction costs that would be required for a form of external regulation offering at least the same level of effectiveness. This form of self-regulation does not mean that lawyers and doctors are any less devoted to their employers or that they will not all engage in forms of malpractice. The power of self-regulation allows professions to create and enforce policies that require their members to meet certain educational and professional licensing requirements to be met in order to become members. Because membership is required to engage in the profession, the threat of disbarment looms large as a hindrance against misconduct as any legal punishment imposed by an outside agency.

In contrast, business chief executives gain membership into their profession through education in business schools, experience in managerial positions of increasing responsibility and selection by their executive predecessors as heirs apparent to the position of CEO. Following Hughes (1965), the absence of any form of self-regulating organisation for business executives suggests that evaluation of the special expertise and training that business professionals possess is easier for others to evaluate their competence for making policy decisions than the professions of lawyer and medical doctor. This theoretical suggestion has clearly not proved to be true in practice. And while lawyers and doctors must meet an ethical code that is required as part of their practice in their professions, business executives may or may not have had a single course in business ethics, and their rite of passage into the profession of business executive is solely incumbent on approval by a company's board of directors: another profession for which there are few generally agreed-upon standards of qualification and performance. Thus, corporations suffer from high market- and bureaucracy-based transaction costs; they have poor corporate governance track records, in part due to the 'liabilities of newness' associated with corporate governance standards and lack of executive training in governance issues; they are led by executives who are under-socialised and under-professionalised relative to practitioners of law and medicine; and, as a result, they lack the ability to self-regulate their profession to help ensure consistency of corporate governance performance. If the occupation of business executive were to become more professionalised and socialised in ways similar to other professional occupations, we might expect that CEOs would develop a shared set of performance standards for ethical and social behaviour and that they would enforce these standards within their professional clan. The shared understanding of acceptable and unacceptable behaviours and the threat of expulsion from the clan for misbehaviour would be expected to reduce the market and transaction costs associated with monitoring CEO behaviour and corporate governance, because the clan of CEOs would provide a lower-cost, equally effective enforcement mechanism. Given these conditions, we should expect two key relations to emerge between corporate governance and the level of professionalisation of the occupation of business executive:

1. The quality of corporate governance guidelines developed under current conditions will be directly related to the extent to which the occupation of business executive is professionalised

2. Market and bureaucracy-based transaction costs associated with corporate governance activities will be inversely related to the extent to which the occupation of business executive is professionalised

As an example, consider the current state of professional sports in the US. The sport of Major League Baseball (MLB) is under fire by fans, the media and the US Congress, because of perceived weak drug testing policies for its players. Until recently, the mandatory penalty for an initial positive test for steroids is counselling and treatment, and no loss of pay. By comparison, the National Football League (NFL) imposes a quarter-season suspension for a first positive test for steroids or any other drug on its list of banned substances. While both sports have seen unionisation and professionalisation of their players, the players of the NFL agreed to and helped to craft the drug testing policies they must follow, because they believed that such a policy would be good for the well-being of the profession and the League. By comparison, players in the MLB have been reluctant to even consider drug testing programmes, citing long-held organisational beliefs in individual rights, protection against unwarranted searches and innocence until guilt is proven. In the US, where sports are seen as a repository of national values and an ultimate form of meritocracy, the proactive clan-like actions of professionals in the NFL have helped to reinforce the positive image of the players and the profession, while sub-optimal behaviours on the part of MLB players illustrate a comparatively inferior form of governance for that profession. As a result, the shared understanding of acceptable and unacceptable behaviours, and the threat of expulsion for misbehaviour should help the NFL to enjoy lower market and transaction costs associated with monitoring player behaviour than those of the MLB.

8.3 Stakeholder management

Obviously, the path toward better governance starts with the executive office, but this step by itself will not lead to a universal governance system applicable to all corporations. The current systems in place for ensuring corporate governance bear significant market- and bureaucracy-based transactions costs, few corporations possess executive management talent that have fully embraced and implemented the principles of corporate governance, and the profession of business executive has no means for policing the behaviour of its own members. The recent failures in governance by corporations such as Enron and WorldCom illustrate how the roles of regulators, institutional investors, shareholders and employees have been just as ineffective in the pursuit of sound corporate governance policies. Given the breakdown in corporate responses to individual interests insisting on various forms of corporate governance, a solution is required that allows corporations and all of their stakeholders to effectively define, implement and monitor corporate governance: stakeholder management. Stakeholder management demands simultaneous attention to the legitimate interests of all appropriate stakeholders, both in the establishment of organisational structures and general policies and in case-by-case decision-making, without necessarily making managers the locus of corporate control, determining the legitimacy of various 'stakes' in the corporation or implying that all stakeholders will be treated equally (Donaldson and Preston 1995). This form of governance loosely reflects the structure of a federation of organisations described by Pfeffer and Salancik (1978), and Provan (1983) without prescribing managerial approaches to structure, function or co-ordination. The modes of structure, organisation and governance emerge from the strategic goals of the firm through participation by all the relevant stakeholders in the firm.

The concept of stakeholder theory has evolved from one of stakeholder management (Freeman 1984) to a formalised framework grounded in organisational behaviour for analysing and evaluating corporate social performance (Clarkson 1995), becoming a standard element of 'Introduction to Management' lectures and writings (Donaldson and Preston 1995). The stakeholder framework is theoretically important due to its ability to relate stakeholder management practices to the achievement of various corporate performance goals (Donaldson and Preston 1995). The definition of stakeholders was originally conceived as 'any group or individual who can affect or is affected by the achievement of the organisation's objectives' (Freeman 1984: 46). Drawing from this definition, a description of classes of stakeholders has been proposed that identifies them through their possession of any of the following attributes: the stakeholder's power to influence the firm; the legitimacy of the stakeholder's relationship with the firm; and the urgency of the stakeholder's claim on the firm (Mitchell *et al.* 1997).

Stakeholder partnerships of regulators, corporations and civil society represent the single best approach toward such a universally effective governance system. Drawing from institutional theory (e.g. Meyer and Rowan 1977), the resource-based view (e.g. Barney 1991) and social network theory (e.g. Burt 1982), the remainder of this chapter argues that the stakeholder partnership framework provides the most effective path for achieving diverse, even conflicting, governance performance goals through transparent, inter-organisational relationships that optimise organisational learning and corporate citizenship behaviour. With this form of theoretical grounding, stakeholder partnerships offer a model of 'competitiveness by co-operation, commensalism, and consensus' (Elkington 2001) with benefits that cannot be achieved through other governance mechanisms.

Stakeholder partnerships allow consensus building around the meaning of effective governance by establishing institutional linkages that lead to institutional isomorphism (DiMaggio and Powell 1983). The stakeholder partnership becomes an institutional 'melting pot' for partners that leads to the crafting of common interests and a common identity in the pursuit of the simple collective goal of corporate governance. Stakeholder partners derive technical, commercial and social capital that can affect their inducements and opportunities to form linkages with other organisations (Ahuja 2000), creating a mechanism that pulls, rather than pushes, the membership base. These inter-organisational linkages allow stakeholder partnerships to yield resources of social capital and increased legitimacy that improve corporate governance performance, financial performance, and public perception and trust.

8.3.1 The stakeholder partnership as institutional melting pot

DiMaggio and Powell (1983) coined the term 'institutional isomorphism' to describe the paradox of how rational managers make their organisations increasingly similar to each other as they try to change them. Thus, processes of bureaucratisation and other forms of organisational change occur as the result of processes that make organisations look more similar without necessarily making them more efficient (DiMaggio and Powell 1983). Thus, corporations will tend to adopt similar forms of bureaucratisation that make them strikingly similar in structure at the same time that they strive to differentiate themselves from each other in competitive terms. Government agencies with completely different functional focuses adopt seemingly identical forms of organisational charts. As non-governmental agencies (NGOs) have matured into organisations that have financial resources on a par with their political clout, they too have come to resemble each other in terms of organisational structure. Following the evolutionary path of for-profit firms, NGOs such as environmental interest groups have increasingly come to view their membership constituencies less as a political base and more of an economic base in which prospective members are seen as customers for their products (Shaiko 1999). The increasing focus on membership constituencies as an economic base by NGOs means that special-interest groups must increasingly look outside their 'movements' for professionally trained managers, and that they must increasingly compete in their market for customers like the organisations against whom they have been created to lobby. This shift from political efficacy to organisational maintenance represents an ironic case of institutional isomorphism (DiMaggio and Powell 1983), as grassroots movements must adopt the organisational forms of their for-profit counterparts in order to maintain legitimacy and ensure their survival as organisations.

With similarities in the training of professional managers they employ, the organisational structures they adopt and the emphasis on financial influence between for-profits and NGOs, it should come as no surprise that these different groups should increasingly be competing for the same customer bases. The increasing overlap in 'customer bases' among corporations, NGOs and government agencies, and the increasing similarity in resource needs in terms of financing and management talent, suggest that these different groups may be far more similar in terms of organisational structure and function than their mission statements imply. By combining these groups into a stakeholder partnership focused on corporate governance, they may be able to share resources and know-how in ways that allow each of them to improve their own forms of governance. These exchanges of resources, know-how and ideologies will cause these organisations to evolve toward a new level of isomorphism, which will improve opportunities for further exchanges. Because organisations with institutional linkages exhibit a significant survival advantage that increases with the intensity of competition (Baum and Oliver 1991), members of a corporate governance stakeholder partnership should experience improvements in their survival advantage that extend to economic, environmental and social dimensions. These same institutional linkages are likely to cause participating firms to exhibit corporate citizenship behaviour and cause all actively participating organisations to develop organisational capabilities for acquiring and transferring forms of knowledge that are created through this unique form of partnership. Thus, the corporate governance stakeholder partnership becomes a valuable resource for its members both in terms of enforcing citizenship behaviour by all stakeholders and in terms of providing financial and other resources to ensure competitive performance.

8.3.2 The stakeholder partnership as a competitive resource

The resource-based view (RBV) of the firm (Barney 1991; Conner 1991; Wernerfelt 1984) provides a framework for explaining the conditions under which a firm may gain a sustained competitive advantage. In this view, a firm's unique tangible and intangible assets, such as management skills, organisational processes and routines, and the information and knowledge under its control, can be 'bundled' and deployed in ways that can lead to sustained superior performance (Barney *et al.* 2001). The expectation that organisations will differ (in and out of equilibrium) in the resources and capabilities they control suggests that they will co-operate with each other to reduce uncertainty, complexity and intra-firm conflict by leveraging each other's unique bundles of resources (Amit and Schoemaker 1993). Importantly, this means that managers will co-operate with each other across organisations *not* to get access to more of the resources they already have, but rather to gain access to complementary resources they do not have. Research in the acquisitions and alliances literature (e.g. Harrison *et al.* 2001) has confirmed that resource complementarity, rather than similarity, produces the potential for greater synergies from organisational co-operation, leading to improved long-term performance as a result. Within the domain of the stakeholder partnership, organisations would be expected to enter into co-operative relationships to conserve resources and gain new competencies (e.g. Hamel *et al.* 1989; Ohmae 1989), promote social learning of adaptive responses (Kraatz 1998) and provide member organisations with legitimacy, which serves as a resource for gaining other resources, such as commercial and technical capital (Zimmerman and Zeitz 2002).

The common goal and common identity of the corporate governance stakeholder partnership serves as more than a resource to its members. The extent to which stakeholder members share common interests and a common identity determines the level of trust within the alliance, to include trust between the major stakeholder groups and individual organisations, such as between participating corporations. A key challenge in assuring the success of the stakeholder partnership is to overcome different ideologies, interests and identities by building common interests, a common identity and trust to enable learning and know-how transfer. Corporations manage relationships with stakeholder groups rather than with society as a whole, and it is important to distinguish between social issues and stakeholder issues (Clarkson 1995), suggesting that successful stakeholder initiatives rely on the commitment and participation of their member groups. Repeat interactions among corporations and stakeholder groups lead to trust, which obliges partners to behave loyally and influences the choice of governance structure for future alliances with each other (Gulati 1995). Interactions at the individual level between alliance partners create a basis for learning and know-how transfer across the exchange interface, while curbing opportunistic behaviour of alliance partners (Kale *et al.* 2000). The creation and reinforcement of such network relationships leads its members to organise and share an unrestrained structure of interdependent activities, enabling them to achieve greater value than would be the case if they did not participate (Holm and Eriksson 1999). The ability of the stakeholder partnership to establish trust therefore rests on the partnership's ability to establish and align the various interests and identities of its strategic group members with a common identity and the alliance's common interests.

The preceding discussion of the stakeholder partnership as an institutional melting pot and nexus of shared resources is based on the argument that, because organisations within similar industries evolve over time to share similar organisational structures and because corporations, government agencies and special-interest groups are increasingly in pursuit of similar resources, they will benefit from co-operative sharing and exchanges of resources through participation in a corporate governance stakeholder group. Thus, we should expect to see three important relationships drive the effectiveness of corporate governance through the stakeholder partnership model:

1. The effectiveness of the corporate governance stakeholder partnership will be directly related to the extent to which its member organisations have established similar organisational structures.

2. The effectiveness of the corporate governance stakeholder partnership will be directly related to the value of the partnership assigned by its members.

3. The success of a stakeholder partnership focused on corporate governance will be positively related to the extent to which its member organisations establish common interests, a common identity for, and trust within the alliance.

The US National Football League provides an illustration of all three of these relationships. Obviously, teams in the League share similar organisational structures, but the NFL's concerted efforts to link each team to its community through outreach programmes gives each team a community identity and creates a value for the League that surpasses the revenues earned from presenting football games. The NFL's community outreach programmes, coupled with the players' willingness to self-govern professional behaviour, help to establish a level of trust among the stakeholder groups of fans, advertisers and communities based on common interests and identity, positioning the League and the profession of football as a repository of national values.

8.4 Opportunism and corporate citizenship

Following the arguments of this chapter, professionalising the occupation of chief executive and pursuing a form of governance based on the stakeholder partnership model would improve corporate governance. Professionalising top-management team roles can provide a common understanding of acceptable social and ethical behaviours that can be policed by the profession's members. Importantly, creating a vehicle for self-regulation of CEOs of public firms provides executives with a tangible arena for owning and addressing the unique challenges of their profession. At the organisational level, public firms, NGOs, regulators and other stakeholders can improve corporate governance through a stakeholder partnership model that creates a melting pot for a shared vision of corporate governance. The stakeholder partnership also provides a venue for sharing complementary resources, improving communications and creating opportunities for organisational learning as rewards for participation.

If governance can be based on the theory of the firm as a series of contracts (Jensen and Meckling 1976), this notion can be extended to a super-organisational level to approach governance as a stakeholder partnership based on a series of social contracts. It is argued, however, that because stakeholder theory prescribes that managers should make decisions so as to take account of the interests of all stakeholders in a firm without specifying how to make the necessary trade-offs among these competing interests, managers are left with a theory that makes it impossible for them to make purposeful decisions (Jensen 2001). In particular, Jensen (2001: 21) argues that:

> stakeholder theory plays into the hands of special interests that wish to use the resources of corporations for their own ends . . . those who wish to use non-market forces to reallocate wealth now see great opportunity in the playing field that stakeholder theory opens to them.

This implies that a new form of agency problems is posed by integrating stakeholders into the social contract of corporate governance, where stakeholder partners may behave opportunistically as duly appointed agents of firm principals.

Despite this threat of opportunism, there is no evidence that boards of directors are replacing professional executives with special-interest groups to run corporations. There is substantially more evidence that corporations are adopting nascent forms of corporate citizenship as they evolve their operating practices to be more in sync with the needs of their primary stakeholders, a group that also happens to be one of the corporation's most valuable resources. The forms of *organising* that arise from stakeholder partnerships represent emergent forms of corporate governance, a process that may 'play into the hands' of those who seek a lasting solution to our recent crisis in accountability and governance.

References

Ahuja, G. (2000) 'The Duality of Collaboration: Inducements and Opportunities in the Formation of Interfirm Linkages', *Strategic Management Journal* 21: 317-43.

Amit, R., and P.J.H. Schoemaker (1993) 'Strategic Assets and Organizational Rent', *Strategic Management Journal* 14: 33-46.

Barnard, C.I. (1968) *The Functions of the Executive* (Cambridge, MA: Harvard, 30th anniversary edn).

Barney, J.B. (1991) 'Firm Resources and Sustained Competitive Advantage', *Journal of Management* 17: 991-1020.

——, M. Wright and D. Ketchen Jr. (2001) 'The Resource-Based View of the Firm: Ten Tears after 1991', *Journal of Management* 27: 625-41.

Baum, J.A.C., and C. Oliver (1991) 'Institutional Linkages and Organizational Mortality', *Administrative Science Quarterly* 36: 187-218.

Burt, R.S. (1982) *Towards a Structural Theory of Action: Network Models of Social Structure, Perception, and Action* (New York: Academy Press).

Business Week (2003) 'Straight Talk from Eliot Spitzer', 6 October 2003: 129-30, 132.

Clarkson, M.B.E. (1995) 'A Stakeholder Framework for Analyzing and Evaluating Corporate Social Performance', *Academy of Management Review* 20: 92-117.

Conner, K.R. (1991) 'A Historical Comparison of Resource-Based Theory and Five Schools of Thought within Industrial Organization Economics: Do We Have a New Theory of the Firm?', *Journal of Management* 17: 121-54.

DiMaggio, P., and W.W. Powell (1983) 'The Iron Cage Revisited: Institutional Isomorphism and Collective Rationality in Organizational Fields', *American Sociological Review* 48: 147-60.

Donaldson, T., and L.E. Preston (1995) 'The Stakeholder Theory of the Corporation: Concepts, Evidence, and Implications', *Academy of Management Review* 20: 65-91.

Eisenhardt, K.M. (1989) 'Agency Theory: An Assessment and Review', *Academy of Management Review* 14: 57-74.

Elkington, J. (2001) *The Chrysalis Economy: How Citizen CEOs and Corporations Can Fuse Values and Value Creation* (Oxford, UK: Capstone Publishing).

Freeman, R.E. (1984) *Strategic Management: A Stakeholder Approach* (Boston, MA: Pitman).

Gulati, R. (1995) 'Does Familiarity Breed Trust? The Implications of Repeated Ties for Contractual Choice in Alliances', *Academy of Management Journal* 38: 85-112.

Hamel, G., Y. Doz and C. Prahalad (1989) 'Collaborate with your Competitors and Win', *Harvard Business Review* 67.1: 133-38.

Harrison, J.S., M.A. Hitt, R.E. Hoskisson and R.D. Ireland (2001) 'Resource Complementarity in Business Combinations: Extending the Logic to Organizational Alliances', *Journal of Management* 27: 679-90.

Holm, D.B., and K. Eriksson (1999) 'Creating Value through Mutual Commitment to Business Network Relationships', *Strategic Management Journal* 20: 467-85.

Hughes, E.C. (1965) 'Professions', in K.S. Lynn (ed.), *The Professions in America* (Boston, MA: Houghton Mifflin).

Jensen, M.C., and W. Meckling (1976) 'Theory of the Firm: Managerial Behavior, Agency Costs, and Ownership Structure', *Journal of Financial Economics* 3: 305-60.

—— (2000) *A Theory of the Firm: Governance, Residual Claims, and Organizational Forms* (Cambridge, MA: Harvard University Press).

—— (2001) 'Value Maximization, Stakeholder Theory, and the Corporate Objective Function', *Journal of Applied Corporate Finance* 14.3: 8-21.

Kale, P., H. Singh and H. Perlmutter (2000) 'Learning and Protection of Proprietary Assets in Strategic Alliances: Building Relational Capital', *Strategic Management Journal* 21: 217-37.

Kraatz, M.S. (1998) 'Learning by Association? Interorganizational Networks and Adaptation to Environmental Change', *Academy of Management Journal* 41: 621-43.

Mayo, E. (1945) *The Social Problems of an Industrial Civilization* (Boston, MA: Division of Research, Graduate School of Business Administration, Harvard University).

Meyer, J., and B. Rowan (1977) 'Institutional Organizations: Formal Structure as Myth and Ceremony', *American Journal of Sociology* 83: 340-63.

Mitchell, R.K., B.R. Agle and D.J. Wood (1997) 'Toward a Theory of Stakeholder Identification and Salience: Defining the Principle of Who and What Really Counts', *Academy of Management Review* 22: 853-86.

Ohmae, K. (1989) 'The Global Logic of Strategic Alliances', *Harvard Business Review* 67.2: 143-54.

Ouchi, W.G. (1980) 'Markets, Bureaucracies, and Clans', *Administrative Science Quarterly* 25: 129-41.

Pfeffer, J., and G.R. Salancik (1978) *The External Control of Organizations: A Resource Dependence Perspective* (New York: Harper & Row).

Pink, D.H. (2001) *Free Agent Nation* (New York: Warner Books).

Provan, K.G. (1983) 'The Federation as an Interorganizational Linkage Network', *Academy of Management Review* 8: 79-89.

Shaiko, R.G. (1999) *Voices and Echoes for the Environment* (New York: Columbia University Press).

US Military Academy (1998) 'Information Paper on "Honor": A Bedrock of Military Leadership' (West Point, NY: USMA).

Van Maanen, J., and S.R. Barley (1984) 'Occupational Communities: Culture and Control in Organizations', in B.M. Staw and L.L. Cummings (eds.), *Research in Organizational Behavior* 6: 287-366 (Greenwich, CT: JAI Press).

Wernerfelt, B. (1984) 'A Resource-Based View of the Firm', *Strategic Management Journal* 5: 171-80.

Williamson, O.E. (1975) *Markets and Hierarchies: Analysis and Antitrust Implications* (New York: Free Press).

Zimmerman, M.A., and G.A. Zeitz (2002) 'Beyond Survival: Achieving New Venture Growth by Building Legitimacy', *Academy of Management Review* 27: 414-31.

9
Adding the stakeholder value
GOVERNANCE CONVERGENCE IN THE PRIVATE, PUBLIC AND NOT-FOR-PROFIT SECTORS

Alison L. Dempsey

Canada

> There is nothing more difficult to carry out, more doubtful of success, nor more dangerous to handle, than to initiate a new order of things. For, those who would institute change have enemies in all those who profit by the old order and only lukewarm defenders in all those who would profit by the new order (Machiavelli 1532).

The absence of 'a level playing field' is cited as one of the obstacles deterring many companies from adhering to higher standards of corporate responsibility than competitors who meet only the minimum standards prescribed by law. Companies observing significantly higher ethical, social and environmental standards without the support and emulation of peers, or reinforcement from enabling policy initiatives, continue to face considerable challenges in terms of realising the return, or gaining the competitive advantage needed to rationalise this approach on purely economic terms.

Similarly, less onerous accountability requirements for civil-society organisations,[1] and the gap between the government's approach to public accountability and its increasing expectations of business, create an uneven platform on which to construct the framework for balanced and constructive engagement between sectors. Raising the bar for business, or setting it substantially lower for those state and non-state entities to whom business is now widely considered to be accountable (in addition to its shareholders), may create a disparity so significant that it undermines the chances for meaningful engagement across sector boundaries.

Ethical processes and standards are core to the establishment of the trust necessary for effective engagement. Where organisations interact without a shared understanding of transparency and accountability, they are unlikely to develop the necessary trust

---

1   See CEC 2002. The term 'civil-society organisations' is used to encompass the range of organisations that includes: labour-market players; organisations representing social and economic players, which are not social partners in the strict sense of the term; non-governmental organisations (NGOs) dedicated to environmental, human rights, charitable and educational causes, etc.; community-based organisations; and religious communities.

to move beyond the pursuit of their own agenda and to co-operate fully in seeking mutually beneficial outcomes.

9.1 Accountability standards

9.1.1 Private sector

The last decade and a half has seen a growing demand from regulators and civil society for corporate executives to demonstrate that responsible governance, increased transparency and greater accountability, are embedded in the policies and practices within their organisations. Moreover, the scope of this responsibility has extended to the need for corporations to ensure the integrity of organisations comprising their supply chain. The recent corporate transgressions in North America, Europe and elsewhere over that period brought about widespread recognition of the economic and legal imperative for establishing consistent standards of acceptable business conduct, along with the means to demonstrate and enforce the observance of legal, financial and reporting requirements.

This period also saw the emergence of an additional ethical dimension to the traditional view of what constitutes acceptable business conduct. This new dimension extends the constituency to who business has traditionally been primarily responsible and accountable—shareholders, regulators, in some cases, employees and suppliers—to include a broader base of external stakeholders encompassing customers, local communities and others on whom the business has an impact in the wider societal context. For the most enlightened of companies, this group extends even further to include *future generations* of stakeholders as envisaged in the Brundtland Commission's definition of sustainability as being responsible for 'meeting the needs of the present without compromising the ability of future generations to meet their own needs' (WCED 1987).

The developing relationships between business and those who make up this constituency are complex and dynamic. In the past, companies used mainly one-way processes of reporting and disclosure at predetermined intervals to demonstrate accountability. This traditional linear approach has been increasingly viewed as insufficient to properly understand and address the diverse and changing relationships with these varied constituents. One approach that provides a framework for greater interaction and ongoing engagement with the diverse constituents is the 'stakeholder engagement' model.

The AccountAbility AA1000 Series, which establishes standards focused on the social dimensions of organisational accountability, envisages in stakeholder engagement 'the reflection at all stages of the process over time of the views and needs of all stakeholder groups . . . the consideration of voiceless stakeholders including future generations and the environment' (Institute for Social and Ethical Accountability 1999). Forward-looking companies are seeing that this model is a basis for an ongoing dialogue that offers the opportunity for increasing awareness and understanding of relevant issues and the evolving context within which they operate. This knowledge can inform and strengthen decision-making processes by enabling a wider consideration of the implications and consequences of decisions on those who will be affected by them. There are also strategic and operational benefits that flow from having a sound consultative framework, which increases the capacity to identify opportunities and innovative means to achieve objectives in ways that are ethical, sustainable and satisfy the 'bottom line'.

9.1.2 Non-profit sector

The not-for-profit sector (comprised of non-governmental and community-based civil-society organisations, but excluding religious congregations) has been estimated at US$1.1 trillion with full-time employees in the region of 19 million. The contribution made by this burgeoning sector, in terms of providing social services and addressing the cultural, educational and development needs of the communities they serve, is not at issue. However, in the wake of government cutbacks, the proliferation of single-focus organisations and the emergence of the anti-corporate, anti-globalisation movement, the sector has become increasingly vocal and influential on issues beyond their traditional milieu, ranging from matters of public policy to corporate conduct. This increased participation has not been accompanied *in the main* by adherence to more rigorous standards of accountability that would increase transparency as to representation and purpose.

The sector's growth in size, scope of influence and increased participation in the policy and operational decisions of public- and private-sector organisations needs to be accompanied by the means to demonstrate an appropriately heightened sense of responsibility that befits this new role. The strength of this sector's claim to a legitimate role in the decision-making processes of public- and private-sector organisations is weakened by the lack of a collective adoption and adherence to good governance practices and a level of accountability and transparency, commensurate (at least in spirit) with recognised best-practice standards for those organisations with whom they are engaging. Many of these organisations receive voluntary donations and enjoy favourable tax status intended to enable their pursuit of worthy causes with impartiality and independence; they must not, therefore, risk abusing this privilege by failing to reciprocate with appropriate levels of accountability to these external corporate, public and private stakeholders.

This shift to uniformly heightened accountability and governance standards in the not-for-profit sector would help to achieve more alignment, and thereby greater credibility *vis-à-vis* the public sector, which has the challenge of assessing the legitimacy of the interests, mandate and representation of these civil-society and non-governmental organisations. It would do the same for relations with the private sector who, as corporations are not only accountable to their traditional shareholder constituency but as corporate citizens are increasingly responsible to an additional constituency comprised of internal and external stakeholders and the wider communities in which they co-exist.

9.1.3 Public sector

Disaffection and lack of trust in the institutions and processes of government continues to grow in many Western democracies. It can be attributed, in large measure according to survey data, to the public perception of a lack of transparent accountability on the part of government and the message being heard at grass roots. In her December 2002 report, the Canadian Auditor General Sheila Fraser defined accountability in the public sector context as:

> a relationship based on obligations to demonstrate, review and take responsibility for performance, both the results achieved in light of agreed expectations and the means used. [It is absent when there is] no reporting or inadequate reporting on performance . . . and no serious informed review of the information reported (Auditor General, Government of Canada 2002).

The authenticity of a system based on accountability depends on the existence of established standards that set out explicit, realistic expectations, support access to complete and reliable information and establish a credible review process. The above definition of accountability with its focus on outcomes would be a strong foundation on which to base the methods and standards for assessing, benchmarking and continuously improving performance within all three sectors and new forms of cross-sector partnerships.

For the system to be truly progressive, however, it needs to go beyond this framework to active and ongoing engagement with those to whom the obligation to account is owed. Without these relationships, it is limited to a linear reporting process that successfully chronicles the delivery and discharge of obligations, but which falls short when it comes to finding new ways to address the interests of multiple stakeholders.

9.1.4 Cross-sector

As corporate governance and accountability frameworks increasingly encompass stakeholders and reflect a growing consciousness of the larger societal context—where individuals, communities and organisations co-exist—there should be less divergence between what is understood as accountability for the private, 'not-for-profit' and the public sectors.

The needs of this emerging stakeholder-based system would benefit from a dynamic and holistic definition of accountability that encompasses responsibility to (and of) stakeholders by organisations in all three sectors with respect to the process by which policy objectives are established, the means used to achieve them and the eventual outcomes. It then becomes possible to contemplate an optimal model of accountability that places this shared responsibility at the core of constructive and meaningful engagement across sectors and with the communities they serve. Ideally in this form of engagement, the sector and socioeconomic boundaries created over the last century blur as the individuals participating in the engagement process develop a shared commitment to achieving the best practicable result for all those who have a legitimate interest, now and in the future.

This process starts with the individuals representing those organisations recognising themselves in the stakeholder community—as members of the public, consumers of goods or services, funders or beneficiaries, investors, suppliers, volunteers or voters.

This enhances their ability to see the intersection of responsibility for making informed, ethical decisions in relation to all interactions: from standards of conduct; discharge of workplace responsibilities; participation within shared decision-making processes; use of finances; to political choices and decisions about the particular issue or non-profit organisation to support. As Ann Svendsen observes in *The Stakeholder Strategy*:

> To identify and establish productive relationships, an organization and its employees must understand how they fit into the larger systems of which they are part . . . the dynamic nature of those relationships and the importance of creating a shared understanding of each others' assumptions and beliefs (1998: 79).

9.2 Demonstrating accountability and stakeholder engagement

The world has witnessed transgressions in business, government and non-profit organisations in the past few years that have served as powerful examples of what happens when the principles of accountability, ethical conduct and individual integrity are absent. The most high profile instances have been in the corporate world, but public-sector and civil-society organisations have not been immune from lapses in conduct and judgement. These transgressions have to some extent acted as catalysts for accelerated change in governance standards and the means by which these are communicated to internal and external stakeholders.

Such changes are reflected in the increasingly stringent external measures for regulating corporations such as those introduced in the United States,[2] and in growing numbers, the strengthening of best-practice standards by which industries and organisations seek to govern themselves.

Governments have made explicit commitments to greater transparency *vis-à-vis* the public through independent audits and external reporting along the lines of that required of the private sector, public consultations and increased access to information. In specific instances of actual or perceived misconduct or unethical behaviour within public-sector institutions, formal investigations and quasi-judicial enquiries have been convened with the proceedings and eventual findings accessible to the public.[3]

Non-profit organisations have started to introduce processes intended to demonstrate ethical conduct and accountability. One area of focus is the, often controversial, area of fundraising, where specific fundraising codes have been developed as a means

2 *The Sarbanes–Oxley Act, 2002, Law HR 3763*, 107th Congress, 2nd Session (Washington, DC: Library of Congress, www.sarbanes-oxley.com).
3 For example, Hutton 2004; and Auditor General, Government of Canada 2003.

of responding to adverse perceptions of how funds are raised and subsequently managed. Organisations, especially those operating in locations far from their donors' view, are increasingly conscious of the need to demonstrate their worthiness to receive and oversee the responsible expenditure of the billions of dollars in donors' funds and government grants that flow to charities and non-governmental organisations to support their growing role in economic and social aid and development.[4]

These various approaches go some way to address accountability lapses and reduce the risks of recurrence. However, the process of building and increasing trust in and between organisations and the communities they serve requires more than rules, linear reporting, and processes developed to deal only with the consequences of unacceptable conduct. The importance of ethics, accountability and responsibility needs to be explicit and embedded throughout the whole process, not just in relation to outcomes.

These principles apply to the interactions between individuals and continue when those same individuals engage as part, or on behalf, of a group within a corporate, institutional or public context. Corporations, civil-society organisations, governments, regulatory bodies and other associations, after all, are the vehicles for formal and informal interactions among individuals.

Those interactions between individuals are the means by which the organisational construct is realised and its culture established. Building a strong ethical foundation within organisations therefore must be an ongoing priority, for there can be little enduring value in investing in communicating the values and responsible practices of an organisation externally, if the internal stakeholders fail to understand the need and perceive the benefits of such practices. An organisation cannot legitimately claim to be ethical or responsible if those within it do not (independently and collectively) 'buy into' the ethical principles and values, or lack the systems and support to put them into effect in their work and interactions with others.

Authenticity and trust are also core requirements of effective engagement. Svendsen states that:

> [F]or relationships to thrive, all partners must have a sense that the other parties have their best interests at heart and that they will act honourably and fairly. Studies show that ethical behaviour is a precursor of trust, and trust is essential for building strong relationships with customers, suppliers, employees, and the public (1998: 80).

In this regard, an increasing number of organisations are explicitly stating their core values in efforts to maintain or restore trust in the integrity of their operations. Many of these statements refer explicitly to individual and collective responsibility and make an express commitment to accountability and transparency that extends well beyond their shareholders and internal stakeholders.[5]

These overarching statements of ethical principles and values create an explicit, shared frame of reference. They help to achieve consistency and common standards of

4 For example, the *Ethical Fundraising and Financial Accountability Code* by the Canadian Centre for Philanthropy (2003) was a response to a perceived need for a credible mechanism demonstrating fundraising accountability to stakeholders.
5 For example: BP, www.bp.com; General Motors, www.gm.com; Scottish Power, www.scottishpower.com; Suncor, www.suncor.com; TransCanada Pipeline, www.transcanada.com.

accountability that constitute a safeguard against dishonest, unethical behaviour within organisations. If these same core principles and values are shared by partners in the community, they form a sound basis for engaging in constructive and respectful dialogue amongst the diverse stakeholders and the varied interests in society. This more cohesive approach to economic and social development is more likely to lead to mutually beneficial outcomes than the pursuit of unilateral objectives without regard for the wider societal implications or impacts.

9.3 Terms of engagement

As with any form of bona fide engagement, it is important to be honest about motivation. From the business perspective it needs to be clear, from the outset, that being a responsible corporation in the wider sense is not something additional or peripheral to the primary purpose of being a good and profitable business. Ethics and integrity are an integral part of how to go about that purpose, while maintaining honesty and observing high standards of accountability. When companies state and exemplify responsible business practices in all decisions and operations and act in good conscience toward stakeholders and the wider community, they exhibit leadership and provide greater certainty about the standards of conduct to be met within their organisations and at the same time influence the standards to be expected of others.

The mandate for government is to act in the public interest. This means playing an active role in the pursuit of the public good—underpinned by an economically, environmentally and socially sustainable society. In practical terms, this means exemplifying the highest ethical standards within the institutions and workings of government and in all dealings with its stakeholders. It also means investing in the development of enabling and creative policies and legal mechanisms that support organisations whose standard of behaviour exceed the prescribed legal minima, at least as much as they invest in policing those who fail to reach the lowest denominator.

Civil-society and non-governmental organisations also need to understand that their integrity, and their commitment, to the primary purposes for which their organisations were formed is not necessarily compromised by seeking out, and participating in, constructive engagement with business and government, aimed at achieving mutually beneficial outcomes. Furthermore, asserting the principles of transparency and accountability as core values within those engagements can provide the desired reassurances as to clarity of purpose and mandate.

Social Ventures Network defines nine principles of corporate social responsibility (Goodell 1999). Along with numerous other examples of such principles (Sherpell *et al.* 2002), they include being accountable to and dealing ethically with stakeholders, and managing resources with regard to stakeholder interests. Despite their corporate-centric perspective, these principles contain little to offend, overburden or, in most instances, substantially alter existing governance models of (or those aspired to by), ethical and responsible organisations in all sectors, especially regarding engagement with stakeholders.

If such principles broadly reflect the terms of engagement and conduct desirable of corporate partners, then arguably they should be mirrored in the reciprocal commitment and explicit expectation of all partners. Otherwise, how can the goal of new forms of true partnership be credible while inherently disproportionate expectations of one partner exist?

Recent years have seen the expectations that corporations, pension and investment funds reveal the environmental and ethical practices that guide their day-to-day operations become increasingly mainstream. For this expectation to be truly fair, the spirit of such disclosure should be observed in turn by all levels of government and the not-for-profit community. After all, governments oversee and are directly responsible for managing and developing the infrastructure and services at the very core of communities and many non-profit organisations now operate along business lines, managing significant funds, conducting marketing campaigns, lobbying for their cause and competing (at times fiercely) to protect and increase cash flow.

9.4 Sector responsibility

9.4.1 Corporate responsibility

Corporate responsibility in the wider sense is not a construct created to meet the unilateral demands of external players or a regulatory environment—nor is it something that can readily be harnessed to accomplish single-minded business objectives. It is about the recognition of common interests and shared responsibilities of companies and the societies in which they operate.

Good environmental and social practices and business success are not mutually exclusive. Attention to the issues and constructive engagement on environmental and community-linked policy and projects can be to the benefit of business, government, civil-society organisations and the interconnected constituency of stakeholders to whom they are all responsible and accountable.

The growing international public opinion that corporations have an obligation that goes beyond the pursuit of profit to the consideration of the social and environmental impacts of their activities constitutes an important stimulus for these changes to occur.[6] Some business reaction downplays the significance of public opinion on the grounds that it generally lacks adequate factual basis or first-hand knowledge. Arguably, the more proactive approach is to recognise this as the 'reality' business needs to address, and to do so by actively engaging with these important stakeholders to narrow the gap between this perception and their corporate reality.

---

6   Environics International Limited 1999. The overall survey was drawn from a total of 25,000 surveys conducted worldwide of approximately 1,000 citizens in each of 23 countries across six continents in May 1999. See also Environics Limited *2003 CSR Monitor* showing over eight in ten Canadians surveyed felt companies should go beyond their traditional economic role. According to Ipsos Reid 2003, of Canadians polled 55% said they had made conscious decisions based on their perception of whether the company was a good corporate citizen; 52% had boycotted a company they believed did not conduct business in a socially responsible way.

One of the ten key findings of the World Economic Forum's 2003 Survey of the initial CEO signatories to the 2002 Joint Statement on Global Corporate Citizenship[7] was the need for effective approaches to communication, consultation and collaboration with external stakeholders (Nelson and Bergrem 2003). Many companies are working toward this. Over half the CEOs surveyed cited personal contact with external stakeholders on corporate citizenship issues, a number of whom gave examples of direct involvement in multi-stakeholder dialogues on these issues.[8] The benefit of this kind of leadership will only be maximised—for these vanguard companies, and for society—through the collective efforts of all who have a vested interest in fundamentally changing the expectations of how *every* business conducts its operations. This means credible endorsement such as the World Economic Forum 2002 Joint Statement, and other such explicit commitments,[9] supported by ongoing, practical embodiment of the elements of corporate responsibility within the wider business community. The 2005 World Economic Forum witnessed a further advancement of this thinking in the unprecedented attention paid to development challenges and the growing recognition that partnerships between business, government and civil society must play a role in addressing key development challenges facing the world.

Companies risk the dilution of their ability to focus on the foremost issues facing their businesses if they seek to be all things to all people. The best places from which to start are those areas where the greatest alignment of business and social needs are readily identified, and where a company is best able to commit the time and resources necessary to ensure the investment is sound. Ideally, these areas would develop from a consultative process involving key stakeholders. The ongoing objective, however, must be to continue to seek ways to advance corporate responsibility to a more comprehensive approach that achieves effective co-ordination of the many dimensions to business interface with society.

At present, however, much of public opinion and expectation with respect to Corporate Responsibility, and the growing body of Socially Responsible Investment (SRI) research, continues to be biased in favour of broad societal perceptions rather than whether and how the principles are applied in practical terms. The extent of a particular company's investment in ongoing stakeholder relations, proactive workplace health and safety practices, decisions made with future environmental impact in mind, and responsible management approaches to the day-to-day conduct of operations are more meaningful measures of commitment than performance against third-party administered criteria. This underlines the importance of engaging directly with internal and external stakeholders in a process that takes communication beyond statements in annual reports to an ongoing dialogue around the particular issues, activities and performance indicators that are most material to all concerned.

---

7   See World Economic Forum Global Corporate Citizenship Initiative 2002.

8   Rio Tinto, Statoil, WMC, EDF, Renault, Merck, Phillips, Van Heusen, Xenel, ING and SC Johnson; see Nelson and Bergrem 2003: 7.

9   For example: Nelson *et al.* 2001; Cragg 2004; World Economic Forum Global Corporate Citizenship Initiative 2002; Business in the Community, www.bitc.org.uk; Caux Round Table, www.cauxroundtable.org; CERES Network for Change, www.ceres.org; European Business Campaign on Corporate Social Responsibility, www.csrcampaign.org; and the Global Compact, www.unglobalcompact.org.

Among the 'front of pack' companies adopting corporate responsibility, some see it as a way to pursue competitive advantage and for others it represents the possibility of achieving business success without compromising integrity. Few define it as a purely altruistic strategy and, as Milton Friedman has suggested in his writings on the subject, to do so would be a failure to have regard for the primary purpose and responsibility of business—to generate value for shareholders. Regardless, for corporate responsibility to become truly mainstream requires sound metrics which send a compelling message, *in the language of business*, that operating with a stronger, wider definition of the responsibilities of business can assist the pursuit of shareholder value over the longer term.[10]

The potential strategic value in corporate responsibility and the ability to communicate this by applying a business case analysis to what has been referred to as the *triple bottom line* (Elkington and Burke 1987) approach is what will keep it on the corporate agenda.[11] A majority of the respondents in the 2003 study by Political and Economic Link (PELC) and *Ethical Corporation* magazine for the World Bank and the International Finance Corporation reported CSR issues to be at least as influential as traditional considerations (e.g. cost, quality, delivery) in new venture assessment and that this influence has grown in the last five years. From this basis of understanding, the need to *justify* corporate responsibility lessens and the ability to acknowledge explicitly the connections and *mutual* benefits for companies, their shareholders, stakeholders, and the wider society in which they co-exist increases. As Hawken *et al.* (1999: xi) observed, '[c]onventional business intuition mistakenly sees priorities in economic and social policy as competing purposes'.

A cogent approach to the quantification and system-based analysis and systematic quantification of the benefits of a triple-bottom-line approach to business is presented in *The Sustainability Advantage: Seven Business Case Benefits of a Triple Bottom Line* in which the author, Bob Willard, builds the case for:

> [A] more accurate frame of reference [which] would . . . acknowledge that the global economy is a small sector within global society, which in turn is within the global environment that is necessary for life as we know it . . . an integrated 'both/and' situation (2002: 146).

9.4.2 Civil-society responsibility

The past decade has seen considerable progress in civil society becoming a legitimate and acknowledged 'partner' with business and government in key areas within the public domain (EESC 1999). Continuing this progress toward equal footing and increasing credibility requires that the majority of these organisations no longer consider themselves to some degree exempt from the increasingly robust standards of governance and accountability they expect from the corporate and public sectors.

---

10 See Webley and More 2003. The IBE studied two groups of companies for the period 1997–2001. One group had a demonstrable commitment to ethical behaviour—the first indicator being a published code of ethics—the other group did not. The results released in 2003 indicated that on EVA, MVA and P/E, there was clear out-performance by the first group.

11 See also www.sustainability.co.uk.

Just as traditional notions of corporate accountability extended no further than shareholders and, sometimes, internal stakeholders and customers, the accountability framework in many civil-society organisations has related primarily to internal stakeholders—staff, members and volunteers—and, to varying degrees, those directly linked to the organisation such as donors and beneficiaries. Civil-society accountability must come to mean demonstrating responsibility for the impact of decisions and actions to a wider stakeholder community that extends to individuals, organisations, businesses and governments who invest their trust in the sector via donations and other support by reference to explicit mutually acceptable standards. Indeed, their continued effectiveness may depend on meeting these accountability standards.

Materiality and sound metrics are as critical to achieving true accountability in not-for-profit organisations as they are for their for profit counterparts. A study conducted by One World Trust's Global Accountability Project (GAP) and released in 2003 showed that the non-governmental organisations (NGOs) surveyed often failed to provide information likely to be material to stakeholders or meaningful assessments of how effectively they have been achieving their stated purpose (Kovach *et al.* 2003).[12] The report observed that, although

> [I]ndividuals and communities . . . affected by these organizations' actions should be able to hold them to account . . . few mechanisms have been identified at a global level to enable these stakeholders to exert such a right . . . These organizations need to become more transparent and accountable (2003: iv).

Of those surveyed most lacked consistency in the manner of their reporting and failed to apply a systematic basis on which the information they did provide could be evaluated. However, the need for adequate, coherent, transparent and scalable systems to report and verify adherence to sound social and environmental practices for civil society organisations is now being recognised. A cross-sectoral partnership of non-profit organisations and civil-society actors—Keystone (formerly ACCESS)—is currently working toward the development of a generally accepted, global reporting standard for non-profit public-benefit organisations. The aim of this initiative is to enhance internal and external accountability, transparency and access to enabling resources by establishing a uniform approach to reporting material, performance-related information and metrics (Keystone 2003: 10).

A similar rationale prompted the UK Charity Commission (the regulator and registrar for charities in England and Wales) to post the accounts for the UK's 400 biggest charities on its website as of March 2004 and eventually those of all UK registered charities. The Commission aims to improve public trust in these organisations by increasing transparency and accountability through timely, standardised accounts and information returns available to the public and funders to gain a better understanding of the work of charities and make more informed decisions about which charities to support (Home Office 2003: 18).[13]

---

12 The study assessed the accountability of three key actors on the global stage: intergovernmental organisations (IGOs), transnational corporations (TNCs) and international NGOs (INGOs).

13 See also Charity Commission of England and Wales 2003.

The allegations of mismanagement recently levied at a number of prominent non-profit organisations in the US in the aftermath of 11 September 2001, and the ensuing loss of public confidence, mirrored recent scandals in the corporate world and are but one example of the dangers inherent in failing to address this issue.

Civil-society organisations that fail to demonstrate competent governance structures and practices risk losing credibility, trust and finding themselves at a disadvantage when seeking the resources, and expertise necessary for sustainable, independent existence. Dr Miklos Marschall, Executive Director of Transparency International (TI) for East and Central Europe in his 2002 article 'Legitimacy and Effectiveness: Civil Society Organizations' Role in Good Governance'[14] suggests that, while

> [t]he varied nature of accountability reflects the different role and functions of governments, businesses, and civil society organisations . . . [t]he best way NGOs can make up the natural 'accountability gap' is to generate public trust by full transparency and high standards of performance.

Furthermore, civil-society efforts such as those promoting sustainable development and corporate responsibility would likely be more compelling to the intended corporate audience when presented from a united front rather than a coalition of groups with divergent ideals, methods of engagement and standards of conduct. It would certainly improve their legitimacy when challenging inconsistent and unaccountable corporate behaviour if their own conduct is supported by consistent, explicit high standards of conduct, transparency and commitment to constructive engagement.

9.4.3 Public-sector responsibility

The enormous economic power of corporations exerts more influence in many parts of the world than traditional governing institutions. Based on 2002 figures, the top ten companies by revenue *alone* accounted for 3.2% of global GDP (or US$1.5 trillion).[15] In the last two decades, corporations have had unprecedented freedom to choose where and, to a significant extent, how they conduct their businesses. These freedoms have been largely unfettered (other than by market regulation), due to a lacuna where otherwise co-ordinated intra- or supra-jurisdictional means by which governments might regulate business activity might exist.

With globalisation lessening the ability of governments to regulate economic activity in the unilateral ways of the past, governments need to engage effectively with business and accept that the investment decisions of private corporations fuel the economic development critical to addressing issues of poverty and under-development, and achieving positive outcomes. If a more equitable distribution of global wealth is ever to be achieved, the responsibility for doing so must be undertaken by the public and private sectors working together to accomplish shared objectives consistent with social and environmental values, as well as sound economics.

Even in purely domestic corporate activity where jurisdictional obstacles are less at issue, government regulation has been cognisant of the vital role of business in local

---

14   This article draws on Marschall 1999.
15   Based on information from *Sydney Herald*, July 2002 and CIA *World Fact Book* 2003. See also: Friedman 2000; Korten 1995; Klein 2002.

economies, with the result that policy has tended to avoid undue constraints on corporate competitiveness in either domestic or international markets. The recent high-profile corporate scandals in the US (such as WorldCom, Enron, Tyco), and elsewhere, are stark reminders of the shortcomings in this approach. Public opinion and the spectre of governmental intervention through unilateral prescription are two *external* influences that keep the terminology of 'corporate responsibility' and 'business integrity' in the corporate lexicon.

To date governments have tended to focus mainly on the environment and the workplace with respect to the wider obligations of business; however, recent regulatory initiatives requiring companies to address social, ethical and environmental considerations such as those in the UK, France, Denmark, Australia, South Africa and the US exemplify a broadening of the scope of public policy interventions. In this regard, governments must recognise that it is imperative that those companies that already set and meet high standards of conduct in their domestic and international operations are not penalised by prescriptive measures intended to police the behaviours of those that do not.

The balance between voluntary and mandatory requirements relating to corporate governance and social responsibility, and the territory to be occupied by state- and non-state-promulgated standards is still being charted. With respect to their interventions in this area, regulators should allow themselves to be guided by the course set by the existing international codes and standards[16] and be cognisant of the value in engaging those stakeholders who are materially affected and represent diverse cross-sector perspectives.

In this regard, it is interesting to consider the correspondence of recent company law reforms such as those in the UK to require the largest 1,000 British companies to report on non-financial material risk extending to social and environmental issues, and similar requirements in France and Denmark for major listed companies to report on the social and environmental consequences or their activities, with the results of recent surveys showing significant support for compulsory reporting among stakeholder groups[17] and the importance placed by these groups on candour and openness regarding challenges and difficulties (Burson-Marsteller 2003) (of which some of the more significant are increasingly likely to be issues of 'non-financial' material risk).

Government also has a key contribution to building a more credible and legitimate role for civil society, levelling the playing field *vis-à-vis* governments and the private sector, and fostering balance and effective multi-sector stakeholder partnerships.

In direct or indirect (through state organisations) dealings with non-profit and other community-based organisations receiving financing and development support from public funds, governments must push for and support the development of greater transparency and strengthened governance practices of NGOs, cause-based and other non-state entities.[18] In some cases this will need to take the form of regulatory inter-

---

16 For a compendium of codes of conduct and Instruments of corporate responsibility see the web-based Voluntary Codes Research Group 2003.

17 ECC Kohtes Klewes GmbH and Fishburn Hedges 2003. The survey found four out of five respondents favouring mandatory reporting for large companies.

18 Voluntary Sector Initiative Secretariat 2001. The Accord is based on five guiding principles: independence; interdependence on shared goals; adherence to the principles of ongoing dialogue, co-operation and collaboration and accountability to Canadians.

vention to ensure standards of conduct and governance oversight in these organisations in the absence of an effective voluntary regime. The United States Congress Finance Committee, for example, has considered introducing regulation that would touch on issues of conduct such as conflict of interest policy and whistle-blower protections.

For its own part, public-sector conduct should be seen as at least as critical as private-sector conduct to safeguarding ethics and integrity and restoring public trust in the sociopolitical and economic systems. Reforms aimed at greater transparency and the development and consistent observance of accountability and disclosure standards (confidentiality rules permitting) within government have been taking place over a number of decades.[19] Credibility and oversight mechanisms commensurate with those increasingly required of the private sector must exist to ensure consistency and fairness in the exercise of discretionary powers and to support open and unbiased competition. These independent checks and balances relating to the discharge of responsibilities in respect of judicial functions, audit, treasury and finance, licensing, procurement and others also need to be monitored for continued effectiveness and independence.

Internal stakeholders are critical to achieving these objectives. Engaging these stakeholders can assist with progressing commitments to embed transparency, ensure accountability and disclosure at policy and procedural levels, overcome institutionalised resistance to change, and co-ordinate practice with the emerging norms of a shared governance model (Nye and Donahue 2000).

Public attitudes constitute an important stimulus for the development of public policy. Governments are increasingly cognisant of the growing public opinion that corporations have an obligation going beyond the pursuit of profit to the consideration of the social and environmental impacts of their activities. Similarly, they are increasingly aware of the public view that government has an obligation to be more accountable to its stakeholders—the present and future generations of electorate—and more transparent in their governance processes. For example, in 2003 Britain's Labour government launched its 'Conversations with the People' initiative as a medium for citizen participation in determining the priorities of government (Labour Party of Britain 2003). By seeking to engage stakeholders in setting the agenda, these types of initiatives go further than the practice of merely inviting public comment on policy decisions.

The European Union's 2002 White Paper on European Governance (CEC 2001) sought to define steps to open up the policy-making process and make EU institutions more accountable to the public (CEC 2002). The paper suggests that good governance takes place mainly in a process of regular and open consultation and dialogue between government authorities and the citizens from whom their power is derived. Many of the ongoing challenges for a new European constitution lie in the need for adequate means to entrench the basis for such democratic accountability.

Accountability and transparency standards need to be stated and compliance enforced. Realistically, these standards need to be sufficiently scalable to accommodate resource and other constraints faced by many of these organisations, but in spirit should be no less than commensurate with the appropriate minimum standards required of the private sector.

---

19 For example, see OECD 1998.

9.5 Conclusion

Engagement between business, civil society and government can be an effective and mutually beneficial strategy for all concerned if the different players are willing to find ways to work together around a shared agenda, and a common set of principles that enable the discussion to encompass broader social and environmental issues.

Clear articulation of generally understood ethical standards to be respected by business, civil society, and government alike creates a common frame of reference and increases certainty in their interactions. Consensus around such standards, underpinned by shared community values, could lessen or eliminate many of the current obstacles to effective multi-sector engagement.

In an increasingly complex, diverse and yet interconnected world, it is essential to be explicit about those values that absolutely need to be shared. Honesty, individual and collective accountability and responsibility, integrity, lawful conduct, mutual trust and respect form the foundation of a fair and ethical society regardless of culture, generation, geography, occupation, race or religion. This is critical for the success of multi-stakeholder engagement that seeks effective means to accomplish such objectives as: addressing and ameliorating poverty, mitigating the negative impacts of globalisation, respecting human rights, and safeguarding the environment, among others.

There has been a proliferation of codes, standards and guidelines worldwide in recent years addressing the many dimensions of corporate environmental and social responsibility. A growing repository of examples can be found on websites maintained by not-for-profit organisations dedicated to corporate responsibility, sustainability and social partnerships.[20] Many companies have published codes of conduct and include stakeholder-related activities in their business practices. Explicit commitments to ethical conduct, integrity, transparency, and greater public and stakeholder accountability are also increasingly prevalent within the public sector.

Starting from the premise that a market-based capitalist economy and a good society are not an 'either/or' proposition, a number of voluntary international initiatives take a multi-stakeholder approach to corporate citizenship issues.[21] Their cross-sector relevance along with the input of representatives from business, unions, non-governmental organisations and international institutions are evidence that it is possible to begin to reconcile opposing perspectives and reach a level of consensus through engaging those who have a stake in the outcomes. While critics will argue that their consensual nature denotes compromise, at minimum they establish a shared framework for ongoing dialogue and evolution.

Of these high-profile initiatives, the UN Global Compact is considered to be the first basis for dialogue on corporate responsibility between for profit, not-for-profit and governmental organisations produced by an institution with such global stature. Notably, the Compact evolved from engagement between all the relevant social actors:

20 Business in the Community, www.bitc.org.uk; Business for Social Responsibility, www.bsr.org; CSR Europe, www.csreurope.org; The Copenhagen Centre, www.copenhagencentre.org.
21 See for example: 'The Global Compact', www.unglobalcompact.org; 'ILO Conventions', www.ilo.org; 'The OECD Guidelines for Multinational Enterprises', www.oecd.org; 'AccountAbility 1000', www.AccountAbility.org; 'The Global Reporting Initiative', www.globalreporting.org; 'The Global Sullivan Principles', www.thegsp.org; 'Social Accountability 8000', www.cepaa.org.

governments, who defined the principles on which the initiative is based; companies whose actions it seeks to influence; labour, in whose hands the concrete process of global production takes place; civil society organisations representing the wider community of stakeholders; and the United Nations, the world's only truly global political forum, as an authoritative convenor and facilitator.

The approach is not prescriptive but based on: 'public accountability, transparency and the enlightened self-interest of companies, labour and civil society to initiate and share substantive action in pursuing the principles on which the Global Compact is based'.[22]

To date, the Compact's primary campaign has been directed to a corporate audience. While more than 1,000 companies support the Compact, arguably greater efforts directed toward the other 'relevant social actors'—governments, labour and civil-society organisations—are now necessary to establish a broad-based credibility which is absent if those who are most vocal, perceived as 'owning' the moral authority, or both, are seen to champion, but not exemplify the standards they expect of corporations.

There is growing consensus that it is not sufficient for the 'terms of engagement' to be mutually understood and standards observed by the relevant party, if there are no consistent means to assure and evaluate adherence. The Global Reporting Initiative (2000) is an example of corporations, NGOs and accountancy organisations reaching broad-based consensus on performance reporting criteria and the metrics for environmental and social performance. As these mechanisms are put into practice, it is critical that the dialogue between reporters and their stakeholder audience continues so as to identify the gaps, make the improvements and develop the enforcement mechanisms that are needed to increase strength, extend reach and maintain relevance amidst an evolving web of relationships.

Whatever the promise of the emerging governance standards and heightened accountability measures directed at corporations, it will only be fully realised when the underlying principles are respected, not only by that community but also the government, civil society and non-governmental entities with whom they engage. Maintaining the economic and social infrastructure of society is increasingly a shared responsibility as traditional silos break down through a shifting balance of power. This requires a heightened understanding, in all of these actors, of their *mutual* accountability and the extent to which it goes beyond their traditional spheres to encompass the wider societal dimension. True stakeholder engagement creates the nexus for this learning and a framework around which organisations in all three sectors can build effective, sustainable partnerships that are economically, environmentally and socially viable.

22   UN Global Compact, www.unglobalcompact.org.

References

Auditor General, Government of Canada (2002) *Report of the Office of the Auditor General to the House of Commons* (Ottawa: Government of Canada, www.oag-bvg.gc.ca).

—— (2003) 'Special Report on the Office of the Privacy Commissioner of Canada by the Auditor General of Canada' (Ottawa: Government of Canada, www.oag-bvg.gc.ca).

Burson-Marsteller (2003) *Building CEO Capital*™ (New York: Burson-Marsteller, www.ceogo.com).

Canadian Centre for Philanthropy (2003) *Ethical Fundraising and Financial Accountability Code* (Toronto: Canadian Centre for Philanthropy, www.ccp.ca).

CEC (Commission of the European Communities) (2001) 'European Governance: A White Paper', europe.eu.int/eur-lex/en/com/cnc/2001/com2001_0428en01.pdf.

—— (2002) 'Toward a Reinforced Culture and Dialogue', europa.eu.int/eur-lex/en/com/cnc/2002/com2002_0704en01.pdf): 6.

Charity Commission of England and Wales (2003) *Corporate Plan 2003–2006* (London: Charity Commission of England and Wales, www.charitycommission.gov.uk/spr/pdfs/corpplan03.pdf).

CIA *World Fact Book* (2003) www.cia.gov/cia/publications/factbook.

Cragg, W. (2004) *Corporate Responsibility and Accountability in the Global Marketplace: A Canadian Vision* (Toronto: York University, www.schulich.yorku.ca/ssb-extra/businessethics.nsf/lookup/CSR_Brief_v5/$file/CSR_Brief_v5.pdf).

ECC Kohtes Klewes GmbH and Fishburn Hedges (ed.) (2003) *Global Stakeholder Report 2003: Shared Values?* (Bonn/London: ECC Kohtes and Fishburn Hedges, www.fishburnhedges.co.uk): 5.

EESC (European Economic and Social Committee) (1999) *The Role and Contribution of Civil Society Organizations in the Building of Europe* (Brussels: European Economic and Social Committee).

Elkington, J., and T. Burke (1987) *The Green Capitalists* (London: Victor Gollancz).

Environics International Limited (1999) 'The Millennium Poll on Corporate Responsibility', as part of *Corporate Social Responsibility Monitor* (in co-operation with the Prince of Wales Business Leaders Forum and The Conference Board; London: Environics International Limited, www.environics.net).

Environics Limited (2003) *2003 CSR Monitor* (Toronto: Environics Limited).

Friedman, T. (2000) *The Lexus and the Olive Tree: Understanding Globalization* (New York: Anchor Books).

Goodell, E. (1999) *Social Ventures Network, Standards of Corporate Social Responsibility* (San Francisco: Social Ventures Network, see www.svn.org).

GRI (Global Reporting Initiative) (2000) *Sustainability Corporate Reporting Guidelines* (Boston, MA: Global Reporting Initiative).

Hawken, P., A.P. Lovins and L.H. Lovins (1999) *Natural Capitalism: Creating the Next Industrial Revolution* (Boston, MA: Little, Brown and Company): xi.

HMSO (1999) *Statutory Instrument 1999 No 1849: Occupational Pension Schemes (Investment and Assignment, Forfeiture, Bankruptcy, etc.) Amendment Regulations, 1999* (London: HMSO, www.hmso.gov.uk).

Home Office (2003) *Charities and Not-for-Profits: A Modern Legal Framework* (London: Home Office, www.homeoffice.gov.uk): 18.

Hutton, The Right Honourable Lord (2004) 'Investigation into the circumstances surrounding the death of Dr David Kelly' (London: House of Commons, www.the-hutton-inquiry.org.uk).

Institute for Social and Ethical Accountability (1999) *AccountAbility 1000 (AA1000): Framework AA1000 Series* (London: Institute for Social and Ethical Accountability, www.AccountAbility.org.uk).

Ipsos Reid (2003) *Corporate Social Responsibility Poll* (Vancouver: Ipsos Reid Corporation, www.ipsos-reid.com).

Keystone (formerly ACCESS) (2003) *An Inception Report* (London: Accountability, www.accountability.org.uk/uploadstore/cms/docs/Keystone%20Inception%20Report.pdf): 14.

Klein, N. (2002) *No Logo* (New York: Picador).

Korten, D. (1995) *When Corporations Rule the World* (Bloomfield, CT: Kumarian Press).

Kovach, H., C. Nelligan and S. Burall (2003) *Global Accountability Report 1: Power without Accountability?* (London: OneWorld Trust).

Labour Party of Britain (2003) 'The Big Conversation', www.thebigconversation.org.uk.

Machiavelli, N. (1532) *The Prince* (New York: Alfred A. Knopf).

Marschall, M. (2002) 'Legitimacy and Effectiveness: Civil Society Organizations' Role in Good Governance' (Transparency International 2002).

—— (1999) 'From States to People: Civil Society and Its Role in Governance', in *Civil Society at the Millennium* (Bloomfield, CT: CIVICUS/Kumarian Press).

Nelson, J., and C. Bergrem (2003) *Responding to the Challenge: Findings of a CEO Survey on Global Corporate Citizenship* (Geneva: World Economic Forum and The Prince of Wales International Business Leaders Forum, www.weforum.org/corporatecitizenship).

——, A. Singh and P. Zollinger (2001) *The Power to Change: Mobilising Board Leadership to Deliver Sustainable Value to Markets and Society* (London: International Business Forum, www.iblf.org).

Nye, J., and J. Donahue (eds.) (2000) *Governance in a Globalizing World* (Washington, DC: Brookings Institution Press).

OECD (Organisation for Economic Co-operation and Development) (1998) *Convention on Combating Bribery of Foreign Public Officials in International Transactions* (Paris: OECD, www.oecd.org).

Political and Economic Link (PELC) and *Ethical Corporation* magazine (2003) 'Race to the Top: Attracting and Enabling Global Sustainable Business' (Business Survey Report; Washington, DC: World Bank and IFC, www.ethicalcorp.com).

Sherpell, S., A. Garner, K. Shergold, P. Davies and M. Baker (2002) *Winning with Integrity* (Business Impact Task Force; London: Business in the Community [BITC], www.bitc.org.uk): Summary 02.

Svendsen, A. (1998) *The Stakeholder Strategy: Profiting from Collaborative Business Relationships* (San Francisco: Berrett-Koehler): 79.

Voluntary Codes Research Group (2003) 'Compendium of Ethics Codes and Instruments of Corporate Responsibility' (Toronto: York University, www.schulich.yorku.ca/ssb-extra/businessethics.nsf/allwebdocuments/links.htm).

Voluntary Sector Initiative Secretariat (2001) *An Accord between the Government of Canada and the Voluntary Sector* (Ottawa: Voluntary Sector Initiative Secretariat, www.vsi-isbc.ca).

WCED (World Commission on Environment and Development) (1987) *Our Common Future* ('The Brundtland Report'; Oxford, UK: Oxford University Press).

Webley, S., and E. More (2003) *Do Business Ethics Pay?* (London: Institute for Business Ethics [IBE], www.ibe.org.uk).

Willard, R. (2002) *The Sustainability Advantage: Seven Business Case Benefits of a Triple Bottom Line* (Gabriola Island, Canada: New Society Publishers, www.newsociety.com).

World Economic Forum Global Corporate Citizenship Initiative (2002) *Global Corporate Citizenship: The Leadership Challenge for CEOs and Board* (Geneva: World Economic Forum [WEF], www.weforum.org).

Part 3
Empirical studies on emerging governance structures and corporate social responsibility

10

Governance via collective learning between corporate and public actors*

Raimund Bleischwitz

Wuppertal Institute, Germany and College of Europe, Belgium

Kristian Snorre Andersen

Wuppertal Institute, Germany and Aarhus University, Denmark

Michael Latsch

College of Europe, Belgium

Our chapter proposes the following thesis: governance of sustainable development goes well beyond traditional, state-centred policy-making, because it aims at proactive changes of the behaviour of private actors at different levels. It necessarily involves the lower levels of policy-making and the activities of private individuals in policy formulation and implementation. Innovations generate positive externalities, which enable corporate actors to play a public role while doing business on competitive markets. The notions of networks and collective learning that we put forward in this chapter do accept profit seeking in emerging markets for sustainability. They further identify this behaviour as a driving force towards policy integration and the internalisation of externalities. Motivated by self-interest and soft incentives, corporate actors transform areas into markets for sustainable development that were previously a part of the public domain. However, the state retains the responsibility for structural conditions and innovation-inducing regulations.

* This chapter has benefited much from a grant provided by the Japanese Economic and Social Research Institute (ESRI), the Mitsubishi Research Institute and the Nomura Research Institute. It was also a part of the Millennium Collaboration Projects (www.esri.go.jp). We owe special thanks to Peter Hennicke, Michael Kuhndt, Holger Wallbaum and Thomas Langrock of the Wuppertal Institute as well as to Kilian Bizer, Carlo Carraro, Frank Convery, Matthias Finger, Hans Nutzinger, Peter Weise, Taishi Sugiyama and one anonymous referee. Nina Hausmann was instructive in language editing.

To test this thesis we discuss the following questions:

- What exactly is the function of networks and regulation?

- What are the characteristics of a system that develops synergies between political and corporate governance?

- If corporate players can play a public role, what conclusions can be drawn for policy-makers?

Methodologically, this chapter refers to recent theories from both political science and economics. The analyses in the discipline of political science look at governance systems with less government activity (Héritier 2002; Majone 1998; Young 1999), while the economic analyses offer findings on firms, market failures and regulatory theories (Williamson 1999; Nelson 2002; Stiglitz 1998). This interdisciplinary approach is valuable because political science has a strong bond with administrations and policy-making, especially in the field of institutionalism, which is actor-centred. Within the economic analyses, the emerging branches of new institutional economics and evolutionary economics prove to be helpful. The analytical framework derived from these theories departs from models of rational choice; that is to say, it does not assume a fully rational actor with perfect information (Ostrom 1998; Mantzavinos 2001). Recent literature on corporate governance is of special relevance here as it provides insights into the motivation and self-interest of firms. This in turn is helpful for the (new) design and reform of policies.

In Section 10.1 we will give a short survey of theories on market and government failures. It is proposed that both types of failures can be compensated between private and public actors in the development of sustainable markets. Section 10.2 outlines a more evolutionary approach on firms and markets. Section 10.3 deals with the policy level while in Section 10.4 we describe a case study on wind energy. Section 10.5 draws conclusions on governance.

10.1 The development of network governance as a response to market and hierarchy failures

Markets are well known for being dynamic and powerful, yet imperfect. These imperfections also have been described as market failures. However, not only the market but also government failures are a field of research for political and economic scientists. Within the sustainability debate the hierarchical mode of failures, or inadequacies of the government to bring about changes, is widely discussed. In this part of the chapter, the market and the hierarchy, the two most dominant government forms, and their failure to bring about sustainability improvements are examined. Subsequently, co-operative governance structures between private and public actors will be presented as a possible solution to correct both these forms of government failures.

10.1.1 Market failures

Markets are often considered to be unable to contribute to sustainability improvements: because such improvements are characterised solely in relation to public goods. They are thereby incompatible with the mandate of profit seeking in a pure free market economy. Public goods are defined as being non-exclusive and non-rival. A good is non-exclusive if nobody can be excluded from the benefits of its use. Further, the good is said to be non-rival if the consumption of one unit of the good does not lower the consumption opportunities still available to others (Sandler 1992: 6). These attributes of non-rivalry and non-excludability make private production of these goods unattractive. However, this standard concept of public goods can be problematic (Nelson 2002). The attributes may change due to technological progress. The examples of harbours and lighthouses illustrate such a conversion from a former public to a private good due to technological improvements and better pricing possibilities. Although citizens are usually taken as one aggregated unit, they benefit from public goods in innumerable different ways. Preferences are often heterogeneous and change over time. The assumption of a fixed borderline between private and public goods seems no longer to be tenable. In fact, the borderline can be argued to be rather blurred. At the same time sustainability improvements often result in certain private benefits (e.g. higher levels of efficiency, lower total costs and a green image). It is often more relevant to regard improvements in sustainability as an impure collective good of the so-called joint product variety.[1] Such a conceptualisation provides a new perspective on the roles of public and private actors in the field of sustainable development.

The notion of *externalities* raises further questions. Third parties that so far have not been involved can be affected by internalisation efforts within Coase-type negotiations. Governments have to serve their respective voters and may tend towards decision-making in favour of certain interest groups. This might lead them to overlook vulnerable groups, inside and outside of the society, that are only modestly organised. Participation is a topic of internalisation strategies that has merits also in other areas of sustainability. Its relevance becomes even clearer when we look at the openness of technological change (Freeman 1998), where mechanisms for absorbing new knowledge are crucial. The acknowledgment that firms pursue these interests of knowledge transformation into business concepts creates the scope for an endogenous internalisation of externalities.

The category of *information and adaptation deficits* refers to the speed at which markets and firms adapt to new circumstances that arise from new legislation and other exogenous factors. The field of evolutionary economics has shown that markets evolve step by step (Witt 2003; Pelikan and Wegner 2003), created by pioneers and early imitators from a variety of firms. However, in the evolution of markets stakeholders are at least as important as the Schumpeterian entrepreneur. In fact stakeholders are central information carriers for the learning processes that drives the evolution of markets. Stakeholder involvement is therefore a key to reduce the information and adaptation deficits.

---

1   A collective good can be defined as a joint product, where the collective activities result in a multiple output.

Based on this overview of different market failures it can be concluded that the correction of unsustainable market behaviour is often a question of learning processes that involve a variety of actors. Collective learning processes, new products and technologies that bring about private and public benefits can be developed through the involvement of different stakeholders. In other words, collective learning processes should be seen as a key factor for the internalisation of externalities and for the provision of collective goods. Therefore, the development of collective learning processes and stakeholder involvement should be a focal point in the governance of sustainable development.

10.1.2 The failures of hierarchy

This chapter proposes that co-operation between private and public actors in the development of learning processes is essential for sustainability improvements, as it responds to a central weakness of hierarchical governance. The problem goes beyond the sometimes too simplistic general view of public choice theories. The fact is that economic actors, and also politicians and bureaucrats, are driven by self-interest. This provides at least some initial insights into why public policies are likely to involve failures (Buchanan and Musgrave 1999). In this context, hierarchical top-down regulation can be seen to be unaware of the interests and knowledge of the actors, and processes in the local networks where the real changes take place. Such forms of regulation can lead to dissatisfaction, conflicts and spore behaviour of self-interest both by private and public actors.

Command-and-control is an example for hierarchical governance. It is often defined as legally mandated standards that are enacted by a series of agency decisions that are enforced by local authorities. In her analysis of German water and air pollution controls, Mayntz (1978) concludes that the environmental standards do not automatically result in the assumed target group behaviour. Further she argues that control, monitoring activities and prosecution of violators are necessary for the effectiveness of such a regulation. However, the possibilities of the public to execute such a required control are limited. For this reason many polluters choose the risk of not complying with the standards.

The top-down approaches suggested by science have been criticised in the general political debate because of their implicit assumption that public authorities control the organisational, political and technical processes that affect implementation. It is also criticised that the approach fails to acknowledge the importance of the interaction between street-level bureaucrats, target groups and other private associations. The knowledge of actual problems within these groups is far better compared to the top level of the hierarchy (Enevoldsen 2001: 88; Jordan *et al.* 2003; Pelikan and Wegner 2003).

10.1.3 The development of co-operative institutions for collective learning processes

The possession of knowledge of private and public actors can be seen as a central cause for the existence of policy networks. Policy networks are therefore proposed as a mode of governance (Börzel 1998; Kenis and Schneider 1991). During the last decade a development and strengthening of the societal organisational structures outside of the state hierarchy has been witnessed (Kenis and Schneider 1991). More resources have come under control or have been produced by private organisations. These changes have developed alongside an increase of new technologies, products and services. This has resulted in higher levels of complexities within policy-making. These complexities require knowledge, expertise and access to resources beyond the scope of public actors. As a consequence, governments have become increasingly dependent on co-operation and joint resource mobilisation between policy actors from sectors outside of the traditional hierarchical control of governments (Börzel 1998: 260). These changes have favoured the emergence of policy networks as a new form of governance. These new forms of governance are different from the two conventional forms of governance (namely, market and hierarchy). These two conventional forms allow governments to mobilise political resources in situations where resources are widely dispersed between public and private actors (Börzel 1998).

On the one hand, we agree with the view that the development of networks between private and public actors is central for the co-ordination and mobilisation of resources that are necessary for the implementation of change. On the other hand, we see the co-operation between private and public actors as the central argument for the development of learning processes that we propose to be a key factor for sustainability improvements. In actor-centred institutionalism interests are treated as exogenous. If preferences are treated as fixed, however, one fails to recognise learning processes as a central driver behind change. In the approach presented here it is assumed that learning processes can change the interests and preferences of actors. We argue that the generation of collective learning processes should be a central pillar in governance strategies.

However, market development instead of policy implementation is the aim of the kind of networks proposed in this chapter. This concept has an influence on the composition of networks and the issues discussed. The networks we analyse deal with the strategic issue of bringing economic activities on paths towards sustainability. It is not the aim of the networks to seek strategic influence on the ongoing national and/or local political agenda. This means that the relevant networks will be made up by business and political actors and consumer groups (both on the decentral and central level). The development of co-operative structures for collective learning processes where the co-ordination knowledge generation involves both private and public actors is a key for the improvement of governments (Dror 2001; Stiglitz 1998; Pelikan and Wegner 2003; Young 1999).

From this viewpoint, the traditional dichotomy between the market and the government, or between *laissez-faire* and intervention, loses importance. The market and the state serve complementary functions that keep the system running. A well-performing market economy is a mixed composition of government regulation and (free) markets. Langlois and Robertson (1995) formulate similar views on business institutions.[2] Governance towards sustainability is a co-evolution between the market and the state, where private and public actors search permanently for market and policy improvements.

2   See North 1990; Pelikan and Wegner 2003.

10.2 Firms and market evolution

How does the behaviour of profit maximisation of firms fit into the approach of collective learning described above? What is the interest of firms to engage in such forms of co-operation and why should they not defect from the co-operation if it pays off? This might well be the case. Corporate behaviour is unlikely to become benevolent for society as a whole or for the global commons. The shadow of hierarchy and co-operation played as a game are two factors that will reduce the likelihood that corporate actors will defect from such relations (Scharpf 1997; Börzel 1998). Another—and perhaps more important—point is that in many cases it proves to be profitable to develop new technologies, products and services that result in sustainability improvements (von Weizsäcker *et al.* 1997). This emphasises the fact that profit seeking can go hand in hand with sustainability improvements. In other words, corporate behaviour can indeed produce sustainability improvements.

Recent economic analysis (Nelson 2002) reveals a shift in the behaviour of profit maximisation. Previously it was quite naturally assumed that businesses are motivated by profits and an optimisation process alongside a sharply defined set of opportunities. Firms were not regarded as groping, experimenting and gradually innovating towards incremental improvements. The idea was that profits were predetermined by the given set of total average cost, marginal revenues and technological choices. The aims of the management were an optimisation towards the market equilibrium. Such companies would obviously have no interest in a contribution towards public goods or the internalisation of externalities.

However, this kind of model could not account for the dynamics of competition and knowledge generation. More recent views established an analytical model of knowledge-based firms (Leonard-Barton 1995; Langlois and Robertson 1995; Grant 1996; Nonaka and Toyama 2002). It is assumed that firms act under uncertainties and information deficits. They rely on permanent knowledge generation provided by outside sources, experiments or internal implementation processes. Firms can also create markets from scratch through co-ordination with others along vertical or horizontal lines. In doing so, firms communicate with stakeholders in order to learn about changes in demand, the development of useful goods and services, and to avoid hostile reactions. Figure 10.1 illustrates that firms make use of a spiral of knowledge generation that helps them to transform information that was generated elsewhere into useful knowledge. Moreover, it transforms into transaction cost-reducing routines.

Does this new model overcome the prevailing assumptions about corporate approaches to sustainable development and the involvement in governance structures? If the model is acknowledged to reflect competitive markets, what are the implications for the questions outlined here? The basis for an answer is: (a) our proposition that there is no fixed borderline between common and private goods; and (b) that there are potential low-cost or even profit-generating options (*low-hanging fruits*). Basically, knowledge-based firms contribute in two respects towards sustainable development while they still serve their own interests: they develop technologies and/or services that are private but contribute to public goals: for example, renewable energies and technologies for clean water. Firms also work on the creation of demand, either by marketing or other professional business forms. An illustration for this are services such as

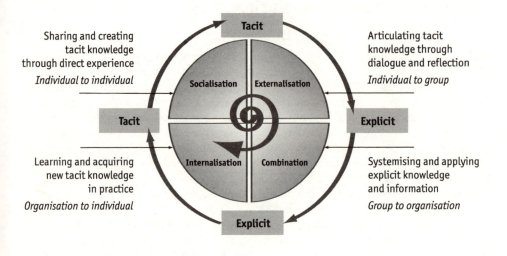

FIGURE 10.1 The spiral of knowledge generation

Source: Nonaka and Toyama 2002

leasing, renting, pooling and sharing of goods that contribute to the commons: for example, the organisation of car-sharing in order to save costs for parking.

In the context of collective learning firms can profit from participation with stakeholders in the evolution of new market rules. This is not only due to the fact that they can influence the outcome. The main reason is, once again, that there exists an advantage to be a forerunner or fast imitator. The adaptation times for participating firms are significantly shorter. Learning during times of governmental reframing can trigger competitive advantages (Porter and van der Linde 2000). In other cases, any further regulation has to rely on the experiences gained by pioneering firms, because they can draw on precise data on the costs and benefits of various institutional mechanisms. Thus, governance systems can rely on exploration and experiments undertaken by corporate actors. The free-riding position to simply wait for the establishment of new market rules is likely to be a competitive disadvantage. Figure 10.2 presents firms as a part of the social environment where the decisions of the firms are likely to be influenced by being embedded into this system of rules.

The tentative conclusion for collective learning is not that the model of the knowledge-based firm reflects the only or dominant form of doing business. Many firms struggle to survive and hardly spend time with learning processes and exploring new opportunities. Though they may be seen as laggards, they are still relevant for an analysis. One also has to take into account that firms do not necessarily act with total consistency. Some operations may become more sustainable than others where asset-specific investments hinder rapid change. We would like to suggest that firms tend to imitate pioneers and successors through benchmarking processes. Incentives for improvements are then easier to understand, if they come from markets and not only from governments or from law. These processes of imitation lead to a horizontal diffu-

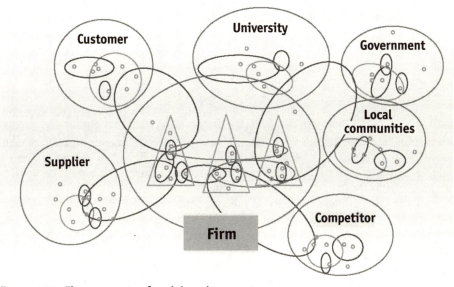

FIGURE 10.2 Firms as parts of social environments

Source: Nonaka and Toyama 2002

sion of best practices that is pivotal for sustainable development (see Fig. 10.3). Of course, governments and the law still have a role to play: for example, by co-financing agencies facilitating horizontal diffusion.

Looking at market evolution altogether, transaction costs associated with research and development as well as with the establishment of new markets have to be taken into account. Markets for sustainability goods involve a multitude of actors. The demand of the consumers needs to be stimulated as they only have a vague idea of some of these goods (Loasby 2001). Firms, markets and institutions can economise these transaction costs. Within the analytical framework outlined here, this process is characterised by public activities that gradually move towards the involvement of profitable markets. A point that gains more and more attention by research is that co-evolving incentives set through governance systems are an essential prerequisite.[3] In terms of market evolution, the following steps can be expected to lower transaction costs:

- Overcoming information deficits

- Improving sustainability management within firms

- Establishing supply chain management among firms (vertical co-operation)

- Opening the supply chain for stakeholder involvement

---

3   See, for example, Bleischwitz 2003a, 2003b; Cashore 200; van Dijken *et al.* 1999; Gabel and Sinclair-Desgagné 1998; Haufler 2001; Héritier 2002; Weizsäcker *et al.* 1997.

- Initiating sequences of incremental innovations or more radical innovations such as functional redesign or system renewal

- Promoting horizontal diffusion of innovations

In some areas in particular, emerging markets for sustainability are obvious, as the case study on wind energy in Section 10.4 shows. But how does this apply to other environmental problems such as climate protection? Is the climate itself not a truly global public good? This chapter does not seek to argue against open access to, and non-rivalry in, consumption of the atmosphere of the Earth. However, the proposed thesis on markets for sustainability may open a new perspective on the problem of non-excludability. The issue of climate protection is closely linked to energy efficiency, increasing shares of renewable energies and growing markets for eco-efficiency that act as a substitute for resource-intensive manufacturing processes. These markets can be made profitable. The marginal cost functions can be modelled as step-shaped functions. Markets for sustainability produce positive externalities together with a learning governance structure, insofar as they have positive impacts on the Earth's atmosphere. Hence, governance for sustainable development becomes a positive-sum game: once markets for energy efficiency, renewable energies and eco-efficiency start to emerge, they can provide public goods or, more precisely, reduce risks and contribute to stabilisation of the atmosphere. It is required to strengthen the processes of search, discovery, innovation and diffusion in order to realise such a scenario. This is an explicit challenge for firms, stakeholders and governments. Figure 10.2 illustrates the double meaning of the environment: firms act as parts of the natural and social environments. Markets for sustainability emerge as a method to provide goods in order to solve co-ordination problems among different actors.

Technological change has a definite bearing on market evolution (Freeman 1998; Langlois and Robertson 1995). Discoveries can set the route to cleaner production, more efficient manufacturing processes, new products that are able to lower environmental pressure, and so on. Technological change can result in a shift of the margin from public towards private goods. As a consequence, goods that were formerly considered to be public can now be provided by private engagements. For that reason private market activities can at least partly provide a clean environment. Firms are interested in these emerging markets as long as they can expect profits. Sequences of incremental technological change can stimulate markets as well as radical innovations can do. Furthermore, incremental changes are more open to flexible incentives that are provided by other firms, stakeholders and regulatory efforts. This fact is important because it proves to be easier to manage changes via improvements in incremental technological rather than a 'backstop technology'. Such changes, however, ought to be embedded in institutional reforms where aspects of sustainability act as a permanent driving force for markets and firms to search for innovation.

10.3 Regulation

Any governance of sustainability has to deal with various forms of doing business as well as with the day-to-day policies of a wide variety of actors. Still, command-and-control approaches and other policies exist that restrict businesses in case of permanent non-compliance or high-risk activities. Our approach of governance becomes especially important if long-term tasks are to be performed: for example, climate protection that requires learning, innovation and change. For such tasks, innovation-inducing regulation (Jänicke and Jacob 2002) fits into our conceptual framework. This type of regulation is not only conducive to innovation but also co-evolves alongside with the specific developments in each case. Such co-evolution between corporate and political actors is based on the insight that important governance functions have to be dealt with at the level of day-to-day governance. They cannot completely be regulated *ex ante* by any political or constitutional order. The reasons for this are uncertainties, knowledge deficits and, by and large, the unpredictable results by human activity. One may note that these uncertainties result from different sources: previously unknown facts and the persistence of market failures that are more difficult to overcome than previously expected. For this reason, innovation-inducing regulation co-evolves with corporate activities and the emergence of new markets for sustainability. In contrast to Jänicke and Jacob (2002), who put great emphasis on political actors, we would argue in favour of collective learning that leads to change. This statement on co-evolution is stronger than the analysis of Jänicke and Jacob (2002) reveals.

Innovation-inducing regulation has a short time horizon of a few months or years. On the other hand, framing efforts have an impact over many years if not decades. Innovation-inducing regulation relates to the governmental functions to absorb problems of the society, to bring together heterogeneous actors and to find solutions for specific problems. At the same time, this type of regulation takes into account that governments do not necessarily have the knowledge of what exactly can be done. The governments only draw business attention to certain problems instead of telling them what to do. Governments help to establish win–win coalitions, but they do not specify which action should be taken. They participate in networks and other forms of multi-actor coalitions without being in a dominant position. There is a shift in the process of policy-making from policy-makers to a multitude of other actors that include corporate actors and environmental and/or social NGOs. Corporate governance and our idea of knowledge-based firms fit well into such a comprehensive governance system.

Figure 10.3 illustrates this view. It basically shows that policies and management develop through different stages, from immediate problem-solving towards institutionalisation to low-cost, innovative and preventative approaches. The meaning of governance is twofold: first, each stage serves a certain function and any institutional leapfrogging strategy may come at the expense of comprehensiveness and that of the major actors. Second, any progress depends on co-evolution, not only on success in policy or management. There is hardly a country in the world where eco-efficient services (stage 4 in environmental management in Fig. 10.3) emerge without incentives being set by governments. Vice versa, there is also hardly a country where without support from vested or newly established interest groups a horizontal co-ordination among ministries and institutional adaptation flexibility improves (stages 3 and 4 in environmental policy).

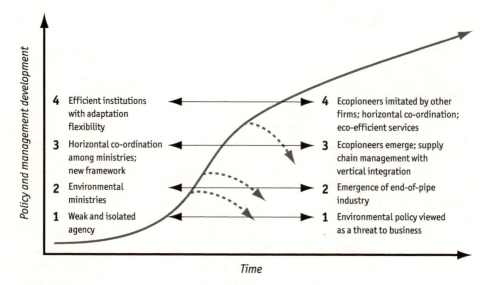

FIGURE 10.3 Co-evolution of corporate and political governance

Source: Bleischwitz 2003a

This figure suggests that participatory and administrative processes in governments and businesses increasingly fulfil important governance functions that were previously devoted to a political framework. Stabilisation not only results from a framework but also from the adaptation towards new conditions. The importance of adaptive flexibility increases with the degree of uncertainty and change. For governance that aims at long-term changes with varied innovations, adaptive flexibility is at least as relevant as an *ex ante* framework. This implies a kind of regulation that is not determined by a rigid framework and that precludes strict regulation that would stifle the adaptive flexibility of markets and societies. Such criteria may become relevant when the European Union uses any kind of 'Sustainability Impact Assessment' in support of its policies.

10.4 The developments of the Dutch, German and Swedish wind turbine industries

The development of the wind turbine industries in Sweden, the Netherlands and Germany illustrates the governance approach we suggest. The German wind turbine industry is now the second largest in the world. The Dutch and Swedish industries only account for very low shares of the world market. These three industries can be connected to the development of different public and private relations and collective learning processes. Johnson and Jacobson (2000) see two phases in the different development paths of the German, Dutch and Swedish industries. The first phase, roughly between 1975 and 1989, was characterised by substantial technological variety (and uncertainty), under-development of markets and the entry of many firms. The second phase, roughly between 1990 and 1999, was characterised by a considerable turbulence, driven by rapid growth in the market and an upscaling of turbines. Further, there were many exits with also some new entrants including some larger firms (Johnson and Jacobson 2002: 7). The differences of the institutional frameworks, both in the first and the second phase, can be seen as a central fact in order to explain the different evolution of the emerging industries in the three respective countries.

At the end of the 1980s, a large number of actors, firms and universities developed and tried out a range of different technological designs both in Germany and the Netherlands. In both countries R&D policies encouraged a broad range of technical experiments that stimulated the creation of new knowledge. In contrast, the funding policies in Sweden were directed towards large turbines (MW-sized) and did not support small and medium-sized turbines. At the same time only a few large firms were involved in the development of the wind turbine industry. Therefore, a great variety in the industry was developed in Germany and the Netherlands with concern towards the generated knowledge and the exploration of it. In contrast, the variety of the technology and the actors in the Swedish industry was low. Only one firm was mainly involved in the development of knowledge and was at the same time focused only on large turbines.

The German market expanded rapidly due to the market formation programme, which included measures affecting the price of wind electricity (Assmann *et al.* 2004). The price regulation for renewable electricity was based on fixed enumeration prices established by law, independent from public budgets. Therefore, the income that was generated by wind turbines was high and predictable and greatly reduced the risk of the investment. Another cause for the rapid expansion of the German market was the fact that it was required to provide property to build wind turbines. This was requested by federal law in 1997 and therefore required by the different federal states (*Länder*). The German wind turbine industry witnessed at the same time the development of two forms of networks that made the market formation possible. First, learning networks that facilitated the diffusion of wind turbines developed between the different actors in the product chain of wind turbine technology. Second, policy networks were created that actively took part in securing wind energy policies within the German wind turbine industry. Large energy companies particularly demanded these networks.

The market formation in the Netherlands failed, however. The investment subsidises implemented by the Dutch government did not have the intended effect. One reason was a problem of the establishment of sites for wind turbines. The building permits were issued under the jurisdiction of local authorities, which were characterised by slow and time-consuming procedures. This therefore blocked the formation of the Dutch market. The failure of the *Windplan foundation*, which was organised by several Dutch electricity distributors, is another cause for the failure of the formation of the Dutch market. The idea behind the project was to co-ordinate procurement and thereby acquire cheaper and better wind turbines. The project was ambitious at that time (measure in MW) and also attracted foreign firms. However, the *Windplan foundation* project was abandoned at a very late phase because the electricity distributors started to question the benefits from joint procurement. Further, the *Windplan foundation* is seen as a central reason why the Dutch wind industry failed to acquire shares of the expanding German market. The Dutch industry concentrated on the domestic market because it looked very promising. Although the opinions on this matter do not concur, it is also argued that technical requirements of the *Windplan project* made the Dutch industry develop a wind technology that followed specific requirements. However, these requirements were not commercially feasible with respect to other markets. Without access to a booming market and the associated economic benefits, the Dutch firms had neither the resources to develop their technology fast enough or to keep up with the German suppliers nor the political strength to influence the vital building permit issue (Johnson and Jacobson 2002: 28).

No virtuous circles for the industry were started in Sweden although a growth in demand developed. An important reason for this was that potential industrial partners were not interested. The Swedish wind industry therefore lacked resources in the development of new technology and market shares. There were also investment subsidies within the facilitation of the Swedish market, even though they were much weaker than in Germany and the Netherlands. The Swedish firms did not have a strong response capacity in the second phase due to the low technology variety during the first phase. This also contributed to the failure of the market formation.

The level of legitimacy of the new technology enjoyed by public and private actors is, according to Johnson and Jacobson (2000), a central explanation in the analysis of the different evolutions of the wind turbine industry in the Netherlands, Sweden and Germany. The legitimacy of a new technology and new ideas can be seen as a part of learning processes where actors develop new understandings and perceptions of human life and market opportunities. In this context, the absence of an interest of potential industrial partners within the Swedish industry was connected to lack of legitimacy of wind power that came due the so-called *nuclear trauma*.[4] On the other hand, there subsisted a political consensus in the Netherlands and Germany in the 1980s that the wind turbine industry should be supported. It was seen as being legitimate for private capital to exploit wind turbine technology. 'The legitimacy meant that firms responded to various stimuli, e.g. the Californian "boom", R&D programmes, etc., by diversifying into wind turbines or by starting new firms' (Johnson and Jacobson 2002: 32). Furthermore, these authors state that the low legitimacy in Sweden caused different responses by Swedish firms to the very same stimuli that made some German firms invest. In addition, the Californian 'boom' did not inspire Swedish firms to the same extent as in the other two countries.

The Dutch government did not find a solution for the problem of the establishment of locations for wind turbines. Johnson and Jacobson (2000) associate this with the fact that the political support for the Dutch wind industry failed in the second phase. This lack of political support is also reflected by the fact that, even after the Dutch market formation failed, no more powerful political measures were taken. The German industry benefited from the highest legitimacy that was reflected in well-designed incentives and in creative corporate networks and demand.

---

4 Johnson and Jacobson (2000) use the term *nuclear trauma* to describe the entrenchment of the Swedish nuclear power debate (pro versus con). Any interest in wind power is automatically taken as being against nuclear power. This was seen by the Swedish industry as a betrayal that benefited cheap nuclear power.

A crucial factor to explain the evolution of the Dutch, German and Swedish wind turbine industries was that the ideas and interests of the three national industries were embedded. A decisive impact on co-operation preparedness, the developed policies, the technology and knowledge generation and the market formation, was the perception of these emerging industries by public and private actors. The case of the wind turbine industry concurrently illustrates the relationship of collective learning between the government and the market mechanisms in the development of new sustainable markets. It further shows what happens if both parties fail to co-operate. At the same time, this case shows the important function of governments in setting the institutional frame for knowledge generation between public and private actors. At last, the expansion of the wind turbine industry in Germany and the development of economic and political networks illustrate the specific dynamics of sustainable markets that are likely to grow as new markets develop.

10.5 Conclusions

Governance, as described in the present chapter, reveals its greatest strength where long-term innovatory tasks with low immediate damage potential are pursued. Such processes usually result in new actor coalitions and the formulation of new rules of the game. Areas of application are climate change policies (beyond the need of the management of specific impacts), eco-efficiency policies, water policies, provision of collective goods, and so on.

In distinction to many other approaches, our conceptual framework on collective learning processes welcomes the self-interest of business as a beneficent force. The self-interest of private business is not content with the exploitation of *low-hanging fruits*. Instead, it promotes the creation of new knowledge because business recognises the changing market expectations and the resulting needs for a market evolution. Yet, business can opt out of the collective learning processes if profits fall short of the expectations. The function of governance is thus to support processes of mutual learning where the governments are in a strong but not (too) dominant position. This function goes well beyond the usual compliance procedures.

Network institutions for collective learning between private and public actors are essential in order to correct market and government failures within the evolution of markets for sustainable products and services. The provision of collective goods and the internalisation of externalities could gradually shift to co-evolutionary processes managed by both private and public actors even though they were thought of as being a core competence of governments.

Our analytical framework for corporate action combines elements of new institutional economics, evolutionary economics and actor-centred institutionalism. Each of these disciplines has been criticised as being heterogeneous and as being too much in line with traditional *unsustainable* approaches. Nevertheless, the overall framework seems to be consistent and well suited for the analysis of the evolution of the Dutch, German and Swedish wind turbine industries and various other case studies.

References

Assmann *et al.* (2004) 'Renewable Energy Act in Germany', in R. Bleischwitz and P. Hennicke (eds.), *Eco-Efficiency, Regulation, and Sustainable Business: Towards Governance of Sustainable Development* (Cheltenham, UK/Northampton, MA: Edward Elgar Publishing).

Bleischwitz, R. (2003a) 'Governance of Eco-efficiency in Japan: An Institutional Approach', *Internationales Asienforum: International Asian Quarterly* 34.1–2: 107-26.

—— (2003b) 'Cognitive and Institutional Perspectives of Eco-efficiency', *Ecological Economics* 46: 453-67.

Buchanan, J.M., and R.A. Musgrave (1999) *Public Finance and Public Choice: Two Contrasting Visions of the State* (Cambridge, MA/London: MIT Press).

Börzel, T.A. (1998) 'Organising Babylon: On the Different Concepts of Policy Networks', *Public Administration* 76 (Summer 1998): 253-73.

Cashore, B. (2002) 'Legitimacy and the Privatization of Environmental Governance: How Non-state Market-Driven (NSMD) Governance Systems Gain Rule-Making Authority', *Governance: An International Journal of Policy, Administrations, and Institutions* 15.4: 503-29.

Dror, Y. (2001) *The Capacity to Govern*. A Report to the Club of Rome.

Enevoldsen, M. (2001) 'Rationality, Institutions, and Environmental Governance', in S. Beckmann and E. Kloppenburg, *Environmental Regulation and Rationality: Multidisciplinary Perspectives* (Aarhus, Denmark: Aarhus University Press).

Freeman, C. (1998) 'The Economics of Technical Change', in D. Archibugi and J. Michie (eds.), *Trade, Growth and Technical Change* (Cambridge, UK: Cambridge University Press): 16-54.

Gabel, H.L., and B. Sinclair-Desgagné (1998) 'The Firm, Its Routines and the Environment', in T. Tietenberg and H. Folmer (eds.), *The International Yearbook of Environmental and Resource Economics 1998/99* (Cheltenham, UK/Northampton, MA: Edward Elgar Publishing): 89-118.

Grant, R.M. (1996) 'Toward a Knowledge-Based Theory of the Firm', *Strategic Management Journal* 17 (Special Issue, Winter 1996): 109-22.

Haufler, V. (2001) *A Public Role for the Private Sector: Industry Self-regulation in the Global Economy* (Carnegie Endowment for International Peace).

Héritier, A. (ed.) (2002) *Common Goods: Reinventing European and International Governance* (Lanham, MD: Rowman & Littlefield).

Johnson, A., and S. Jacobson (2000) 'The Emergence of a Growth Industry: A Comparative Analysis of the German, Dutch and Swedish Wind Turbine Industries' (Mimeo; Department of Industrial Dynamics, Chalmers University of Technology, Sweden).

Jordan, A., R. Wurzel and A. Zito (2003) 'New Instruments of Environmental Governance? National Experiences and Prospects', *Environmental Politics* 12.1: 201-24.

Jänicke, M., and K. Jacob (2002) *Ecological Modernization and the Creation of Lead Markets* (FFU rep 03/2002; Research Centre for Environmental Policy: FU Berlin).

Kenis, P., and V. Schneider (1991) 'Policy Networks and Policy Analysis: Scrutinizing a New Analytical Toolbox', in B. Marin and R. Mayntz, *Policy Networks: Empirical Evidence and Theoretical Consideration* (Oxford, UK: Westview Press).

Langlois, R.N., and P.L. Robertson (1995) *Firms, Markets, and Economic Change: A Dynamic Theory of Business Institutions* (London: Routledge).

Leonard-Barton, D. (1995) *Wellsprings of Knowledge: Building and Sustaining the Sources of Innovation* (Boston, MA: Harvard Business School Press).

Loasby, B. (2001) 'Cognition, Imagination and Institutions in Demand Creation', *Journal of Evolutionary Economics* 11: 7-21.

Majone, G. (1998) 'From the Positive to the Regulatory State: Causes and Consequences of Changes in the Mode of Governance', *Journal of Public Policy* 17.2: 139-67.

Mantzavinos, C. (2001) *Individuals, Institutions, and Markets* (Cambridge, MA: Cambridge University Press).

Mayntz, R., *et al.* (1978) *Vollzugsprobleme der Umweltpolitik* (Wiesbaden, Germany: Kohlhammer).

Nelson, R. (2002) 'The Problem of Market Bias in Modern Capitalist Economies', *Industrial and Corporate Change* 11.2: 207-44.

Nonaka, I., and R. Toyama (2002) 'A Firm as a Dialectical Being: Towards a Dynamic Theory of a Firm', *Industrial and Corporate Change* 11.5: 995-1,009.

North, D.C. (1990) *Institutions, Institutional Change and Economic Performance* (Cambridge, UK: Cambridge University Press).

Ostrom, E. (1998) 'A Behavioural Approach to the Rational Choice Theory of Collective Action', *American Political Science Review* 92.1: 1-22.

Pelikan, P., and G. Wegner (eds.) (2003) *The Evolutionary Analysis of Economic Policy* (Cheltenham, UK/Northampton, MA: Edward Elgar Publishing).

Porter, M., and C. van der Linde (2000) 'Green and Competitive: Ending the Stalemate', in E.F.M. Wubben (ed.), *The Dynamics of the Eco-Efficient Economy* (Cheltenham, UK/Northampton, MA: Edward Elgar Publishing): 33-55.

Sandler, T. (1992) *Collective Action: Theory and Applications* (New York: Harvester Wheatsheaf).

Scharpf, F.W. (1997) *Games Real Actors Play: Actor-Centered Institutionalism in Policy Research* (Oxford, UK: Westview Press).

Stiglitz, J. (1998) 'The Private Use of Public Interests: Incentives and Institutions', *Journal of Economic Perspectives* 12.2: 3-21.

Van Dijken, K., *et al.* (eds.) (1999) *Adoption of Environmental Innovations: The Dynamics of Innovation as Interplay between Business Competence, Environmental Orientation and Network Involvement* (Dordrecht, Netherlands: Kluwer).

Von Weizsäcker, E.U., A. Lovins and L.H. Lovins (1997) *Factor Four: Doubling Wealth: Halving Resource Use* (London: Earthscan Publications).

Williamson, O.E. (1999) 'Strategy Research: Governance and Competence Perspectives', *Strategic Management Journal* 20.12: 1,087-108.

Witt, U. (2003) *The Evolving Economy: Essays on the Evolutionary Approach to Economics* (Cheltenham UK/Northampton MA: Edward Elgar Publishing).

Young, O. (1999) *Governance in World Affairs* (Ithaca, NY/London: Cornell University Press).

11

CSR in the Scandinavian countries

A REVIEW OF VOLUNTARY VERSUS REGULATED

Eli Bleie Munkelien

DNV Research, Norway

Pia Rudolfsson Goyer

University of Oslo, Norway

co-author: Izabela Fratczak

Technical University of Lodz, Poland, and Turku Polytechnic, Finland

Corporate social responsibility (CSR) is becoming increasingly important in the sphere between government, society and corporations. Today corporations are expected to do more than make a profit, and in fact performance in the non-financial field has become a criterion against which corporations are measured.

There are several definitions of CSR in use: the World Business Council for Sustainable Development (WBCSD) defines CSR as 'the commitment of business to contribute to sustainable economic development, working with employees, their families, the local community and society at large to improve their quality of life' (WBCSD 2000). The European Union emphasises that CSR is about taking responsibility beyond legal requirements (CEC 2002).

The accelerating activities linked to CSR show us that it is here to stay, and it is now clear that the integration of social issues into business practices was not a passing phase of the 1990s. The most profound drivers for CSR are government actions, pressure from society and the importance for corporations to attain and retain goodwill. Governments around the world applaud and encourage business actors to take increased responsibility for the environment and society surrounding the corporations (McClure 2000). The result is that businesses today need to take a stronger social responsibility to uphold or to gain their 'licence to operate' or their 'licence to sell' from all their stakeholders. This is becoming increasingly more challenging and complex (Zadek 2001). The term 'stakeholder' is defined by Freeman (1984: 108) as 'any group or individual who can affect or is affected by the achievement of the organisation's objective'. The number of variables that could affect the financial bottom line appears to be growing rapidly, and losing the trust of stakeholders can be fatal (Hatcher 2002: 32-38). Stakeholders' preferences are increasingly affected by the perception of a company and its brand, with the company's reputation for social responsibility as one aspect in their choices (Brønn 2002).

The constantly growing number of non-financial reports show that such reporting is gaining support (Holland and Gibbon 2001). However, the status of extended reporting in volume and maturity varies widely between countries. The evolvement of reporting is strengthened by governments introducing regulations or laws requiring corporations to report on their environmental and social impacts, as well as their financial impact. The extent to which corporations actually engage in non-financial reporting can serve as a good indicator when examining the degree of CSR evolvement. A process of maturity is often illustrated by a pyramid; the top level of the 'CSR pyramid' would in this case indicate the reporting phase.

The main focus of this chapter is to review the extensiveness and development of CSR in the Scandinavian countries. The focus lies on the similarities and differences, but also on the question of whether governments are among the major motivating factors influencing corporations to apply CSR and issue triple-bottom-line reports.

The empirical data supporting this study was obtained through interviews with representatives from corporations and governments in the Scandinavian countries. The 20 interviewees are anonymous. They represent the following industries: retail, energy, telecommunications, forestry and manufacturing, as well as the Swedish, Norwegian and Finnish governments. Three main questions were asked: what does the government do in the CSR field?; what role should the government have in the CSR field?; what are your opinions on CSR reporting—do you think such reporting should be mandatory or voluntary? In addition, we have analysed several international surveys on non-financial reporting referred to in this chapter.

11.1 Sustainable development and CSR

Sustainable development and CSR are concepts that play an increasingly important role for governments, business and society within the 21st century. The link between these two concepts is important because governments are responsible for achieving the goals of sustainable development by signing international agreements; though it is not possible to achieve these goals without the contribution and effort of industry.

The idea of sustainable development has survived nearly a decade of rhetorical excess and academic criticism. The Brundtland Report, *Our Common Future* (WCED 1987), has remained the central goal and guiding norm of environment-and-development policies (Lafferty and Langhelle 1999). The underlying idea of sustainability existed, of course, long before this report. It is, however, only since the publication of the report that sustainability has been strongly coupled with the notion of 'development'.

Further involving industry in the work towards sustainable development was one of the driving forces behind the rise of the CSR concept. There are two nuances worth noting about the relationship between sustainable development and CSR. First, sustainable development has been understood to be dependent on a strong involvement from governments. An active governmental role has not been emphasised to the same extent with regard to CSR. On the contrary, CSR is often defined as business contribution 'beyond legal requirements' and at the same time described as a 'business contribution to sustainable development'.[1] We argue that governments have a clear task of involving, encouraging and clarifying the expectations they have in relation to the industry. To what degree this takes place varies even between the Scandinavian countries.

Second, CSR is sometimes defined as the social dimension of sustainable development, while at the same time sustainable development can be understood as solely environmental. Economists' response to the CSR phenomenon was to introduce the concept of the triple bottom line, which came into play as an attempt to try to encapsulate for business what are defined as the three spheres of sustainability; the economic, environmental and social. Bebbington and Thomson (1996) stated that this concept challenges the traditional understanding of 'sustainability' as concerning only environmental aspects, and underlines that all three spheres are important to a successful business and that they can be accounted for.

11.2 Triple-bottom-line reporting

In an explanation of the terminology we use throughout this chapter, it should be noted that non-financial reports are more commonly referred to as triple-bottom-line reports or sustainability reports. As outlined by John Elkington in his book *Cannibals with Forks* (Elkington 1998), the term 'triple bottom line' refers to social, environmental as well as financial impacts and achievements of a corporation. A company's bottom line is an economic term, used by standard accounting practices. This approach is, however, seen as a model for environmental and social reporting.

Before presenting the surveys on non-financial reporting it is necessary to briefly mention the best known and most important CSR reporting initiative—the Global Reporting Initiative (GRI).[2] The GRI gives guidelines on reporting principles and universal indicators. It aims at delivering comparable data on CSR performance. This has, however, proven difficult. A positive sign, however, is the increasing number of corporations applying the guidelines as far as they find feasible, in addition to the current development toward sector-specific guidelines within this framework. The GRI guide-

---

1 Such as in one communication from the European Commission concerning 'Corporate Social Responsibility: A Business Contribution to Sustainable Development'. This understanding of CSR and sustainable development is also supported by the WBCSD (see the definition on page 182).

2 GRI was instigated in 1997 (by CERES and UNEP) and the initial work has included hundreds of partners contributing on a voluntary basis (GRI 2002).

lines encompass the triple bottom line, though not the traditional financial indicators (information on the profitability of an organisation). 'By contrast, economical indicators in the sustainability reporting context focus more on the manner in which an organisation affects the stakeholders with whom it has direct and indirect economic interaction' (GRI 2002: 46).

Following this, the term 'triple-bottom-line reporting' is throughout this study equated with non-financial reporting. The term 'non-financial' will, however, be applied when the reporting does not encompass the entire triple bottom line, but instead covers specific aspects such as health, safety or environment.

11.2.1 The extent of non-financial reporting

There exist a large number of surveys on the development of triple-bottom-line reporting. To give an impression of the development of such reporting, some of the international surveys are given in Table 11.1.

Survey conducted by	Year	Who was surveyed	Findings
MORI	2001	World's 100 largest corporations	50% report, up from 44% in 2000
KPMG	2002a	Top 100 in 19 countries	23% social reports, 16% HSE reports
PWC	2003	1,000 CEOs from 43 countries	66% report, 37% in separate report
NextStep	2003	FTSE100	90 report, 72 in separate reports, up from 66/55 in 2002
Context and SalterBaxter	2003	FTSE 250	132 report on environment, 100 also on social issues, up from 30 in 1998

TABLE 11.1 Selected surveys on non-financial reporting

According to the GRI, as of May 2003, there are 260 GRI reporting businesses spread over 27 countries (see Fig. 11.1), including 26 of the Global *Fortune* 100 as well as 20% of Dow Jones Average and the FTSE 100 companies.[3] The geographical dispersal of GRI usage in the Scandinavian countries is that between one and 15 corporations use the GRI.[4]

With regard to such international surveys as cited in Table 11.1 it is important to take account of the number of replies to the survey—but even more so the number of corporations not replying. One has to assume that the corporations not responding in these surveys do not report on aspects other than their financial performance. Even though the response was as high as 97% in the survey conducted by MORI, it is important to keep this in mind.

3   Presented by GRI in the Corporate Governance and Globalisation forum in Oslo, 10 June 2003.
4   It should be noted that these figures are based on companies having published a report (current or previous) referencing the GRI Guidelines. By listing a company name, GRI does not certify the report's conformance to the guidelines.

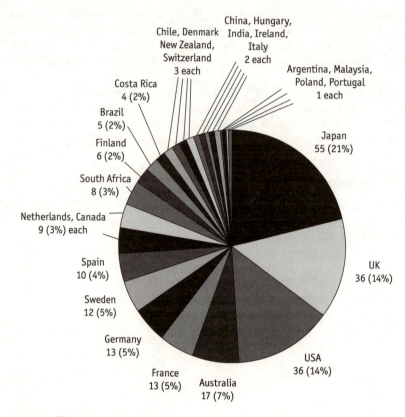

FIGURE 11.1 GRI reports by country

Another aspect is the diversity of these reports: no two of them are alike. The international surveys cited above also reflect this through their usage of different names on the surveys: KPMG, 'corporate social responsibility reporting'; PwC, 'Sustainability survey report'; and others using 'triple-bottom-line reports' or 'environmental and social reports'.

One explanation of the surprisingly high numbers of non-financial reporting may also be that these surveys include absolutely all aspects exceeding pure financial reporting. This means that countries with binding regulation requiring reporting on health, safety and environmental issues will come out disproportionately high. Therefore, many of the reports included in the surveys cannot automatically be categorised as triple-bottom-line reports. One must also take into account that all the corporations surveyed are large and transnational. If we were to look at medium-sized corporations, the reporting rate would be much lower, even more so for small businesses.

Nevertheless, all these surveys show an increase in number of non-financial reports and an increase in the coverage of CSR issues. The demand and focus of such reporting is not decreasing. This is also evident when analysing the Scandinavian countries.

11.3 CSR in the Scandinavian countries

A debate on whether governments should take the lead in promoting CSR and whether the method should be stick or carrot is not concluded. Neither are the roles of civil society, government and corporations in the field of CSR cemented. These uncertainties create opportunities for many possible models.

The Scandinavian countries are known for their common history, strong social democracy, similar culture and scattered demographic settlements. Another important similarity is the phenomenon of developing industry close to natural resources, forcing the corporations to take on total responsibility for their employees by providing houses as well as schools and infrastructure. Today many of these corporations still have a reputation for taking on social responsibilities. Considering the homogeneity of the Scandinavian countries, it is probable that they would choose a common path when dealing with CSR.

With the aim of shedding light on the actual situations, we have conducted case studies showing the different corporate and governmental CSR approaches in Norway, Denmark, Finland and Sweden (between 1999 and 2003). As will be shown below, the Scandinavian countries are not taking a common path as would be expected.

11.3.1 CSR in Norway

The Norwegian Accounting Act makes it mandatory for corporations to include issues relating to health and safety in their annual reports. Norwegian corporations are exceeded only by the UK in the survey comparing the inclusion of information on health, safety and environment (HSE), or sustainability in annual reports (KPMG 2002b: 16). Of the Norwegian annual reports, 81% include health and safety issues (KPMG 2002b: 16).

The Norwegian Accounting Act also requires corporations to include in their annual reports information on their environmental impact when this impact becomes 'more than insignificant'[5] (Regnskapsloven 1999: §3-3). This requirement is not met to the same degree. In 2001, only 35% of the top 100 corporations were actually fulfilling the requirements of the Accounting Act (Ruud and Larsen 2002)—the loophole being the wording 'more than insignificant'. The same survey was conducted in 2002, and the findings show a decrease: that only 28% of the largest and most polluting corporations satisfy the requirement (Ruud and Larsen 2002). Hopefully this is about to change.

The latest development is an evaluation of the accounting law, acquired by the Norwegian parliament and circulated for comment in September 2003. The evaluation committee's recommendation is a clear weakening in the HSE and environmental reporting requirements and a move away from the general trend in other countries. The suggested wording is that corporations should only report on such issues 'as far as it is found necessary to understand the corporation's financial position, risks, development and results' (NOU 2003: 23 §3.3).[6]

---

5   Our translation.
6   Our translation. The committee's recommendations were not accepted but rather a new requirement for reporting on gender equality was added and made valid from financial year 2001.

In Norway the responsibility for CSR has been placed within the Ministry of Foreign Affairs. This is characteristic of the general CSR focus in Norway today where CSR is perceived to be relevant only when doing business in developing countries. In co-operation with NHO (Confederation of Norwegian Business and Industry) the Ministry of Foreign Affairs initiated a discussion forum called KOMpakt (the Consultative Body for Human Rights and Norwegian Economic Involvement Abroad) in 1999, which has also produced a number of valuable reports and guidelines for corporations.[7]

Even though the Organisation for Economic Co-operation and Development (OECD) guidelines and the United Nations (UN) Global Compact are emphasised by the Norwegian government as the major initiatives in the CSR field, these are not known in the Norwegian business community. This became evident through a survey of Norwegian top managers, when 42% stated that they had never or barely heard of CSR or knew the concept (Argument 2003). The fact that the questionnaire was sent out to 300 CEOs in the largest Norwegian corporations and only 63 responded also supports the notion of little knowledge of CSR in Norway.

Through an interview with an official from the Norwegian government, it became clear that the government is aware of this situation; the need for closer dialogue between the government and the corporations is one element that has been part of the revitalisation of the CSR process. Another element in this process is to broaden the mandate to include all aspects of CSR and to make sure that several ministries have an active share in the CSR work. Action taken in this regard has so far been to extend the number of participants from business and relevant ministries in the KOMpakt forum. Whether or not this measure is sufficient, and if there are further initiatives planned to meet these challenges and goals will be interesting to observe in the future.

All interviewees in the Norwegian corporations recommended a clearer and stronger governmental involvement (DNV Research 2002). The role of the government, both as regulator, co-ordinator and as an information provider, was thought to be very important. According to the interviewees, the government should take a larger and more prominent role, assist corporations, push for some unifying standards or principles and co-operate with corporations to a larger extent. Another point raised was that the government should act as a good example and lead the way by applying stricter requirements when inviting tenders and when purchasing.

11.3.2 CSR in Denmark

The Danish government has actively promoted CSR through different initiatives such as having;

- Funded a CSR project developing a human rights impact assessment (HRIA) (Aaronsen and Reeves 2002)

---

7   Those are: (1999) *Article 1: Business Aspects of Human Rights Work*; (2001) *Article 2: Normative Aspects of Human Rights Work; Article 3: Political Measures to Ensure that Business Take Responsibility for Human Rights; Article 4: Corporate Responsibility in the 21st Century*; and *Article 5: Socially Responsible Companies. What? Why? How?* (Ministry of Foreign Affairs, Norway).

- Funded the development of a social impact assessment[8] in 2000 (Beskæfti-gelsesministeriet 2003a)

- Established a certification scheme for the working environment develop-ment.[9] The certificate requires that the corporation or the actual workplace implements a management system for protecting the working environment. This includes internal and external reporting of policy, plans and performance (Beskæftigelsesministeriet 2003b).

- Established the organisation The Copenhagen Centre (TCC) to promote vol-untary partnerships between business, civil society and governmental agen-cies. TCC is a partner in CSR Europe which is well known in international CSR arenas but less well known in Denmark.

- Established mandatory meeting place for governmental–private partnerships in local authorities (some were perceived to be a success while others were no— a comment made in an interview).

The focus of most of the initiatives from the Danish Government has been concerned with work environment-related issues. Their work on this started as early as 1994 with the Ministry of Social Affairs initiating the campaign 'Our Common Concern: The Social Responsibility of the Corporate Sector'. The Danish Ministry of Labour (Beskæftigelses Ministeriet) is now responsible for CSR within the government. In offi-cial speeches on CSR only topics of the inclusive labour market (*det rommelige arbeid-sliv*) are elaborated on.

The Danish government was the only one of the Scandinavian governments not will-ing to participate in this study; all inquiries for an interview were responded to with a reference to their web page.[10] Through the information on their web page one can read that it perceives its role to be an: organiser, decrease bureaucracy, give information, be a good example for corporations themselves, and encourage corporations to take vol-untary action.

Denmark has two relevant laws: the Annual Accounts Act (2001) and the Green Accounts Act (1996). The Annual Accounts Act's reporting requirements on intellectual capital resources and environmental aspects are applicable only if material in provid-ing a true and fair view of the company's financial status. The Green Accounts Act applies only to certain listed activities. These laws therefore have little implication for general non-financial reporting in Denmark.

There has been some confusion as to whether the Danish government requires triple-bottom-line reporting or not. In the newsletter *Business Respect* (2001) it is written:

> The Danish Government is to introduce a set of legal measures to encourage companies to report on issues of wage disparities, ethnic representation, acci-dents at work, CO_2 emission and companies' policies on child labour . . . Companies that do not achieve the proposed standard by 2003 will face finan-cial penalty (article source: CSR Europe).

---

8   Our translation of 'Det Sociale Indeks'.
9   This was announced by the Danish Minister of Labour on 21 October 2001.
10   www.bm.dk

This was allegedly stated by the Danish Department of Trade and Industry. We have, however, not been able to verify this, nor seen any traces of this on the Danish Ministry's website. The only information accessible on this subject from the Danish Department of Trade and Industry is a speech held at the IBC Euroforum conference on 20 September 2001 on the theme 'From Financial Reports to Annual Reporting'.[11] Social reporting is here presented as part of the 'Governmental Industry Strategy'[12] called *dk21* where the development of voluntary codes for triple-bottom-line reporting is part of a project running until October 2003. While working on this chapter we have tried to obtain more information regarding the outcome of this project and the actual governmental requirement on triple-bottom-line reporting in Denmark, regretfully without success.[13]

The perception of CSR solely being a 'labour market' issue was also supported through the process of interviews with Danish corporations. It was very difficult to get in contact with those responsible for or working with CSR/sustainability in the corporations. Regretfully, only two interviews were possible. These interviews confirmed that CSR in Denmark is perceived to evolve around internal labour issues and did not include international challenges or topics such as corruption and human rights. Information, engagement and help on international-related CSR issues from the government were thought to be lacking.

11.3.3 CSR in Sweden

In Sweden, the government seems to have a pragmatic and well-defined approach towards CSR. All its activities were, in March 2002, gathered under the same umbrella when the Swedish government launched its initiative called 'Swedish Partnership for Global Responsibility' (Swedish Ministry for Foreign Affairs 2002). The foundation for this new initiative was the government's international commitments under the OECD Guidelines for Multinational Enterprises[14] together with its active support of the UN Global Compact.[15] The Swedish government clearly emphasises that its role is different from that of the business community. While the government enacts laws and regulations, corporations will supplement this work, of course, by adhering to these laws, but also by acting as good ambassadors abroad applying the same basic values no matter where they do business. Furthermore, the government has taken on the task of clearly communicating what is expected from corporations, by stating what corporations should and should not do, by offering assistance and advice, and by presenting good examples showing how they can develop their social commitments.[16]

---

11   Our translation of 'Fra årsregnskap til årsrapport', Økonomi og Erhvervsministeriet.
12   Our translation of 'regjeringens erhvervsstrategi'.
13   The Danish Department of Trade and Industry has not replied to emails and phone messages, and no further information has been available on their web page.
14   See www.oecd.org/document/28/0,2340,en_2649_34889_2397532_1_1_1_1,00.html, accessed 1 April 2004.
15   The Global Compact is an initiative made by the UN Secretary General, where he encourages the business community to take larger responsibilities in the field of environment, labour issues, human rights and corruption. See www.unglobalcompact.org.
16   Information on 'Globalt Ansvar' is to be found at the government's website: www.utrikes. regeringen.se/ga.

There are no laws in Sweden obliging corporations to report on their activities in the social field. However, corporations that, because of their environmentally hazardous activities, are required to have environmental permits or to keep the environmental authorities notified, have a certain duty to report on their activities in their annual report (Annual Accounts Act 1995).

'The Swedish Export Credits Guarantee Board' is an agency that in its daily work has to relate to CSR when financially supporting Swedish corporations operating abroad. This governmental agency offers corporations, banks and other finance institutions doing business with other countries a guarantee, securing these against losses made in connection with export transactions and investments. This board's policy is to not grant any guarantees to projects that obstruct social and/or economic development or have negative effects on the environment of the foreign country in question.[17] From a CSR point of view, this policy is certainly the most interesting Swedish example where social responsibilities and corporate activities are formally linked and applied in practice.

Interviews with representatives from three large Swedish corporations were carried out. All interviewees expressed that the Swedish government has chosen the right path when giving support to the business community instead of creating binding regulation. However, all interviewees were of the opinion that the initiative 'Swedish Partnership for Global Responsibility' was probably more important for small or medium-sized corporations than for the very large ones, many of which often already have a social agenda. Two of the respondents emphasised that the government should discuss frequently appearing problems facing corporations doing business in developing countries, with colleagues in other governments. Local business partners neglecting national legislation were claimed to be a problem that creates situations where Swedish corporations find themselves trying to convince local subcontractors to adhere to their own national laws. This was considered both frustrating and time-consuming. The fact that the Ministry for Foreign Affairs has now gone public with its report on the human rights situation in different countries was seen as a good example showing how governments can contribute to increased knowledge about foreign countries' situations.[18]

Despite the fact that progress has been made in the CSR field in Sweden, there are still business representatives holding the opinion that CSR involvement can be bad for business. As has been shown above, the view of the government is the complete opposite: that the connection between CSR and the label 'Made in Sweden' can be a competitive advantage for Swedish corporations operating abroad. The first and necessary step of the Swedish government has therefore been claimed to be to convince the business community of the 'CSR business case'.

11.3.4 CSR in Finland

This case study differs markedly from the other country analyses, due to difficulties in attaining documents, surveys or academic papers on CSR in Finland.

---

17   See www.ekn.se/cgi-bin/om/hipc_lander.pl, accessed 1 April 2004.

18   See 'Landrapporter' (our translation: 'country reports') written by officials at Sweden's embassies around the world, at www.manskligarattigheter.gov.se/extra/page, accessed 1 April 2004.

Finnish corporations think of CSR as something natural—like a core value. They underline the voluntary nature of integrating social and environmental concerns into their operations, and the importance of interaction with stakeholders. The interviewees considered CSR as necessary when doing business but stressed that as long as it is based on voluntarism it endows them with valuable freedom of operating, and that this in fact encourages them to increase their involvement in this field. Although many Finnish corporations appear to have knowledge of CSR, some of them have problems explaining their understanding of it. A similar situation came to light when contacting the government's office—they had problems finding who was responsible for CSR issues.

Through an interview with a governmental official, it became clear that the Finnish government also supports the voluntary character of CSR. It hopes that the discussion on the Green Paper from the EU will lead to recommendations for measures, with the aim of establishing a framework for the development of CSR at European and national levels (Finnish Government 2001). According to the government, this would not require the creation of separate EU standards—the content of CSR was considered as being sufficiently covered in the UN, ILO and OECD instruments. Neither the government nor the business community expect any legal framework on CSR.

The Finnish corporations' representatives interviewed explained that they would like to see the government providing guidelines on CSR and taking part in the CSR debate. They also expressed that the government should take measures to influence customers, so that they will appreciate more socially responsible companies and stimulate development of CSR by using financial tools (e.g. extra tax deductions). Finnish companies experience problems with practising CSR while operating abroad. They believe that the Finnish government could assist them in doing business responsibly abroad by negotiating with foreign authorities, and giving guidance on how to develop a socially responsible way of operating.

The Finnish government seems to meet some of these expectations: for example, by supporting the Finnish Ethical Forum which brings together different members of society to discuss CSR issues, and by arranging a contest for best environmental and social report. These incentives stimulate competitiveness among corporations and draw public attention to corporations doing well in the CSR field.

Generally, Finnish corporations see social policy statements as unnecessary since activities in this field are considered 'self-evident and obvious'. They realise that there is a new market demand for reporting in this field, but they stress that such reports should only have the status of 'light documents' and be limited only to certain major issues. They meet no demands on this issue from Finnish accounting acts, but the interviewees were in favour of standardised reporting guidelines (such as the GRI) in order to obtain more knowledge on how to report and on what issues. According to one of the interviewees, reporting demands a lot of effort and incurs expense. From that perspective, it was considered unfair to make it mandatory particularly for small or medium-sized corporations.

11.3.5 Reporting: a comparative analysis of the Scandinavian countries

A survey from KPMG analyses the sustainability reporting habits of the top 100 companies in 19 countries, out of which 14 were European (see Fig. 11.2; KPMG 2002a). The survey shows that the number of reports containing more than financial data are increasing. It also indicates a clear trend toward including performance on more issues than HSE. The reporting of social issues has clearly risen every year for ten years, since 1993; when these surveys were initiated (KPMG 2002a).[19]

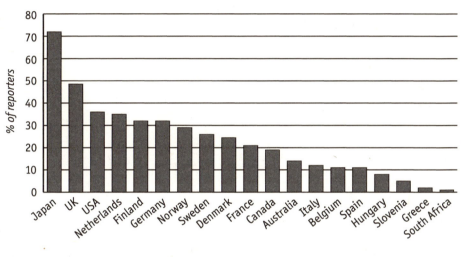
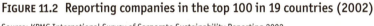

FIGURE 11.2 Reporting companies in the top 100 in 19 countries (2002)

Source: KPMG International Survey of Corporate Sustainability Reporting 2002

What is the status of triple-bottom-line reporting in the Scandinavian countries, and is it possible to draw links to the respective governments' initiative and focus on CSR?

Of the 100 largest Norwegian companies, 29% issued a separate non-financial (HSE or sustainability) report in 2002. This is only 1% above the average for the 11 countries surveyed (28%) (KPMG 2002b). Norway is 7th, exceeded by Japan, UK, USA, the Netherlands, Germany and Finland. Norway is also among the six countries that have seen a decrease in number of reports from the last such survey in 1999 (explained by foreign mergers and acquisitions). Non-financial reports cover primarily environment-related issues (49%), though it is interesting to notice that 34% of the reports have transformed into triple-bottom-line ones.

---

19 When correlating for the rise in number of countries being looked at in the last year (19 instead of 11).

Of the 100 largest Danish corporations, 25% issue non-financial reports today, about the same rate as Norway and Sweden (KPMG 2002); three are using the GRI guidelines.

A survey was made in 2003 examining the extent to which Swedish corporations listed on the Stockholm stock exchange actually have policies and issue reports in the non-financial fields.[20] The survey showed that 50% of the corporations questioned claimed to have an ethics policy, 45% issue environment reports, but only 6% make some kind of social reporting. There were 5% saying that they had some kind of sustainability reporting, and 8% were in the process of developing one (CKS Sustainability 2003).

According to the survey conducted by KPMG, 32% of Finnish corporations have published CSR reports. It is the highest rate among Scandinavian countries and ranks Finland 5th on the list. There are eight GRI reporters in Finland.

11.4 Conclusion

Even though all governments in Scandinavia have endorsed the Global Compact, and encourage corporations in the respective countries to sign the ten principles, very few have. In Sweden 17 corporations have signed them, in Denmark 13, in Norway nine and in Finland only four.[21] When compared with countries such as Brazil where 76 have signed, or France where 180 have signed, the Scandinavian numbers are not very impressive (even when taking into account the differences in size).

The Norwegian companies are above average in surveys listing numbers of companies publishing other than financial reports. But the numbers are based on the effects of laws and regulations. The number of corporations involved in GRI and the number of corporations reporting on the whole triple bottom line is still low. So are the number of corporations that are familiar with the CSR concept. Of the many important issues addressed through CSR, the Norwegian government has focused on transnational corporations' behaviour when operating in developing countries, and the concern for human rights. This was also reflected through interviews with corporations' representatives saying that they miss a stronger and clearer governmental engagement covering the entire CSR agenda.

Denmark differs from the other Scandinavian countries with regard to their internal focus of CSR. One reason could be the Danish government's campaign to enlist corporations' help in solving the social problem of high unemployment in the 1980 and 1990s. The Danish government has not extended the concept of social responsibility beyond the issues of the labour market and this is clearly mirrored in the Danish corporations' understanding of CSR.

The Swedish government appears to have the most active and conscious approach to CSR compared to the other governments in Scandinavia. Despite this, the level of triple-

20   20% of the corporations (66 in number) were randomly selected and data was gathered through telephone interviews; 60 of these corporations replied to all questions in the survey.
21   The numbers were taken from the Global Compact web page, 26 September 2003.

bottom-line reporting is still quite low. Swedish corporations concentrate their CSR efforts on policy-making instead of reporting, and existing reports deal almost exclusively with environmental issues. As in the case of Norway, legal requirements are the most probable explanation for the strong environmental focus of the reports.

For Finnish corporations CSR is, by and large, something perceived as a core value. That is why they claim that they do not need any mandatory regulation regarding CSR. No form of non-financial reporting is mandatory in Finland, but still such reporting is quite common and more common than in the other Scandinavian countries. The government's role in Finland has rather been to inform and give incentives, such as the competition for the best triple-bottom-line report.

Even though the Scandinavian countries in many ways appear quite homogenous, there are vast differences concerning the CSR approaches chosen, both by the governments and the corporate sector. Quite surprisingly, the CSR focus chosen by the different governments ranges from no particular focus (Finland) to a purely national focus (Denmark), to a strong focus on corporate activities in the developing countries (Norway and Sweden). There are also variations in the field of legislation requiring non-financial reporting: where Finland has no such legislation, where the situation in Denmark is uncertain (unverifiable), where Norwegian law prescribes mandatory reporting for corporations in general and where Swedish legislation prescribes mandatory reporting for certain kinds of corporations. It is rather striking that the corporate sector in the Scandinavian countries spoke almost with one voice, saying that it prefers a stronger involvement from government—not necessarily more regulation but more support and dialogue.

The reasons for the large variations of the CSR focus among the Scandinavian countries have not been looked at in depth in this study. Rather we have tried to confirm whether there are differences and what these differences consist of. A link between mandatory reporting and corporations involved in CSR was not found, but the study shows a close link between what the government chooses to focus on and their degree of action and what activities the corporations respond with.

References

Aaronsen, S.E., and J.T. Reeves (2002) *Corporate Responsibility in the Global Village: The Role of Public Policy* (Washington, DC: National Policy Association).

Annual Accounts Act (2001) Denmark, www.retsinfo.dk.

Annual Accounts Act (1995) Sweden, 1554, ch. 6, § 9, www.riksdagen.se.

Argument (2003) *Topplederundersøkelse om Corporate Social Responsibility (CSR)* (Oslo: Argument Gruppen).

Bebbington, J., and I. Thomson (1996) *Business Conceptions of Sustainability and the Implications for Accountancy* (ACCA Research Report; London: ACCA).

Beskæftigelsesministeriet (2003a) *Beskæftigelsesminister Claus Hjort Fredriksens tal ved lanceringen av Det Sociale Indeks*, 19. og 21. august 2003 (third version).

—— (2003b) 'Værktøj til virksomheder til at arbejde med socialt ansvar', *Nyt fra Beskæftigelsesministeriet—Nr. 9 September 2003*.

Brønn, P. (2002) 'Corporate Communication and the Corporate Brand', in P.S. Brønn and R. Wiig (eds.), *Corporate Communication: A Strategic Approach to Building Reputation* (Oslo: Gyldendal).

Business Respect (2001) *Business Respect—CSR Dispatches* 14/6 (October 2001), www.mallenbaker.net/csr/nl/14.html#Anchor-Denmark-58019v.

CEC (Commission of the European Communities) (2002) *Communication from the Commission concerning Corporate Social Responsibility: A Business Contribution to Sustainable Development,* COM(2002) 347 final, 2 July 2002.

CKS Sustainability (2003) *Undersökning: CSR i börsnoterade svenska företag* (Spring 2003).

Context and SalterBaxter (2003) *Trends in CSR Reporting 2002-03* (London: Context).

DNV Research (2002) *A Pilot Survey on CSR* (Report no. 2002-0873; Norway: DNV Research).

Elkington, J. (1998) *Cannibals with Forks: The Triple Bottom Line of 21st Century Business* (Oxford, UK: New Society Publishers).

Finnish Government (2001) Response to the Commission's Green Paper on Corporate Social Responsibility COM(2001)366 final, 12 December 2001, Helsinki, Finland.

Freeman, R.E. (1984) *Strategic Management: A Stakeholder Approach* (Boston, MA: Pitman).

Green Accounts Act (1996) Denmark, www.retsinfo.dk.

GRI (Global Reporting Initiative) (2002) *Sustainability Reporting Guidelines,* www.globalreporting.org.

Hatcher, M. (2002) 'New Corporate Agendas', *Journal of Public Affairs,* 3.1: 32-38.

Holland, L., and J. Gibbon (2001) 'Processes in Social and Ethical Accountability: External Reporting Mechanisms', *Perspectives on Corporate Citizenship* (Sheffield, UK: Greenleaf Publishing): 278-95.

KOMpakt (1999) *Article 1: Business Aspects of Human Rights Work* (Norway: Ministry of Foreign Affairs).

—— (2001) *Article 2: Normative Aspects of Human Rights Work* (Norway: Ministry of Foreign Affairs).

—— (2001) *Article 3: Political Measures to Ensure that Business Take Responsibility for Human Rights* (Norway: Ministry of Foreign Affairs).

—— (2001) *Article 4: Corporate Responsibility in the 21st Century* (Norway: Ministry of Foreign Affairs).

—— (2001) *Article 5: Socially Responsible Companies. What? Why? How?* (Norway: Ministry of Foreign Affairs).

KPMG (2002a) *KPMG International Survey of Corporate Social Responsibility Reporting 2002: Environmental Social Economic* (available at www.wimm.nl).

—— (2002b) *KPMGs Internasjonale Undersøkelse om Bærekraftighetsrapportering 2002, Norske Resultater,* Oslo, Norway.

Lafferty, W.M., and O. Langhelle (eds.) (1999) *Towards Sustainable Development* (London: Macmillan).

McClure, P. (2000) *Participation Support for a More Equitable Society* (Canberra, Australia: Reference Group on Welfare Reform).

NextStep (2003) www.nextstep.co.uk/overviewpub.php.

NOU (Norges offentlige utredninger) (2003: 23) *Evaluering av regnskapsloven.* Utredning fra utvalg oppnevnt ved kongelig resolusjon 7 June 2002.

PricewaterhouseCoopers LLP (2003) 'Leadership, Responsibility, and Growth in Uncertain Times', in *6th Annual Global CEO Survey,* in conjunction with the World Economic Forum, www.pwcglobal.com/extweb/pwcpublications.nsf/4bd5f76b48e282738525662b00739e22/595a8807a38c1ae685256cb70042ob5a/$FILE/CEO_Survey_2003.pdf, accessed 1 April 2004.

Regnskapsloven (1999) Norway, §3-3, www.lovdata.no.

Ruud, A., and O.M. Larsen (2002) Miljørapportering i årsberetningen; Følger Norske bedrifter Regnskapslovens pålegg?, Rapport nr. 2/02, www.prosus.uio.no/publikasjoner/Rapporter/2002-8/Rapp8.pdf.

Swedish Ministry for Foreign Affairs (2002) *Open Letter of 6 March 2002 from the Ministry of Foreign Affairs to the Swedish Business Community.*

WBCSD (World Business Council for Sustainable Development) (2000) *Corporate Social Responsibility: Making Good Business Sense* (Geneva: WBCSD): 10.

—— (2001) *The Business Case for Sustainable Development: Making a Difference toward the Johannesburg Summit 2002 and Beyond* (Geneva: WBCSD; www.wbcsd.org/web/publications/business-case.pdf).

WCED (The World Commission on Environment and Development) (1987) *Our Common Future* ('The Brundtland Report'; Oxford, UK: Oxford University Press).

Zadek, S. (2001) *The Civil Corporation, The New Economy of Corporate Citizenship* (London: Earthscan Publications).

Interviews performed in September 2003

Norway: Energy 2, forest 1, telecommunications 1, retail 1 and government.
  (See DNV Research, A pilot survey on CSR, Report no. 2002-0873 [2002])
Denmark: Retail 1, pharmaceutical 1, Copenhagen Centre and government.
Finland: Energy 1, forest 1, telecommunications 2, retail 1 and government.
Sweden: Telecommunications 1, retail/process 2 and government.

12
Governance and management of protected areas in Canada and Mexico

Angeles Mendoza Durán and Dixon Thompson
University of Calgary, Canada

Krahmann (2003) suggests that, globally, 'governance' is defined by the fragmentation of political authority in seven dimensions: geography, function, resources, interests, norms, decision-making and policy implementation. He also indicates that few studies have been done on how the rise of governance arrangements at different levels might be linked. The concept of governance has been applied to private and public organisations, and in areas such as commerce or the privatisation of public services. Discussions about how governance is changing in areas of the public administration responsible for natural resources and how this is linked to other governance levels are rare. This may be in part because governance and management effectiveness are two interdependent concepts recently introduced into natural resource management theory and because new arrangements are rising in this field. The current debate turns around how to improve Protected Areas (PAs) governance and management. Given that governance involves different actors, this chapter addresses what the public sector is doing to improve PAs governance and management and what can be done to improve in these aspects. To answer these questions, this chapter discusses the following points, based on lessons from Canada and Mexico:

- What factors influence PAs governance and management?

- What interrelationships exist among governance at global, national and corporate levels and PAs management and governance?

- What schemes have been adopted for assessing governance and management effectiveness for PAs?

- What elements could be incorporated in future schemes?

12.1 Methodology

This chapter is based on four main sources:

1. Case studies (Yin 1994). Five PAs in Canada and five in Mexico were selected based on their relevance for biodiversity conservation, the presence of endangered migratory species shared by both countries, and the existence of a management team and a management plan. Mexico and Canada were chosen because they represent two different tendencies in management of Protected Areas, and two levels of governance and economic development within North America. Governance indicators for 2002 put Canada in the 93rd percentile worldwide and Mexico in the 57th percentile (Kaufmann *et al.* 2003).

2. Key informant interviews (Punch 1998; Yin 1994). Managers and staff of case studies and national agencies were interviewed between November 2002 and November 2003. Topics included, but were not limited to: governance; management; legislation; stakeholders; ecosystem-based management; environmental management systems; operations; management effectiveness; and barriers and driving forces to achieve social, environmental and social objectives. A deep analysis of the whole network shaping PAs governance is beyond the scope of this chapter. The names of key informants and their affiliations are not disclosed to respect anonymity requests. Throughout the document, the information provided by interviewees is referred to only as 'Informant'.

3. Literature search and document review (Strauss and Corbin 1998; Yin 1994). The review covered laws and documents related to management of PAs in both countries, technical and non-technical literature related to the case studies, and guidelines for assessing governance and management of Protected Areas endorsed by the World Commission on Protected Areas (WCPA).

4. Observations and notes (Punch 1998; Yin 1994). One of the authors (Mendoza) visited the case studies and both authors participated in international conferences on PA management. These included the World Park Congress (Durban, South Africa, 8–17 September 2003) and the V Science and Management of Protected Areas Conference (Victoria, BC, Canada, 11–16 May 2003).

12.2 Protected Areas

Protected Areas (PAs) are areas of land and/or sea, managed through legislation or other means, and especially dedicated to the protection and maintenance of biological diversity, and natural and associated cultural resources (IUCN 1994). Nowadays, PAs are promoted as a strategy to achieve sustainable development that seeks to balance local development needs and biodiversity conservation at national or global levels (Sayer 1999; WCPA 2003). However, they were created for other purposes originally. Banff, the first Canadian National Park, was created for recreation and business in 1885 (Bella

1987). Desierto de los Leones, the first Mexican protected area, was created for protection of water springs in 1876 (SEMARNAT 2001).

Two trends have dominated among PAs management. Paper parks, the first trend, consisted of lands protected in name only. Paper parks experienced continuing degradation due to illegal uses, lack of effective governance and management, and lack of resources or political will (Dudley *et al.* 1999a, 1999b). This trend characterised most Mexican PAs (SEMARNAT 2001). Parks for profit, the second trend, emphasised managing parks as recreation businesses to promote economic development and generate revenue. This characterised Canadian parks during the 1980s (Bella 1987; Searle 2000). Both trends led PAs to become an area of public administration characterised by inadequate governance, lack of management, low funding and low accountability (Dudley *et al.* 1999b). The pressure for overcoming these deficiencies has led PA authorities and funding organisations to propose ways to improve management effectiveness. However, progress in this aspect may be limited by other factors influencing governance and management at various levels.

12.3   Factors affecting governance and management of Protected Areas

12.3.1   Issues

Downsizing and privatisation

The focus on conservation and not on profit is one reason why the trend to manage government as a business has not always been successful (Kaufmann and Kraay 2003; Thompson 2002). During the 1990s, Parks Canada adopted an entrepreneurial approach looking for strategies to generate more revenue and cut costs. Changes included: reducing staff; attracting more visitors; increasing fees; pursuing partnerships with the public sector; privatising selected services; and restructuring the parks as business units, each with its own investment and revenue targets (Searle 2000). Repercussions for Parks Canada were: the confusion about whether conservation or recreation was the priority for management, demoralisation of staff due to job insecurity and conflicts between personal and corporate ethics, loss of intellectual capital, and an ageing workforce (Informant; PC 2000; Searle 2000). To reverse these consequences, in 2000 Parks Canada was restructured as an agency and ecological integrity was emphasised in the Canadian Parks Act (GC 2000) as a priority for managing parks.

Financing

PAs are a luxury that is hard for poor countries to afford (De Lopez 2001; Ferraro 2001) and one of the first areas affected by cuts in budgets. However, allowing corporate sponsorship in PAs raises concerns because of potential conflicts between private and conservation interests (Barton 2000). In Mexico, the creation and maintenance of PAs rely on foreign assistance through contributions from the Global Environmental Facility, The Nature Conservancy and the World Bank (Informant). In Canada, PAs operate with a mix of federal budget, revenues and donations (Informant). In Mexico, the federal laws and structure of the public administration did not allow for charging fees in PAs until 2002. Now it is possible to charge user fees (CAN$1.20/day) and use tax incentives to attract corporate sponsorship (Informant). In Canada, parks have been charging fees for visiting parks and historic sites (CAN$5.00/day on average). Federal policies have not been modified to allow corporate sponsorship. Federal budgets and fees are not sufficient to provide services to visitors, capitalise infrastructure and implement conservation plans (Informant).

Land tenure

In Canada and Mexico, land expropriation to create PAs caused conflicts between PA managers and former landowners. In Mexico, most decrees did not come with the economic compensation for previous owners or the allocation of resources for managing PAs. This brought a lack of control on protected lands that translated into land invasions and illegal uses. In Canada, PAs were usually created on crown lands or by purchasing private lands. However, there are pending aboriginal land claims affecting various PAs. Thus, new PAs consider co-management with aboriginal groups.

Law enforcement

PAs governance relies on enforcement of existing laws, but enforcement is complex and bureaucratic in Mexico. PAs lack the equivalent of a warden service. Prosecution involves different agencies and support from armed forces to confront armed groups engaged in illegal activities. Inspectors from the Procuraduría Federal de Protección al Ambiente (Federal Environmental Attorney, PROFEPA) are the prosecutor arm of the Secretaría del Medio Ambiente y Recursos Naturales (Ministry of Environment and Natural Resources, SEMARNAT), but they are few and lack appropriate training. Local people hired as wardens lack adequate training or equipment, and their role is limited to filing complaints. Having staff with prosecution authority would speed up enforcement (Informant). Canada has a well-established park warden service, and wardens are professionals with training in different aspects of law enforcement and safety. Nevertheless, there are pending issues concerning the reorganisation of responsibilities between park wardens and the Royal Canadian Mounted Police.

12.4 Multi-level governance and Protected Areas

The quality of governance determines PAs' ability to set and meet conservation objectives to benefit society. Governance applies at all levels: site, national, regional and global (WCPA 2003). Governance is the sum of the many ways in which individuals and public and private institutions manage common matters. It is a continuous process to accommodate diverse interests and take co-operative action (CGG 1995). Governance is a tool to achieve three ends (Albert 1999; OECD 1998):

- Improve competitiveness and access to finance

- Provide a structure to set objectives and targets and define means of achieving them

- Set the basis for monitoring and auditing performance

Thus, governance and management are interdependent: efficient and effective management is not possible without strong governance, and governance is not successful without effective management.

The basic principles of good governance such as decentralisation, participation, transparency and accountability are valid worldwide (Albert 1999). Although governments', corporations' and PAs' concerns overlap, their governance principles emphasise different aspects (see Table 12.1). Thus, governance models developed for one are not fully applicable to the other (Mintzberg 1996). PAs are on the intersection of interdependent governance types acting as nested geographical scales: protected areas, economic and environmental (see Fig. 12.1).

Corporations	Internal means by which corporations are operated and controlled (OECD 1999)
Countries	Traditions and institutions by which authority in a country is exercised for the common good (WBG 2003)
Protected areas	Interactions among structures, processes and traditions that determine how power and responsibilities are exercised, how decisions are taken, and how citizens or other stakeholders have their say (Graham *et al.* 2003: 2)

TABLE 12.1 Governance definitions for corporations, governments and protected areas

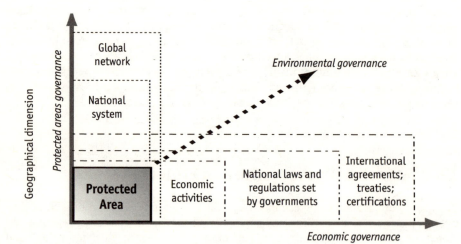

FIGURE 12.1 Protected areas and governance levels

12.4.1 Global PA governance

In 1988, the WCPA created the Task Force on Management Effectiveness to improve the selection and management of PAs and provide managers and decision-makers with tools for assessing management effectiveness (IUCN 2003). Accountability in PAs, as in other natural resource agencies, has been limited mainly to reporting on budget expenditures; auditing and monitoring of conservation programmes, evaluation of outcomes and effectiveness are missing (Dudley *et al.* 1999b; Kleiman *et al.* 2000; Pullin and Knight 2001). As an organisation, the WCPA can look for ways to improve its own governance. For instance the WCPA Steering Committee is responsible for ensuring adequate planning, implementation and evaluation of the Strategic Plan (WCPA 2002). By improving its own governance, the WCPA can have a positive influence in improving governance at other levels. As leader and generator of principles and guidelines, it sets the basis to improve governance in national systems and individual PAs within member countries (e.g. Hockings *et al.* 2000; Pomeroy *et al.* 2002).

12.4.2 Corporate governance

For corporations, actions take place at headquarters, business units and operations levels (Pearce and Robinson 1997, in Thompson 2002: 80). Since governance influences the corporation's external social and natural environment, good governance should consider the interests of constituencies and communities affected by their operations in addition to ensuring good return on investment (OECD 1998).

12.4.3 National governance

Corporations and PAs operate within the legal, institutional and regulatory context set by governments (OECD 1998), but often governments lack the ability to monitor their performance. Unlike private corporations, governments and public organisations are not driven by competition or profit (Wirtz 2001). Public organisations such as PA agencies deliver intangible products or services and have outcomes that cannot be measured monetarily. PAs generate revenues but their main goal is conservation, which causes conflicts between public and private interests.

A country's governance determines the ability of the public administration to deal with issues such as accountability, corruption, culture, decentralisation, democracy, rule of law and globalisation (Daily *et al.* 2003; WBG 2003). Giving financial aid to countries with governance problems may be discouraged in the near future (Kaufmann and Kraay 2003; Werlin 2003). Inconsistent policies generate conflicts among governments, corporations, civil society and protected areas. Increasing population, poverty, and uncontrolled economic growth have placed additional pressure on natural resources (CGG 1995) and increased illegal uses within PAs (PC 2000; Sayer 1999). Inadequate governance raises questions about PAs' ability to reduce pressures that affect natural resources and to get foreign funds (Kaufmann and Kraay 2003; Werlin 2003).

Therefore, consistency among governance of governments, corporations and protected areas is needed to achieve PA objectives efficiently and effectively. PAs by themselves can do little to improve governance if there is not co-ordination with other actors to draft policies and set rules to govern economic activity that pay attention to social, economic and environmental needs. These examples show how inadequate governance hinders PAs' performance.

12.4.4 Balancing control and collaboration

Government control over PAs created conflicts because it acted both as regulator and manager. The focus on short-term yield compromised ecological and social goals (Holling and Meffe 1996; Phillips 2003; Sundaramurthy and Lewis 2003). Long-term survival of PAs depends on gaining stakeholder support by promoting ecological and social benefits of PAs (IUCN 2003). Stakeholders include users, adjacent landowners, non-governmental organisations, corporations and citizens that may never have a direct contact with PAs. Government-managed, co-managed, privately managed and community-managed are new governance types for PAs (Graham *et al.* 2003). The ability to deal with these is key to implementing ecosystem-based management, decentralising management and involving stakeholders (WCPA 2003).

PAs have to be open to these governance types and incorporate stakeholders' interests and values (CGG 1995; WCPA 2003). Governance is not restricted only to the relationships among managers. Thus, PA agencies have to change their structure and culture to work simultaneously with various governance types on a more co-operative basis. Parks Canada is taking steps in that direction.

12.4.5 Changes in national governance structure

The changing structure in federal governments can be either a barrier or driving force to improve governance. In Mexico and Canada, the agencies responsible for managing PAs have undergone major reorganisations in the last five years. Table 12.2 presents the main characteristics of these agencies. Parks Canada was a department within Canadian Heritage and was elevated to an agency in 1998. It is expected that this change will give it more autonomy to operate and draft policies (Informant). In Mexico, the structure of the federal government and the administration of PAs changes with every presidential period (six years). The Comisión Nacional de Áreas Naturales Protegidas (National Commission of Natural Protected Areas, CONANP), created in 2000, is the merger of an advisory body, the Consejo Nacional de Áreas Naturales Protegidas (National Council of Protected Areas) and the previous Dirección de Áreas Naturales Protegidas (Directorate of Protected Areas). CONANP is now a decentralised agency that belongs to SEMARNAT. Constant change from one Ministry to another and deficient relationships among departments have slowed down agency progress (Informant).

12.4.6 Examples of governance interdependence at various levels

PA

Inadequate control of traffic and visitor access to breeding areas inside national parks may influence the distribution of species and decrease population size (Informant).

	Mexico	Canada
Responsible agency	National Commission of Natural Protected Areas	Parks Canada Agency
Reorganised	Created in 2000	1998 (created in 1911)
Ministry	Secretaría del Medio Ambiente Recursos Naturales	Ministry of Canadian Heritage
Mission	To conserve Mexico's natural heritage and the ecological processes through protected areas and sustainable development programmes	To present and protect natural and cultural heritage, foster public understanding, appreciation and enjoyment, and ensure ecological and commemorative integrity of national parks and historic sites
Sites administered	148	187
Emphasis	Natural heritage	Natural and cultural heritage
Governance	• President • Directors General (Institutional Development and Promotion, Conservation Management, Conservation for Development) • Executive Director of Administration and Institutional Effectiveness • Director of Legal Matters • Director of Evaluation and Monitoring	• Chief Executive Officer • Directors General (Strategy and Plans, National Historic Sites, National Parks, Western and Northern Canada, Eastern Canada) • Chief Administrative Officer • Executive Directors (Quebec and Mountain Parks) • Executive Director on Ecological Integrity • Chief Human Resources Officer • Senior Financial Officer • Director of Communications • Senior Legal Counsel
Priorities	• Consolidate the priority regions for conservation • Promote the sustainable use of ecosystems and their goods and services	• Complete the system of national parks, historic sites and marine conservation areas • Maintain or restore ecological integrity • Increase the public's awareness and understanding

TABLE 12.2 **Protected Areas in Canada and Mexico**

Source: based on GC 2000; PC 2002; SEMARNAT 2001

Corporations

Tourism, logging, mining, and oil and gas exploration and production are among the activities affecting PAs in Mexico and Canada (PC 2000; SEMARNAT 2001). Governments play a key role in drafting environmental laws and giving transnational corporations concessions to exploit natural resources (Informant). Especially in developing countries, concessions granted based on private interest cause socioeconomic and environmental impacts (Informant). Governments can improve law enforcement and corruption control, while the WCPA can negotiate adoption of best practices and trade-offs with corporations.

National governments

In Mexico, PAs located within priority areas for conservation were given the responsibility for promoting sustainable development projects among neighbouring communities. Although this is an opportunity to promote sustainable practices among neighbouring communities, programmes promoted by other governmental agencies promote short-term gain rather than sustainable use (Informant).

International

Inadequate forest policies and lack of enforcement allow the destruction of forest in central Mexico. This threatens Monarch butterflies which migrate between Mexico and Canada. Despite the existence of bilateral agreements, there has not been co-ordination among PAs that share this species to reduce threats affecting its population (Informant).

12.5 Assessing governance and evaluating management effectiveness

Krahmann (2003: 327) indicates that governance represents political systems where the authority is fragmented among multiple actors. In the case of PAs, the increased reliance on external funds and a limited success in achieving and reconciling conservation, social and economic goals determine the need for systems to evaluate management effectiveness, report on progress and enhance governance. Certifications and frameworks to assess governance and management effectiveness are two current trends among PAs.

12.5.1 International standards and certifications

The existing global environmental management system has been inadequate in solving environmental problems that affect shared resources such as biodiversity, fisheries or water (Esty and Ivanova 2001). Environmental management systems (EMSs) and tools have been developed to assist with establishing goals and objectives, improving performance, and working with stakeholders. However, a key factor in the successful use of EMS and tools is understanding and support from senior management: the governance of the organisation, the rules, regulations and practices at the upper levels that guide the organisation (Thompson 2002). Adopting EMS standards helps improve management through the adoption of practices such as document control, record keeping, management system audits and feedback. Although it may look like the scope of an EMS is limited to the organisation's boundaries and that it does not have influence beyond those boundaries, EMSs help to link PA managers with other actors. By adopting EMS tools and principles, corporation and PA managers can make improvements in the following aspects.

Public participation

Management tools (Thompson 2002) have helped corporations enhance communication with stakeholders and can do the same for PAs. Adaptive management requires public involvement in the planning and decision-making processes to incorporate stakeholders' values and interest, and decide on limits of acceptable change (Shindler and Cheek 1999). However, previous frustration with government reduces stakeholders' trust in consultation processes. There is the perception that agencies do not walk the talk in public participation and that outcomes do not improve (Holliday *et al.* 2002). For PA managers and staff, reaching out to neighbouring landowners and local communities is a key element in gaining public support and create partnerships. Better communication strategies and reporting by PAs could provide stakeholders and citizens with opportunities to give feedback on their issues of concern. Similarly, corporations can get feedback from civil society, PAs and non-governmental organisations. Improvement on accountability, disclosure and transparency enhance collaboration and trust between regulators, PAs, corporations and civil society. This, in turn, increases PAs governance and management effectiveness.

Environmental performance

Different certification standards and codes of conduct apply to ecotourism, golf, skiing, or extractive industries operating inside and near PAs (Mendoza *et al.* 2003). These include environmental management systems such as ISO 14001 (ISO 1996). PAs are adopting EMS standards to improve management effectiveness and accountability and to share the benefits associated with such standards. For instance, Parks Canada adopted ISO 14001 as a model for its EMS. This is helping the agency minimise environmental impacts, save on operation costs and demonstrate environmental stewardship (Snell 2003). The Parque Natural de la Zona Volcánica de la Garrotxa in Spain is certified under ISO 9000 and used ISO 14001 to reorganise its management structure (Falgarona 2003).

Despite the calls for certifications, a scheme for PAs has not been developed. A proposal to certify PA categories did not gain support because categories within national systems in member countries do not follow IUCN categories or definitions (WCPA 2003). ISO 14000 and 9000 standards, although flexible, have been designed for corporations whose main goal is profit, not conservation. Despite bringing tangible benefits to PAs, the application of ISO standards to PAs has been limited, because aspects such as biodiversity, natural areas and non-contingent values are outside their scope (Mendoza *et al.* 2003; Quinn 2002).

12.5.2 Proposals to assess governance and management effectiveness

The WCPA has endorsed two frameworks to evaluate management effectiveness that include governance indicators. The first one, by Hockings *et al.* (2000), is a general framework for national systems that emphasises evaluating outcomes. It was later applied to World Heritage Sites. The second one, by Pomeroy *et al.* (2002), is specific for Marine Protected Areas and includes governance indicators that evaluate aspects such as management planning, legislation, stakeholder participation and training, enforcement, and communication with stakeholders. In addition, Parks Canada has proposed a framework specifically for assessing PA governance (PC 2003). It focuses on national systems and assesses aspects such as leadership, performance against mandate, accountability and financial accountability. Their characteristics are shown in Box 12.1.

It is expected that these proposals will help to improve governance and management of PAs. However, interviews with managers and interventions of participants during the World Park Congress in 2003 indicated that it would be necessary to overcome the following barriers for effective adoption of the frameworks:

- Lack of awareness among managers of PAs about the existence of the frameworks

- Lack of capacity to modify existing national reporting schemes already developed

- Reluctance to increase reporting demands for PA managers

- Inappropriate baseline knowledge to measure indicators

- Use of indicators of interest to international organisations, which do not reflect activities and reporting needs of individual PAs

- No emphasis on auditing the management system, which makes it difficult to target areas for improvement

- Low applicability of frameworks to other categories or socioeconomic contexts

12.6 Suggestions for future schemes

The success of governance and certification schemes will depend on overcoming those barriers, but also on their ability to satisfy two management needs. The first one, mentioned by Hockings (2000) and PC (2003), is the need to measure governance and man-

Hockings *et al.* 2000

Focus: management effectiveness; it includes governance

Indicators:

- Context: importance and values of sites, stresses and threats, government support, stakeholders
- Planning: legal status, design, management planning
- Inputs: resource use and needs
- Process: definition of best practice
- Outputs: management plan implementation
- Outcomes: achievement of management targets and objectives

Pomeroy *et al.* 2002

Focus: management effectiveness; it includes governance

Indicators:

- Biophysical: characteristics of focal species and their habitat
- Socioeconomic: socioeconomic characteristics, knowledge, income, and local use patterns
- Governance: legislation, management and decision-making, stakeholder training and involvement
  - Adoption of a management plan
  - Community understanding of rules and regulations
  - Decision-making and management body
  - Existence and adequacy of legislation
  - Stakeholder satisfaction regarding participation in management
  - Management and sustainability training of resource users and community organisations
  - Community organisations
  - Human resources and equipment for surveillance and monitoring
  - Definition of enforcement procedures
  - Information to enhance stakeholders' compliance
  - Staff meetings with stakeholders
  - Stakeholders' involvement in monitoring and enforcement

Parks Canada 2003

Focus: Governance

Indicators:

- Leadership
  - Long-range system plan
  - Management plans for individual sites
  - Protection and sustainability of natural resources, monitoring systems, partnerships
  - Visitor services, control of commercial and visitors' impacts, positive return on investment
- Accountability
  - Annual corporate plan, public accessibility and input
  - Corporate leadership
  - Achievement of mandate
- Financial accountability
  - Availability of financial plans and audits
  - Capacity to sustain operations, adequate investment rates to support infrastructure

Box 12.1 Elements proposed for assessing governance and management for Protected Areas

agement effectiveness for both national systems and individual areas. The second one is the need to consider the individual PA management needs—and social, environmental and economic conditions—as they vary from PA to PA within a national system, and from country to country on the world network of protected areas. Our analysis identifies the following aspects that have been mentioned in the current debate about improving governance and management for PAs, which should be incorporated in future evaluation schemes:

12.6.1 Working outside boundaries

The above-mentioned proposals are a good beginning. However, they still portray PAs as islands by focusing on what is happening inside the PA boundaries. Agencies and managers have jurisdiction only inside the PA boundaries. However, fulfilling their mandate requires working outside those boundaries to reduce threats, promote sustainable land use practices and achieve management objectives. The work PA managers and staff do in this regard remains outside reporting schemes and is not rewarded. Nevertheless, evaluations punish them for aspects outside their control, such as the adequacy of laws or regulations or impacts on the PA due to activities outside.

12.6.2 Valuation of goods and services provided by PAS

Although important for demonstrating the benefits of PAs to society, the proposals do not include indicators to report on the variety of ecosystem goods and services provided by PAs and their relevance for human quality of life. In addition to services, PAs preserve populations of species that are disappearing in non-protected lands that can provide genetic resources, new drugs or materials, and other products that represent future revenues and improvements in the quality of life for human communities (Good 2003).

12.6.3 Need to integrate social, economic and environmental indicators

'PAs have focused on conservation objectives but PAs' contribution to sustainable development should be measured through social, economic and environmental indicators and should reflect the benefits to indigenous and local communities in these aspects' (Griffiths 2003). Staffs of PAs are dealing with two main approaches to developing indicators:

- OECD's Pressure–State–Response framework for developing sustainability indicators (Schuh and Thompson 2002)

- WCPA's outcome-based approach (Hockings et al. 2000)

Despite WCPA's recommendations, PA staff are having difficulties in developing indicators to evaluate outcomes and rely mainly on input or output indicators (Informant). For instance, for marine PAs, one indicator measures the amount and quality of training provided to community organisations, and another the number of community organisations that are created (Pomeroy *et al.* 2002). Possible outcomes could reflect how training and organisation help to improve the quality of community involvement. PA agencies could benefit from using existing reporting schemes such as the Global Reporting Initiative (GRI 2003), or the ISO 14031 standard on Evaluating Environmental Performance (ISO 1999).

The diversity of needs and conditions of PAs has made it difficult to propose standards for monitoring or sharing best practices. Two options are to modify existing standards to suit the needs of protected areas or to design standards that focus on the priorities of PAs. Mendoza *et al.* (2003) followed the second option. Since EBM is the current paradigm in PAs and natural resource management (Quinn 2002), they combined the strengths of both EMS and ecosystem management to propose an Ecosystem-Based Management (EBM) System for PAs. To increase data verification and repeatability, this system emphasises the documentation of monitoring and auditing protocols, and of operational procedures. Additionally, it integrates monitoring, auditing and performance evaluation into management reviews to provide information for adaptive EBM. The model takes the PA management plan as the basis for evaluating effectiveness and allows for the use of different types of indicators and performance measures. Therefore, it accommodates social, environmental, economic and operational goals.

12.6.4 Factors influencing the development of governance and management schemes

The application of the concept of governance to Protected Areas is a new trend. This makes it difficult at this point to provide an abundantly clear analysis of how it will evolve. The following four factors influence the development of governance structures for Protected Areas at local, national and global levels.

1. The formerly clear distinctions among the roles of governments, civil society (including NGOs) and corporations have become blurred. In part, this is due to the application of the Washington Consensus (downsize governments and give corporations a larger role; Williamson 2000), to globalisation, through the Internet, trade agreements (such as NAFTA) and a shrinking world. The fiscal reforms promoted by the Washington Consensus influence the design of policies for protected areas based on business-like and market approaches.

2. The theory and practice of governance and environmental and natural resource management are in a state of flux because of the above-mentioned factors. The fragmentation of governance suggested by Krahmann (2003) obstructs the application of theoretical developments to strengthen the role of protected areas and their benefits to populations from local to global level.

3. The Washington Consensus has failed in delivering the promises of development (e.g. the Report of the Meeting of the Hemispheric Leaders held in Monterrey, Mexico, 12 January 2004, SOAIN 2004). The revisions to the Consensus, as a response to the pressures to broaden concerns beyond economic growth, and to increase the roles for civil society and governments, will likely modify the influence different stakeholders have in shaping new policies for natural resource and PAs development.

4. National, corporate and global governance are linked and influence Protected Areas policy and implementation. Currently, the debate around Protected Areas governance has centred on Protected Areas themselves. However, local and national governments, international organisations, and national and transnational corporations can either facilitate or hinder the achievement of Protected Areas' goals through their practices. Therefore, further research could focus on two points. First, how the ability of Protected Areas to achieve their mission and deliver public goods and services is influenced by the good or bad governance at these other levels. Second, what is being done to ensure that governance structures among those levels include adequate representation of stakeholders' needs and values.

12.7 Conclusion

PAs by themselves can do little to improve governance if there is no co-ordination with governments and corporations to work at multiple levels simultaneously. Governance for PAs involves different actors and this determines the need to pay attention to social, economic and environmental needs. Achieving conservation objectives for a given PA is not feasible if governance at global or national levels is deficient. Similarly, it is not possible to gain public support for PAs if the mistakes of past PA policies that excluded people are not corrected and the benefits are not shared with local communities. Agencies and staff had to be flexible enough to work using different styles according to the type of governance dictated by stakeholders' involvement. The adoption of EMS and other certification mechanisms can help PAs improve management and governance by establishing sound working relationships with stakeholders on surrounding lands and demonstrating PAs' contribution to the quality of life locally and nationally. However, managers of PAs will have to improve their ability to measure, assess and report on the contributions to improving quality of life outside PA boundaries. Most certifications used in PAs have been created for corporations to enhance profit. Thus, there is need to modify such certifications or develop others to suit PA needs. Finally, evaluation and certification schemes developed for PAs specifically should combine bottom-up and top-down approaches to appropriately reflect the variety of categories and conditions within PAs.

References

Albert, M. (1999) 'Principles of Good Governance', Global Corporate Governance Forum Library of Speeches, 29 September 1999, Launch Ceremony speech, Washington, DC, 19 August 2003, www.gcgf.org/ifcext/cgf.nsf/AttachmentsByTitle/Forum_Creation_1999_Michael_Albert/$FILE/Michel_Albert_Principles_of_Good_CG_Sep_1999.pdf.

Barton, R. (2000) 'The Implications of Sponsorship for State Park Management', *The George Wright Forum* 17.3: 40-6.

Bella, L. (1987) *Parks for Profit* (Montreal: Harvest House).

CGG (Commission on Global Governance) (1995) *Our Global Neighbourhood: The Report of the Commission on Global Governance* (Oxford, UK: Oxford University Press).

Daily, C.M., D.R. Dalton and A. Cannella Jr (2003) 'Corporate Governance: Decades of Dialogue and Data', *Academy of Management Review* 28.3: 371-82.

De Lopez, T.T. (2001) 'Stakeholder Management for Conservation Projects: A Case Study of Ream, National Park, Cambodia', *Environmental Management* 28.1: 47-60.

Dudley, N, B. Gujja, B. Jackson, J.P. Jeanrenaud, G. Oviedo, A. Phillips, P. Rosabel and S. Stolton (1999a) 'Challenges for Protected Areas in the 21st Century', in S. Stolton and N. Dudley (eds.), *Partnerships for Protection: New Strategies for Planning and Management for Protected Areas* (London: IUCN/Earthscan): 3-12.

——, M. Hockings and S. Stolton (1999b) 'Measuring the Effectiveness of Protected Areas Management', in S. Stolton and N. Dudley (eds.), *Partnerships for Protection: New Strategies for Planning and Management for Protected Areas* (London: IUCN/Earthscan Publications): 249-57.

Esty, D.C., and M.H. Ivanova (2001) 'Making International Environmental Efforts Work: The Case for a Global Environmental Organization' (Working Paper 2/01; New Haven, CT: Yale Center for Environmental Law and Policy).

Falgarona, J. (2003) 'Parc Natural de la Zona Volcánica de la Garrotxa', personal communication, 15 August 2003.

Ferraro, P.J. (2001) 'Global Habitat Protection: Limitations of Development Interventions and a Role for Conservation Performance Payments', *Conservation Biology* 15.4: 990-1,000.

GC (Government of Canada) (2000) 'Canada National Parks Act. Bill C-27. Assented to 20 October 2000', *Canada Gazette*, Part III, 23.4: Ch. 32.

Good, L. (2003) 'Financing Protected Areas in the New Millennium: The Role of the GEF', open ceremony speech, *Vth World Parks Conference*, Durban, South Africa, 8–17 September 2003.

Graham, J., B. Amos and T. Plumptree (2003) 'Governance Principles for Protected Areas in the 21st Century', prepared for the *Vth World Park Congress*, Durban, South Africa, 30 June 2003 (in collaboration with Parks Canada and Canadian International Development Agency).

GRI (Global Reporting Initiative) (2003) *The GRI: An Overview* (Amsterdam: Global Reporting Initiative).

Griffiths, T. (2003) *A Failure of Accountability: Indigenous Peoples, Human Rights and Development Agency Standards* (A Forest Peoples Programme Briefing Paper; Moreton-in-Marsh, UK: Fosseway Business Centre).

Hockings, M., S. Stolton and N. Dudley (2000) *Evaluating Effectiveness: A Framework for Assessing the Management of Protected Areas* (Cambridge, UK: IUCN Publications Services Unit).

Holliday, C.O., S. Schmidheiny and P. Watts (2002) *Walking the Talk: The Business Case for Sustainable Development* (Sheffield, UK: Greenleaf Publishing).

Holling, C.S., and G.K. Meffe (1996) 'Command and Control and the Pathology of Natural Resource Management', *Conservation Biology* 10.2: 328-37.

ISO (International Organisation for Standardisation) (1996) 'ISO 14001:1996(E). International Standard ISO 14001', *Environmental Management Systems—Specifications with Guidance for Use*, 1 September 1996 (Geneva: ISO).

—— (1999) 'ISO 14031:1999(E). International Standard ISO 14031', *Environmental Management—Environmental Performance Evaluation—Guidelines*, 15 November 1999 (Geneva: ISO).

IUCN (The World Conservation Union) (1994) *Guidelines for Protected Area Management Categories. Part II: The Management Categories* (Cambridge, UK: IUCN Publications Service Unit).

—— (2003) 'World Commission on Protected Areas', The World Conservation Union, www.iucn.org/themes/wcpa, 12 October 2003.

Kaufmann, D., and A. Kraay (2003) 'Governance and Growth: Causality Which Way? Evidence for the World, in Brief' (World Bank Group Working Papers and Articles; Washington, DC: World Bank Group).

——, A. Kraay and M. Mastruzzi (2003) *Governance Matters. III. Governance Indicators for 1996–2002* (Draft for Comment, Washington, DC: World Bank Group).

Kleiman, D.G., R.P. Rading, B.J. Miller, T.W. Clark, J.M. Scott, J. Robinson, R.L. Wallace, R.J. Cabin and F. Felleman (2000) 'Improving the Evaluation of Conservation Programs', *Conservation Biology* 14.2: 356-65.

Krahmann, E. (2003) 'National, Regional and Global Governance: One Phenomenon or Many?', *Global Governance* 9.3: 323-46.

Mendoza, D.A., M. Quinn and D. Thompson (2003) 'An Ecosystem-Based Management System for Protected Areas', presented at the *V International SAMPAA (Science and Management of Protected Areas Association) Conference*, Victoria, British Columbia, 11–16 May 2003.

Mintzberg, H. (1996) 'Managing Government, Governing Management', *Harvard Business Review* May/June 1996: 78-84.

OECD (Organisation for Economic Co-Operation and Development) (1998) *Principles of Corporate Governance* (Paris: OECD).

PC (Parks Canada Agency) (2000) *'Unimpaired for Future Generations' Protecting Ecological Integrity with Canada's National Parks. Report of the Panel on the Ecological Integrity of Canada's National Parks* (Ottawa: Minister of Public Works and Government Services).

—— (2002) *National Environmental Management Framework* (Ottawa: Internal document).

—— (2003) 'A Framework for Protected Area Governance for the Twenty-first Century', discussion paper for the *Vth World Parks Conference*, Durban, South Africa, 8–17 September 2003.

Phillips, A. (2003) 'Turning Ideas on their Head: The New Paradigm for Protected Areas', in H. Jaireth and D. Smith (eds.), *Innovative Governance: Indigenous Peoples, Local Communities and Protected Areas* (New Delhi, India: Ane Books): 1-27.

Pomeroy, R.S., J.E. Parks and L.M. Watson (2002) *How is Your MPA Doing? A Guidebook. Biophysical, Socioeconomic, and Governance Indicators for the Evaluation of Management Effectiveness of Marine Protected Areas* (Working draft; Silver Spring, MD: IUCN World Commission on Protected Areas-Marine, World Wildlife Fund for Nature—Endangered Seas Programme, National Oceanographic and Atmospheric Association).

Pullin, A.S., and T.M. Knight (2001) 'Effectiveness in Conservation Practice: Pointers from Medicine and Public Health', *Conservation Biology* 15.1: 50-54.

Punch, K. (1998) *Introduction to Social Research: Quantitative and Qualitative Approaches* (Thousand Oaks, CA: Sage).

Quinn, M. (2002) 'Ecosystem-Based Management', in D. Thompson (ed.), *Tools for Environmental Management: A Practical Introduction and Guide* (Gabriola Island, Canada: New Society Publishers): 370-82.

Sayer, J.A. (1999) 'Globalisation, Localisation and Protected Areas', in S. Stolton and N. Dudley (eds.), *Partnerships for Protection: New Strategies for Planning and Management for Protected Areas* (London: IUCN/Earthscan): 28-38.

Schuh, C., and D. Thompson (2002) 'Environmental Indicators', in D. Thompson (ed.), *Tools for Environmental Management: A Practical Introduction and Guide* (Gabriola Island, Canada: New Society Publishers): 174-208.

Searle, R. (2000) *Phantom Parks: The Struggle to Save Canada's National Parks* (Toronto: Canadian Parks and Wilderness Society/Key Porter Books).

SEMARNAT (Secretaria del Medio Ambiente y Recursos Naturales) (2001) *Programa de Trabajo, Comisión Nacional de Áreas Naturales Protegidas 2001–2006* (D.F., México: SEMARNAT).

Shindler, B., and K.A. Cheek (1999) 'Integrating Citizens in Adaptive Management: A Propositional Analysis', *Conservation Ecology* 3.1: 9.

Snell, J. (2003) Parks Canada Sustainability Advisor, personal communication, 21 January 2003.

Strauss, A., and J. Corbin (1998) *Basics of Qualitative Research: Techniques and Procedures for Developing Grounded Theory* (Thousand Oaks, CA: Sage).

SOAIN (Summit of the Americas Information Network) (2004) 'Special Summit of the Americas', 12–13 January 2004, Monterrey, Mexico, www.summit-americas.org/SpecialSummit/mainpage-eng.htm, 4 April 2004.

Sundaramurthy, C., and M. Lewis (2003) 'Control and Collaboration: Paradoxes of Governance', *Academy of Management Review* 28.3: 397-415.

Thompson, D. (2002) *Tools for Environmental Management* (Gabriola Island, Canada: New Society Publishers).

WBG (World Bank Group) (2003) *About Governance* (Washington, DC: World Bank Institute, www.worldbank.org/wbi/governance/about.html, 30 July 2001).

WCPA (World Commission on Protected Areas) (2002) 'Strategic Plan 2002–2012' WCPA/World Conservation Union, www.iucn.org/themes/wcpa, 28 December 2003.

—— (2003) *Vth World Park Congress Recommendations* (Durban, South Africa: WCPA/World Conservation Union).

Werlin, H.H. (2003) 'Poor Nations, Rich Nations: A Theory of Governance', *Public Administration Review* 63.3: 329-42.

Williamson, J.H. (2000) 'What should the World Bank Think about the Washington Consensus?', *The World Bank Research Observer* 15.2: 251-64.

Wirtz, R.A. (2001) 'Icebergs and Government Productivity', *The Region* 15.2: 16-19.

Yin, R.K. (1994) *Case Study Research: Design and Methods* (Thousand Oaks, CA: Sage).

13

Putting governance to work in a US company
THE CARRIS EXPERIENCE*

Cecile G. Betit

Independent researcher, USA

This conceptual paper, based on a case, examines the Carris Companies' corporate citizenship efforts—as they moved toward full employee ownership and employee governance—in the context of basic questions involving the nature of corporations, the manner in which they should be governed, their roles within civil society[1] and how they should be held accountable for the common good. Such a focus examining one corporation's efforts is in keeping with Derber's ideas of empowerment and participation presented in *People before Profits* (2002) and Williamson's observation concerning the need for microanalysis in the study of alternative forms of corporate governance (1996: 357).

Fisher puts forward the need for 'clear, self conscious organizational commitment' (2003: 29) in the context of organisational autonomy as one of the serious change elements within the discussion of governance and civil society. Hertel (2003: 42) notes the importance of companies facing questions (in the sense of developing shared norms that could guide joint thinking and actions) of legitimacy, transparency, accountability

---

* The assistance of the following is gratefully acknowledged: William H. Carris for providing full access to the Carris Companies; Michael Curran, named corporate President on 1 January 2005, formerly Vice President and Chief Operating Officer, for raising and answering questions in a manner that challenges and expands; Karin McGrath, Human Resources Director, for the above-and-beyond provision of ongoing status information (so essential in keeping the research current); and the employee-owners of the Carris Companies whose efforts in providing information and materials for this work are absolutely essential to its success. I am grateful to Professor Sandra Waddock (Boston College) for her insight and suggestion of resources and to the anonymous reviewer whose recommendations I have incorporated in this revision.

1 While some consider civil society a contentious term, within this chapter it is used to mean the 'non-market, non-state sphere of human interaction' (see Hertel 2003: 42). It can be considered to be that sector of co-operative relationships emerging between business and government. Of specific interest here is Bruyn 2000 and Zadek 2001. (See Bruyn 2000: 63 for a description of civil society and page 104 for his characterisation of the transition at Carris as social entrepreneurship. Bruyn gives numerous examples of corporations providing the impetus for social change.)

and the role of representation in decision-making. The latter, involving the role of rights (with property rights often the most clearly defined) and responsibilities, is put forward as foundational to democratic and participative governance (starting at home and having broad international influence) within the companies driving change—significant aspects being the shift from shareholder to stakeholder and the sharing of profits with employees. The challenge of extending, in practical and appropriate ways, the principles of participatory democracy to firms and civil society was noted. Employees are not citizens of corporations though corporations operate in a social setting.

In addition to the recommendation to balance its accountability to stakeholders with a broader civic responsibility, Andreadis takes a position congruent with that of Harman and Hormann (1990), who saw the growing potential for corporate and business power to be the dominant and central social institution for creating positive social change:

> Increasingly, the business sector is being called on to provide leadership, to use its enormous reach, knowledge, problem-solving skills and access to capital in service of society's greatest dilemmas. Many in the public sector suggest that, with the growing wealth enjoyed by business, comes a responsibility of a higher order, a civic responsibility in addition to its traditional responsibility to shareholders (Andreadis 2002: 143).

In the following section, we present an interpretation of the Carris Companies' mission and discuss the firm's origins, current structure, products and locations.

13.1 The Carris Companies[2]

13.1.1 Mission

The Carris mission 'to improve the quality of life for our growing corporate community' was interpreted within the *Long Term Plan* (*LTP*) in a manner that denoted relationship and responsibility within the local corporate community and its external communities:

- The term 'quality of life' means anything that serves to better oneself—be it spiritual emotional, physical or material betterment.

- 'Growing' means ever expanding. The company . . . will have growth as a goal so that . . . it can serve to have a positive effect on an ever-increasing number of people—an ever-expanding community of interconnected people.

- People and organisations involved with and affected by Carris Reels, such as our families, customers, suppliers, neighbors, civic leaders and fellow citizens are part of our Corporate Community. Community spirit and loyalty should prevail . . . [T]he most meaningful form of 'membership' in this corporate community should be employee-owners. As we, a community of companies, are united in our business and common interests

2   For additional corporate information, see www.carris.com.

toward the common good, so too should our dedication and concern encompass the outside community—those towns or districts where we live—(the general public) and thereby society as a whole . . . [T]o one degree or another, anyone could fall within the corporate community, with corporate loyalty to its members being proportional to their own conceptual degree of ownership in the organisation.

- There is an implied statement of the common good having the highest priority. Each individual is of equal importance, but in order to maximize the effect, the common good has to come first. Common good means that which is best for the most people as opposed to that which is best for an individual (Carris 1994: 6).

For the Carris Companies, there were interests beyond those of the individual (and the company) to be served. As will be seen further in this chapter, engaging employees as owners, broadened the governance structure to include elements of civil society not usually included (community interests in certain types of decisions, as well as employee interests). Employee participation in decision-making as these led to corporate changes reflected the kind of local democracy emphasised by Charles Derber (2002) and promoted the balance between the needs of individuals and the community suggested by Waddock (2002: 48).

13.1.2 Henry Carris, founder

On 1 June 1951, when Henry M. Carris started Carris Reels in Rutland, Vermont, USA, to manufacture hardwood and plywood reels (for steel and wire cable), there were two employees. The first order involved 5,000 reels constructed according to his patented design. Of Carris Reels' first 22 employees, 4 were handicapped (its first hard-working 57-year-old sawyer was blind and worked with special fixtures and precautions) (Billings 1976: 13). The company made money. Its growth was steady. Henry Carris's civic contributions at the local and state (Vermont) levels and his appreciation and commitment to the arts were matters for awards outside the company and of emphasis in the unpublished history prepared for Carris Reels' 25th anniversary in 1976 (Billings 1976).

13.1.3 William H. (Bill) Carris, CEO

With the exception of a few years away for education and military duty, Bill Carris lived in the Rutland area. Bill and Barbara (Tracy) Carris had four children. During his childhood in the 1950s, the Vermont way of life was rooted in a predominantly agricultural lifestyle and strong sense of stability, egalitarianism, independence, fiscal conservatism, fair play and social concern (Bryan and McLaughry 1989). These were also Carris family characteristics and values. Bill Carris brought these forward when he took over from his father as CEO in 1980. He had grown up with the company, learning reel manufacturing and its administration.

Not only did he bring management skills to his leadership role, he brought a desire to bring the Carris employees into the company as owners and participants in designing their own future. As the company grew, he worked to make his vision for 100% employee ownership and governance of the company a practical reality. He wrote several drafts, asking for feedback from colleagues and friends of the document that he would later name the *Long Term Plan* (discussed later in the chapter). In order to get more feedback and to prepare for the transition, he attended the Harvard Business School programme for CEOs, worked with consultants and had deep conversations with those inside and outside the company.

13.1.4 The Carris companies: Carris Reels and Carris Plastics

Carris Reels and Carris Plastics manufactured wood, plastic and metal reels in six US locations and one in Mexico:

- Carris Reels: California, Connecticut, North Carolina and Vermont—as needed to be near customers, plants' added assembly/warehouse locations. In 1970, New Carlisle, Indiana, opened as a permanent assembly site. That site and the one in Galien, Michigan, are assembly sites for the Midwest market.

- Carris Plastics: Vermont, Virginia and Mexico.

From its beginnings, the company had a flat organisation within manufacturing: workers, supervisors and managers. Corporate management travelled as needed from Vermont.

13.2 Methodology

The study of the transitions at the Carris Companies began in 1996. This chapter draws primarily from conversations, interviews and meeting notes over a nine-year period. Conversations with Bill Carris about his goals and plans for employee ownership and governance were routinely scheduled. The change co-ordinator provided information about the training activities and other efforts moving forward to increase participation and those employee skills foundational to employer ownership and governance. Conversations with managers provided background on Carris Companies operations and suggested additional indicators for tracking corporate change. Regular attendance at employee-owners training activities, Corporate Governance meetings, North Carolina Governance meetings, State of the Company meetings (Vermont and Connecticut), Strategic Planning meetings, Task Force meetings, Human Resource presentations and information sessions, and so on, provided a direct means of keeping abreast of changes. From its onset, Bill Carris provided an open environment for the research process. No restrictions were placed on access to information or personnel or to materials published.

The next section will address the question regarding the nature of the corporation from the perspectives of the traditional legal definition and of current challenges to widen the responsiveness of corporations to their constituencies. It will conclude with an application from the Carris Companies.

13.3 What is the nature of the corporation?

Several of the traditional elements of the corporation within the following definition posed by Chief Justice Marshall in the landmark US Supreme Court case *Dartmouth College v. Woodward*[3] are problematic and in question today. While legally correct, most notably absent are those relational aspects that are emphasised in this chapter and underpin so much of the conversation about corporations in our time:

> A corporation is an artificial being, invisible, intangible, and existing only in contemplation of law. Being the mere creature of law, it possesses only those properties which the charter of its creation confers upon it, either expressly or as incidental to its very existence. These are such as are supposed best calculated to effect the object for which it was created. Among the most important are immortality, and, if the expression may be allowed, individuality; properties by which a perpetual succession of many persons are considered as the same, and may act as a single individual . . . a perpetual succession of individuals are capable of acting for the promotion of the particular object, like one immortal being. But this being does not share in the civil government of the country, unless that be the purpose for which it was created. Its immortality no more confers on it political power, or a political character, than immortality would confer such power or character on a natural person. It is no more a state instrument than a natural person exercising the same powers would be (1819).

Post, Preston and Sachs consider the 'conventional concept of the corporation . . . descriptively inaccurate and ethically unacceptable' (2002: 16), a position supported in *The Divine Right of Capital* (Kelly 2001). In the introduction (to that work) and further in *The Soul of Capitalism* (Greider 2003), William Greider notes that 'the problem is not the free market but the design of the corporation' (Kelly 2001: 3). Separating these two concepts, though not always *au courant*, seems in keeping with the original thought of Adam Smith (1952, 1969) whose writings are considered foundational to capitalism. He did not foresee, nor seemingly encourage, the modern complex corporation with its global reach and impacts.

Greider explores the idea that the market is a relatively innocent concept where buyers and sellers have equal footing in setting prices 'with the primary form of regulation that of property rights' (Kelly 2001: 4). The relationship between capitalism and property rights is described at length by DeSoto (2002) who noted that an under-studied aspect in the export of capitalism from the West is the stage of development of a given region's property rights. He notes that, without legal underpinnings clarifying property rights, there is no equity (or capital arising from it).

Though a thorough discussion of capitalism and economic democracy is beyond the scope of this chapter, it deserves to be mentioned that reconceptualising the corporation does not require turning away from capitalism but rather, as also suggested by Zadek (see below), recognising the financial as simply one of the forms of capital.

---

3   *Dartmouth College v. Woodward*, 17 US 518 (1819) Marshall, C.J. accessed 26 September 2003 available at www.ku.edu/carrie/docs/texts/drtmouth.htm.

> We think of this [property rights] as inherent in capitalism, but it may not be. It is true that throughout history capitalism has been a system that has been largely served through the interest of capital. But then, government until the early twentieth century largely served the interest of kings. It wasn't necessary to throw out government in order to do away with monarchs—instead we changed the basis of sovereignty on which government rested. We might do the same with the corporation, asserting that employees and the community rightfully share economic sovereignty with capital owners (Kelly 2001: 4).

In addition to financial capital, Zadek lists the human (health, knowledge and motivation), natural (environmental or ecological), social (the value added from relationships and co-operation) and manufactured capital (the infrastructure of the production process) (2001: 117).

For Greider such an evolution in historical context would parallel the shift in government from the monarchy to democracy. He suggests a similar path may be possible for the economic system:

> What we have known until now is capitalism's aristocratic form. But we can embrace a new democratic vision of capitalism, not as a system for capital, but a system of capital—a system in which all people are allowed to accumulate capital according to their productivity, and in which the natural capital of the environment and community is preserved. At the same time we might also preserve much of the wisdom that is inherent in capitalism . . . supply and demand, competition, profit, self-interest, wealth creation, and so forth . . . most concepts are . . . healthy and worth keeping (Kelly 2001: 4).

Greider is not advocating an overturn of capitalism but, in a very real sense, expanding its base so that all forms of contributed capital are duly acknowledged by the corporation. To recognise only the financial is inconsistent:

> It is the lever that keeps the lock and dam functioning, and it is these four words: *maximizing returns to shareholders* . . . When we . . . turn it over in our hands—really looking at it, as we so rarely do—we will see it is out of place. In a competitive free market, it decrees that the interest of one group will be systematically favored over others . . . it says corporations will consciously serve one group alone. In a system rewarding hard work, it says members of that group will be served regardless of their productivity. Shareholder primacy is a form of entitlement. And entitlement has no place in a market economy. It is a form of privilege. And privilege accruing to property ownership is a remnant of an aristocratic past (Kelly 2001: 4).

This view regarding the nature of the corporation with its interconnectedness, interdependence and interactive quality within the larger civil society is noted by Simon Zadek who also notes its characteristic dominance within the interactive settings creating change:

> Business is increasingly moulding societal values and norms, and defining public policy and practice, as well as being the dominant route through which economic and financial wealth is created. How business is done will underpin how local and global communities of the future address social and environmental visions and imperatives. This is true whatever one believes to be critical in creating a just and sustainable world (2001: 1).

These elements are also addressed within the very opening words of *Redefining the Corporation*:

> For more than a century the business corporation has been a successful and widely adopted institutional arrangement for creating and distributing wealth. But the power and purpose of corporations and of the entire corporate system has been continuously questioned and debated. The interaction between global economic growth and global social challenge has led to changes in the character and behavior of corporations and in public expectations about the role and responsibility of corporations within society . . . [W]e present the corporation as a collaboration of multiple and diverse constituencies and interests, referred to as *stakeholders*. Our *stakeholder view* of the corporation integrates stakeholder relationships within the firm's resource base, industry setting, and sociopolitical arena into a single analytical framework. Our central proposition is that organizational wealth can be created (or destroyed) through relationships with stakeholders of all kind— resource providers, customers and suppliers, social and political actors. Therefore effective *stakeholder management*—that is managing relationships with stakeholders for mutual benefit—is a critical requirement for corporate success (Post *et al.* 2002: 1).

Later, the authors suggest that a 'stakeholder perspective is developed through strategies, structures and policies over the long-term'. They note, 'Our redefinition of the corporation rests on the maxim that "Corporations ARE what they Do" ' (2002: 2). Their alternative definition of the corporation is decidedly relational:

> The corporation is an organization engaged in mobilizing resources for productive uses in order to create wealth and other benefits (and not to intentionally destroy wealth, increase risk, or cause harm) for its multiple constituents or stakeholders (2002: 17).

In this context, corporate survival is dependent on its responsible relationship to its constituents and the larger society:

> The corporation cannot and should not—survive if it does not take responsibility for the welfare of all of its constituents and for the wellbeing of the larger society within which it operates (2002: 16).

The Carris Companies' vision grew out of a similar view of the nature of the corporation as broadly responsible to its constituents and the larger society in which it operates.

13.3.1 The Carris Companies

The LTP (Carris 1994) described not only the road leading to employee ownership and employee governance, but the values and qualities required to go the distance. From the outset, Bill Carris distanced his vision from the traditional view of the corporation. He noted:

> The traditional view is that employees exist to benefit the company: i.e. the owners. My view is that the organization should exist to benefit those who work there from a financial, skill development, emotional and spiritual standpoint (Carris 1994: 3).

In another section, Bill Carris spoke of bringing together emotional and actual ownership suggesting an expanding view of capital to include 'sweat equity'. While this may seem an unusual stance, Greider (2003: 75) points out that 'owning your own work' has a base in several occupations. It is not part of the tradition for manufacturing which continues a more feudal relationship.

Throughout the *LTP*, Bill Carris noted the role of trust and the importance of equality, commitment and daily effort. He shared with employees that though he started out to implement employee ownership, the idea of an employee stock ownership Plan (ESOP)[4] came later. Its tax incentives for individuals and the company made the choice an obvious one (Carris 1994). At the end of 2004, employees shared 43.2% ownership with plans going forward to move beyond 50%.

In an act that seemed the beginning of their joining the democratic process to their economic benefits, the Carris employees voted (one person–one vote) to accept the *Long Term Plan* (LTP) leading to 100% employee ownership through the employee stock ownership plan (ESOP) and a practice-based transition to employee governance. The *LTP* Steering Committee designed the ESOP and put forward allocation structures to be voted on by the employees.

The discussion in the section below on corporate governance will incorporate relationship, theoretical trends, a micro-analytic perspective and decision-making.

13.4 How should corporations be governed?

Anticipated in the discussion above on the nature of the corporation is corporate governance's concern 'with the relationship between business and society' (McIntosh *et al.* 1998: 284). Bandori in a tight summary of theoretical trends connects 'the theory of governance to the theory of rationality both in organisational theory' as put forward by March and Simon (1958) and as 'organisation economics' put forward by Williamson (1975).

> The divide between 'absolute' and 'bounded' rationality, the attribution of these forms of rationality to be contrapposed models of the 'economic' and 'administrative' man respectively, has generated a further divide between 'markets' and 'firms' as different and even antithetic worlds, with little if anything in common. A third model of man, and a basic form of rationality is sometimes called the social man . . . It is a *programmed man*, obeying to norms and rules, applying a logic of appropriate action, non calculative, constrained by the past experience of self and others . . . Correspondingly, 'third' governance forms have been added (Bandori 2000: 1).

For purposes of this chapter the third model might be considered a prototype of citizenship at least from a micro-analytic perspective.

---

4   Technically, an ESOP is a deferred benefit plan in which a company purchases shares of its own stock and places them in trust for its employees who may claim their shares or sell them back to the company when they quit or retire. See Lawrence 1997: 198.

13.4.1 Micro-analytical perspective of governance

A micro-analytical perspective can be seen in Amin and Cohendet's work which seeks to bridge the 'traditional transactional approach' with a more qualitative co-ordinating aspect. In this latter instance, 'the co-operating parties align not their incentives but their knowledge and expectations'. Within the firm there is a need for a governance structure that deals with its core activities as well as the non-core domain (Amin and Cohendet 2000: 94). Working with this possibility using more anthropological theories of the firm, they speak of 'communities of practice' as sources of routine and strategic learning distributed within the organisation. The following finding has implications for the practical outcomes for the Carris Companies' transition:

> We tentatively conclude from the analysis of learning in communities of prac-tice, that in practice, firms might not tackle the two imperatives through two separate structures of governance. This is partly because the implementation of priorities through groups of people along the firm's hierarchy and across its divisional structure which both routinely behave as unitary transactional and knowledge-generating communities, and regularly communicate with the rest of the organization as functional and governance domains (2000: 95).

'Communities of practice are the shop floor of human capital, the place where the stuff gets made' (Stewart 1997: 96). They are ubiquitous (though not always obvious), defined by the history they develop over time, the enterprise they share (rather than one specific agenda), the shared learning and culture developed and experienced through the long term with a product recognised as shared (Stewart 1997: 97).

Looking at communities of practice, within the context of corporate governance, cre-ates an opportunity to look at the horizontal dimensions of governance and widens the opening beyond the traditional sense of 'shareholders', which usually denotes financial interest. Moving toward stakeholders, who may be employees, offers a more pluralistic understanding of resource contribution (Charreaux and Desbrieres 2001: 108). In the case of employee ownership, the polarities between shareholder and employee and management and employee are, of course, considered to be greatly reduced. In the average ESOP company, there are only a few matters of long-range impact requiring an employee vote. As will be seen below, Carris employees are directly involved in gover-nance. In the section below on Carris Companies' structures of governance are several groups whose formation can be considered a 'community of practice'.

13.4.2 Carris Companies' structures of governance

Discussion involving Carris Companies' governance needs to emphasise that employee governance was both a source for and a recipient of corporate change. It was one of the more unusual facets of the Carris Companies' transition. The first transition group was the *Long Term Plan* Steering Committee comprised of a cross-section of Carris Compa-nies' roles. Its work is described in the first decision milestone below. At the first meet-ing after the first stock was issued, corporate and site management joined the repre-sentatives (one employee-owner elected for every 50) to form the Corporate Steering Committee (CSC). This became the decision-making group guiding the transition and implementing change.

The CSC delegated work to ongoing and ad hoc committees (Corporate, North Carolina, Corporate Management and Office Governance Committees), study groups (management for compensation), task forces (Health Care), sites (North Carolina as prototype for site implementation of the decision-making model; local sites gift committees), and so on.

In addition to the information moving through the CSC, there were various interactive communication vehicles within the company. Prior to each CSC meeting, there were a series of meetings at each of the sites to prepare and to go over the agenda. The State of the Company meetings were held at least once annually but more often as necessary. Usually, Bill Carris and at least one corporate manager (usually the Chief Financial Officer or Human Resources Director) travelled to the sites and met with small groups to go over the financials, corporate performance data, the ESOP stock valuation and to talk over new directions and concerns. From 2001 to 2003, with the downturn in the economy, these took on a more serious quality. Rather than offering a report designed at corporate headquarters, employees' questions were solicited from each of the sites. These became the backbone for organising the State of the Company meetings. At the end of the fiscal year, Bill Carris wrote shareholder letters to the employees reviewing the previous year's performance. In early 2004, as hopes for a speedy economy recovery dimmed, a series of conversations were held to gather and to answer questions rather than to wait for the State of the Company meetings.

13.4.3 Governance and decision-making

Daily, Dalton and Cannella define governance within a context that implies decision-making:

> We define governance as the determination of the broad uses to which organizational resources will be deployed and the resolution of conflicts among the myriad participants in organizations (2003: 371).

Within the frame of means and order, Williamson also implies that decision-making is at the root of governance:

> Governance is . . . an exercise in assessing the efficacy of alternative modes (means) of an organization. The object is to effect good order through the mechanisms of governance. A governance structure is thus usefully thought of as an institutional framework in which the integrity of a transaction or related set of transactions is decided (1996: 11).

Pound clearly notes that 'Corporate governance is not about power but about ensuring that decisions are made effectively' (2000: 79). Further he states, 'A number of companies have already made progress toward governance that focuses . . . more on the effectiveness of the organization' (2000: 80). Doppelt does not dodge the power issue. He notes governance's relational qualities, its importance and pervasiveness:

> The term 'governance' refers to the way any organization, public or private, small or large, distributes power and authority through its information, decision-making and resource allocation mechanisms. An organization's governance system plays a major role in shaping the ways its members view the world, interact with each other and the external environment, and perform

their tasks. Whenever people choose to live or work together, some type of governance system evolves (2003: 17).

13.4.4 Governance systems as three-legged stools

To decision-making, Doppelt adds the manner in which information is gathered and shared and how resources and wealth are distributed:

> In other words, governance systems are three-legged stools that shape the way information is gathered and shared, decisions are made and enforced, and resources and wealth are distributed. These factors shape the way people perceive the world around them, the way they are motivated, and their power and authority. These are the drive shaft and steering mechanisms of an organization (2003: 78).

In the following sections, the Carris governance systems will be seen to have the components of Doppelt's three-legged stool: information, decisions, and resources and wealth distribution.

13.4.5 Carris Companies share information

Through bulletin boards, meetings, and print media, Carris Companies' employees received information on matters that affected them on a regular basis. For example, when there were changes in compensation, the retirement programme and healthcare insurance, Human Resources personnel met with small groups of employees to go over the information and to receive and answer questions.

Meetings were held with employees on a regular basis to keep employees informed during the recent downturn in the US economy. The telecommunications industry problems at the turn of the century directly affected the sale of reels for wire and cable. Less directly affected were sales to those customers in the energy industry. In spite of the loss in sales, Carris Reels maintained market share and continued as the second-largest reel manufacturer in the US—profitable in that core business. With problems in their other industries because of expansion just prior to the downturn, their financial institution directed that two of the companies be sold or closed. It was very difficult for the Carris Companies to reduce their size for the first time in their history.

An interim goal was set to sustain and maintain good corporate health, rather than to grow. The process involved months of seeking buyers for two of the companies: Killington Wood Products (which ultimately closed) and Vermont Tubbs. With a great deal of effort on the part of corporate management, help was received from state and federal governments for loan guarantees to help buyers purchase Vermont Tubbs, which was the largest business with the largest employee group. At the end of September 2003, the Carris Companies and number of employees approached half of what they were in 1999. Given the long time-line for the transactions, most employees (with company and Vermont state assistance) were able to find other employment either within Carris or local businesses.

In the 2005 State of the Company meetings, solid profits were reported with plans to move employee ownership beyond 50%.

13.4.6 The Carris Companies: building participation for governance

In the opening memorandum to the LTP written for Carris employees, Bill Carris noted the participation required to bring to life employee ownership and employee governance with shared rewards: 'I am searching for the working mechanism to make an ideal concept such as this a reality here, at our company, and I need your help' (Carris 1994: i); and later 'The conversion to employee governance is everyone's project' (Carris 1994: 23). The Carris Companies built participation through conversations with small groups about work and the agenda for the CSC meetings; committee structures such as those directing the overall and site implementation of the decision-making model and local site gift giving committees; training for the governance decision-making model and other corporate and governance needs; task forces to review major challenges such as healthcare; and the CSC. Three of the five ESOP trustees were elected employee-owners who also served as representatives on the CSC.

Within ESOPs, participation is important. Early efforts to mount employee ownership in manufacturing settings had disappointing results in areas involving productivity. Analyses suggested that multifaceted approaches for employee participation must accompany employee ownership (Blasi 1990). For example, Marens *et al.* found that ESOPs 'can be a useful mechanism for building a stakeholder relationship'. That usefulness might be in 'anchoring participation programmes in a tangible and credible manner' (1999: 73). Employing meta-analysis (a statistical technique for distilling a single estimate from a number of studies) of 43 studies, Doucouliagos estimated the 'average correlation between productivity and various forms of participation'. He found that

> profit sharing, worker ownership and worker participation in decision-making are all positively associated with productivity. All the observed correlations are stronger among labor-managed firms (firms owned and controlled by workers) than among participatory capitalist firms (firms adopting one or more participation schemes involving employees, such as ESOPs or quality circles) (1995: 58).

13.4.7 Selected milestones toward 100% Carris corporate governance

Presented below are selected milestones for Carris corporate governance. Note the information sharing, the decision-making role, the allocation of resources and the distribution of wealth moving through the Corporate Steering Committee

- In 1994, the LTP and ideas for moving into corporate governance were shared broadly.

- In 1995, the *Long Term Plan* Steering Committee (LTPSC) as an ESOP Advisory Committee was comprised of management and employees (15 to start and later five site representatives added). It was formed to work with the attorney to make the decisions for the ESOP; to ensure participation; to establish criteria for selecting ESOP trustees; to advise trustees and seller on 18 key decisions. Of the 18 Bill Carris could have made, he made two (one person–one vote and continuing the corporate tithe). The LTPSC made the other 16 which involved allocation of shares. Great effort was made not to favour management. The Committee established $30,000 (with annual CPI adjustments; $37,550 at the end of 2004) as the salary ceiling for allocation. This was in sharp contrast to settings in which management was favoured in allocations. Consensus was used for decisions.

Selected committee members attended NCEO meeting in Chicago.

Trustees were selected for ESOP.

Bill Carris suggested to LTPSC that it should act as if it were the corporate Board of Directors. Sometime in the future, that would very likely occur.

Closing on the initial ESOP transaction began the process for the actual transfer of ownership.

- In 1996, a survey of all employees was conducted before the stock certificates were issued. The first stock certificates were issued to employee-owners. At the joint meeting of the LTPSC and managers, the decision was made to form the Corporate Steering Committee (CSC).

Established goal of three meetings each year.

Corporate information, site reports and decisions were brought forward within the joint group for discussion and action—a practice that became precedent and tradition.

At the end of the meeting, Bill Carris put attendance policy into the hands of the sites.

A survey was given to members following the meeting. Results indicated a great deal of anticipation and expectancy about the possible impact of CSC on the corporation.

- In 1997, CSC adopted the mission statement with community principles, corporate purpose and company goal for prominent posting at every location. The CSC recognised that the stock transfer rate needed to be slowed. Per person limits within Section 415 of the federal income tax code were causing long-term employees retirement and ESOP benefits to be placed into excess benefits with the return of 401K contributions.

Grants and gifts distribution involved site employee committees. The idea of distribution of the wealth of the corporation was basic to the idea of ownership.

Training for new CSC members was put forward.

Greg Zlavor provided training in decision-making—procedures for polling, voting or consensus, and guided the process for development of the agenda flow for CSC.

In the nomination for the ESOP Association national award, it was noted that the Carris ESOP was the only one ever so designed.

The decision was made to move forward with implementation of incentive compensation beginning January 1998.

- In 1998, CSC compensation research was delegated to a committee of managers.

CSC meetings changed to two per year; discussion regarding number of floor workers to managers at the meetings.

100 to 1 stock split recommended.

Recommendation that stock allocation be changed to reflect less seniority; new allocation structure put to a vote of all employees.

Two company-wide surveys were conducted on the Carris employees' views of the company, the LTP and employee ownership.

- In 1999, Strategic Planning is initiated. N. Berg (consultant from HBS) and C. Wise (local planning consultant) provided training at the CSC meeting.

  Dave Tabor reviewed healthcare.

  Health Care Task Force formed to reduce rising healthcare costs.

  Retirement benefits analysis was put forward.

  Continued effort to explain Workers' Compensation expenses.

  Decision was made to have members complete terms after the Fall meeting.

  Time off and its costs were made part of compensation study.

  In study of LTP noted that profit was mentioned 101 times.

- In 2000, CSC discussed Strategic Planning.

  Feedback on survey results and impacts for the Carris Companies.

  Training by Ownership Associates to the CSC for decision-making: 'Frontiers and Boundaries'.

  Decided that those running to be CSC reps should be employee-owners (employed for one calendar year beginning 1 January through end of the year).

  Compensation plan unveiled.

  Performance evaluation model unveiled.

  Health Care Task Force recommendations received and decision made to put them to an employee-owner vote.

- In 2001 Ownership Associates (OA) worked with the CSC to develop the corporate Influence Allocation Chart at the meeting. This chart showed who and where in the company decisions were made as well as how to gain input. It is the foundation of the process to make decision-making transparent to all employee-owners. Any employee can begin the process.

  OA presented the Six-Step Decision-Making model.

  NC decided to be the pilot site to introduce the decision-making model.

  Corporate Governance Committee formed.

  Scholarship Task Force reported to CSC.

  Lean manufacturing presented to CSC.

- In 2002, Corporate Governance Committee and North Carolina Governance Committee work to complete grids.

  CSC received several reports showing how the companies were handling the recession.

  Information provided regarding change in bank for 401K and retirement.

  Review of decision-making model.

- In 2003, Bill Carris, Mike Curran (VP) and Dave Fitz-Gerald (CFO) reviewed carefully the current status of the company, its sales and plans. It was noted that, from 2000, debt level had been reduced by nearly two-thirds. Fixed costs were reduced to levels appropriate to sales. The companies had returned to their core business which was profitable in spite of downturn in the economy. Maintained commitment to 100% employee ownership and 100% employee governance.

One full day was devoted to elements in the LTP, the ESOP, and hearing of the pilot project in North Carolina.

Those present chose to move forward with the decision-making model.

Site reports included safety, sales, employee ownership activities.

Bill Carris announced that, as soon as possible after 1 January 2004, employees will own 50% of the company.

• At the March 2004 CSC meeting:

Consensus was reaffirmed as the decision-making method of choice.

Discussion was continued from the meeting in September 2003 and the assignment on the LTP review. Affirmed was the continued movement towards 100% employee ownership and the ESOP—with the understanding that the ESOP is a vehicle for employee ownership and increased participation.

Rationale for the change of banks was presented; reviewed were overall company finances with its increasing financial health.

The number of employees was at 1993 levels.

Health Care Task Force Update was presented.

Decision was made to go forward with the decision-making process in Connecticut and in Rutland—corporate, the office and the mill.

Discussed was the management of the repurchase liability of participants eligible for a distribution at the end of 2003.

HR posed the question for discussion: 'How do we find what works for everybody or individually at each site: tying the ownership and day-to-day performance—education, technical, historical and essential skills and ongoing communication?'

Site reports included education, employee involvement, employee participation and decision-making.

• At the September 2004 CSC meeting:

Financial reports indicated that company was on track for its 2004 goals—success was noted to come from doing many small things well.

Change in healthcare provider was meticulously reviewed. Extensive discussion ensued concerning efforts to maintain solid coverages while picking up efficiencies and reducing administrative costs.

Safety continued as an area emphasis within all site reports.

Communication exercise clarified differences in styles, some of which were humourous.

Efforts to contain material costs in light of the market were presented and discussed at length.

Each site reported on its progress toward implementing the LTP.

Bill and Barbara Carris reported on their meetings at each of the sites.

Bill Carris presented a handout suggesting processes for increased visibility for the CSC employee representatives and increased employee involvement with ways to increase accountability for these processes.

- At the March 2005 CSC meeting:

   The announcement was made that Mike Curran was named President by the Board of Directors. Discussed was the importance of this succession in terms of the transfer of ownership to the employees and the successful management of the company. It was noted that Bill Carris would continue as Chair of the Board leading the transition process.

   Discussed was strategic planning going forward later in the year.

   Reported were the good financial results for 2004.

   Savings for the new healthcare plan were noted.

   Continued was the reporting on the LTP implementation at the local sites and the discussion on the role of the CSC representative.

   Implementation of the decision-making model was discussed by the sites involved.

   The decision was made to go forward with the remaining sites: California, Michigan and Plastics.

   Bill and Barbara Carris reported on their second round of meetings at each of the sites.

In the following section, corporate citizenship will be described in the context of corporate roles within civil society with an application from the Carris Companies.

13.5 What are corporations' roles within civil society?

Though there may be additional roles, for purposes of this chapter corporate citizenship is highlighted. Sandra Waddock's observations regarding corporate citizenship clearly delineate the interconnectivity, interdependence and interactive quality of business:

> Corporate citizenship really means developing mutually beneficial, interactive and trusting *relationships* between the company and its many stakeholders—employees, customers, communities, suppliers, governments, investors and even non-governmental organisations (NGOs) and activists through the implementation of the company's strategies and operating practices. In this sense, being a good corporate citizen means treating all of a company's stakeholders (and the natural environment) with dignity and respect, being aware of the company's impacts on stakeholders and working collaboratively with them when appropriate to achieve mutually desired results (2003a: 3).

The values of corporate citizenship seem particularly clearly stated here:

> Good corporate citizenship is fundamentally about respect and integrity: respect for stakeholders and the Earth from which we draw life and breath; integrity both internally and, in reporting out, externally. Integrity—wholeness, soundness, healthfulness, firm adherence to a code (2003b: 3).

Waddock notes that good corporate citizens

> live up to clear constructive visions and core values. They treat well the entire range of stakeholders [defined below] who risk capital in, have an interest in,

> or are linked to the firm through primary and secondary impacts through developing respectful, mutually beneficial operating practices and by working to maximize sustainability of the natural environment (2002: 5).

Waddock places good corporate citizenship within the operating practices and long-term viability of the corporation:

> Becoming a good corporate citizen thus means defining, and achieving, responsible operating practices fully integrated into the entire corporate strategy, planning, management, and decision-making processes. Such practices need to give due consideration of the impacts of all operating and policy decisions on each of the corporation's stakeholders. Responsibility to all these constituents *in toto* constitutes responsibility to society, especially as government and community are critical secondary stakeholders . . . Corporate responsibility is fundamental not only to the corporation's citizenship as we define it, but perhaps more importantly also to its economic viability long-term, particularly as demands for accountability and transparency of corporate action increase (2002: 7).

Corporate citizenship is about the corporate lived experience. It is

> not about philanthropy, it is not about attaching a glossy community affairs report to the annual financial report as an afterthought managed by public relations. [It] is about citizenship at the heart of strategic planning . . . [O]ne of the qualities of the current corporate citizenship situation is its post-modernity—that there is no clear view of the future and that rationality in management decision-making must be tempered with caution, emotion, and unreason (McIntosh *et al.* 1998: 284).

13.5.1 Carris Companies: practice-based rather than a blueprint

Rather than a full-blown step-by-step blueprint, in the LTP Bill Carris offered his thoughts as a practice-based view of the change. Waddock notes the relational quality and interconnectivity of such an approach.

> Taking a practice-based stakeholder view . . . significantly alters the approach to the firm and its responsibilities, broadening the understanding of those to whom a firm is accountable. It moves the conversation . . . toward the quality and nature of the relationships that companies develop with stakeholders and the assessment of the impacts of corporate activities on those stakeholders' (2002: 9).

Before 1994, the idea of employee ownership churned in Bill Carris as he worked with consultants and Carris corporate management to find the best vehicle to make his vision of shared ownership of the company reality. He wanted to create the space for the employees to participate fully in the rights and responsibilities within the company.

> Companies that take advantage of the intelligence and ideas of all their employees will be much more successful than those that rely on a few people to lead. In conventional companies, it is up to the leaders (managers) to both generate the information needed to make changes and then to come up with the ideas for making improvements. The process may involve moving infor-

mation up and down several layers of the organization, slowing the process of decision-making considerably. Companies can no longer afford to be so limited. Employees are the best and most timely source of information, so this power should be utilized. The most effective organizations are those that strive to find ways to generate and process this knowledge in practical, efficient ways. This will happen when employees are owners and we move away from 'monarch-type' leadership to where everyone *participates* in decision-making. A structure for this to work still needs to be defined . . . The winners of the next decade will be those companies who have more people processing more information and making decisions faster. These will be the companies that stay ahead of the market (Carris 1994: 5, 7).

The next section briefly discusses corporate accountability for the common good with an application from the Carris Companies.

13.6 How should corporations be accountable for the common good?

Accountability in the relational sense means 'companies need to assume responsibility for the impacts of their practices, policies, and processes and the decisions that stand behind those practices' (Waddock 2002: 219).

> The true test of an accountable organization is specific: whether it measures performance quantitatively—with financial and non-financial numbers— and reports it publicly to audiences inside and outside the organization. Anything less than hard numbers broadly disclosed, reveals an organization hesitant to commit to full accountability. The act of one party answering to another in qualitative terms alone is not enough. Accountability requires data (Epstein and Birchard 2000: 5).

13.6.1 Carris Companies accountable in relationships to internal and external communities

The Carris Companies' quantifiable accountability involved areas of compensation, employee benefits, financial and in-kind gifts to the communities surrounding the site. Regarding community, Bill Carris explained that 'to improve the quality of life for our growing corporate community' (Carris 1994: 1) included the 'common good' in the context of the many and varied internal corporate relationships but also those relationships with the 'outside community—those towns or districts where we live—(the general public) and thereby society as a whole' (Carris 1994: 2). The Carris Companies used a pebble-in-the-pond approach to examine impact of actions within its companies and the larger society.

In a September 1996 payroll 'stuffer', Bill Carris defined community:

> as a group of people who are committed to a common purpose, depend on one another, make decisions together and identify themselves as part of

something larger than the sum of their individual relationships. They make a long-term commitment to their own wellbeing, the wellbeing of others in the community and the health and vitality of the community itself. Community embodies friendship (Carris 1996).

At the 50th anniversary celebration, the mayor of Rutland spoke of his gratitude for the prompt response he had received from the many calls requesting advice or assistance he had made to Bill Carris. Among others ways of being corporate citizens, Carris employees were released for service to volunteer fire departments and to donate blood. Local not-for-profits used the office facilities for meetings and fundraising calls. The Rutland sites were selected as participants in the Vermont State Welfare to Work programmes. The Carris Companies supported many local efforts to 'improve the quality of life' corporately and through their foundation which is supported through a tithe of 7.5% of corporate profits. Employee committees at each of the sites shared in the distribution of foundation monies with Bill Carris. During the last quarter of 2003 fundraising for the United Way,[5] the Carris Companies expected that Rutland gifts might be greatly reduced because of the reduction in size and economic problems in the area. The HR director noted her surprise that the employees had reached the previous year's goal and surprised everyone with their generosity.

US corporations have several oversight government groups. One of the groups that the Carris Companies worked with closely was the Occupational Safety and Health Administration (OSHA). Because the Companies saw its mandates and requirements as reducing injuries and making the work environment healthier and more productive, they consulted frequently. Stretching exercises and other wellness programmes were put forward on a regular basis.

The importance of balancing 'soft' and 'hard' aspects of community building, recognised before the LTP, was incorporated within it. Sites were encouraged and supported to create opportunities for participation. The longevity of employee-owners within the company at the older sites may be reflective of the strong relationships experienced. For example, at a September 2003 meeting, it was reported that for its 90 employee-owners the average length of service in the Rutland mill (Vermont) was 17 years and eight months.

13.7 Conclusions

An emphasis within this chapter was the interconnected, interdependent, interactive and pervasive nature of business within the global economy. In addressing the basic relational questions it was suggested that the view of corporations being reframed was more inclusive and of service to the common good; corporate governance needed to involve stakeholders through information, decision-making and resource allocation; consideration of the principles of corporate citizenship could be used as a guide for corporations in their roles within civil society and that accountability for the common

---

5   The United Way is a not-for-profit that has local bases throughout the US to raise funds for local charities.

good involves relationships, information and qualitative and quantitative aspects. Examined, as application, were the Carris Companies efforts in their transition toward full employee governance and employee ownership. Employee governance was seen to be both a source for and a recipient of corporate change. Within the governance process, information, decision-making and resource allocation were key elements. In spite of the financial distractions caused by the downturn in the US economy, and most notably in telecommunications, the Carris Companies continued their commitment to 100% employee ownership and governance. They continued to move toward their goals and maintained relationships within the companies and to their communities even as declining sales made it more difficult to be responsive. In early 2005, the companies were planning beyond 50% employee ownership.

References

Amin, A., and P. Cohendet (2000) 'Organisational Learning and Governance through Embedded Practices', *Journal of Management and Governance* 4: 93-116.

Andreadis, N.A. (2002) 'Leadership for Civil Society: Implications for Global Corporate Leadership Development', *Human Resource Development International* 5.2: 143-49.

Bandori, A. (2000) 'Conjectures for a New Research Agenda on Governance', *Journal of Management and Governance* 4: 1-9.

Billings, C.C. (1976) *Carris Reels Inc. History* (unpublished).

Blasi, J.R. (1990) *Employee Ownership: Revolution or Ripoff?* (New York: HarperCollins/Harper Business).

Bruyn, S. (2000) *A Civil Economy: Transforming the Market in the Twenty-first Century* (Ann Arbor, MI: University of Michigan Press).

Bryan, F., and J. McLaughry (1989) *The Vermont Papers: Recreating Democracy on a Human Scale* (Chelsea, VT: Chelsea Publishing).

Carris. W.H. (1994) *The Long Term Plan* (Rutland, VT: Carris Financial Corporation).

—— (1996) 'CCC Payroll Stuffer', 24 September 1996 (unpublished).

Charreaux, G., and P. Desbrieres (2001) 'Corporate Governance: Stakeholder Value versus Shareholder Value', *Journal of Management and Governance* 5: 107-28.

Daily, C.M., D.R. Dalton and A.A. Cannella (2003) 'Corporate Governance: Decades of Dialogue and Data', *Academy of Management Review* 28.3: 371.

Derber, C. (2002) *People before Profits: The New Globalization in an Age of Terror, Big Money, and Economic Crisis* (New York: St. Martin's Press).

DeSoto, H. (2002) *The Mystery of Capitalism: Why Capitalism Triumphs in the West and Fails Everywhere Else* (New York: Perseus Books).

Doucouliagos, C. (1995) 'Worker Participation and Productivity in Labor-managed and Participatory Capitalist Firms: A Meta-analysis', *Industrial and Labor Relations Review* 49.1: 59-77.

Doppelt, B. (2003) *Leading Change toward Sustainability: A Change-Management Guide for Business, Government and Civil Society* (Sheffield, UK: Greenleaf Publishing).

Epstein, M.J., and B. Birchard (2000) *Counting What Counts: Turning Corporate Accountability to Competitive Advantage* (New York: Perseus Publishing).

Fisher, J. (2003) 'Local and Global: International Governance and Civil Society', *Journal of International Affairs* 57.1: 19-40.

Friedman, M. (1970) 'The Social Responsibility of a Business is to Increase its Profits', *New York Times Magazine*, 13 September 1970: 32-33.

Greider, W. (2003) *The Soul of Capitalism: Opening Paths to a Moral Economy* (New York: Simon & Schuster).

Harman, W., and J. Hormann (1990) *Creative Work: The Constructive Role of Business in a Transforming Society* (Munich: Schweisfurth Foundation).

Hertel, S. (2003) 'The Private Side of Global Governance', *Journal of International Affairs* 57.1: 41-51.

Kelly, M. (2001) *The Divine Right of Capital* (San Francisco: Barrett-Koehler).

Lawrence, A.T. (1997) 'Employee Stock Ownership Plans', in P.H. Werhane and R.E. Freeman (eds.), *The Blackwell Encyclopedic Dictionary of Business Ethics* (Malden, MA: Blackwell Business): 198-99.

March, J.G., and H.A. Simon (1958) *Organizations* (New York: John Wiley).

Marens, R.S., A.C. Wicks and V.L. Huber (1999) 'Co-operating with the Disempowered: Using ESOPs to Forge a Stakeholder Relationship by Anchoring Trust in Workplace Participation Programs', *Business and Society* 38.1: 51.

McIntosh, M., D. Leipziger, K. Jones and G. Coleman (1998) *Corporate Citizenship: Successful Strategies for Responsible Companies* (London: Financial Times Prentice Hall).

Post, J.E., L.E. Preston and S. Sachs (2002) *Redefining the Corporation: Stakeholder Management and Organizational Wealth* (Stanford, CA: Stanford University Press).

Pound, J. (2000) 'The Promise of the Governed Corporation', in *Harvard Business Review on Corporate Governance* (Cambridge, MA: Harvard Business School Press): 79-104.

Smith, A. (1952) *An Inquiry into the Nature and Causes of the Wealth of Nations* (Chicago, IL: Encyclopedia Britannica, Inc.).

Smith A. (1969) *The Theory of Moral Sentiments* (New Rochelle, NY: Arlington House).

Stewart, T.A. (1997) *Intellectual Capital: The New Wealth of Organizations* (New York: Doubleday).

Waddock, S. (2002) *Leading Corporate Citizens: Vision, Values, Value Added* (Boston, MA: McGraw-Hill).

—— (2003a) 'Editorial', in *Journal of Corporate Citizenship* 9 (Spring 2003): 3-8.

—— (2003b) 'Editorial', in *Journal of Corporate Citizenship* 10 (Summer 2003): 3-5.

Williamson, O.E. (1975) *The Economic Institutions of Capitalism* (New York: The Free Press).

—— (1996) *The Mechanisms of Governance* (Oxford, UK: Oxford University Press).

Zadek, S. (2001) *The Civil Corporation: The New Economy of Corporate Citizenship* (London: Earthscan Publications).

14

Networks for environmental management

INVOLVING PUBLIC AND QUASI-PUBLIC ORGANISATIONS FOR MARKET DEVELOPMENT TOWARDS SUSTAINABILITY IN RIO DE JANEIRO, BRAZIL

José Antônio Puppim de Oliveira*

Brazilian School of Public and Business Administration—EBAPE
Getulio Vargas Foundation—FGV, Rio de Janeiro, Brazil

Economic development and environmental protection are intimately linked in developing countries. Those countries have two kinds of environmental problems. First, there are problems related to the lack of economic well-being of a large part of their populations. Poor peasants practise slash-and-burn agriculture, which in turn leads to deforestation. Water streams in poor urban areas are polluted due to the lack of infrastructure for sanitation. Second, the affluent part of the society has similar problems to those in developed economies, such as high patterns of consumption and waste generation.

Economic development is necessary to improve the life of the majority of the population. However, economic development strategies as practised by developed economies can increase those environmental problems. Therefore, new alternatives for the management of economic development are important to improve the quality of life of the population, and at the same not aggravate environmental problems.

Industrial ecology initiatives can provide an alternative to generate economic development to alleviate poverty and, at the same time, solve environmental problems in developing countries. Nevertheless, the implementation of policies based on industrial ecology has some tremendous obstacles in those countries. The difficulties for policy

*   I would like to thank the Department of Environmental Management of the Federation of the Industries of the State of Rio de Janeiro (FIRJAN) for providing information and data. I am also indebted to Christianne Maroun, who participated in the early versions of this chapter, as well as the reviewers for their insightful comments. However, the responsibility of all the ideas and opinions are those of the author solely.

implementation range from financing to lack of technical capacity and information (Puppim de Oliveira 2002b). Sometimes technical solutions do exist, but due to lack of economic viability they are difficult for firms to put in practice.

Markets can improve the economic viability of some industrial ecology alternatives. However, markets do not work simply when sellers and buyers exist. Transactions need to be made efficiently (Williamson 1994). The development of well-functioning markets is fundamental to make some transactions economically viable. Information is an important part of the puzzle to make markets work, such as technical information, price information and customer information.

This chapter examines the importance of public and quasi-public organisations, as providers of information to development markets, to making the alternatives of industrial ecology viable. It analyses the case of solid-waste management by the initiatives of the Federation of the Industries of the State of Rio de Janeiro (FIRJAN) in Brazil.

14.1 The rise of economic and market mechanisms[1]

Market-oriented approaches to environmental policy have become increasingly popular in the environmental policy-making arena. For a long time, these approaches have been preferred and advocated by many groups, including people from academia, the government, the non-governmental sector and multilateral agencies.[2] Proponents of economic regulation[3] have constantly claimed that direct regulation[4] is too costly and does not achieve the proposed environmental goals (Anderson and Leal 1992). Also, it is argued that command-and-control regulations have an inappropriate incentive structure (Barde and Pearce 1991), are generally too far from the people (Commoner 1987), favour certain interest groups (Anderson and Leal 1992) and are too confrontational (Vig and Kafts 1994). With the increasing recognition of some of the weaknesses of command and control, which are addressed below, more policy-makers have been tempted to support economic regulation as an alternative or complement to direct regulation (Fiorino 1995; Vig and Kraft 1994). Economic mechanisms have been used from forestry to energy and waste management (Richards 2000; Puppim de Oliveira 2000, 2002a).

The main argument supporting the use of economic regulation over the use of direct regulation is the presupposed higher economic efficiency to achieve environmental goals. It is argued that economic regulations can achieve more in terms of improving environmental quality and can cost much less. Supporters of economic regulation propose that governments should try to bring 'unpriced assets' (environmental assets, unowned or common properties) and market externalities into the pricing system, in

---

1   Some parts and ideas relating to this section were originally published in Puppim de Oliveira 2001.
2   For example, Baumol and Oates 1979; Panayotou 1993; Pearce and Turner 1990; OECD 1991, 1994; Repetto *et al.* 1992; World Bank 1992; Richards 2000.
3   The chapter uses the terms 'economic regulation' and 'market-oriented approaches to environmental regulation' interchangeably as synonyms throughout.
4   The chapter uses the terms 'direct regulation' and 'command-and-control approaches to environmental regulation' interchangeably as synonyms throughout.

order to internalise social costs. In doing this, a market system would be created and 'the invisible hand' would help to achieve environmental goals more efficiently (Anderson and Leal 1992). However, things are not that simple, as I will explain below.

Many of the criticisms (on efficiency or effectiveness) of command-and-control mechanisms are relevant. Additionally, economic incentives or market mechanisms may be part of the solution to many environmental problems. One branch of the literature, mostly composed by economists, argues that distorted markets are the cause of most environmental problems, or that market mechanisms can prove significant in tackling environmental problems, even in developing countries (Panayotou 1993; Anderson and Leal 1992; Pearce and Turner 1990). Although economic or market mechanisms may contribute to improving environmental management and industrial ecology initiatives, they can not be viewed as the only alternative for solving environmental problems. Indeed, some authors are sceptical that governments that fail to implement other kinds of policies may be effective in creating the institutions to implement market mechanisms (Puppim de Oliveira 2002b). Many governments have problems in implementing public policies, ranging from lack of political support to lack of financial resources or technical capacity.

These problems seem to be more critical in developing countries. The literature is proficient in documenting the lack of effectiveness in implementation of environmental policies in developing countries, especially in Asia, Eastern Europe and Latin America.[5] However, though the descriptions of failures are important to understand the problems, they do not point out effective and viable solutions. Thus, how to tackle these problems?

First, the implementation process involves several organisations in general. In order to search for viable solutions to environmental problems, we have to understand the political economy of the policy process. This varies from country to country, or from context to context. Many solutions come from experiences in developed countries, and may not fit in a different context, so we need more experiences from developing countries. Second, the understanding of successful examples of policy implementation in developing countries can direct the solutions. Although there are few studies of successful implementation of environmental policies in those countries, some authors have recently contributed to the literature (Brinkerhoff 1996; Lemos 1998; Puppim de Oliveira 2002b). Third, the same concerns described above are valid for the implementation of market-based environmental policies. Markets do not work automatically; they should be created and developed. The understanding of cases in developing countries where market-based policies succeeded can lead to practical solutions in other less developed countries.

5   Shams 1994; Vyas and Reddy 1998; Reich and Bowonder 1992; Ross 1988; Jan 1995; Hardi 1992; Klarer and Francis 1997; Pichon 1992.

14.2 The importance of public and quasi-public organisations to developing markets

Business people, politicians and academics have increasingly recognised the need for innovative management models to deal with the complexity of the inter- and the multidisciplinary nature of economic, social and environmental problems. In the new paradigm of sustainable development, the implementation of environmental policies needs intricate relations, not only intra-organisational but especially inter-organisational. Nowadays, any effective environmental action involves several individuals and organisations in private, public and civil society. Hierarchy (command and control) and markets may be forms of institutions to control behaviour and to mediate the relations among those individuals and organisations. However, the creation and maintenance of well-functioning hierarchy and market institutions needs a series of actors outside the system such as individuals and organisations that involve more horizontal or co-operative relations. For example, civil society actors can provide information for well-functioning markets, or for the enforcement of command-and-control regulations. These outside actors may easily mediate many horizontal interactions in the hierarchy and market institutions. Those horizontal relations are called networks (Powell 1990). Networks have been important in many theories. For instance, the theory of 'clusters' has recognised the importance of co-operation networks to develop firms and make regions and companies more competitive (Piore and Sabel 1984; Porter 1998). In this chapter we will concentrate on studying how quasi-public organisations support the development of market institutions only, though some of the lessons could be adapted to hierarchies.

Public and quasi-public organisations (e.g. NGOs and unions) are important to develop markets institutions and make them work in such way that make firms more competitive and innovative. They can 'lubricate' the market relations by providing information and stimulating the exchange of goods. These organisations are also important in providing technical advice to the potential demanders and suppliers of goods in this market.

In solid-waste management, several examples demonstrate the role of public or quasi-public organisations in developing markets to alleviate environmental problems. Some states in the United States provide incentives to the creation of markets as demanders of recyclable products ('Buy Recyclables Initiatives') and stimulate the work of recycling firms (Puppim de Oliveira 2000). In Europe, the Green Dot system reduced drastically the environmental problems caused by packaging. Initially developed in Germany, the Green Dot system is a non-profit organisation that integrates the activities of producers of packaging material, firms that use packaging, and recycling and processing industries. The system is such that firms have economic incentives to reduce their packaging material (Polzin and Puppim de Oliveira 2001).

In the state of Rio de Janeiro in Brazil, the state's federation of industries (FIRJAN[6]) is playing an important role in creating the means to catalyse the market for industrial

---

6   FIRJAN = Federação das Indústrias do Rio de Janeiro (Federation of the Industries of Rio de Janeiro State). The union affiliates more than 16,000 medium and large industries in the state of Rio de Janeiro.

solid waste. Several actions for providing market information, technical advice and mediation of commercial relations among buyers and sellers of solid material have been undertaken in a general programme created by the Federation.

14.3 Industrial solid-waste management in Rio de Janeiro: the role of FIRJAN

This chapter examines the role of quasi-public organisations in the development of markets for solid-waste management. It uses case-study methodology (Yin 1994) applied to the case of industrial solid-waste management in Rio de Janeiro and the role of its federation of industries (FIRJAN).

According to the State Environmental Agency of Rio de Janeiro State (FEEMA),[7] industries generate six million tons of solid waste per year in the state. A portion of this material goes through the municipal waste systems. Another large part of the waste produced needs specialised environmental management and final destination, which can be made by companies accredited by FEEMA. Nevertheless, special waste management can be quite expensive. On top of that, Brazilian regulations for waste disposal and management have become increasingly strict since 1981, when the National Environmental Policy was promulgated. Besides, there were some accidents involving solid waste in the last few years, which increased pressure from civil society. As a result, scrutiny by law enforcement and by civil society, in addition to the unwanted results of a major accident, have also increased pressure to the companies to find innovative and new ways to conduct adequate solid-waste management.

Additionally, several companies throughout Brazil started to find that recycling, re-use and waste reduction (pollution prevention) can result in real economic benefits. A few firms have specialised in solid-waste management to help those companies to implement the challenge. Other firms have focused on recycling or re-using solid waste. A potential solid-waste market started to form. To catalyse this market, FIRJAN created programmes to facilitate interchanges among suppliers and demanders of solid materials and to help companies in Rio de Janeiro to deal technically with their solid-waste management.

In 1998, FIRJAN's Department of Environmental Management created the Environmental Exchange Program (EEP), which organises tours to industries in Rio State that have innovative solutions in waste. Members of other companies are invited to attend the tours and learn through experience of these 'cutting-edge' firms. The programme started with 52 companies in 1998 and reached more than 230 participants in 2001 (see Fig. 14.1). Besides learning about new processes, the visits are opportunities for networking on environmental management and business. Participants in the programme are composed mostly of medium-sized and large companies' managers (33%) and small business owners (54%) looking for business opportunities in waste management.

Another FIRJAN initiative to stimulate the market for solid materials (waste) is the Waste Exchange Market (WEM), which was created in 2000. FIRJAN encourages its affil-

---

7 Personal consultation in 2002.

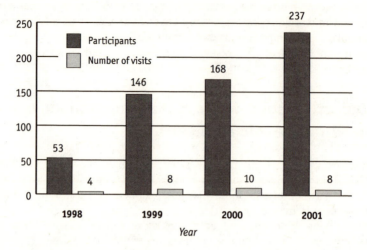

FIGURE 14.1 Evolution of participation in the Environmental Exchange Programme

Source: FIRJAN, direct consultation in an interview in August 2002

Product	Number of ads	%
Acid solutions	31	13.5
Rubber	7	3.1
Sludge	11	4.8
Wood	11	4.8
Textiles	10	4.4
Leather materials	1	0.4
Non-metallic minerals	2	0.9
Used oils	16	7.0
Paper and cardboard	14	6.1
Plastic	32	14.0
Organic chemical products	15	6.6
Paints	7	3.1
Solvents	3	1.3
Scrap metals	22	9.6
Glass	4	1.8
Other	43	18.8
Total	229	100.0

TABLE 14.1 Advertisement by the type of product offered in February 2002

Source: table generated by the author from FIRJAN 2002

iated members to advertise 'wastes' they have available for donation or sale in FIRJAN's monthly environmental newsletter.[8] Moreover, companies are allowed to advertise for their material supplies in the newsletter, which reaches more than 3,000 subscribers, mostly environmental managers of large and medium-sized companies, throughout Brazil and Latin America. The information is also available online at FIRJAN's homepage[9] where companies can advertise their offers and demands directly. The offers vary widely regarding the type of material (Table 14.1), from solvents to wood and plastics.

The Waste Exchange Market has become very popular and the number of adverts has grown steadily. In the February 2002 issue, more than 260 adverts were placed in the newsletter (see Fig. 14.2; FIRJAN 2002). Moreover, adverts have been quite effective. In a survey in 2002, 54% of the advertisers were contacted by people interested in their offers and 30% (of the total number of adverts) resulted in an actual deal being done. Recently, FIRJAN has focused on another kind of initiative to help corporations to manage and minimise (through pollution prevention) their waste generated in the industrial process. In addition to the legal counsel it provides, FIRJAN created a Centre for Environmental Technology (CET). CET, which is a result of an investment of more than US$ 1.5 million, all contributions from Rio de Janeiro-based industries, aims at assisting companies in finding technical advice to develop their projects for improving environmental management. These projects include solid-waste management programmes and market solutions.

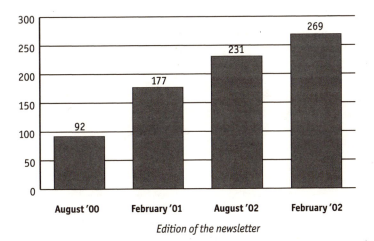

FIGURE 14.2 **Number of advertisements in the Waste Exchange Market**

Source: FIRJAN, direct consultation in an interview in August 2002

---

8 The newsletter, *Súmula Ambiental*, deals with environmental issues for industries in Rio de Janeiro (new laws, experiences, opportunities, concepts, etc.).

9 The website is www.firjan.org.br, click on Meio Ambiente and then Bolsa de Residuos; or go to www.firjan.org.br/notas/cgi/cgilua.exe/sys/start.htm?infoid=4036&sid=33.

14.4 Conclusions

The existence of potential suppliers and customers does not mean that a market exists. This is also true that market mechanisms can improve the management of 'environmental goods' and the search for solutions in industrial ecology. However, the development of markets is complex and needs an interdisciplinary approach. Markets are not *laissez-faire* and do not appear instantaneously; they are institutions (North 1990). Well-functioning markets require the development of a series of rules, formal and informal, and organisations that promote and enforce those rules, as well as providing information and organising the players in the market.

Developed markets can make eco-efficiency and industrial ecology solutions economically and financially viable. In the case of solid waste, there are several examples around the world that are technically feasible (Puppim de Oliveira 2000). Nevertheless, many of these solutions are not economically viable because the market institutions are not well developed, especially in developing countries.

Public and quasi-public organisations have an important role as facilitators to create and develop market institutions and find solutions for environmental problems. These organisations can provide information to make technical solutions economically viable. They can facilitate the relation between supply and demand, thus diminishing the transaction costs for helping markets solve environmental problems more effectively. Therefore, as the FIRJAN case demonstrates in this chapter, quasi-public organisations can play a crucial role in solid-waste management. Similarly, other public and quasi-public organisations, such as local governments, NGOs and unions, can also play important roles and help markets for environmental products and services to develop by, for example, organising suppliers or customers and providing information.

Bibliography

Anderson, T.A., and D.R. Leal (1992) 'Free Market versus Political Environmentalism', *Harvard Journal of Law and Public Policy* 15.2 (Spring 1992): 297-310.

Barde, J.P., and D.W. Pearce (1991) *Valuing the Environment: Six Case Studies* (London: Earthscan Publications).

Baumol, W., and W. Oates (1979) *Economics, Environmental Policy, and the Quality of Life* (Englewood Cliffs, NJ: Prentice Hall).

Brinkerhoff, D.W. (1996) 'Co-ordination Issues in Policy Implementation Networks: An Illustration from Madagascar's Environmental Action Plan', *World Development* 24.9: 1,497-510.

Commoner, B. (1987) 'Reporter at Large', *The Environment, New Yorker* (n.d.): 46 and 62.

Fiorino, D. (1995) *Making Environmental Policy* (Los Angeles: University of California Press).

FIRJAN (Federação das Indústrias do Estado do Rio de Janeiro) (2002) 'Bolsa de Resíduos', *Súmula Ambiental*, February 2002.

Hardi, P. (1992) *Impediments on Environmental Policy-making and Implementation in Central and Eastern Europe: Tabula Rasa vs Legacy of the Past* (Berkeley, CA: University of California Press).

Jan, G. (1995) 'Environmental Protection in China', in O.P. Dwivedi and D. Vajpeyi (eds.), *Environmental Policies in the Third World: A Comparative Analysis* (Westport, CT: Greenwood Press).

Klarer, J., and P. Francis (1997) 'Regional Overview', in J. Klarer and B. Moldan, *The Environmental Challenge for Central European Economies in Transition* (Chichester, UK/London: John Wiley).

Lemos, M.C. de Mello (1998) 'The Politics of Pollution Control in Brazil: State Actors and Social Movements Cleaning up Cubatão', *World Development* 26.1: 75-88.

North, D.C. (1990) *Institutions, Institutional Change, and Economic Performance* (Cambridge, UK: Cambridge University Press).

OECD (Organisation for Economic Co-operation and Development) (1991) *Environmental Policy: How to Apply Economic Instruments* (Paris: OECD).

—— (1994) *Environment and Taxation: The Cases of the Netherlands, Sweden and the USA* (Paris: OECD).

Panayotou, T. (1993) *Green Markets: The Economics of Sustainable Development* (San Francisco: ICS Press).

Pearce, D.W., and R.K. Turner (1990) *Economics of Natural Resources and the Environment* (New York/London: Harvester Wheatsheaf).

Pichon, F.J. (1992) 'Environmental Policies in Ecuador', *Policy Studies Journal* 20.4: 662-78.

Piore, M., and C. Sabel (1984) *The Second Industrial Divide: Possibilities for Prosperity* (New York: Basic Books).

Polzin, D.A.O.F.M., and J.A. Puppim de Oliveira (2001) 'Buscando Alternativas para o Gerenciamento de Resíduos Sólidos: O Caso das embalagens na Sociedade Ponto Verde, Portugal' ('Searching for Institutional Alternatives for Solid-Waste Management: The Case of Packaging Material in Portugal'), paper presented at the *VI Meeting on Business Management and the Environment*, São Paulo, 26–28 November 2001.

Porter, M.E. (1998) 'Clusters and the New Economics of Competition', *Harvard Business Review* 76.6 (November/December 1998): 77-90.

Powell, W.W. (1990) 'Neither Market nor Hierarchy: Network Forms of Organization', *Research in Organizational Behavior* 12: 295-336.

Puppim de Oliveira, J.A. (2000) 'Study on Recycling Program Cost-effectiveness: The Case of Municipal Recycling Programs (MRPs) in the Commonwealth of Massachusetts, USA', paper presented at the *Conference of the Association of European Schools of Planning (AESOP)*, Brno, Czech Republic, 20 July 2000.

—— (2001) 'Command Control versus Economic Mechanisms: What Is the Evidence for Efficiency and Effectiveness in Environmental Management?', *International Journal of Environmental Creation* 4.1: 27-33.

—— (2002a) 'The Policymaking Process for Creating Competitive Assets for the Use of Biomass Energy: The Brazilian Alcohol Programme', *Sustainable Energy Reviews* 6.2: 129-40.

—— (2002b) 'Implementing Environmental Policies in Developing Countries through Decentralization', *World Development* 30.10 (October 2002): 1,713-36.

Reich, M.R., and B. Bowonder (1992) 'Environmental Policy in India: Strategies for Better Implementation', *Policy Studies Journal* 20.4: 643-61.

Ross, L. (1988) *Environmental Policy in China* (Bloomington, IN: Indiana University Press).

Repetto, R., R.C. Dower, R. Jenkins and J. Geoghegan (1992) *Green Fees* (Washington, DC: World Resources Institute).

Richards, M. (2000) 'Can Sustainable Tropical Forestry be Made Profitable? The Potential and Limitations of the Innovative Incentive Mechanisms', *World Development* 28.6: 1,001-16.

Shams, R. (1994) 'Environmental Policy and Interest Groups in Developing Countries', *Intereconomics*, January/February 1994: 16-24.

Vig, N., and M. Kraft (eds.) (1994) *Environmental Policy in the 1990s* (Washington, DC: CQ Press).

Vyas, V.S., and V.R. Reddy (1998) 'Assessment of Environmental Policies and Policy Implementation in India', *Economic and Political Weekly* 10 (January 1998): 48-54.

Williamson, O.E. (1994) 'The Institutions and Governance of Economic Development Reform', proceedings of the *World Bank Annual Conference on Development Economics* (Washington, DC: The World Bank).

World Bank (1992) *World Bank Development Report 1992: Development and the Environment* (Oxford, UK/New York: Oxford University Press).

Yin, R.K. (1994) *Case Study Research: Design and Methods* (Vol. 5. Applied Social Research Methods Series; Thousand Oaks, CA: Sage, 2nd edn).

Part 4
Corporate governance and its implications for regulators and civil society

15

Corporate governance models
INTERNATIONAL LEGAL PERSPECTIVES

Željko Šević *

University of Greenwich, UK

The concept of **corporate governance** should be understandable by itself. One can say that it is about governing (steering) the corporation as a major business form since the late 19th century. However, diverse practices have shown that the obvious is *finally* not so obvious. Usually a system of governance is perceived as a set of rules that govern the way people interact and how decisions are made within an organisation (both private and public). The rules generally reflect the organisational aims, size of the organisation and sector within which it operates and, finally, the macro conditions such as culture, values, legal system, political regime and so on. Although we try to group governance models into different types, every national system has its specifics, where national culture and the system of enrooted values dominate the nuances, which quite often can be crucial.

The corporate governance systems have been the focus of research interests for a number of years, but the term 'corporate governance' got its citizenship rights in the last decade or two (Tricker 1997). Unfortunately, corporate governance comes into the public focus only after a major scandal or a series of corporate failures and scandals. The fall of Barings Bank and more recently the 'implosion' of Enron and WorldCom have attracted the attention of not only investors but also regulators and governments. In the US, the *Sarbanes–Oxley Act of 2002* was triggered by the Enron scandal and was primarily passed to restore confidence in American corporate governance; but it has a more far-reaching impact. In fact, the US government is set to exercise not only *regulatory leadership*,[1] but also regulatory control over a number of business entities that are very remotely connected with the US (Vagts 2003). This is not just a phenomenon of the early 21st century. The Berle–Dodd debate (Macintosh 1999) and the initiation of a set of security laws in the US were triggered by the failure of the Kreuger and Toll group of companies in 1931. Price, Waterhause & Co. blamed, in their final report on the Kreuger

---

* The author is grateful to anonymous referees, editor Professor Istemi Demirag, Lawrence E. Mitchell and Nicholas G. Hand, for their comments on the previous versions of this chapter. However, the usual disclaimer remains.

1 Understood here as being first in regulating this obvious 'market failure', setting the agenda for other countries or intergovernmental organisations.

& Toll, secrecy and the lack of transparency as the main reasons for this large failure (Price Waterhause & Co. 1932). The New York Stock Exchange (NYSE) immediately required all companies applying for listing to ensure that their financial reports were 'certified' by an independent public accountant and that all subsidiary (dependent) companies were covered in the financial reports (*Journal of Accountancy* 1933).

However, while all the company laws and regulations that were passed regulated some aspects of what we call nowadays corporate governance, in fact 'no laws were passed on how corporations should be governed' (Estes 1980: 50). To a large extent corporate governance remains in the domain of 'good practice' and recent moves on the both sides of the Atlantic support this claim. The promotion of the OECD *Principles of Corporate Governance* and *American Law Institute Principles of Corporate Governance* (in further text 'ALI Principles of Governance') has clearly shown that (potential) regulators are aware of possible differences in apprehension of the concept and are therefore willing to put forward a set of expectations and standards that are to be observed. In a mature institutional structure, the power of 'moral suasion' cannot and should not be neglected, as it may have more far-reaching consequences than the simple introduction of law. Only where the regulator expects serious distortions in comparison to standards should the law or other compulsory regulation be promulgated (Kelsen 1945; or in fact any Theory of Law text).

For the purposes of this chapter, we may perceive governance as an institutional framework within which the 'integrity of the transaction is decided' (Williamson 1996: 11), or the 'relationship among various participants in determining directions and performance of corporations' (Monks and Minow 2001: 1). As the corporate governance system is a part of the social infrastructure, it has to fit in with the rest of the institutional framework. This very framework is decided by the economic structure. It is very difficult to have a socially based model of corporate governance in an economy that is exclusively (or predominantly) profit-oriented. Economic theory recognises three dominant economic structures: social-market economy, administratively guided economy and consumer-driven economy (Ostry 1990; Marer 1991; Šević 1999). Social-market economy is characteristic of the continental European tradition; the administratively guided economy blueprint has been used in Japan, while the US is the most important representative of the consumer-driven economy. Whereas the former two take a somewhat longer view of company and societal performance, the last is short-term-driven, and profit maximisation in the short run is the most important task of a corporation. Social-market and administratively guided economies resort more to social planning and better social co-ordination of allocation of (scarce) resources, while in the consumer-driven model the market is seen as the most important (if not the only) and the most effective regulator. If the market does not recognise the results of a company, this will inevitably lead to its removal from the market (bankruptcy).

Nevertheless, all these economic structures are not so clear now when compared to the time when the models were regarded as 'cleaner', such as in the 1980s (Ostry 1990). Today's extensive regulation of business activities cannot be neglected and regulatory attempts in the countries where the models evolved have led to model modification through cross-fertilisation. The liberal American model is becoming more 'socially responsible' (although slowly), while the European and Japanese non-liberal models are trying to achieve the efficiency benchmark set by the American model. Regulatory attempts embodied in the legislative efforts to prevent serious corporate failures, large-scale fraud and system deficiencies have made the American traditionally highly liberal model more constrained and 'socially guided'.

This chapter compares two (ostensibly) opposing models of corporate governance: the Anglo-American (i.e. American) and the European model, and analyses how different legal traditions and experience have influenced the manner in which the model has been designed and operates. First, we look at the American model and how various events in American legal and corporate history contributed to the current type of model. Then, we will look at the main features of the European model and what the prospects of its future development might be. Finally, we compare the two models and bring this chapter to its conclusion.

15.1 Corporate governance: an American way

Dominant theory perceives the American model to be highly liberal (see Jackson 2002). However, the history of corporate law shows that there have always been different views as to the purpose of modern corporations and the means of governing them. The American (liberal or authority[2]) model is traditionally derived from a contract and the property conception of a corporation. Initially, this view claimed that a corporation was a merely an extension of shareholders' rights to own (private) property, their freedom of association and finally their freedom of contract (to be able to transfer property if and when required). This was reaffirmed by the court ruling *Trustees of Dartmouth College v. Woodward* (17 US [4 Wheat] 518 [1819]). However, the concentration that arose in the US economy in the late 19th century required a systemic regulatory intervention. Even historically, corporations had some public character as they required a charter that, in fact, gave them some social monopoly, enabling them to work. As property rights became cherished as the predominant social value, corporations lost their public role and became purely profit-making enterprises. Again, with the concentration of power, a challenge emerged for the state, as the social costs of market failure were (and still are) picked up by the state and implicitly by the taxpayers. The initial lack of differentiation between public and private corporations disappeared.

In the late 19th and early 20th century, the judiciary delineated private and public business undertakings (*Munn v. Illinois*, 94 US 113, 1 [1877], *Lochner v. New York*, 98 US 45, 25, S.Ct. 539 [1905]). In the 1920s, property law supremacy was still mainly present. In *Dodge v. Ford Motor Co.* (204 Mich. 459, 170 N.W. 668 [1919]), the Michigan Supreme Court clearly stipulated that shareholders' rights were in the primacy. Henry Ford's claims that Ford Motor Co.'s large profits should be reinvested to create new jobs, and to benefit consumers by reducing car prices, were refuted by the Court. It was said that 'a business corporation is organised and carried on primarily for the profit of shareholders' and that 'the powers of the board of directors are to be employed to that end'.

---

2   The authority model assumes that the property rights concept is strongly applied, emphasising that governing rights stem from the ownership over the company (Jackson 2002).

However, the economic crisis of the 1930s, the New Deal and the more proactive public policy undertaking clearly called for the redefinition of business corporations and
their relationship with wider society. The debate in the 1930s between Berle and Dodd
clearly demonstrated that there were irreconcilable differences between the property
concept of a corporation and that of a corporation as a social entity with definable
social purposes. Dodd saw the corporation as a social service with profit-making functions. Despite this fairly appealing approach put forward by Dodd, Berle and Means's
(1932) concept of a corporation based on property rights remained dominant in American theory and practice almost until the end of the 20th century. Although the 'prop-
erty-authority model' remained dominant throughout the 20th century, it did not mean
that corporations themselves could decide not to sponsor and support social actions
deemed by them to be worthy of supporting. Immediately after WWII (as always after
large conflicts when social cohesion was put to the test), the government showed more
interest in strengthening social trust and supporting social causes. This immediately
triggered large public policy actions, and Berle himself claimed, in the early 1950s, that
'corporate powers are held in trust for the entire community' (Berle 1954: 169).

Modern US judiciary practice has supported the concept of the corporation as a social
entity that should respect the public interest.[3] In *Theodora Holding Corp. v. Henderson*,
the Court recognised the authority of company directors to use corporate funds for
charitable, civic, educational or humanitarian purposes, while in *Shlensky v. Wrigley*,
the board of directors was supported in rejecting business strategies that would
increase profits at the expense of the local community. Although this is certainly an
improvement on the liberal-authority model, the changes are not so radical. The American judiciary supports the board of directors, which traditionally represents predominantly shareholders' interests, and does not grant *co-determination rights* to other possible stakeholders.[4] Workers' participation in decision-making is still something that
corporate America is uneasy with. In the American model, even workers' participation
in management is to be based on their ownership of a corporation's shares.

In the US, efforts to promote worker ownership have focused heavily (if not exclusively[5]) on employee stock ownership plans (ESOPs), under which workers can invest in
shares of their own company (see Hansmann 1990). Anti-takeover statutes and constituency statutes permit (again) boards of directors to consider the effect of any corporate action on non-shareholder interests (employees, customers, creditors, suppliers,
regional and local economy, community interests, interest corporation per se, etc.).
Despite these 'extensions', the US model is still based on a property conception of the
corporation, underlined by individualism, property rights and free markets (Allen

---

3 See *Theodora Holding Corp. v. Henderson* (257 A.2d 398 Del. Ch. 1969); *Shlensky v. Wrigley* (237 NE
   2d 776 III.App. Ct. 1968); *Credit Lyonnais Bank Nederland, NV versus Pathe Communications Corp.*
   (1991. Del. Ch. 15); *Paramount Communications Inc. v. Time, Inc.* (571 A.2d 1140 Del. 1989).

4 Co-determination is a notion of workers sharing in the management of enterprises. This can be
   done either through consultative workers' councils or through workers' representatives sitting on
   management or supervisory boards. This, theoretically, should not affect the position of trades
   unions in the process of collective bargaining, as the process of collective bargaining is usually
   decentralised in the models where workers can locally participate in management of their enterprises. For co-determination in Europe, see Levinson 1994; Gunn 1994; Frege 2002; etc.

5 The author is very grateful to Larry Mitchell and Michael Selmi of the George Washington University Law School for pointing this out (see Mitchell 2002).

1992). Individual shareholders are seen as dispersed, passive investors with a primary concern for financial returns and a 'fixation on a firm's financial capital' (Rubach and Sebora 1998). To conclude, the American model of corporate governance is dominantly ownership-based with the shareholders having the final say in the way the company is governed. This is increasingly moving towards the point where companies will be governed by large institutional investors who will be able to exercise significant powers within the company, even if they do not have a controlling package.

15.2 Corporate governance: a European model

In contrast, the European model of corporate governance is (or was) more socially oriented.[6] Corporate governance is seen as a combination of various interest groups whose goals have to be co-ordinated in the national interest (Schneider-Lenne 1993). The interface between all major groups of participants in the process of corporate governance (individuals, institutional investors, businesses, creditors, employees and governments) is much more intensive, and all of them should act in the social interest. Of course, the government remains the ultimate guardian of social interests. Socially responsible ownership has found ways to be transformed from theory to real life. The owner has to hold in his or her heart and mind the values and welfare of society. Certainly, profit maximisation is one of the motives, possibly the dominant one, but by no means the exclusive one. In the European model, which favours large institutional investors and banks (creditors) as important players (voters), an important role is reserved for the employees.[7] The policy of co-determination gives the workers the right to information, hearings and participation, emphasising the importance of industrial democracy, which is still absent in the US (see, for instance, Pedersen and Thomsen 1997).

The European model has been characterised by five main features encompassing: the two-board model (French law favours a single board); employee co-determination; concentration of shareholdings and a less developed stock market; dominance of banks and creditors orientation; and the lack of public hostile takeover bids. The two-board model worked well in the past, but now demonstrates significant weaknesses in a time of harsh international competition (Mallin 2004). A supervisory board consisting only of non-executive directors controls and dismisses the management. However, not in all countries will the supervisory board be given powers to dismiss management, as this right may rest with the annual general shareholders' meeting. Co-determination of

---

6   For the purpose of this chapter we consider the European model to be monolith, as this is increasingly the case in the textbook literature (i.e. Mallin 2004). It is evident that the European (EU) model is emerging as a result of cross-fertilisation of various national models on the European continent and the British model.

7   Recent research in financial history claims that the historians failed to recognise the role of banks in pre-1930s corporate finance in the US. Namely, the claim is that J.P. Morgan and other investment banks played a prominent role in corporate governance through their proxy votes and trusteeship over shares. See Bricker and Chandar 2000 and Baskin and Miranti 1997 for a background.

employees is again predominantly in the German tradition, where, in firms with more than 500 employees, one-third of the supervisory board will be elected by the employees, rising to one-half in firms with over 2,000 employees (Hopt 1994).

Concentration of shareholding is another important feature of the European model. For instance, 85% of 171 industrial German companies quoted in 1990 had at least one large shareholder owning more than 25% of voting shares (Franks and Mayer 2001). In contrast, in the UK only 13% of 173 companies had one shareholder owning more than 25% of issued equity (Franks and Mayer 2001). Banks are the most important source of business finance in continental Europe. Therefore, the overall system of corporate governance holds a particular position for banks (creditors), reducing the importance of a financial market. Consequently, legal protection of outside shareholders is less developed in continental European law than in Anglo-American countries (primarily the UK, the US, Australia, Canada and New Zealand) (Shleifer and Vishny 1997). The flow of information is less transparent, and only the minimum of information is publicly disclosed. There is very little market activity and there is a strong bank presence, so consequently there is very little hostile takeover activity. If the company is taken over, then it is more a result of negotiation than of the acquisition of a controlling package through financial market activities.

The particular pattern of attracting external finance determined the organisational infrastructure (Frank and Mayer 2001). German separation between management and supervisory board dates back to the 19th century, while co-determination has been around since the 1920s and the Weimar Republic. The whole legal structure favoured debt finance, and to a large extent protected debtors in the bankruptcy procedures. The pension system was mainly based on company reserves and/or state pensions financed from the budget. With only small activity in the financial market, very little pension money has been invested in financial markets. Although there is a noticeable increase in financial market activity, the German stock market is still perceived to be under-capitalised and small, and consequently cannot play a role in corporate control. Large government shareholdings and strong creditor protection add to the existing problems (Francke and Hudson 1984; Šević 1997). Banks are not prevented from owning shares in other banks or other corporations, and have proxy votes taking care of their clients' interests if the client has entrusted his or her share to their custody (*Depotgesetz*). The close relationship with the bank ensures that the management can build a longer (medium- or long-term) perspective on business, as they can rely on the bank supporting their efforts (Šević 1999).

The continental European model is closer to becoming a European hybrid model that takes into account developments on the Continent and in the countries of the Anglo-American tradition (sometimes including the Netherlands). The supranational European regulations should result in a longer run with a unique European model, which should embrace different experiences and traditions. In earlier drafts, the Fifth EU Directive argued for the introduction of a two-tier company structure and the Dutch and German-type co-determination decision-making systems. As this was opposed by, primarily, the British and French, the document later put forward a model with a one-tier board system, but still with obligatory participation of employees on the bodies of the company. On the other side, the Germans and Dutch successfully opposed a takeover code that closely resembled the current British model. As experience with other EU directives has shown, it will be very difficult to introduce a directive to satisfy all the opposing sides, and many options will be exercised. This is the main weakness of the European law-making process. While regulatory competition should satisfy all the parties involved, as it does in the US, European regulatory competition is rather limited by a cumbersome reconciliation process. Furthermore, EU member states may easily diverge from the standards set out by the EU. A high degree of centralisation of law-making in a fairly large territory with different cultural and social experiences may show very little respect for the competing ideas initiated by these local differences.

Yet another problem for the European legislator can be the phenomenon of *legislative evasion*.[8] Many European firms, especially those that are global players, opt to follow the American model of corporate governance (especially with respect to transparency), and prepare accounts in accordance with the US GAAPs in order to be listed on a US capital market and to be able to raise finance there. This opens the question as to whether G7 countries' regulators should compete or collaborate. An international regulatory co-operation model developed by Colombatto and Macey (1996) demonstrates the clear advantages of wider international co-operation, even for a country that is clearly a dominant business leader (the US). However, the change in the American way of tackling regulation, with the US now more proactive in the protection of the weaker contractual side (to be read as customers) through court actions initiated by a number of state Attorneys General, makes it difficult to predict how the US federal government will behave. Interestingly, there is an ever-increasing level of co-ordination between state Attorneys General, who traditionally have shown very little co-operation, let alone co-ordination, as they opted to remain strictly within their territorial jurisdiction. It seems that their co-ordinated action may give even better results than federal action (*Economist* 2003).

15.3 Corporate governance: competing models or long-term convergence?

Regulation has been traditionally seen as the American way of dealing with market failures, in contrast to the European model of the public provision of (public) goods through public enterprises (Šević 1999). Often the Americans would see European industries as largely under-regulated, while believing their regulatory levels to be essentially optimal. However, it came as a shock in the 1970s when it was realised that many industries were over-regulated, hampering innovation and entrepreneurship, and preventing further growth and development. The response was, in fact, very American—large-scale deregulation, which in turn created mayhem of its own. Deregulation was primarily in the form of price competition, and the result was a long-term decrease in prices, which in turn led to serious under-investment and damage to the existing infrastructure. In the face of serious failures, the response was again more than

---

8 Understood here as a phenomenon where the firm decides to formally move its headquarters to benefit from a more favourable legal regime in another country. This move should be legally allowed, not to trigger prosecution or other retributory action taken by the government.

robust—regulatory capture[9] was widened, so many areas previously unregulated or self-regulated suddenly became the focus of regulation, often through the enactment of new statutes.

One of the acts swiftly pushed through the legislative body was the *Sarbanes–Oxley Act of 2002* (HR 3763), which aimed at strengthening the protection of investors 'by improving the accuracy and reliability of corporate disclosures made pursuant to the securities laws, and for other purposes'. However, a 'collateral damage' of the act was the self-regulation of the accounting profession. Instead of looking at licensing rights for practising accountancy, the Act created another body to oversee not the practising of accountancy, but actually controlling the profession itself (although in a very American way—indirectly). Statutory intervention in Anglo-American countries has been a characteristic of *institutional capitalism*[10] but, until recently, the traditional areas of self-regulation were not interfered with. In principle, only when the natural order cannot secure the socially desired results is there room for the legislator to interfere in social relations. However, self-regulation (*autonomous law* in Continental European legal theory) is a form of outside intervention which is closer to the moral equilibrium as all the involved parties are searching for the best social outcome.

However, this does not mean that there is insufficient grounds for intervention in the field of corporate governance. Traditionally, the practice of corporate governance rarely conformed to the theoretical model of division of powers between different social players (shareholders, directors, management). Often minority shareholders were left on the margins. They usually did not select the management nor determine company policy, besides formally confirming, legitimising or ratifying matters already decided by either management or the board of directors. Even in publicly listed companies with a number of outside directors, they often do not play an effective role in the management of the company, due to time constraints, lack of professional support, 'over-digested information' or simply the lack of personal professional expertise. Although the law cannot rectify these problems, it can provide the framework to ensure that the system is fairly effective, stipulating the minimum legislative requirements that a company has to meet. However, regulation understood as a set of prescriptive and proscriptive rules has to be enacted and enforced in a manner that will not unduly restrict or interfere with exploring the opportunities for fostering both efficiency and the ultimate purposes of the corporation recognised by law as a social entity. In the social context, the corporation has to provide employment, goods and services, and serve as a *locus* for social interaction. So, is it possible to ensure better protection of small shareholders? It seems that the government may opt for *regulation by litigation* which would allow the authorised government body to challenge under-performance in corporate governance, challenging unsound decisions of the boards of large corporations which can undermine the general public trust.[11] This, however, would not pre-

9 Regulatory capture is understood here as a set of social relation targeted by the government in its regulatory action. It does not have the same meaning as classical regulatory theory of capture (Kolko 1963).

10 See more on 'varieties of capitalism' in Hall and Soskice 2001.

11 For instance the US government has decided to resort to regulation by litigation in the case of protection the environment (diesel engine emission control). See more in Viscuzi 2002.

vent the possibility of minority shareholders initiating a 'class action' to protect their rights on a more individual (and group) basis.

It seems that a modified stakeholder model offers a reconciliatory position necessary to both systems.[12] The American model of corporate governance is *short-term* and overly optimistic, while the European is overly socially embedded, and therefore hampers efficiency. With the introduction of a *modified stakeholder model* (as a result of 'natural convergence'), the American 'extreme' becomes more socially responsible, taking more serious consideration of signals from the environment, while the European model becomes more effective, as the introduction of (primarily hostile) takeover possibilities forces existing management teams to be more careful in accepting risks (both risk pooling and risk sharing). The board of directors in both modified models will have to take into consideration the impact of any corporate action on a wide range of stakeholders. These include employees, customers, creditors, suppliers, the national and regional economy, the immediate and wider community and their legitimate social interests, both implicit and explicit, and the long-term and short-term interests of the corporation. Finally, a possibility of 'regulation by litigation' where the government body may sue all those who do not comply with the principles may be a 'last (regulatory) resort'.

Profitability can be both a long-term and short-term goal in the converged model, but in either case will not be as prevalent as in the basic American model. To a large extent American ALI Principles of Corporate Governance collated best practices and ensured that the American model has become more social-centred, moving from its classical position, often perceived as the ruthless profit-above-all model of corporate governance, centred on shareholders and the sole maximisation of their wealth. A perspective on welfare, both social and individual, had been lost somewhere. So, bringing social responsibility and accountability into the analysis enables the American model of corporate governance to move with the times. Traditionally, both the absoluteness of property rights and the freedom of contracting enforced social cohesion and ensured social stability; but the postmodern society requires more than mere stability. It seeks a sustainable community as an output of modern public policy processes (including the redefinition of corporate governance principles).

Furthermore, the social responsibility (advanced stakeholder model) of corporate governance is based on the premise that public corporations exist to serve a broader social purpose beyond the simple maximisation of shareholders' wealth. So, the cross-fertilisation between the two models should deliver both in terms of social desirability and efficiency. Finally, it should not be forgotten that even Ford in the 1920s believed that the corporation had a social responsibility to create jobs, and not only to increase dividend payments. At the time, as we have already said, the Court overruled this approach, but it seems that, in the 21st century, social motives will be more attractive to the modern judiciary.

---

12   Stakeholder theory in corporate governance takes account of a wider group of constituents rather than focusing on shareholders (Mallin 2004; Puri and Borok 2002). However, some recent developments in stakeholder theory attempt to reconcile value maximisation and stakeholder interests (Jensen 2001).

15.4 Conclusion: does (corporate) governance really matter?

Governance, understood broadly as a way one organisation (institution) makes decisions, is something debated both in political and business theory. Political scientists are interested in how to make decision-making models more democratic in modern states, while management scholars are interested in developing a model of corporate governance that would ensure the social responsibility of corporations, especially large ones, and protection of minority shareholders' rights. In fact, both groups are searching for a sustainable model of decision-making that can reinforce social stability in the 21st century.

In this chapter I have focused on the basic legal framework of two, currently, competing models of corporate governance. Initially, I assumed that models of corporate governance occur because of the way in which ownership and control are distributed (Franks and Mayer 2001). However, I have not focused on the analysis of ownership and the exercise of control, but on the formal legal framework for corporate governance looking at the main (legal) features of the two models. The American model has developed largely spontaneously with limited legislative interventions of regulatory bodies. Even the introduction of a set of securities laws in the 1930s was the result of one-off state interventionism, rather than premeditated legislative strategy. In contrast, Europe is more statutory-based and whatever has to be socially regulated will preferably be embedded into the law. The common law model is more prone to support non-government professional regulation and self-regulation, while European countries are more inclined towards codification. However, the situation may be changing in Europe as well. European law, that is to say law, is largely a result of the compromise of two legal systems (Common Law and *Civil Law*). With the promotion of New Public Management (NPM) which professes that 'less government is better government', government may now play a role in shaping the legal, institutional and administrative environment in which corporate governance and control are developed, but the main *responsibility is to remain with the private sector* (OECD Principles of Corporate Governance). The adoption and enforcement of the OECD Principles allows a more creative legislative approach in continental European countries, enforcing the principle 'comply or explain', which allows an application of various legislative and regulatory instruments and voluntary codes and practices.

This newly defined complexity should preserve diversity, but also ensure convergence through the spreading of 'best practices' that are internationally renowned and endorsed. Certainly, the growth in the relative importance of *international institutional investors* (primarily US and UK pension funds) will support the spreading of positive Anglo-American practices in the countries with a primarily Continental European legal tradition. Voluntary principles (both national and international) enable development and modification of directions taken in order to accommodate changes and facilitate innovations. Although a relatively small number of countries currently go for 'principle-based laws'[13] accompanied by detailed best-practice guides (guidelines), it is prob-

---

13 'Principles-based laws' are understood here as laws that have embedded into themselves largely tested principles and standards, ensuring that the enforcement will be done directly by the government apparatus.

ably the path that the future will support. The basis is to be set out by the legislation, while the standards are upheld by the guidelines and principles that cherish best national and international practices. But this process will not be smooth. Many countries of continental European tradition will certainly have problems endorsing the model. The usual argument may be that the legislation regulates the corporate governance matters in great detail anyway, so why bother with promoting (rather than enforcing) principles? Or it may be argued that principles and guidelines are simply of a voluntary nature, and therefore the government may not require that they will be applied. However, it is an additional challenge for countries with a Civil Law legal system to find a pragmatic and reasonable balance between the issues that necessarily should be regulated by legislators and those that should be left to corporations and their associations to regulate (Hommelhoff 2000).[14]

Notwithstanding, one should not underestimate the emerging concept of *political delegation* within the EU, where the government (politicians) delegates the performance of particular functions to professional organisations, which will be contractually held liable for performance. Modern central banking is one of the best examples of this. However, the growth in non-departmental independent public bodies is expected, as well as 'contracting out' of public functions to private organisations. If this trend is to continue, then it is most likely that in the future 'private production of law' (Šević 2002) will be increasingly important, which would allow even the countries of the Civil Law system to be more flexible about the timely evolution of rules and regulations. This will certainly lead to even more (legislative) convergence of currently 'competing' models: Anglo-American and European. The flexibility of new arrangements should enable the European model to be more adaptable, while bringing it closer to the Anglo-American one. Over time, this cross-fertilisation is the only credible path leading to the emerging universally accepted model of corporate governance.[15]

---

14   The discussion along these lines in the German Parliament, initiated by the German Panel on Corporate Governance (Grundsatzkommission Corporate Governance), did not lead, as yet, towards the significant changes in company law. However, the adoption of standards at European level may lead to changes introduced by the back door, via widely accepted practices and codes of conduct.

15   Although it is very difficult to see what will be the cross-fertilisation influence on the US model, in the light of the renewed nationalism and 'legislative sovereignty' exercised by Congress when the Sarbanes–Oxley Act of 2002 was adopted, as we have noted above (Vagts 2003).

References

Allen, W. (1992) 'Our Schizophrenic Conception of the Business Corporation', *Cardozo Law Review* 14.2: 261-81.

Baskin, J.B., and P.J. Miranti, Jr (1997) *A History of Corporate Finance* (Cambridge, UK: Cambridge University Press).

Berle, A.A., Jr (1954) *The Twentieth Century Capitalist Revolution* (New York: Harcourt Brace).

—— (1959) *Power without Property: A New Development in American Political Economy* (New York: Harcourt Brace).

—— and G. Means (1932) *The Modern Corporation and Private Property* (New York: Macmillan).

Bricker, R., and N. Chandar (2000) 'Where Berle and Means Went Wrong: A Reassessment of Capital Market Agency and Financial Reporting', *Accounting, Organizations and Society* 25.6: 529-54.

Colombatto, E., and J.R. Macey (1996) 'A Public Choice Model of International Economic Co-operation', *Cardozo Law Review* 18.6: 925-65.

Economist (2003) 'American Business and the Law: Enemy of the States', *The Economist* 368.34 (6–12 September 2003): 67-68.

Estes, R.M. (1980) 'Corporate Governance in the Courts', *Harvard Business Review*, July/August 1980: 50-64.

Francke, H.H., and M. Hudson (1984) *Banking and Finance in West Germany* (London: Croom Helm).

Franks, J., and C. Mayer (2001) 'Ownership and Control of German Corporations', *Review of Financial Studies* 14.4: 943-77.

Frege, C.M. (2002) 'A Critical Assessment of the Theoretical and Empirical Research on German Work Councils', *British Journal of Industrial Relations* 40.2: 221-48.

Gunn, C. (1994) 'Workers' Participation in Management: Capital's Flexible System of Control', *Review of Radical Political Economy* 26.3: 119-26.

Hall, P.A., and D. Soskice (eds.) (2001) *Varieties of Capitalism: The Institutional Foundations of Comparative Advantage* (Oxford, UK: Oxford University Press).

Hansmann, H. (1990) 'When Does Worker Ownership Work? ESOPs, Law Firms, Codetermination and Economic Democracy', *Yale Law Journal* 99.8: 1,749-816.

Hommelhoff, P. (2000) 'The OECD Principles on Corporate Governance: Opportunities and Risks from Perspective of the German Corporate Governance Movement', *International and Comparative Corporate Law Journal* 2.4: 457-81.

Hopt, K.J. (1994) 'Labor Representation on Corporate Boards: Impacts and Problems for Corporate Governance and Economic Integration in Europe', *International Review of Law and Economics* 14.2: 203-14.

Jackson, G. (2002) Organizing the Firm: Corporate Governance in Germany and Japan, 1870–2000 (unpublished PhD thesis; New York: Columbia University).

Jensen, M. (2001) 'Value Maximization, Stakeholder Theory and the Corporate Objective Function', *Journal of Applied Corporate Finance* 14.3: 8-21.

Journal of Accountancy (1933) 'Editorial', *Journal of Accountancy*, September 1933: 14-16.

Kelsen, H. (1945) *General Theory of Law and State* (Cambridge, MA: Harvard University Press).

Kolko, G. (1963) *The Triumph of Conservatism: A Reinterpretation of American History, 1900–1916* (New York: Free Press).

Levinson, K. (1994) 'Codetermination in Sweden: From Separation to Integration', *Relations Industrielles: Industrial Relations* 49: 131-42.

Macintosh, J.C.C. (1999) 'The Issues, Effects and Consequences of the Berle–Dodd Debate, 1931–1932', *Accounting, Organizations and Society* 24.2: 139-53.

Mallin, C.A. (2004) *Corporate Governance* (Oxford, UK: Oxford University Press).

Marer, P. (1991) 'Models of Successful Market Economies', in P. Marer and S. Zecchini (eds.), *The Transition to a Market Economy* I (Paris: OECD): 108-14.

Mitchell, L.E. (2002) *Corporate Irresponsibility: America's Newest Export* (New Haven, CT: Yale University Press).

Monks, R.A., and N. Minow (2001) *Corporate Governance* (Malden, UK: Blackwell).

O'Sullivan, M. (2000) 'Corporate Governance and Globalization', *Annals of the American Academy of Political and Social Sciences* 570 (July 2000): 153-70.

OECD (Organisation for Economic Co-operation and Development) (2004) *OECD Principles of Corporate Governance* (Paris: OECD; www.oecd.org).

Ostry, S. (1990) *Government and Corporations in a Shrinking World: Trade and Innovation Policies in United States, Europe and Japan* (New York: Council on Foreign Relations).

Pedersen, T., and S. Thomsen (1997) 'European Patterns of Corporate Ownership: A Twelve-Country Study', *Journal of International Business Studies* 28.4: 759-79.

Price Waterhause & Co. (1932) 'Conclusion of the Final Report of Price, Waterhause & Co. on the Kreuger and Toll Group of Companies', in *Stock Exchange Practices* (1933) 22nd Congress, Part IV: 16-64. Reprinted in B.C. Hunt (ed.), *George Oliver May: Twenty-five Years Accounting Responsibility, 1911-1936, Vol. 2* (New York: The American Institute of Publishing, 1936): 49-59.

Puri, P., and T. Borok (2002) 'Employees as Corporate Stakeholders', *Journal of Corporate Citizenship* 8 (Winter 2002): 49-61.

Rubach, M.J., and T.C. Sebora (1998) 'Comparative Corporate Governance: Competitive Implications of an Emerging Convergence', *Journal of World Business* 33.2: 167-84.

Schneider-Lenne, E. (1993) 'Corporate Control in Germany', *Oxford Review of Economic Policy* 8.3: 11-23.

Šević, Z. (1997) *Financial Reform in a Transitional Economy: Some Conceptual Issues* (Tokyo/Belgrade: Ryoichi Sasakawa Young Leaders Fellowship Fund and Yugoslav Association of Sasakawa Fellows).

—— (1999) *Restructuring Banks in Central and Eastern European Countries as a Part of Macroeconomic Changes towards Market-oriented Economy* (Belgrade: BCPPRS and Čigoja štampa).

—— (2002) 'A Law and Economics of Public Policy Process in a Polycentric Federation', *Commentaries on Law and Economics* 2: 1-35.

Shleifer, A., and R.W. Vishny (1997) 'A Survey of Corporate Governance', *Journal of Finance* 52.2: 737-83.

Tricker, R.I. (1997) 'Editorial: Where do We go from Here?', *Corporate Governance: An International Review* 5.4: 177-79.

Vagts, D.F. (2003) 'Extraterritoriality and the Corporate Governance Law', *American Journal of International Law* 97.2: 289-94.

Viscuzi, K. (2002) *Regulation through Litigation* (Washington, DC: AEI–Brookings Joint Center).

Williamson, O.E. (1996) *The Mechanisms of Governance* (New York: Oxford University Press).

16

Conflicting and conflating interests in the regulation and governance of the financial markets in the United States

Istemi Demirag and Justin O'Brien
Queen's University Belfast, UK

This chapter examines several recent financial scandals in the United States, which have implicated various key actors in the corporate arena, from the boardroom to outside legal counsel, from the auditors to the federal regulators, from the self-governing policing of the markets to the politicians who ostensibly guard the guardians. It argues that the complexities of the malfeasance and misfeasance cannot be understood without reference to the wider structural environment in which the market operates. A more robust and complementary theoretical framework is needed.

The chapter has five main parts. In Section 16.1, the changing nature of economic governance as a consequence of 'private interest' government is critiqued, with particular reference to the social-order framework developed by Streeck and Schmitter (1985). The conflicting and conflating objectives of the key societal actors—the state, the market and the associational community mediating the demands of the communities that make up civil society—identified in the model are indicated along with its failings. In Sections 16.2 and 16.3, empirical evidence is provided to demonstrate how these conflicting and conflating interests manifest themselves in the governance of Wall Street. This is achieved through an analysis of the limitations placed on the most important regulatory forces in the United States, the Securities and Exchange Commission (SEC) and the New York Stock Exchange (NYSE). Section 16.4 illustrates the point that, when markets fail, state intervention may become necessary to maintain social order in the financial markets, although the form that intervention takes is conditioned by the relative power of the competing actors that design public policy. Section 16.5 synthesises the argument. It argues that blaming excesses on corrupted individuals has a distinct purpose: continued misplaced faith in the efficacy of self-regulation. In doing so, it calls for a more robust theoretical framework in order to better understand the complex shifting power structures, myths and rhetoric, which determine how governance is constructed.

16.1 Association democracy or capture

In the context of advanced industrialised societies, Streeck and Schmitter (1985) developed a model addressing the question of how social order is created and maintained. Three principal models—the state, the market and the community—provide the bedrock on which competing theories of social order are built. The complex relationship between the state, the market and civil society is not static, however. Rather, it is in constant flux. The asymmetrical nature of the dynamic relationship within economic governance is conditioned by the interplay of beliefs with the power capacity of corporate actors to effect change. Streeck and Schmitter articulate the need to give due cognisance to this interpenetration. They go on to tentatively posit the existence of a fourth institutional base that has, through the principle of 'private-interest government', the ability to ensure equilibrium: the association. The authors argue that their fourth institutional order 'is more than a transient and expedient amalgam of the three others and, hence, capable of making a lasting and autonomous contribution to rendering the behaviour of social actors reciprocally adjustive and predictive' (Streeck and Schmitter 1985: 2). The resulting social order is based on tactical rather than strategic management. It is predicated on 'disparate, uneven and pragmatic responses to particular dysfunctions and conflicts' (1985: 8) as and when they occur. For Streeck and Schmitter, by elevating pragmatism, the associational model vouchsafes stability by limiting the destabilising effect of changes in the ideological superstructure, while simultaneously increasing the public policy repertoire (1985: 14). As we will argue below, this approach can result in the granting of excessive powers over financial regulation to private-interest groups, leading to precisely the kind of malfeasance and misfeasance seen in the United States.

A combination of ideological and pragmatic imperatives provided the dynamic for the shift away from formal state oversight of the capital markets in the United States. Professional associations—accountants, lawyers, corporate directors—acting as political groupings, emphasised the wider benefits accruing to society from liberalising still further the market system. Once oversight of regulation is relinquished to private-interest government, this penetration by cross-cutting alliances, conceived at the market and forged in the political arena, has profound implications for state capacity. Fiduciary intermediaries, or gatekeepers, play a significant role in their own right as the most influential sectoral lobby grouping in the United States. In the next sections, we explore the extent to which the Streeck and Schmitter model helps us to understand the crises in the capital markets by applying it to two of the most important regulatory authorities in the United States.[1]

---

1   The Streeck and Schmitter model has been adopted to explore the regulation of the accounting profession in the UK and other developed countries (for example, see Wilmott *et al.* 1992). It has also been applied to the governance of the University of Oxford (Jones 1994). This is the first time that the explanatory power of the model has been explored in the context of financial regulation in the United States.

16.2 Formal oversight: the Securities and Exchange Commission

The Securities and Exchange Commission overarches the regulatory structure of the financial markets in the United States. Established as a consequence of catastrophic market failure associated with the Great Crash, the SEC performs a dual function. It interprets legislation and acts as a civil authority in the policing of the market. Despite its considerable power, throughout the long years of the bull market and in its immediate aftermath, it lacked the political muscle or enforcement resources to deal with a confluence of internal and external flaws.

In the mania that accompanied what Stiglitz (2003) terms 'the roaring nineties', no credible restraint was placed on the operation of the market, certainly not by the self-regulating associational bodies, nor by an emasculated SEC, whose capacities were severely limited by congressional figures who transferred the oversight function into a clientelist service available to the highest bidder (Levitt 2002). Attempts by the SEC in 1998 to limit the provision of auditing and consultancy by accountants to whom self-regulatory authority had been delegated were rebuffed by a concerted campaign led by Harvey Pitt. Pitt was to become chairman of the SEC in 2000. He made a priority rapprochement with the organisations he was charged to regulate.

A similar rationale pervaded relationships with the Wall Street investment banking system. The collapse of the dot.com market in 2000 and the implosion of confidence it engendered were dismissed merely as greed, an impoverished account of the structural dynamics inherent in the system. It was indicative of the growing power of the securities industry that any official probe into the workings of Wall Street focused on actors, not systems. Congressional hearings were scheduled at which politicians and regulators alike collectively wrung their hands at the reality of conflicts of interest over analyst research and their inability to do anything about it. It is a point conceded by the Director of Enforcement at the SEC, Steve Cutler, in a recent interview with the authors (13 May 2003): 'Systemic is a good word. There were many places where the system failed and Wall Street research was only one of those places.'

The range of policy options was circumscribed precisely because financial engineering had displaced manufacturing as the driving force of the American and indeed the international economy. The centrality of liquid equity markets as a source of capital reinforced the short-term nature of American business, making trading of stock and financial services rather than product the primal generator of wealth (Demirag *et al.* 1994; Demirag 1995a, 1995b, 1996; Philips 2002). Further, it was no accident that the sectors most associated with malfeasance and misfeasance in the late 1990s—telecommunications, banking and energy—were also subject to the most far-reaching regulatory reform in the preceding years (Clark and Demirag 2002; O'Brien 2003b; Krugman 2003).

In evidence to the Senate, the Executive Director of the Council of Investor Relations likened the operation of the securities market to a perverse racetrack scam (Teslik 2002). Teslik's evidence provides support for the view that there are systemic roots to the crisis in the functioning of the financial markets. Moreover, it highlights who benefited from ensuring the centrality of Wall Street's preoccupation with short-term financial performance measures (Demirag 1995a, 1996) as the key determinant for economic governance. It also focuses attention on where responsibility lies for ensuring that the political discourse accepted uncritically the ideological underpinning of Wall Street dominance. The crucial effect of politics on the make-up and shifting power structures of the regulatory authorities and the wider economic market in the United States is central to the arguments advanced in this chapter.

These serve to highlight structural problems affecting both state and non-state regulatory organisations. The SEC faces acute difficulties in securing a mandate from its political masters and enforcing its authority on actors with direct and continuing privileged access to the legislative elite. While the 'state', manifested in institutional form by the SEC, has the residual power to regulate the markets, its form and function is dependent on wider strategic, political and financial considerations. Precisely the same dynamic afflicts the NYSE, at once, both market maker and market regulator.

In the Streeck and Schmitter formulation, the state is defined, somewhat narrowly, as an ideal bureaucracy that is buffeted by pressures exerted by an economic and political market. This is achieved by stripping the 'private-interest government' component of their framework from association with potential, or actual, illegitimate, abusive use of power (Nadel 1975). This conflation serves to constrain the definition of state capacity, while sidestepping the thorny issue of bureaucratic capture through the deployment of ideological and financial capital.

16.3 Self-regulatory failure: the case of the New York Stock Exchange

Responsibility for negotiating the granularity of the new rules on corporate liability, discussed below, now passes to the very bodies that failed to exercise internal or regulatory oversight: the corporate boards, auditing and legal associations and self-regulatory bodies. Most notable in this regard is the New York Stock Exchange, whose own deeply flawed internal corporate governance structures led to the departure of chief executive (and chairman) Dick Grasso in September 2003. An editorial in the *New York Times* at the height of the crisis over Grasso's tenure was indicative of a change in the public discourse. It opined that the corporate governance structures of the exchange are 'a threat to the entire financial system . . . When reckless chief executives are able to raid their institutions at will and enrich themselves beyond reason, it's a sure sign that corporate governance has been corrupted to an alarming degree' (*New York Times* 2003). A year-end profile in the *Wall Street Journal* took an even more uncompromising approach, in which it likened the former chairman to 'an old-time political boss' who acted as if he owned the venerable institution (*Wall Street Journal* 2003a).

Like the Securities and Exchange Commission, the NYSE performs a dual function: enhancing the trading volume on the exchange for the benefit of its owners and regulating the operation of that market to ensure probity. As such, it has to manage a profound conflict of interest between market making and market restraining. This conflict magnified rather than receded during the diverse investigations into the corporate malfeasance and misfeasance scandals (Krugman 2003; Stiglitz 2003).[2]

The NYSE played a major role in mediating the dispute between the combative New York Attorney General, Eliot Spitzer, and the powerhouses of Wall Street, although, crucially, the exchange did not play a role in prosecuting the problems in the first instance. Indeed, a confidential SEC report, leaked to the *Wall Street Journal* in November 2003, castigated the NYSE for failing to police the specialist firms trading on the market. According to the *Journal*, the SEC estimated that '2.2 billion shares were improperly traded over the past three years, costing investors $155m' (*Wall Street Journal* 2003b).

Grasso was to be one of the highest-profile corporate casualties in the search for scapegoats following the sharp deterioration in confidence, a search that also brought down the sector's highest-paid Internet and telecommunications analysts (Henry Blodget of Merrill Lynch and Jack Grubman of Citigroup subsidiary Solomon Smith Barney, respectively) and investment banker (Frank Quattrone of Credit Suisse First Boston).

Throughout the crisis, Grasso maintained that there was an acute responsibility to improve internal corporate governance rules of those companies listed in order to restore confidence in the probity of the market. Yet the NYSE itself under Grasso was a paragon of bad practice (*Wall Street Journal* 2003a). Notoriously secretive, it refused to divulge details of revenues and earnings, its governance structure or the process through which it nominated members or compensated top executives. Dick Grasso was chairman and chief executive of a board that included 12 directors from firms directly regulated by the exchange. The board resembled a club, in which elevation depended on contacts and perceived acceptability. The management of reputational risk, a key role performed by the board, was simply ignored. Grasso did not demur when the Chief Executive (and Chairman) of Citigroup, Sandy Weill, was nominated to the NYSE board to represent shareholder interests at precisely the time that his corporation was mired in controversy over analyst conflicts of interest. Weill withdrew but not before the SEC had expressed its unease at the nomination process at the prompting of the New York Attorney General, Eliot Spitzer, a pivotal figure in the exposure of systemic problems in the governance of Wall Street (Sarkin 2002).

The SEC was forced to intervene a second time following publication of the details of Grasso's remuneration package. The SEC demanded to know how the remuneration committee justified a deferred benefits package valued at US$139.5 million and annual pay in 2001 of US$30 million. With excessive levels of executive pay widely seen as one of the contributing factors leading to corporate scandal, the example set by the NYSE remuneration committee is an important indicator of how seriously—or otherwise—the financial community has taken the crisis. The dispute deepened when the powerful Californian-based institutional investor, CalPERS, called for the chairman's resignation and threatened to take its business to other exchanges if the NYSE board did not act. While many commentators agreed that Grasso was an exceptionally successful

---

2 Here it is important to spell out the difference between the two concepts. The first refers to illegality while the second refers to a moral laxity in conducting legal acts in a wrongful manner. While malfeasance undoubtedly occurred within the corporations who benefited most from lax oversight, for the NYSE the charge is that its lack of meaningful enforcement amounted to a form of misfeasance.

chairman of the 'Big Board', the tone that was set by the board, some of the members of which claimed they did not know how much Grasso was being compensated, was indefensible. Charges may yet be brought against both Grasso and the NYSE board for inappropriate pay awards over the past three years, with separate investigations opened by the SEC and the New York Attorney General (*Wall Street Journal* 2004).

Grasso and his entire board were forced to resign because the misfeasance exacerbated the perception of a voracious, unreconstructed capitalism, which was detrimental to the smooth operation of the market. The board of the NYSE contained some of the most influential corporate leaders in America. The failure to reform its practices is not a single actor failure but a collective one, leaving one sceptical of the efficacy of William Donaldson's call for a transfusion of corporate DNA to cleanse the economic body politic of a particularly virulent strain of corporate greed (O'Brien 2003a: 17). A senior investment banker in New York, speaking on condition of anonymity, told the authors that 'the entire system is broken and self-regulation is fatally flawed',[3] a view endorsed by one SEC Commissioner (*Wall Street Journal* 2003c) and the authors of the SEC confidential report into the lax policing of the specialist firms in the market, which was leaked to the *Wall Street Journal* in November.

Despite the rhetoric of investor protection, both the NYSE and the SEC have long suffered budgetary shortfalls and none of the other regulating bodies has a good record in exposing systemic fraud. Skocpol (1985) has argued that, if government, operating at federal or state level, or its franchised subsidiaries, no longer retains the means to ensure a level playing field because of a lack of skilled personnel or budgetary depletion, a key safeguard is destroyed. The problem of wider state capacity is, however, even more problematic. By successfully engaging in a bargaining process with the state across the ideological spectrum, private-interest government effectively depoliticises economic policy. The result of what Vogel (1998: 31-32) terms 'regulatory arbitrage' is a form of private-interest governance that can be impervious to control. The central question to resolve is whether government, operating at either federal or state level, has been rendered incapable of adjudicating disputes because of corporate dependency of its political parties and a revolving door between Washington and the citadels of Lower Manhattan (Clark and Demirag 2002).

16.4 State intervention in corporate governance

In the United States, the preserve of the state as the arbiter of competing demands has been substantially weakened through the institutionalisation of the concept of governance and in particular its application to the capital markets, one of the primary sources of political funding. While the Streeck and Schmitter model draws attention to how the complexity of economic governance necessitates pragmatic interaction, the model overestimates, when applied to the American context, the capacity of private interests to set aside narrow self-interest. The misfeasance is inextricably linked to the moral failure of gatekeepers, to whom regulatory authority was franchised, to tran-

3   Interview, New York City, 25 October 2003.

scend this narrow self-interest, thereby falsifying the normative assumptions of the model. We now seek to demonstrate this by showing how political pressures created and delineated the actual impact of the Sarbanes–Oxley Act on corporate liability.

The passage of the Sarbanes–Oxley Act, which, on paper, amounts to sweeping reform to corporate liability within 90 days of the collapse of the telecommunications giant WorldCom, is testament to the political imperative to demonstrate robust action (for a discussion of why legislation alone cannot be seen as a panacea, see Morrison 2004). The policy was driven, in part, by the desire to reassure the investing public that policy-makers were just as shocked by the scale of the malfeasance. It was also designed to provide a soothing balm to the ragged erosion of confidence in the probity of the market itself. If each political goal is at once a name and a metaphor to create reassurance, the official title of the legislation—the Public Company Accounting Reform and Investor Protection Act of 2002—serves a deeply symbolic purpose. This purpose is further ensconced by the creation of a new regulatory organisation, the Public Company Accounting Oversight Board, a nomenclature that again provides reassurance.

In attempting to restore confidence in the probity of the markets an easy target was found in ineffective boards of directors. The institutional weakness, combined with corporate governance problems associated with the hierarchical nature of much of American business, certainly exacerbated the crisis. The inability of firms to detect illicit management decisions is a defining defect of the hierarchical model, a process worsened by a business culture that fostered the imperial rule of powerful CEOs who faced little opposition from subservient boards. There is considerable merit in the argument, however, that blaming the malfeasance and misfeasance on either executives or compromised boards alone is a stunted theory of causation (Coffee 2003). It is a point conceded by a senior investment banker interviewed by the authors, who accepts that a systemic dynamic induced people to act in their own self-interest, which, in turn, allowed people to become bad actors.

> Corporate officers panicked that they are not going to meet the quarterly numbers because if you don't make the quarterly numbers the stock price is going to plummet so the incentive is built into the system that you meet the numbers. [This imperative] drives people to become bad actors.[4]

The necessity to meet quarterly share price targets thus elevated short-term tactics in preference to long-term strategy, a move mirrored in the *de facto* if not *de jure* downgrading of corporate legal and compliance programmes. Corporate policy was defined by enhancing short-term profit, a policy that in the most egregious circumstances turned legal departments into profit centres rather than gatekeepers of reputational integrity. The result was an institutionalised propensity among those in whom fiduciary trust was placed to engage in what the Deputy Head of Investigations at the New York District Attorney's Office, John Moscow, describes as a deliberate 'gaming of the system'.[5]

In order to understand the purpose of the legislative reforms, it is necessary to examine, therefore, how they address the role of the gatekeepers and their responsibility in

4   Interview with one of the authors, New York City, 7 February 2003.
5   Interview with one of the authors, 9 April 2003.

the corporate scandals. The Sarbanes–Oxley reforms speak to only one aspect of the associational matrix: the accountancy profession. This is, in part, a consequence of successful lobbying by other key associations, such as the legal profession and business associations, which combined under the associational social-order model to deflect responsibility away from their own profession.

The result of this is a distortion both of the nature of the problem and of its resolution. While the associative model, as predicted by Streeck and Schmitter, has restored social order in the financial markets, on a temporary, ad hoc basis, it fails to take into account why and how that process occurred. In mapping the changing governance of Wall Street, change has not been achieved solely to improve the operation of the market, thereby improving the effectiveness of public policy. Rather, as a consequence of the shifting power relationships within and between the principals—state, market, associations—responsibility for the underlying causes of the malaise, which remain in place, is merely obfuscated.

These include excessive executive compensation, perverse incentives built into the corporate model by placing inordinate focus on short-term share values and the lopsided deliberative impact of the financialisation and securitisation on both the economy and the political process itself. As Steve Cutler, Director of Enforcement at the SEC, explained in a recent interview,

> we have so many breakdowns: corporate governance, the gatekeepers, the auditors, the lawyers and the research analysts. So many corners of the market seem to have been affected. In that way it is different from prior scandals, which were focused on one kind of conduct or one set of actors.[6]

The case studies of the SEC and NYSE failure in this chapter have illustrated that concerted effort has been taken in the United States to blame the excesses on corrupted individuals. The political framework adopted through the Sarbanes–Oxley Act legislation has targeted only one component of the associational matrix. It leaves intact the structural power displayed by other key sectoral actors, including the investment banks and the lawyers. Through their funding of the political process, these have become predominant players, retaining the capacity to distort the deliberative process in profound ways.

16.5 Summary and some concluding remarks

This chapter has been chiefly concerned with the regulation of Wall Street in the aftermath of the major financial crises in the United States. In trying to explore the causes of recent financial scandals and their potential resolution, we refer to the explanations provided by the mainstream media and published literature. In seeking to explore both the causes and the legislative response, the chapter used Streeck and Schmitter's model of social order (1985) as the primary analytical lens. We conclude that its explanatory power is extremely weak. These preliminary findings necessitate a reassessment of the

---

6   Interview with one of the authors, Washington, DC, 13 May 2003.

entire Streeck and Schmitter putative paradigm. This study has shown with reference to the corporate malfeasance and misfeasance scandals in the United States that any analysis of corporate failure must take into account the complexity of political power in operation. It highlights that the key intersection between the state, the economic market and the community/association takes place within a distinct political market, the outcome of which is determined by shifting powers within and between the principal actors. We posit that this framework, which we are in the process of developing, not only provides a more powerful lens to capture where power lies but also, more importantly, an opportunity to explain how and why it shifts between these principals.

By its very nature, power is a complex phenomenon that reveals itself in a multiplicity of forms. While we have attempted to explore a particular form of power in operation, the model's applicability is limited to the principal actors identified in our empirical studies. Further analysis is required before the validity of our results can be expanded to other countries or other sectors.

Bibliography

Clark, W., and I. Demirag (2002) 'Enron: The Failure of Corporate Governance', *Journal of Corporate Citizenship* 8 (Winter 2002): 105-22.

Coffee, J. (2003) 'What Caused Enron?', in P. Cornelius and B. Kogut (eds.), *Corporate Governance and Capital Flows in a Global Economy* (Oxford, UK: Oxford University Press): 29-52.

Demirag, I. (1993) 'Development of Turkish Capitalism and Accounting Regulation in Turkey', *Research in Third World Accounting* 2: 97-120.

—— (1995a) 'Assessing Short-Term Perceptions of Group Finance Directors of UK Companies', *British Accounting Review* 27: 247-81.

—— (1995b) 'An Empirical Study of Research and Development Top Managers' Perceptions of Short Term Pressures from Capital Markets in the UK', *European Journal of Finance* 1: 180-202.

—— (1996) 'The Impact of Managers' Short-Term Perceptions on Technology Management and R&D in UK Companies', *Technology Analysis and Strategic Management* 8: 21-31.

—— and J. Solomon (2003) 'Developments in International Corporate Governance and the Impact of Recent Events', *Corporate Governance: An International Review* 11.1: 1-7.

——, A. Tylecote and B. Morris (1994) 'Accounting for Financial and Managerial Causes of Short-Term Pressures in British Corporations', *Journal of Business Finance and Accounting* 21: 1,195-213.

Jones, M.J. (1994) 'Accounting Change, Communitarianism and Etatism: The University, and Colleges, of Oxford 1800–1923', *Critical Perspectives on Accounting* 5: 109-32.

Krugman, P. (2003) *The Great Unravelling* (New York: Penguin).

Levitt, A. (2002) *Take on the Street* (New York: Pantheon).

Martinussen, J. (1997) *Society, State and Market: A Guide to Competing Theories of Development* (London: Zed Books).

Morrison, J. (2004) 'Legislating for Good Corporate Governance: Do We Expect Too Much?', *Journal of Corporate Citizenship* 15 (Autumn 2004): 121-33.

Nadel, M. (1975) 'The Hidden Dimension of Public Policy: Private Governments and the Policy-Making Process', *Journal of Politics* 37.1: 2-34.

New York Times (2003) 'Fixing a Tarnished Market', *New York Times*, 21 September 2003.

O'Brien, J. (2003a) *Wall Street on Trial, A Corrupted State* (Chichester, UK: John Wiley).

—— (2003b) 'Profits with Integrity: The Lessons of Enron', *11th International Anti-Corruption Conference*, Seoul, South Korea, 26 May 2003.

Philips, K. (2002) *Wealth and Democracy: A Political History of the American Rich* (New York: Broadway Books).

Sarkin, A.R. (2002) 'How Wall Street Was Tamed', *New York Times*, 22 December 2002.

Schmitter, P., and W. Streeck (1985) 'Community, Market, State and Associations?', in W. Streeck and P. Schmitter (eds.), *Private Interest Government* (London: Sage).

Skocpol, T. (1985) 'Bringing the State Back In: Strategies of Analysis in Current Research', in P. Evans, D. Rueschemeyer and T. Skocpol (eds.), *Bringing the State Back In* (Cambridge, MA: Harvard University Press).

Stiglitz, J. (2002) 'The Roaring Nineties', *Atlantic Monthly*, October 2002.

—— (2003) *The Roaring Nineties* (New York: W.W. Norton).

Streeck, W., and P. Schmitter (eds.) (1985) *Private Interest Government* (London: Sage).

Teslik, S. (2002) 'Evidence to Senate Hearings 16 May 2002', commerce.senate.gov/hearings/051602teslik.pdf.

Thompson, L. (2003) 'Principles of Federal Prosecution of Business Organizations', *Department of Justice Sentencing Guidelines*, 20 January 2003.

Vogel, S. (1998) *Freer Markets, More Rules: Regulatory Reform in Advanced Industrial Countries* (Ithaca, NY: Cornell University Press).

Wall Street Journal (2003a) 'How Grasso's rule kept NYSE on top but hid deep troubles', *Wall Street Journal*, 30 December 2003.

—— (2003b) 'SEC blasts big board oversight of specialist firms', *Wall Street Journal*, 3 November 2003.

—— (2003c) 'NYSE turmoil poses question: Can Wall Street regulate itself', *Wall Street Journal*, 31 December 2003.

—— (2004) 'Spitzer and SEC open probes into Grasso's pay', *Wall Street Journal*, 9 January 2004.

Wilmott, H., A.G. Puxty, K. Robson, D.J. Cooper and E.A. Lowe (1992) 'Regulation of Accountants: A Comparative Analysis of Accounting for Research and Development in Four Advanced Capitalist Countries', *Accounting, Auditing and Accountability* 5.2: 32-36.

17

A systemic view of US government in market governance
LESSONS LEARNED FROM THE CALIFORNIA ELECTRICITY CRISIS

Kimberly Samaha

AMP Consulting, France

The traditional role of public policy and management has changed fundamentally at the local, state, federal and global levels. The era of government jurisdiction based on separate and autonomous entities has been replaced with an inter-governmental and inter-sectoral network of industry, regulators, special interest groups and individual citizens. This decentralised, networked, oversight system coupled with the complexity and uncertainty of newly reformed markets has given new meaning to 'chaos theory'. Everything seems in motion. And change, in its extreme form, has become the overriding theme.

In this new context, government's role in corporate governance is undergoing what evolutionary biologists call anagenesis: a sudden, qualitative shift in evolutionary development. This anagenesis was first triggered by the 'globalisation' wave of the Thatcher–Reagan administrations. Their promotion of free-market ideals created a worldwide movement within the public and private network industries to move government out of the way and usher in competition under the broad banner of 'deregulation'. This new era of globalisation operates through a web of tightly connected, loosely regulated networks. The prevailing force of interconnectedness has manifested its societal effect through the emergence of massive Internet and communication networks, international finance and monetary flow, multinational corporations and brand homogeneity, and inter-regional trade blocs.

Globalisation has also created a far different environment for administration and decision-making in public-sector governance. Interconnectedness dramatically contracted geographic and social distance, which in turn increased the dynamic of interdependence. Government and its regulatory institutions have traditionally depended on a reality of separate, independent administrators and policy systems. Under the effects of the new paradigm, public-sector officials are finding the simple distinctions between borders, cultures and political ideologies are increasingly blurred, forcing them to manage and lead in an environment of augmenting complexity and turbulence.

The California energy crisis of 2000–2001 is a perfect illustration of the consequences of the systemic changes that occur in opening tightly controlled regulated industries, such as the electric utility industry, to the dynamics and complexity of free-market competition. In the United States, California was one of the first states to push for radical reform of their electric utility industry. The ideals of deregulation soon gave way to a more conservative form of restructuring resulting in a complex and still highly regulated scheme. The non-linear characteristics of this new multi-variable structure manifested themselves in an industrial, financial and political crisis that many have termed 'the perfect storm'.

This chapter will evaluate the California energy crisis, using a framework derived from the theories of complex adaptive systems (CAS). The basic 'system theory' principles of interdependency, feedback loops and emergent properties will be grounded in the real-life example of the California energy crisis.

17.1 The background

California began to consider deregulation of its electricity market in the early 1990s. The original plans were drafted in response to the strong criticism that high electric prices were hurting the state's large industrials and curbing new business investment. Before restructuring, California's electricity supply was provided by three large private investor-owned utilities (IOUs) and a mix of municipal power companies, owned by cities and counties. Over 70% or roughly 20 million Californians were served by the three IOUs in the $20 billion electric services market (Smeloff and Asmus 1997). The generally held belief was that electricity prices were high in California partly because of the regulated market, which afforded utilities a high rate of return on their investments.

Effects of 'deregulation' in other industries, such as telecommunications, airlines and gas, had sufficiently proved the point that competition and open markets lowered consumer prices. Deregulation as defined by the electric industry meant removing the monopoly controls on prices and allowing the entry of competing suppliers. Removing regulation was never the intent as the transportation functions (transmission and distribution) were accepted as natural monopolies. Competition in the electric industry applies only to the generation of electricity and the commercial functions of selling electricity at the wholesale and retail level. What came to be termed 'deregulation' was actually an attempt to restructure the market and secure the benefits of competition, thus lowering electric prices.

The prescription of restructuring followed a basic formula that consisted of breaking up the vertically integrated, state-regulated monopolies to create more wholesale suppliers and by giving retail customers the choice of power suppliers. The expected benefits of opening the wholesale and retail commodity markets to competition were twofold: pricing becomes more efficient and costs are lower. The ideal sales price is set at the efficient level and is beyond the influence of the utility, giving maximum incentive to reduce costs and innovate as the only ways to increase profit. This ideal is realised only when there are many new competitors to avoid collusion among firms and the exercise of market power.

In April 1992, the California Public Utilities Commission (CPUC) initiated a review of trends in the electric industry. A continued set of hearings and public discussions led to a final CPUC restructuring order issued in December 1995, often referred to as 'the preferred policy decision'. The plan expected that both regulated and competitive retail utilities would co-exist and that wholesale prices would be kept 'just and reasonable' by the discipline of competitive market forces. This set of regulatory changes promised to fundamentally change the electricity system from one that is strictly regulated—to one in which market forces would play the primary role.

Crafting the energy bill had been a function of bringing together stakeholders, holding open hearings and debating the policies. Incumbent utilities, alternative suppliers, consumer and environmental groups all weighed in before the legislators and regulators formed their decisions. Acknowledging this open process, Robin Jan Wather, a regulatory expert in Menlo Park, California, commented:

> A review of history of the development of the rules for the California market indicates the rules, both the initial and modified rules, were the result of a substantial amount of lobbying on the part of all the stakeholders, including those representing the interests of suppliers and buyers (Silverstein 2002).

In the end both political parties, the Republicans and the Democrats, crafted California's flawed deregulation structure. The final bill known as the Electric Utility Industry Restructuring Act, AB 1890, was unanimously passed in September 1996. At the signing ceremony, Governor Pete Wilson called the initiative 'landmark legislation' that would 'guarantee' lower rates. AB 1890 worked politically because it satisfied all parties. Political promises became a complex and divisive set of rules that was left to market participants to work out, including:

- Prohibition of long-term competitive contracts for investor-owned utilities

- Mandatory purchasing of electricity through power exchange (PX) with bidding rules that require paying the highest bid price

- State-mandated sale of utility generation assets

- Retail price caps, mandating a 10% rate cut, which eliminated the market's ability to respond to supply-and-demand pricing dynamics

- Mandated recuperation of utility stranded costs, which created financial barriers to new competitors entering the market

- An exemption to government-owned utilities from buying and selling power exclusively through the PX

There was enormous faith in the power of the market to sort itself out without the interference of government regulation. Yet pure market dynamics were already polluted in the fact that AB 1890 injected a set of politically driven criteria into an open market design. Its rules created systemic dysfunction, which surfaced dramatically as soon as the system was put under pressure. In reality, the final plan for 'deregulating' the California energy market was a far more complex 're-regulation' plan. Instead of removing controls, the restructuring actually created an entirely new system: a new centrally planned market, loosely combining free-market theory with political imperatives.

17.2 The outcome

The competitive market for wholesale power was opened in April 1998. The first 18 months of operation went relatively smoothly. Wholesale prices of electricity declined, customers benefited from the rate decrease and utilities were able to pay off their stranded costs. The system was operating in a mode of excess supply, which naturally kept the commodity price low. However, spring 2000 found the system in a supply shortage without any control over lowering demand. Wholesale prices began to jump dramatically triggering the period now referred to as 'the energy crisis'; and, by early 2001, wholesale prices were ten times higher than normal, consumers were experiencing numerous rolling blackouts and two of the three state investor-owned utilities proclaimed insolvency.

The most critical element to understand about the crisis was the non-linear dynamics that were unleashed when the system began operating in a supply deficiency mode. Figure 17.1, taken from the New York market, illustrates the exponential nature of the pricing of electricity when demand exceeds supply, which is applicable for all energy markets.

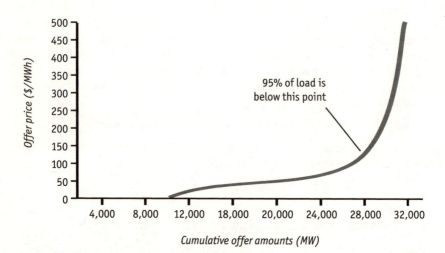

FIGURE 17.1 **Supply and demand curve of electricity**

Source: NY ISO annual assessment of the NY electricity market 2000

The industry crisis rapidly provoked a full-scale political crisis. The blame game began, and consumers were looking to the government to intervene and 'fix' the problem. Under the direction of the governor, the state began to take steps to secure electricity supplies and stabilise prices. The state assumed the central role of purchasing wholesale power on behalf of the insolvent private utilities. It also moved toward establishing a state-owned utility that would not only buy power but also would own an extensive transmission grid and build new generation plants.

The state government took the position that the main problem was market manipulation and advocated wholesale price caps. The state, however, did not have jurisdiction over wholesale prices and spent many months convincing the national regulatory body, the Federal Energy Regulatory Commission (FERC), to order wholesale price caps. The FERC, on the other hand, declared the problem to be the poor market design, in particular the use of retail price caps. The FERC strongly advocated the market principles that claimed true competition would level the pricing field if allowed to operate correctly.

In the middle of a crisis situation, the two regulatory bodies were enmeshed in an ideological debate, preventing them from working together. The FERC had adopted wholeheartedly the deregulation mantra that Nobel prize-winning economist Joseph Stiglitz summed up as a

> Manichean view of the world: they saw the wonders of the free market, over here, and evils of government, over there . . . it had become an article of faith with many Republicans and quite a few Democrats that the market, by itself, could handle almost any problem—that government, by definition, made things worse (Stiglitz 2003: 102).

The state regulators had historically been in the position of price setting. Their role in the electricity market had been in the name of an essential public service. In California, about 25% of power comes from municipal utilities and co-operatives. Government's regulatory role extended beyond price regulation to include subsidised financing to expand generation capacity, increasing green power sources and offering tax exemptions to keep power prices low. During the crisis the California government was put in the untenable position of sorting out the cause-and-effect relationships of a flawed market design, with only partial regulatory control.

In the end both California regulators and the FERC relented, adopting a policy of compromise. The CPUC ratified two price increases of historic proportions: one of 10% in January 2001 and a second larger increase averaging 46% in March. At the federal level, the FERC switched its anti-regulatory stance and imposed effective regional price caps in 19 June 2001 (Weare 2003: 46). Even with these measures the state spent $9.5 billion from its general fund in the first seven months (recouping only about $1.5 billion from reselling that power to utilities) and had to float a $13.4 billion bond to cover the costs. It entered into $45 billion in long-term (up to 20 years) contracts with generators (Congressional Budget Office 2001). To put these numbers into perspective, the $45 billion bill incurred by the state was the equivalent of 3.5% of the yearly total economic output of California. The Savings and Loan debacle was considered a staggering deregulatory failure, but its total cost of about $100 billion amounted to only one half of 1% of the total US economy (Weare 2003).

By the summer of 2001, the California energy crisis was over. Blackouts ceased and wholesale prices returned to their pre-crisis level. The sudden reversal in the situation should have been obvious to see from a fundamental economic perspective. The supply shortage moved out of the critical range with more capacity made available through fast-track regulatory processes. The number of unscheduled outages of generating plants dropped and customers responded to the state's plea to reduce demand. Even though the summer of 2001 was on average hotter than the summer of 2000, electricity demand decreased considerably (8.4%) (Weare 2003: 53).

The financial crisis abated, but it did not end without a high price to pay. California energy users saw prices jump 40% over pre-deregulation rates and may see tax increases to cover the remaining debt incurred. The state had responded to the crisis by directly intervening in the market and, in essence, returning to a closed, centrally planned, vertically integrated system. California's blunt solution to the energy crisis has submerged it into many of the same problems that deregulating was intended to solve. This search for simple answers missed the intricacies of the overall systemic failure of the initiative. Understanding how the system operated as a whole and the dependency of the interconnections inherent in the system may shed light on a number of factors and possible solutions.

17.3 System dynamics—prior to deregulation

Electricity sectors worldwide evolved with vertically integrated geographic monopolies that were either publicly owned or subject to public regulation of prices, service obligations, major investments, financing and expansion into unregulated lines of business (Joskow 2001). The classic structure of vertical integration included controlling the physical functional areas of generation, system operation, transmission and distribution. Utilities built their own generating plants and co-ordinated all aspects of making and delivering electricity.

Nationwide, utilities were established as monopolies and given a geographic service area to exclusively serve (see Fig. 17.2). Their prices and operations were regulated at

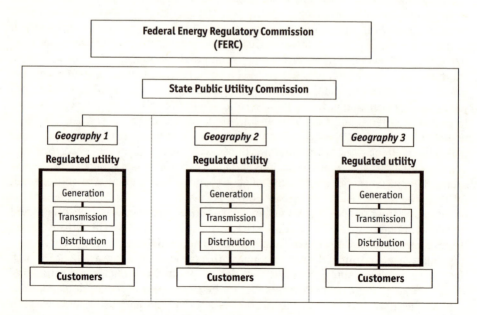

FIGURE 17.2 Vertically integrated electric utility system

the state level with an agreed-upon focus—to have enough electricity to serve all of their customers all of the time. The states' Public Utility Commission (PUC) approved the retail prices that private utilities could charge for electricity and oversaw the reliability of their service. The Federal Energy Regulatory Commission (FERC) was responsible for approving wholesale prices that electricity producers could charge utilities for power and the rates that utilities could charge for the use of their transmission lines.

Inherent in this market structuring was the ability to create boundaries and fix variables to constants, creating an essentially 'closed' system. With many variables held constant, the system exhibits near-linear dynamics enabling cause-and-effect relationships to be established, creating predictability. Policy-making under this traditional system was relatively straightforward, where both the needs of the consumer and the investor were met. Customers used regulators to protect them from the utilities' potential exploitative power, where utilities used regulators to protect the future profitability of their large sunk investments. The private utilities were allowed to charge prices that recovered their costs of production and gave investors a large enough return to attract capital for the building of new infrastructure. This formula worked quite well while new demand continued to outpace supply.

By the 1970s, however, most of the infrastructure in the US was completed, and rapidly increasing demand was tapering off with the introduction of energy conservation programmes. In addition, the national movement toward nuclear power and the formation and subsequent mandates of the Environmental Protection Agency (EPA) meant for the first time utilities' marginal costs, the cost for producing additional power, became higher than average costs. The utilities were faced with growth forecasts that were shrinking from an annual 7–8% to a low average of 2% (Smeloff and Asmus 1997).

Utility executives faced with the reality of stalled growth, began to increase in size through mergers and acquisitions, ushering in a stage of market consolidation. Instead of building new plants in isolation, many utilities invested jointly in remote plants, began sharing transmission lines and creating a new level of interconnection and interdependency. The system began to open up, bringing with it a new order of complexity.

California's electricity market is currently part of a larger, interconnected electricity grid called the Western Interconnect. The Interconnect comprises 11 western states (as well as parts of western Canada and northern Mexico) that effectively constitute one large market for electricity. What happens to supply or demand in one part of the region will influence prices in other parts. California is a net importer of electricity and is highly dependent on sufficient over-supply within the western system.

In this new highly interconnected reality, the California PUC had no authority over municipal utilities in the state, utilities in neighbouring states, federal power agencies or interstate transmission companies—all of those entities were subject to local and federal controls. When the call for deregulation came, its authorship was given to the PUC which found itself in the position of trying to isolate a part of a complex, highly interconnected system for radical change while the rest of the system was supposed to maintain the status quo.

17.4 System dynamics after deregulation

The new market design disintegrated the closed vertically integrated system of the regulated monopolies and replaced it with an open, highly adaptive system that operated at an entirely new level of complexity (see Fig. 17.3). The design of opening the California energy system followed an approach known as 'shock therapy'. The previous system operated with many fixed variables and a relatively straightforward rules and reward system. The new system introduced unknowns at many levels. Classic Cartesian thinking broke the system into five distinct parts. Each part was treated individually with regard to its structuring, geographical reach and regulatory oversight, as illustrated in Table 17.1. The fundamental focus of interconnection of the parts was essentially overlooked and the non-linear dynamics of this open system were severely underestimated.

Unfortunately, while non-linear systems can sometimes yield chaos, they always breed complexity. The California energy system was an ideal model of a complex adaptive system (CAS). CASs are 'adaptive' due to the fact that their participants are thinking emotional humans and, as such, often change their actions as a result of their inter-

Competitive market

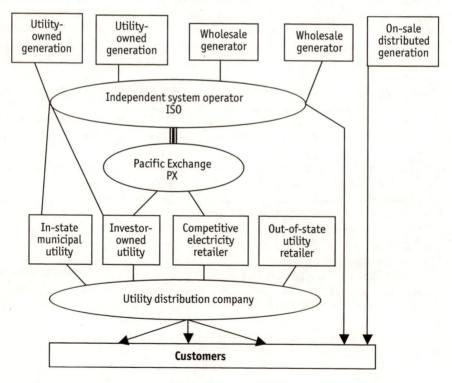

FIGURE 17.3 Distributed open-market electricity system

Functional area	Competitive or regulated	Geographical constraints	Governing organisation
Generation	Competitive	Open	FERC PX
Transmission	Regulated	State—ISO Regional—RTO	ISO/RTO FERC/EOB
Market	Competitive	State—PX	PUC
Retail	Competitive	Open	Unregulated
Distribution	Regulated	State	PUC

EOB = Electricity Oversight Board; RTO = Regional Transmission Organisation

TABLE 17.1 Functional areas of the electricity market

action with the environment. As a CAS begins to undergo change, it often takes on a life of its own, an autonomous nature that allows it to continuously self-organise and evolve. This is explained more clearly in Figure 17.4 using the spiral as an image to illustrate the dynamics of a CAS.

The process of changing from a closed regulated system to an open competitive system is always an evolutionary experiment. The thrust of evolution is oftentimes driven by the volatile nature of positive feedback. It is in an open system's non-linear nature, which allows the system to build upon itself and emerge. The phenomenon of emer-

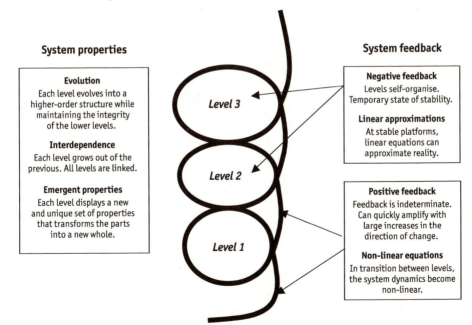

FIGURE 17.4 Evolutionary spiral model of complex adaptive systems

gence takes place at critical points of instability that arise from fluctuations in the environment amplified by feedback loops. Feedback is directional by nature. It is called negative or regulatory feedback when it creates a relatively predictable decrease in the direction of change. It is considered positive or self-reinforcing when change is relatively indeterminate and can quickly amplify, resulting in runaway effects.

Government regulation in a complex adaptive system can be seen as a stabilising feedback loop. If regulation creates too much stability, the system will often settle into a state of equilibrium, run down and stagnate. Scientifically known as entropy, the second law of thermodynamics states that energy is dissipative in nature and any isolated or closed physical system will precede the direction of ever-increasing disorder until it loses its energy and ceases to exist. Regulation under the cost-of-service monopoly regime created a closed insulated system with all of its associated bureaucracy and inertia—a system that often stifled innovation and the motivation to produce at the lowest cost.

The regulatory function of state Public Utility Commissions (PUCs) tried to create self-stabilising feedbacks to correct and compensate for deviations from established norms. In the past, the regulators governed through instituting rules and oversight boards to prevent any potentially corrupt behaviour from the market participants. As the California system opened up, the governing role of the state changed significantly. The need to prevent corrupt behaviour did not disappear through the magic of free-market dynamics—quite the contrary, the need for additional regulatory oversight increased substantially.

This new open system was multivariate, without one central controller. It was a distributed system, which constantly processed a variety of inputs and discharged a variety of outputs in real time. Complex open systems maintain themselves far from equilibrium and find a steady state only characterised by a dynamic balance of continual flow and change. A system undergoing such dramatic change oftentimes exhibits nonlinear dynamics, meaning the result of an action on a system's part may or may not be responsive to its cause.

Outcomes are highly unpredictable, meaning a slight increase in intensity somewhere in the system may lead to an unexpectedly large increase in response. As economist Joseph Stiglitz summed up the dynamics of open markets:

> Problems of periodic excess volatility and capacity have plagued capitalist economies since time immemorial. Simplistic economic theory envisions the economic system as a self-regulating mechanism: when supply exceeds demand, prices fall, reducing supply and the converse. But while such adjustments do indeed occur, they do not happen smoothly, nor without costs (Stiglitz 2003: 113).

17.5 A systemic analysis of the crisis

Systems can be thought of as big nets where there are a network of connections between subsystems. The subsystems act as building blocks for higher more evolved levels. Physicist Albert-Laslo Barabasi argued that in networks independent actions combine to form 'spectacular emergent behaviour' that, while conforming to a self-replicating fundamental structure, are contingent on complex interactions with other networks (O'Brien 2003: 15). The result of 'spectacular behaviour' in the California energy crisis (see Fig. 17.5) best illustrates that real networks are dynamic and it is in the links and interactions between the many nodes of various companies, governments, special-interest groups and consumers that the evolution occurs.

In California, a newly created system was exponentially more complicated than the original structure and it required time to find a new point of equilibrium. The fundamental problem was the necessary period of volatility and instability that precedes a systems evolution. The regulators in California had envisioned a market transformation with an orderly succession of transitions and a great deal of flexibility at each level. The system certainly required stability at the various regions in order to undergo qualitative change, but the balance of positive and negative feedback was stunted by the politics in the system.

Nobel prize-winning physicist Illya Prigogine studied open chemical systems far from equilibrium. His major contribution to the field of science is also applicable to social systems. He found that in classically closed systems, where many variables are held constant, fluctuations play a minor role. In open systems far from equilibrium, minor fluctuations accelerate and generate significant changes in spatiotemporal structure (Daneke 1999). He found order to come through these fluctuations, which he called symmetry-breaking bifurcations. A more careful look at the subsystems and their critical bifurcation points in the California energy system illustrates this dynamic.

17.5.1 Supply shortages: generation costs increase

California is a net importer of electricity and is highly dependent on sufficient over-supply within the Western Interconnect. Weather patterns such as a drought in the northwest reduced the available hydroelectric power and extreme heat in the south-west reduced power imports from that region. The differential in supply was met with increased operation of natural-gas-fired plants both in California and surrounding states. Natural gas storage reserves were severely depleted resulting in the subsequent hike in natural gas prices (see Fig. 17.6). Compounding the problem were existing environmental regulations limiting run hours or adding significant operational costs to existing plants, which were forced to operate to meet the increased demand.

Given these physical limitations in supply and demand, the California system under any regime would have experienced price increases. In a normally operating market, increasing price signals cause a decrease in demand. The real-time nature of electricity causes a critical bifurcation point when demand outpaces supply.

Electricity is arguably the only commodity that cannot be effectively stored. To handle the schedules of electricity to be generated, sent over limited transmission systems and delivered to millions of points with constantly changing load demands, is a daunting task. Add to the complexity the real-time nature of the electricity and its large dependence on weather, and the wholesale market promises to continue to be highly volatile. Capacity limitations of electricity generation implied that if the system were to approach capacity, marginal costs would increase sharply and all spot sales of electricity would sell at a price equal to this marginal cost.

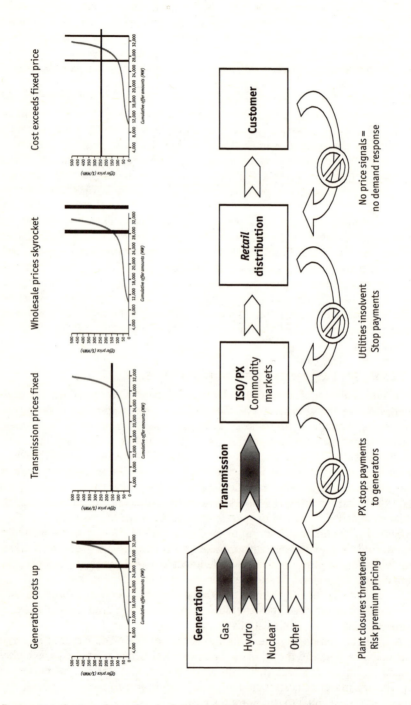

FIGURE 17.5 System dynamics during the California energy crisis

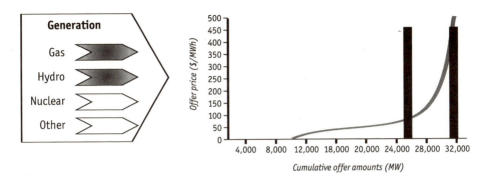

FIGURE 17.6 Supply shortage and generation cost increase

This system dynamic creates a dangerous bifurcation point. When the system is near capacity a very small difference in requirements for electricity could lead to a very large increase in the spot wholesale price. Wholesale markets work reasonably well when demand is low to moderate, generating resources are not too highly concentrated and there is little congestion on the transmission network. The challenge arises during a relatively small number of hours each year when demand is high creating an inelastic market and high transmission congestion.

17.5.2 Transmission grid in California becomes dangerously strained

The transmission grid in California was designed to bring bulk power in from the northwest and the south-west corridors. Most California based gas generation plants connect into the transmission grid in areas of higher congestion. While supply from the two routine routes dwindled, congestion at points of the transmission system became dangerously constrained.

Transmission congestion triggers the same bifurcation point as reduced supply. The inability to store electricity at key points in the network causes an inelastic pricing curve when there is more supply than demand. Compounding the problem with the transmission system was the inability of the Independent System Operator (ISO) to price according to congestion. The ISO charges a flat rate for the wheeling of power (see Fig. 17.7), thus offering no incentive to companies to supply power from points of less congestion. It is the state's ISO that calls for the series of blackouts when the transmission system can no longer safely handle the load at certain congestion points.

17.5.3 Wholesale prices skyrocket

The performance of market institutions under these tight supply conditions is highly strained. Requiring system operator discretion to balance the network's physical parameters to an acceptable level. It is also during these conditions when prices reach astronomical highs reflecting scarcity conditions. The design of the wholesale market greatly determines the opportunities individual suppliers have in moving prices signif-

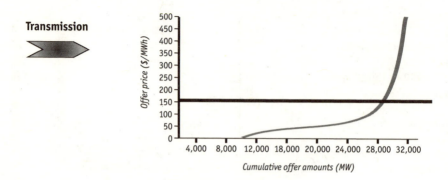

Transmission

FIGURE 17.7 Transmission grid strained and prices remain fixed

icantly (see Fig. 17.8). The California electricity market had two basic markets: the day-ahead market and a real-time market. In California these two markets were separated through the PX and the ISO, respectively.

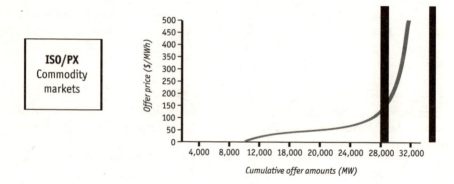

ISO/PX
Commodity
markets

FIGURE 17.8 Commodity market, wholesale prices skyrocket

Given the nature of electricity, a market must be designed to account for the technical limitations. Some generating plants, such as coal and nuclear, have very long and very costly periods of ramping up from no capacity to full capacity. These plants can be most profitable if they can schedule and sell their load as 'base load' in advance and concentrate on maximising operations. Other plants such as gas-fired turbine plants can be ramped up relatively quickly and can offer pricing at any hour. Consequently, generators do not have to worry that new supplies will flow into the market, under-cutting their high bids. The increase in price can be so large that a single firm that owns several plants can profit from shutting down one plant (Weare 2003; Joskow 2001).

There is now little doubt that the bidding strategies of the electricity generators amplified prices beyond a reasonable level. Enron's trading strategies are exemplary of how an open market can be easily manipulated, as capital flow is virtual, even though the commodity is physical. In one strategy, Enron played the California market against regulated transmission in neighbouring states. It would claim to ship energy through California counter to the direction of congestion, thereby collecting payments for congestion relief. It would then sell that power back to the original location through regulated transmission in neighbouring states. No net energy was moved or congestion relieved, but Enron profited from the spread between California congestion payments and tariffed transmission charges (Weare 2003: 48).

Enron's strategy known as 'round-trip' trades has been made public through the guilty pleas of traders such as Timothy Belden of Enron. Other companies including Cynergy Corp and El Paso Corp have acknowledged providing phoney data to pricing indexes. Williams Companies has finalised a settlement with California in an agreement that cuts $1.4 billion off the cost of a $4.3 billion, ten-year power contract (Silverstein 2003).

17.5.4 Costs exceed fixed prices

The natural buying patterns for retail utilities would be to enter into long-term contracts directly with generating plants and purchase their short-term needs on the spot market. The California regulators, fearing the incumbent utilities' market power, forbade the use of long-term contracts. The utilities were forced to make all of their purchases through the PX on short-term basis. This fundamental flaw ran counter to both the financial and technical reality, creating a bifurcation point where the utilities were driven into insolvency, continually paying more for their wholesale purchases than they were able to collect in their retail sales.

The natural economic process of open competitive markets was further stunted with the guaranteed rate decrease. The automatic 10% rate decrease and protective rate freeze dulled consumers' incentive to change providers, undermining competition. New entrants found it difficult to undercut the utilities prices and could offer few value-added services to justify a higher price. The effect of the rate freeze was the most pronounced when prices began to experience the reality of volatility in the spring of 2000 (see Fig. 17.9). Customers flocked back to utilities in essence putting new market entrants out of business.

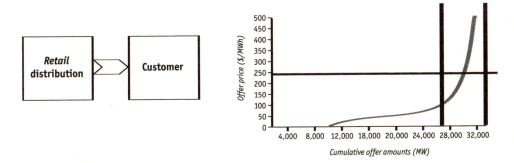

FIGURE 17.9 **Distribution and fixed consumer prices**

Governor Gray Davis's political promises not to raise retail-pricing levels led to the most critical bifurcation point. The cap on consumer prices disabled a central adjustment mechanism. Typically, production costs are translated through wholesalers and retailers into consumer price increases, which motivates reductions in demand. This self-correcting feedback loop translates lower demand back to lower prices at the wholesale level. With consumers completely unaware of the need to reduce demand in response to increasing prices, the risks associated with large wholesale price increases was amplified.

The final blow to the financial solvency of the IOUs was a direct result of this flaw in the system dynamics. With wholesale costs soaring higher than retail prices, negative margins were piling up. Normally a company in this situation would cease selling in the market. The utilities were still held to the public good responsibilities, which forced them to continue to keep the lights on, putting them in an untenable risk-bearing position. This spiral of losses led to defaults on payments to generators who in turn raised prices further to cover the risk premium they incurred in selling to insolvent entities (see Fig. 17.10). By the time the state stepped in to assume control over the situation, wholesale prices were at their justifiable peak.

Plant closures threatened   PX stops payments   Utilities insolvent   No price signals =
Risk premium pricing   to generators   Stop payments   no demand response

FIGURE 17.10 Arrested feedback within the system

17.6 Summary

The California market system did not reach order through its fluctuations. The necessary system of positive and negative feedbacks were stunted causing the system functioning to break down. Resilience to transformation was built in through politicians and special-interest groups, trying to lock in the sense of security and certainty that was part of the static regulated system. The result was that the existing norms of the regulated regime were reproduced versus absorbed into the emergence of a new order. A summary of the subsystems and their critical bifurcation points is provided in Table 17.2.

Compounding the daunting technical challenges in the newly designed system was the human and political challenges. The restructured system was a politically designed system, a 'grab bag' of directives, designed to please effective lobbying groups. The reality is that electricity systems are, by design, complex, interdependent systems. Decisions concerning generation, transmission, distribution and the delivery of inputs

Regulated market	Functional area	Competitive market	Critical bifurcation points
• Utility-owned assets • Seasonal scheduling • Guaranteed investments	**GENERATION**	• Multiple asset owners • Daily/hourly scheduling • High-risk investment	• Few new plants built • Real-time scheduling: a. Limits competitors to gas-fired turbine plants b. Creates unpredictable maintenance downtimes
• Utility-owned transmission • Voluntary membership in Regional Transmission Organisation (RTO)	**TRANSMISSION—ISO**	• Transmission system open to all generators and out-of state utilities—free-wheeling • Mandatory co-ordination through ISO	• Wheeling of non-state power overburdens transmission system • ISO competes with PX in day-ahead and hourly auctions—inviting gaming of the system • No financial incentive or responsible party to build new infrastructure
• No formal commodity market existed • Long-term contracts for additional supply	**MARKET—PX**	• Mandatory use of PX for IOUs only • Prohibition of long-term contracts for IOUs only	• Market structure encourages manipulation and gaming • Unhedged financial risk for IOUs
• All services, billing, maintenance bundled • Monopoly geographic territories • Known number of customers makes planning possible • Public service, environmental and DSM programmes part of tariff	**DISTRIBUTION**	• Utilities still responsible for all billing, metering and maintenance • Number of customers changes daily • Competitive rates make DSM and green programmes unattractive	• Metering and billing confusion hurts new entrants and switching customers • DSM programmes as a safety valve in supply and demand are ignored
• Retail services were bundled into distribution	**RETAIL**	• Many new entrants • Little value-added services available • Difficult for consumers to differentiate between competitors	• Retail price cap makes market dynamics dysfunctional • Guaranteed discount and stranded cost recuperation leaves little room for real competition

TABLE 17.2 Bifurcation points in the competitive electricity market

such as gas must be co-ordinated in real time under tight constraints of reliability. The non-linear dynamics associated with an open system manifested themselves at identifiable bifurcation points creating what has been called the 'perfect storm'. The high risks were not inherent to the economic system but were the results of definable design flaws in the regulatory system. Neither the regulatory agencies nor the major utilities understood how radically their roles had changed when the market deregulated. All parties missed the paradigm shift to the complexity unleashed in an open competitive market.

17.7 Role of government in corporate governance

The electric power industry in the US has been historically regulated by the states. Unlike other countries that have embraced 'deregulation', the US has no clear national laws or national policies addressing a competitive market for electricity. In most other countries, deregulation has been bundled with the privatisation of state-owned assets, clearing the messy issue of government taking of private property.

Instead the US has relied heavily on individual state initiatives and efforts by the FERC to use its limited authority to encourage states to create competitive markets. The FERC has had to rely on a variety of alternative regulatory and institutional arrangements and various regulatory carrots and sticks to provide incentives for co-operation with the states. These institutional and political realities have significantly complicated the kind of industry restructuring that is necessary for effective implementation of what is already the very significant technical challenge of creating a well-functioning, competitive market for electricity.

In California the discussion of alternative institutions was polluted by an unfortunate overtone of ideological rhetoric that attempted to characterise the debate about wholesale market institutions as one between 'central planners' and 'free market' advocates (Joskow 2001). The underlying trend that drove the movement of deregulation was that markets worked better than government regulation. With a view that markets are the paramount objective from which other benefits will flow, many policy decisions were made supporting the creation of markets as the only goal. While it is true that governments often fail, so do markets. This reality is the fundamental reason why the two cannot function in isolation but require a true partnership.

It is therefore necessary to factor into the analysis a systematic examination of the structural bias in American politics. The traditional distinctions between the roles of political parties and interest groups have blurred as interest groups increasingly fund candidates on the basis that their political agendas are enforced. Enron revealed that corruption was not simply the result of corrupted individuals manipulating their companies. Enron is a symptom of the corrupting tendencies endemic in the political model—a point underscored by the fact that 212 of the 248 senators and representatives who investigated Enron also received campaign contributions from the company (O'Brien 2003: 25). While there has been no serious investigation into the role played by the politicians themselves, owing to their subservience to 'interested money', the adverse effect of political funding plays a significant role in market system failures.

The failure of the California energy market and the subsequent findings of illegal and highly unethical corporate behaviour in companies such as Enron and others has put corporate governance at the top of recent political issues in the US. While recognising the need for a more heavy-handed approach to government's role in corporate governance, SEC commissioner Paul Atkins rightfully pointed out that 'morality and ethics' cannot be legislated into existence. Government controls alone—too often paternalistic—will never be the solution if individuals and individual firms are not upholding their own end of simple business ethics through their own effective compliance (O'Brien 2003: 20).

Clearly this illustrates the intersection of oversight between government regulators and corporate organisations. While it is easy to find fault with government leaders who helped design and monitor the new energy market, it is also corporate organisations that need to implement strong ethical codes and steer their workers in the right direction. The unfortunate reality in California was the combination of greed-driven individuals and their companies finding a loose market structure with little oversight, and an inability of regulators to enforce control.

Viewed systemically, the California energy policy resulted from an environment where economic, environmental and social problems formed a layered filter. Each new problem became linked to every other problem, interweaving and causing unpredicted new problems. These dispersed policy aims and agendas exponentially increased the probability of unintended consequences that easily took on a life of their own. Indeed, any flaws in the system's design cannot justify the illegal behaviour of traders and wholesale generators. Yet clearly the imperfect market and regulatory model allowed participants to work out schemes to their advantage, as Jeremy Pope concluded in his analysis of the systemic corruption on Wall Street:

> The problems are structural and not the isolated actions of individual 'rotten apples'. When there is an acceptance that these threats must be countered by strengthening systems, not simply by prosecuting those who step out of line. And when ideologues forsake their unquestioning mantra that deregulation improves all things in favour of a mindset that accepts the eternal fallibility of humankind. Then and only then, will political institutions endorse the consequential and continuing need for strong, independent and effective regulation (O'Brien 2003: ix-x).

The mantra of deregulation has not abated in light of the events in California. Globally, the electric utility industry is undergoing monumental change, ushering in competition and market-based regimes. The lessons learned from the California energy crisis re-emphasise the fact that markets by themselves do not work and there is a real role for government regulation. Getting that balance wrong, veering either toward too much or too little government, inevitably leads to disaster. For the most part this change is in its embryonic stage and due to the number of variables in flux—the entire system needs to be studied in a holistic manner to garner any meaningful analysis of the situation.

Examination of the system from a linear cause-and-effect basis leaves but a partial understanding of how the complex weave of system networks influence the wider system of decision-making, policy formulation and societal structures. The systems approach to finding patterns in apparent chaos is highly suited for this challenge. The subsequent use of dialectic feedbacks serves to both test the accurate interpretation of the situation and provide direction for the establishment of concrete action plans. For in real life, it is not an isolated group of variables that unlocks a 'magic formula' and solves generalised problems, it is the intersection of a group of interested people within a changing environment that really causes change.

References

Bay Area Economic Forum (2002) *California's Energy Future: A Framework for an Integrated Power Policy*.

Bell, S. (2002) *Economic Governance and Institutional Dynamics* (Victoria, Australia: Oxford University Press).

Bertalanffy, L. (1968) *General Systems Theory* (New York: George Braziller).

California Independent System Operator (2002) Market Design 2002 Project (MD02).

Congressional Budget Office (2001) *Causes and Lessons of the California Electricity Crisis*.

Daneke, G. (2001) *Systemic Choices: Nonlinear Dynamics and Practical Management* (University of Michigan).

Gharajedaghi, J. (1999) *Systems Thinking: Managing Chaos and Complexity* (Boston, MA: Butterworth Heinemann).

Hirsh, R. (1999) *Power Loss* (Boston, MA: MIT Press).

Hirst, E. (2001) 'The California Electricity Crisis: Lessons for Other States', prepared for Edison Electric Institute, July 2001, www.eei.org.

Hunt, S. (2002) *Making Competition Work in Electricity* (New York: Wiley Finance).

Joskow, P. (2001) 'California's Electricity Crisis', Working Paper, MIT, 28 November 2001.

Laszlo, E. (1996) *The Systems View of the World* (Cresskill, NJ: Hampton Press).

McNamara, W. (2002) *The California Energy Crisis: Lessons for a Deregulating Industry* (Tulsa, OK: Penwell Publishing).

Moore, A., and L. Kiesling (2001) *Powering Up California: Policy Alternatives for the California Energy Crisis* (Policy Study 280; Los Angeles, CA: Reason Public Policy Institute, February 2001).

O'Brien, J. (2003) *Wall Street on Trial* (Chichester, UK: John Wiley).

Silverstein, K. (2002) 'Recalling California's Energy Crisis', Electric Energy Online, www.electricenergyonline. com/detail_industry_news.asp?ID=9119.

Smeloff, E., and P. Asmus (1997) *Reinventing Electric Utilities* (Washington, DC: Island Press).

Stiglitz, J. (2003) *The Roaring Nineties* (New York/London: W.W. Norton).

Sweeny, J. (2002) *The California Electricity Crisis* (Stanford, CA: Hoover Institution Press).

Taylor, J., and P. Van Doren (2001) 'California's Electricity Crisis: What's Going On, Who's to Blame, and What to Do?', *Policy Analysis* 406 (3 July 2001).

Weare, C. (2003) *California Electricity Crisis: Causes and Policy Options* (San Francisco: Public Policy Institute of California).

18

Good governance and anti-corruption mobilisation
DO RUSSIAN NGOs HAVE ANY SAY?*

Diana Schmidt
Queen's University Belfast, UK

Sergey Bondarenko
Centre for Applied Research on Intellectual Property, Russia

> Since most cases of corruption involve public officials and private companies, civil society as an independent actor representing the interests of the general public is uniquely positioned to investigate and bring to light cases of corruption (World Bank 2003).

A transnational advocacy network has been emerging since the mid-1990s, which presents corruption as a major global problem that raises economic, political and moral concerns. It has thereby turned to framing this phenomenon in a negative way, underlining the corrosive effects of high levels of corruption on economic growth, foreign investment and good governance.[1] Particular concerns have been raised regarding the prevalence of corruption in the post-communist countries of Eastern Europe, with Moldova, Ukraine and Russia at the bottom end of most international rankings.[2] At the same time, within the context of a globalising political system, it has become commonly acknowledged that new forms of transnational governance require the participation of the third sector, represented by a strong community of non-governmental organisa-

---

* For comments on previous drafts, we thank Alex Warleigh, Kate Farrell and an anonymous referee. The chapter also benefits from various suggestions from our Russian colleagues and discussions at international conferences with Russian and Western academics and practitioners. Financial support of the Queen's University Belfast, through its Support Programme for University Research (SPUR), is gratefully acknowledged.

1 This shift in the treatment of corruption as a 'global problem' and the need for anti-corruption initiatives has been noticeable only in the last decade, on both academic and policy fronts, from an understanding of corruption as a mere 'domestic phenomenon', with attention to its forms, causes and consequences—including positive side-effects.

2 See, for example, indexes and surveys published by Transparency International at www.transparency.org/surveys/index.html.

tions (NGOs), especially for 'filling the niches' in issue areas where both states and markets have failed (e.g. Bode 2002; Carroll 1992; Rosenau 2000). Since both governments and liberal markets in many countries have failed to respond to high corruption levels, civil society is viewed as a principal agent in counteracting corruption and providing checks and balances on the entangled political and business sectors (e.g. ACN 2003; OECD 2003b; TI 2002a; World Bank 2003).

However, there is a stark contrast between the way the international community asks us to think about the role of NGOs, as part of transnational networks, and the domestic reality in post-communist countries today, where corruption is more entrenched and NGOs are less institutionalised within the societal system than is commonly assumed. In the case of contemporary Russia, we have to ask whether NGOs can match up to the normative claims of the international community regarding their engagement in lobbying good governance and struggling against corruption. On the one hand, they have benefited much from Western financial assistance, and their agendas have been significantly shaped by the interests of Western donors. With the current trend towards re-centralisation under the Putin administration, however, increasing state influence is compromising much of the potential of domestic organisations to actively further transnational anti-corruption advocacy. Russian NGOs are trapped between foreign expectations to promote good governance, and domestic commitments to a system characterised by an increasingly non-democratic governance style as well as entrenched corruption.

This chapter begins with the observation that an international anti-corruption advocacy network is emerging as part of the international community's striving promotion of good governance.[3] It does not aim to provide a comprehensive evaluation of such international efforts and their effectiveness in post-communist Russia: rather, our objective is to emphasise the conflicting role of NGOs and business communities.

The first part of the chapter discusses the theoretical foundation developed in the literature on transnational human rights and environmental advocacy. The second part explores similarities and differences between these advocacy fields and the transnational anti-corruption realm. The third part evaluates empirical findings from the Russian case with a view to governmental, NGO and business actors. The final part reflects on implications of our observations for the study of domestic actors involved in transnational good governance and anti-corruption advocacy reaching in post-communist countries.

18.1 Studying transnational advocacy

Looking at evidence from transnational human rights and environmental advocacy, international relations scholars have shown how transnational advocacy networks

3   A vital role in the prevention of corruption is attributed to the World Bank and the IMF. With their recent emphasis on the importance of 'good governance', they started to promote a wider range of public-sector reform activities to increase transparency, accountability and participation in lending countries (see Pieth 1997; Wolf and Gürgen 2002).

effectively promote the institutionalisation and implementation of international principles in states that have been accused of norm deviation (Finnemore and Sikkink 1998;
Keck and Sikkink 1998a; Risse *et al.* 1999). Transnational advocacy networks are made
up of domestic and international NGOs, intergovernmental organisations and national
governments who are working internationally on an issue, 'bound together by shared
values, a common discourse, and dense exchanges of information and services' (Keck
and Sikkink 1998a: 2). Such networks participate in processes linking transnational
and domestic politics and are most prevalent in areas of global relevance, devoted to
'public interest causes—the environment, human rights, women's issues, election monitoring, anti-corruption, and other "good things" ' (Carothers 1999, 2000). Their main
goal is to change the behaviour of states and of international organisations, which is
pursued using the strategies of framing the common issue to legitimate and motivate
collective action (Keck and Sikkink 1998a: 3) and shaming, that is to say denouncing,
norm-violating states as pariah states, which do not belong to the 'community of
civilised nations' (Risse and Sikkink 1999: 14). NGOs, as principal network agents, are
associated with fostering the transfer of international principles to the domestic arena
and exerting pressure on governments (e.g. Keck and Sikkink 1998a, 1998b; Risse and
Sikkink 1999).

For studying domestic change due to transfer of internationally promoted ideas, the
scholars have elaborated approaches such as the 'boomerang model' (Keck and Sikkink
1998a) or the 'spiral model' (Risse *et al.* 1999), which highlight the relations between
international and domestic groups and the target state. A boomerang pattern of influence exists when domestic NGOs bypass their government and link with foreign members of the transnational network, who then convince international organisations,
donor institutions or great powers to put pressure on the norm-violating state. Advocacy networks prove to serve three purposes for inducing domestic change in the
human rights area (Risse and Sikkink 1999): they put norm-violating states on the
international agenda in terms of moral consciousness-raising; they mobilise domestic
NGOs and social movements; and they create a transnational structure pressuring
norm-violating governments simultaneously 'from above and below' (Brysk 1993).
Risse argues that the evolution of domestic practices according to promoted ideas
resembles 'not a single boomerang throw but a whole spiral of boomerangs repeatedly
crossing national borders' (Risse 2000: 190). Along this spiral, the accused state usually responds to the pressures by denying the domestic applicability of international
norms and raising a plea for non-interference in domestic affairs. If the transnational
advocacy network can keep the government's failings on the international agenda, the
government will be forced to make tactical concessions to the international community
to accept the prescriptive validity of the norms, embedding them in its rhetoric and
institutions and finally implementing them through rule-consistent practice.

This theoretical foundation is useful for studying transnational advocacy against corruption. However, the major shortcoming of international relations approaches is that
they place heavy emphasis on investigating the final stage of advocacy processes, which
are internalisation of norms and policy outcomes. Norm-creating effects of transnational activities 'on the ground' (Risse 2000: 179) are thus understood as domestic
implementation of international standards leading to governmental compliance with
these standards. We reinforce the argument made by Keck and Sikkink (1998b: 218)
that greater attention to mechanisms involved at earlier stages should precede attempts

to characterise the results of advocacy networking. In particular, the roles of the NGOs and business communities are often misconceived. With a view to the domestic arena in post-communist transformation countries, conventional approaches need to be complemented with insights from sociology and transformation studies. On the one hand, advocacy is fundamentally a social process, heavily influenced by personal relationships. The latter are central to the process of how people in countries with no democratic tradition reconcile ideas and practices common in democracies with their long-held domestic beliefs and customs (Mendelson 2002: 241). An analysis of processes within interpersonal networks, such as reciprocal services and the flow of information and ideas, Granovetter (1973: 1,360) argues, 'provides the most fruitful micro–macro bridge'. On the other hand, the case of Russia suggests that the precise role of powerful governmental decision-makers needs to be better identified (Mendelson 2002: 244). Whatever their platform, advocacy organisations usually need to secure the support of state actors to endorse their ideas and make them part of their agenda (Finnemore and Sikkink 1998). It is thus important to conceptualise states as actively shaping their relationships with domestic actors and international organisations. Recent transformation studies provide valuable insights into the role of newly authoritarian states within a domestic context of constant transformation and reformation.

18.2 A transnational advocacy network against corruption?

Regarding the international arena, a process paralleled to that in the realm of human rights has been set in motion during the 1990s.[4] To a degree comparable with the acknowledgement of human rights as a universal good, a fairly cohesive international discourse on corruption as a global crisis has emerged. While campaigns against corruption are hardly new, in the last decade we have witnessed the emergence of corruption as a truly global political issue that has received response through integrated anti-corruption efforts on a global scale (Glynn et al. 1997; Naim 1995). Within a relatively short time, international organisations and the 'community of liberal states' (Risse and Sikkink 1999) were mobilised.

Civil-society mobilisation started with the foundation of Transparency International (TI) in 1994—a transnationally operating NGO set up as a coalition of national chapters in more than 90 countries. Transparency International is publishing annual corruption perception indices (CPIs), which bring domestic conditions in various countries to the attention of the international community. TI also lobbied for furthering the international OECD anti-corruption convention, which prohibits the practice of bribery by member nations and is often referred to as the strongest international anti-bribery

4   The 1948 Universal Declaration of Human Rights was followed by numerous conventions, specific international monitoring organisations and regional arrangements, the emergence of a huge network of transnationally operating advocacy coalitions and NGOs, as a result of which a global human rights polity emerged, which 'made real differences in the daily practices of national politics' (Risse and Ropp 1999: 234).

instrument (see Eigen 2003; Elshorst 2003; Galtung 2000).[5] Together with the CoE and UN conventions,[6] other international agreements and codes of good practice, such as those developed by the OECD, the IMF and the World Bank—the three leading 'anti-corruption crusaders' (Williams and Theobald 2000)—the international community is being provided with common sets of principles against which domestic practices can be measured. Although these are not always legally binding, they can be considered as 'the seeds of an international legal system' (Risse and Ropp 1999: 234) in the anti-corruption realm, similar to the early UN proposals for legal and policy reforms in the human rights field. Many of the international bodies involved have also proceeded to closer co-operation with each other, contributing to the formation of a true transnational advocacy network.

Regarding post-communist countries, regional agreements and networks are emerging, such as the Anti-Corruption Network for Transition Economies in 1998.[7] Building on the guidance of this network, a special sub-regional Anti-Corruption Action Plan was presented by four transformation countries—Armenia, Azerbaijan, Georgia and the Russian Federation—in September 2003. Apart from the TI country chapters, domestic NGOs emerge in various countries and link up with international network members in order to initiate actions and urge their governments to take positions on the corruption issues in their countries. The transnational anti-corruption mobilisation has clearly benefited from the favourable international climate of the last decade, which was characterised by a spread of democracy and capitalism that marked the 'beginning of a trend towards imitation and transnational encouragement' (Naim 1995: 275). But is this international anti-corruption climate favourable enough, and the corruption-related discourse on post-communist countries 'shaming' enough to induce domestic responses on the part of authorities, NGOs and the business community?

As in the realm of human rights, we can observe that the emergence of anti-corruption advocacy networks is significantly driven by NGOs, both international and domestic, putting anti-corruption principles on the agenda of intergovernmental organisations and bringing 'deviant states' (Risse *et al.* 1999), with high levels of corruption, to the attention of the international public. The example of Transparency International demonstrates that, in the initial phase, NGOs play a particular role for agenda setting, information and documentation, networking between international and domestic levels, and pressuring national governments simultaneously 'from above and below' (Brysk 1993). Yet processes of denial and tactical concessions, coming from the governments, are more entwined than suggested in the literature (see Risse and Sikkink

---

5 The OECD Convention on Combating Bribery of Foreign Public Officials in International Business Transactions (OECD 1998) was already signed in 1997 and tightened in 1999.

6 The Convention on the Fight against Corruption involving officials of the European Communities or Officials of Member States of the European Union (CoE 1997) was adopted by the Council of the European Union in 1997. Negotiation on the United Nations Convention against Corruption (United Nations 2003) started in 2000, and this convention was adopted in 2003.

7 Involving following countries: Albania, Armenia, Azerbaijan, Belarus, Bosnia and Herzegovina, Bulgaria, Croatia, Estonia, Former Yugoslav Republic of Macedonia, Montenegro, Georgia, Kazakhstan, Kyrgyz Republic, Latvia, Lithuania, Moldova, Romania, the Russian Federation, Serbia, Slovenia, Tajikistan, Turkmenistan, Uzbekistan and Ukraine. Collective members of the Network are the EU, CoE, OECD, UN, EBRD, World Bank, Transparency International and Open Society Institute (OECD 2003a).

1999).[8] Especially in transformation countries, regardless of the international anti-corruption climate, governments often have ambivalent positions on the presence of corruption in their country and may accordingly react in contradictory ways to accusations brought forward by the international community. On the one hand, political corruption may be to the benefit of governing or aspiring heads of state, who then speak up for non-interference into domestic affairs.[9] On the other hand, there is reason for them to be concerned about foreign aid and investment, so that they may prefer to make tactical concessions to the international (donor) community. It is possible that the first reaction of accused governments is one of denial, as much as it is possible that they 'make the clever move' (Risse and Ropp 1999: 243) by skipping the assumed denial phase. Further, it is possible that their reactions are inconsistent, depending on local political circumstances and interpersonal relations. With regard to further mobilisation, concessions prove to be a crucial part of the whole process, but also, as in the field of human rights, a remarkably 'Janus-faced' one (Risse and Ropp 1999: 246).

Regime vulnerability constitutes one of the most important conditions under which a move towards tactical concessions is likely (Keck and Sikkink 1998a; Risse and Sikkink 1999). Evidence suggests that two main forms of vulnerability referred to in the literature—dependence on foreign assistance and vulnerability to moral pressures—are significant prerequisites, particularly for post-communist regimes to make tactical concessions. Just as transnational advocacy networks use the moral power of human rights principles not only to shame deviant states directly but also to persuade Western states to apply additional economic and political pressures, we can observe similar mechanisms of successfully pushing Eastern European countries with high levels of corruption towards making concessions: moral consciousness-raising is pursued by the community of liberal states, involving strategies of shaming—in other words, denouncing transformation countries in view of their exceptionally high levels of corruption, starting from assumptions about corruption and communist, capitalist and democratic ideas. Economic pressure is closely linked to post-communist countries' dependence on foreign aid and investment and based on evidence about detrimental effects of corruption on private-sector growth and foreign investment.[10] Political pressure, exerted by Western governments focusing on democratisation, good governance and the rule of law, is often coupled with economic pressures on transformation countries seeking integration into international political systems such as the EU.[11]

---

8   Risse and Sikkink (1999) argue that there are subsequent stages of denial and concessions and treat them as analytically separate phases.

9   On election fraud and corruption related to pre-election campaigns in post-communist Russia, see, for example, Rose and Munro 2002 and White et al. 1996.

10 Hopes that marketisation and privatisation alone would attract substantial flows of foreign direct investment have not been met more than a decade after the collapse of communism (see Hellman et al. 2002). Russia, for example, experienced external pressure when the IMF had stopped disbursements for several years, because the Russian government and the IMF, after a series of discussions, could not reach an agreement on matching the domestic structural reform programme with IMF targets (EBRD 2002: 57).

11 For example, the new TACIS regulation concerning the provision of assistance to states in Eastern Europe and Central Asia conditions assistance to progress towards free and open democratic societies, and towards market-oriented economic systems (EC 2000). The EU Commission cited pervasive corruption as one of the obstacles to the Czech Republic's bid for EU membership (Appel 2002). Consequently, in the Czech Republic, an Anti-corruption Commission as well as a Govern-

Once concessions are made they are used as another window of opportunity for intensified advocacy, and continued transnational mobilisation may eventually have effects on governmental policy. Transnational mobilisation also turns out to be an important means of strengthening domestic NGOs advocating good governance and anti-corruption reforms. However, introduction of anti-corruption principles according to international standards, even through reformed legislation, is no guarantee for actual domestic change in economic, political and social practices in a post-communist country. Even if anti-corruption issues eventually become part of the domestic discourse, the further development in the realm of anti-corruption advocacy in transformation countries deviates from the triumphant process of norm diffusion described in the human rights literature.

The anti-corruption network is indeed a form of transnational advocacy, related to and often overlapping the human rights and environmental networks that have been analysed earlier. However, despite confident transnational lobbying and myriad policy statements and legal reforms, we consider it too early to speak of a strong international social structure of anti-corruption norms and institutions as exists in the field of human rights. To understand the mechanisms of successful advocacy through these networks it is also important to understand differences associated with the issue area and the domestic conditions in contemporary post-communist countries.

Regarding the global level, the evolution of a common international agenda, with policy effects in certain countries, proceeded much faster in the anti-corruption realm, having only started in the 1990s whereas transnational human rights mobilisation started at the UN level as early as 1948. The same applies to the Eastern European transformation after the breakdown of the Soviet regimes, which for the main part took place during the 1990s. The simultaneity of international efforts to promote anti-corruption principles—especially in Eastern Europe—and the societal transformation in the countries concerned makes a combined analysis of both processes particularly interesting. Drawing on empirical findings from post-communist Europe and Central Asia, some scholars have recently come to argue that both the pro-democratic role of civil society and the likelihood of international norm transfer may be overstated in the literature (Henderson 2003; Kopecký and Mudde 2003; see contributions in Mendelson and Glenn 2002; Thomas 2001). We endorse such critique since our findings from the Russian case demonstrate that, apart from the parallels explicated above, aspects of corruption combined with the post-communist transformation context complicate the processes of mobilisation and norm diffusion, in praxis and analysis.

18.2.1 Anti-corruption: a complex issue area

Although corruption is considered as a kind of norm deviation—namely, deviation from rules of law, official ethics or common principles of human morality (INDEM 2001: 5)—it is different from repression, which is the main topical focus of human rights advocacy. Corruption in a particular country is a complex set of offences, from crimi-

ment Council for the Non-Profit Sector (RNNO) has been established. In the case of Poland, explicit legislation was adopted, which does not exempt small facilitation payments from the offence of bribery, although such legislation is not compulsory under the OECD Convention.

nal to unethical, which can be committed by individuals and groups at all levels and in all sectors of a society. Therefore, regarding countries with high levels of corruption, not only *governments* are targeted by or respond to network pressure. In this case, introduction of international principles on the domestic level involves all societal sectors.

Considering the dependence of transformation countries on foreign investment and grants, economic pressure may even outweigh intergovernmental political or moral pressure. Closely related to this, tracing precise mechanisms linking foreign assistance with good governance is a tricky undertaking. Particularly in the field of international anti-corruption initiatives, the degree of overlap, complex interrelations and contradictions between the various actors, their strategies and potential impacts is high. International anti-corruption assistance, for example, is usually incorporated within other assistance programmes devoted to governance, civil society and media, public–private coalitions and legal reforms. At the local level, joint measures of civil-society and business actors can be observed: for example, the development and introduction of codes of conduct, or organisation of training courses for entrepreneurs.

Moreover, rather than successful 'cascading' (Keck and Sikkink 1998a) of international ideas through the 'international community' to the domestic level, non-linear diffusion, as well as non-compliance among the diverse actors involved, can be observed. In the post-communist East, recent evidence suggests that foreign donors and NGOs tended to overestimate the role of democratisation and good governance assistance in fostering positive change and thus helped create expectations that contrasted negatively with what actually happened in the recipient countries. Both administrations and NGOs tended to discuss success stories, because they feared losing funding from international agencies if the latter would change their agendas following open discussion of the limited role that good governance assistance plays in the transformation process (see, for example, Henderson 2002, 2003; Mendelson and Glenn 2002). But local norms may have much more powerful effects on Western principles than conventionally assumed (Höhmann 2002). For example, a recent assessment of the business environment in 22 transformation countries has shown that transnational legal restrictions to prevent bribery have not guaranteed 'good' standards of corporate conduct among foreign investors bound by their provisions.[12]

Finally, the matter of corruption is different from the matter of human rights violations in that post-communist countries are vehemently repelling accusations by pointing out that the phenomenon is universal and also widespread in Western democracies. Indeed, this argument has changed attitudes among Western anti-corruption advocates as well, with increasing attention to Western states and frequent revision of promoted international ideas.

18.2.2 Post-communist transformation: specific domestic context

Key peculiarities that are embedded in the complexity of ongoing post-communist transformation and reformation processes, as well as legacies of the communist past, have not received sufficient attention in the analysis of advocacy networking between

12 Evidence from data up to 2000, with a view to governance, corruption and transnational legal provisions such as the US Foreign Corrupt Practices Act and the OECD Convention on Bribery of Foreign Public Officials (see Hellman *et al.* 2002).

international and domestic levels. If the study of a complex issue, such as the fight against corruption, is coupled with a focus on post-communist societies, tightly interwoven political, economic and social transformation processes make the analysis even more complicated.

A major shortcoming of conventional approaches is the lack of distinction between forms of pressure related to transnational advocacy and the 'upsurge of pressure on the state' (Theobald 2003: 155) that is part of the overall systemic transformation. Future studies in this field would benefit from cross-fertilisation with the recent transformation literature, which investigates how the process of overall systemic transformation is ongoing in the three dimensions of (1) political transition from communist authoritarian rule towards democracy, (2) marketisation and privatisation of the planned economy, and (3) civil society formation where no or little bottom-up public engagement in the form of Western democratic practices existed before. Transformation periods thus involve all levels and sectors of society and are characterised by a lack of institutional strength, commitment and legitimacy (e.g. Dawisha and Parrot 1997; Grugel 2002; Haerpfer 2002; Höhmann 2002).

Besides transformation-related circumstances, the legacy of the communist past matters to transnational advocacy networks where civil society is only emerging and corruption is entrenched. Foreign assistance and democracy promotion projects that are limited in time and scope have shown little influence on these underlying conditions. In societies without civic-democratic traditions, NGOs are new societal entities, and mechanisms of state–civil society interaction are yet to be developed before domestic NGOs will be in a position to engage in advocacy processes according to conventional models of transnational networking.

Corruption in transformation societies is not only a major target, but simultaneously constitutes one of the biggest obstacles to transnational assistance and networking efforts. Both local and international actors must operate, on a day-to-day practical basis, in a system where corruption is the norm. Moreover, when studying transformation societies, we have to carefully distinguish between old and new forms of corruption as well as between grand and petty corruption. As Pope (2000: 20) remarks: 'While the basic source of corruption in communist times was primarily the rigidity of the system, it is now the uncertainty surrounding it'. New forms of corruption often result from transformation processes such as the introduction of new property relations through privatisation or through provision of foreign assistance. Old forms of corruption include various kinds of informal relations between local authorities and the population, which have always been part of the system (Bondarenko 2002). Gifts, bribes and 'misuse' of public goods are often 'socially acceptable norms of behaviour' (Lízal and Kocenda 2001), which local actors do not necessarily consider as being corruption—let alone a 'thread' or 'cancer' as the international discourse currently frames the phenomenon (Johnston 1997; Miller *et al.* 2001; Theobald 2003).

Apart from that, post-communist societies are undergoing transitions from systems characterised by information secrecy and state control on information flows. The endurance of this historical legacy definitely matters to the actors involved in advocacy networks, reaching into post-communist countries, because 'their main currency is information' (Keck and Sikkink 1998b: 218). In Russia and other re-centralised post-communist countries, public access to information remains denied to citizens. For anti-corruption advocacy in particular, information is a central issue since essential institutional pillars of any coherent domestic approach against corruption are independent media and civil society, complemented by the practices of access to information and freedom of speech (TI 2003; USAID 1999). Yet, in post-communist countries, not only the ability of advocacy networks to gather and spread information but also efforts to introduce media and anti-corruption legislation conforming to EU or other international standards prove to be problematic.

18.3 Fighting corruption: the Russian puzzle

Empirical findings from contemporary Russia will illustrate in more detail the above-mentioned aspects of anti-corruption advocacy and transformation mechanisms in a post-communist context.[13] Evidence from this case demonstrates that the combination of authoritarian governance, weak civil society and business sector, and entrenched corruption affects the domestic anti-corruption mobilisation potential in ways that are insufficiently addressed by conventional transnational advocacy studies.

18.3.1 Transformation and good governance promotion—Western perspectives

As part of Russian democratisation efforts pervading the 1990s, much international assistance was devoted to good governance programmes, including those targeted at strengthening civil society and counteracting corruption. EU assistance alone amounted to more than €4 billion between 1991 and 2000.[14] However, the balance drawn today looks rather sobering with civil society remaining weak and levels of corruption high. Furthermore, democracy assistance itself has been acknowledged to have the potential to increase social inequality and foster favourable conditions for corruption. Moreover, the current return to authoritarianism is being watched with mixed feelings by the international community. With President Putin in office since 2000, Russia has finally experienced political stability and strengthening of the state—after

13 The focus here is only on the Putin era (since 2000), since it constitutes a different domestic governance system from that of the 1990s period of democratisation and liberalisation, which has been the subject of most of the literature on corruption and civil-society development in post-communist Russia. Our data result from extensive field research, including numerous qualitative interviews with local and international NGOs, in various parts of Russia as well as personal experience within the communities of Russian NGOs and social scientists.

14 EU assistance was €2.3 billion in support of economic and democratic reform processes. Additionally, there have been US$4.5 billion US assistance and more than €2 billion from EBRD credits, EU member-states, and the European Initiative for Democracy and Human Rights (EIDHR), which assisted the development of democracy and civil society in the period between 1996 and 2000. The EIDHR has designated Russia as a focus country for the period 2002–2004. For details on the impressive numbers reflecting Western support of marketisation and democratisation, specifically assistance in the development of democracy and civil society in Russia, see EBRD 2002; United Nations 2001; www.state.gov/p/eur/rls/rpt and europa.eu.int/comm/external_relations/russia/intro/ass.htm.

it went through one decade of democratisation, which was characterised by economic decline and weakening state power. As recent surveys have shown, the majority of the Russian population welcomes this development. The international community, however, is expressing unease concerning the implied tendency towards decreasing civil-society and media independence.

In response to the unexpected procrastination and changing course of the democratisation process, most donors have readjusted their agendas away from initial structural reform to expanded programmes of good-practice advice and the strengthening of public debate on reforms (e.g. EC 2001; World Bank 2000). Still, the EU expresses further interest in the consolidation of democratic institutions, the strengthening of the rule of law and the continuation of political and economic reform in Russia, making these the top-priority issues to be supported in 2002–2006. Some of the key assistance areas are projects around civil-society capacity building, human rights education and training, freedom of expression and independent media. The main implementing partners for these projects are domestic and international NGOs as well as EU and UN organisations (EC 2001). The commitment to NGOs shows that the latter are recognised as important democracy promoting actors, and an alternative for funnelling development aid, from the perspective of transnational networks today.

Up to now, however, attempts by international anti-corruption organisations to create domestic networks against corruption have failed in Russia. Most of the anti-corruption programmes developed with significant support of Western grants were not effectively or consistently implemented. For example, as part of the federal programme 'South Russia', with a financial volume of almost US$5 billion provided by foreign sponsors, reasonable anti-corruption measures were developed and adopted. Yet the suggested measures remained merely declarative, and related projects to improve the investment climate appear rather unlikely from an anti-corruption point of view.[15]

18.3.2 The position of the government

Russia is perhaps the most convincing example of a government mixing strategies of denial and tactical concessions, thus making it impossible not only for the international community but also for the public 'to separate the real and fake values of their leaders' (Shlapentokh 2001). When President Putin assumed office in 2000, he immediately moved towards tactical concessions and declared the fight against corruption a primary goal of the state, in order to restore Russia's international reputation. After the presidential election, a liberal ten-year strategic programme was approved together with a short-term action plan. The programme has won the broad backing of the international community. It recognises a better investment climate as key to reversing the trend of capital flight and identifies measures to ensure transparency, introduce good corporate governance, and encourage compliance and enforcement. Accordingly, key objectives in the plan are to reduce bureaucratic interference, cut transaction costs and the scope for corruption, make taxation more transparent, and adopt international accounting standards (EC 2001). Several draft codes were set up for ethics, civil servants' conduct and corporate conduct. However, on the international level, the CoE Convention (CoE 1997) has not been signed by the Russian government, and the UN

---

15 For more details on the experience in the Russian South, see Bondarenko 2001.

Convention (United Nations 2003) not been ratified so far. On the national level, practical moves basically only consisted in direct actions against the 'oligarchs' and members of the 'Family', the group of Yeltsin-era Kremlin insiders (Sakwa 2004; Shevtsova 2003). In his 2003 State of the Nation Address, the president did not mention the issue of corruption at all (JRL 2003). When he resumed anti-corruption activities with the establishment of an Anti-Corruption Council in November 2003, shortly before the end of his term, it was widely interpreted as mere re-election propaganda (e.g. Medetsky 2003), all the more so since Putin dismissed his prime minister, Michail Kasyanov, who was also chairman of the council, shortly after.

Not only have the president's tactical concessions repeatedly fallen short of their mark, they have always been accompanied by counterproductive and contradictory reforms. For example, part of Putin's political agenda is the stabilisation of the political system by controlling the formation of civil-society groups (e.g. Meier 2003) and the flow of information to the public (Oates and White 2003; Sakwa 2004). Media pluralism has been considered one of Russia's most significant democratisation achievements in the 1990s. Yet the most sinister aspect of Putin's reform practice is the tendency towards authoritarian solutions, despite a declared commitment to democratisation. A series of investigations and attacks, directed at critical media, journalists and NGOs, raises considerable concern about underlying political motivations. At present, Russia is one of the lowest-ranking countries in the world in terms of press freedom. Journalists who are engaging in legitimate reporting on issues such as corruption and human rights violations are subject to numerous forms of pressure including criminal libel suits, state inspections, or restrictive legislation on campaigning (Black and Tarassova 2003; RSF 2002; 2003). In the words of President Putin, 'there never was freedom of speech in Russia, and consequently we have nothing to trample on in this respect'.[16]

Reactions from the international community show that there is concern about the Russian government's non-democratic behaviour. The international press watchdog Reporters Sans Frontières has set up a gallery of 'predators of press freedom', headed by Vladimir Putin.[17] The OSCE is critical about the Russian 'censorship by killing' strategy[18] and, together with the CoE, called on the Russian authorities to bring the Russian criminal code into line with European press freedom standards.[19] A statement made by the OSCE media freedom representative demonstrates the relevance of close interrelations between corruption, the media and mobilisation:

> What does censorship by murder mean? The corruption mafia kills one journalist, one person, and simultaneously kills the courage of many other people, thus organising a plot of silence. If we organise a plot of silence around corruption we lead the country in a trap. This is not only personal crime it is also a crime against patriotism. And consequently Russia cannot survive as a normal state if, in many regions, not the Constitution but corruption operates.[20]

16   Speech to students of the University of Columbia, 25 January 2003.
17   See: www.rsf.fr/article.php3?id_article=1075, accessed 8 March 2004.
18   Freimut Duve, OSCE media freedom representative, quoted in *The Associated Press* (2003).
19   Article 130 of this law says libel can be punished by up to one year imprisonment at hard labour and article 129 provides for a jail term of up to three years without hard labour. Full text: www.consultant.ru/popular/ukrf.
20   Freimut Duve made this statement at a press conference in Moscow on 16 September 2003.

18.3.3 The position of local authorities

Experiences from the Russian South will illustrate the equally contradictory behaviour of the political leadership at the local level. Frequent statements concerning the need to attract foreign investment are hardly matched by real steps against widespread corruption at the municipal level towards implementing new federal legislation or protecting foreign investors against corruption. In practice, local officials usually prefer to refrain from active involvement in anti-corruption efforts. Consider, for example, the trade in pirate music and software CDs, carried out openly in the streets—despite recently adopted laws. Such business could not exist without corruption among the police and local authorities. Activities of Southern NGOs to protect intellectual property rights have encountered rigorous unwillingness by the police to observe federal laws. Several actions towards revealing corrupt officials have been initiated, and information on corrupt policemen was made public in 2003. As surveys have shown, however, the majority of the population would interpret such reporting in the media as nothing more than propaganda with a view to the forthcoming parliamentary elections.

The most prominent example illustrating gaps between leadership rhetoric and practice, as well as the importance of political interests and interpersonal ties for the ongoing privatisation of locally important corporations and behind-the-scenes reorganisation of the administration, is the case of the representative of President Putin in the Russian South, plenipotentiary Victor Kazantsev. He repeatedly declared civil-society participation necessary in the struggle against corruption.[21] Yet his words have not been translated into action. Not only that, he left unanswered several suggestions for anti-corruption measures directed to him on the part of NGOs. Employees of his own office were accused of corruption by the Russian media. Although he shifted his attention to cadre reform through personnel reorganisation as well as to economic questions, he was dismissed—without any explanation of the reasons—by President Putin shortly after the local Duma elections.[22] Kazantsev's removal has not shown any effect on the local level of corruption so far, and critics of Putin's method of persecuting individuals in his fight against corruption, without any policy or judicial backing, may find themselves confirmed. There is no systemic approach to administrative reform with local bureaucrats remaining resistant to reducing opportunities for corruption. Expert opinions about the leadership commitment to administrative reorganisation are divided. While it can be argued that it is 'the most profitable and least risky business' if responsibility stays with the government,[23] top-down action is widely interpreted in connection with the re-election campaign of the Russian president (e.g. Shlapentokh 2003). Nevertheless, since the present system of local executive authority is so corrupt, there is need to accelerate reform, not only through top-level decision-making, but also from below.[24]

---

21 Among others, such announcements have been made in conversations with one of the authors of this chapter.

22 For details on this particular case, see Bondarenko and Serenko 2004a; 2004b; Serenko and Schapovalov 2004.

23 Statement made by G. Satarov, president of the INDEM foundation, quoted in Tkatshuk 2004.

24 According to a statement made by Sergey Frolov, Thule regional Duma deputy, quoted in Kachiani and Kriutshkov 2004.

18.3.4 The position of non-governmental actors: NGOs and corporations

Within the NGO community, a flurry of activity around research on corruption and anti-corruption measures was noticeable in the late 1990s. There have been a number of international conferences, local 'anti-corruption weeks', and reports on progress in this field. The INDEM Foundation's studies (INDEM 1998; 2001) have received considerable domestic and international attention. Most recently, however, anti-corruption activities of Russian NGOs are decreasing and corruption is not the activity field anymore.[25] Whether the apparent decline in NGO activity against corruption is due to increasing intervention on the part of the government or decreasing enthusiasm on the part of the international donor community remains debatable. Yet it is obvious that transnational anti-corruption initiatives have hardly had long-term network effects and that domestic NGOs find themselves in a weak position. Among the key conditions hindering continued NGO advocacy and networking are lack of political will, transparency and freedom to receive and disseminate information, as well as weak organisational and institutional capacities, lack of finances and high-quality research.

In the period 2000–2002, according to the NGO Sustainability Index (USAID 2002), the Russian NGO sector remained weak, after having seen a temporary improvement in its input into the development of local and national policy in the late 1990s. In terms of strategies, NGOs lobbyism has become more sophisticated thanks to their moving away from ineffective models of public campaigning and working with other professional lobbying or research groups as well as with the business sector. However, partly because of the severe competition for funding, the third sector at large remains rather fragmented and resistant to joint activity programmes. Furthermore, the lack of good-quality research on business and social community development makes it difficult for NGOs to use factual data to back up their advocacy and to design convincing arguments for policy recommendations. In contrast to public education programmes existing in the field of ecology, another problem is the lack of trained personnel for teaching and assisting citizens in counteracting corruption from below.

It is often maintained that domestic NGOs provide valuable linkages between local communities and transnational actors promoting good governance, because both sides trust them (Marschall 2002: 2). Russian NGOs, however, constitute new societal entities, the emergence of which has been significantly fuelled by Western assistance, rather than resulting from bottom-up civil-society formation, thus lacking legitimisation and trust from below (Henderson 2002). Increasing debates about whether Russian NGOs are actually 'representing the interests of the general public' (World Bank 2003) indicate a need to better understand local organisations within the various social milieus in their home countries, following social embeddedness approaches in social research (e.g. Granovetter 1973).

It would be incorrect to assert that NGOs operating in an environment of endemic corruption are not themselves affected by it. Evidence from Russian organisations does not support the portrayal of NGOs as ideal corruption watchdogs or assumptions about their 'uncompromised moral and professional authority' (Marschall 2002: 1). On the contrary, NGOs are equally struck by systemic corruption. The Russian NGO sector is

25   Interview with Elena Panfilova, director of TI Russia, Moscow, 6 August 2003.

notorious for its disproportionate share of pseudo-NGOs, set up for the purpose of benefiting from grant money. There have been numerous cases where NGOs used funding or sold donated equipment for personal enrichment. There are examples of outright norm-violating behaviour, as in the case of the largest organisation for the protection of authors' rights, the Russian Authors' Society, a member of which was arrested in summer 2003 for taking a bribe from one of the central Russian broadcasting companies. Yet there are also discrepancies between abstract policy goals of international actors and the pragmatic means used by domestic partners to promote them, such as, for example, paying bribes for the registration of an NGO. Many cases of bribery within the NGO sector would fall into the category of facilitation payments, usually termed 'speed', 'tea' or 'grease' money, necessary for accelerating the issuance of licences, the processing of official documents and the provision of public services, such as communications, electricity or police protection.

The role of facilitation payments is so far only studied as a phenomenon associated with the business sector. While there is no approved definition, they are often excluded from the definition of bribery. Facilitation payments are generally not covered by anti-bribery conventions.[26] Some researchers understand such payments as 'the low-level, visible manifestation of hidden criminal hierarchies of extortion' (TI 2002b). Others view corruption in this form as a lubricant necessary to grease the wheels, especially in countries where effective market and democratic systems are yet to emerge. Yet critics warn that a 'de-facto tolerance of corruption' will in the end prove socially catastrophic, through massive protest or anti-democratic regimes, in post-communist "infant democracies" ' (Hessel and Murphy 2000; see also Kaufmann 1997; Miller *et al.* 2001).

In Russia, both companies and NGOs are in many cases forced to take similar measures for inducing public officials to perform functions that are part of their routine duties. Experts confirm that local NGOs struggle under the burden of constant demands for unofficial payments. Transparency International's (TI 2002b) conclusion regarding the business sector, that facilitation payments can create more problems than they solve, may also apply to the NGO sector: in theory they save time but in practice they can actually cause delays by giving officials an incentive to create obstacles so that they can be paid off for removing them.

As for the Russian business community, the very existence of corruption is a problem. However, more importance is ascribed to the international perception of Russia as a completely corrupt country. They criticise international rankings set up on the basis of experts' perceptions, such as the CPI annually published by Transparency International. Russian corporations, represented by the Union of Industrialists and Entrepreneurs (RSPP), are instead calling for more attention to legal reform within the country. They are also concerned with conveying positive trends in the investment climate to the international public. In autumn 2002, for example, RSPP promised provision of considerable funds for international PR measures such as an English-language Internet portal

---

26 Facilitation payments are, according to paragraph 9 of Commentaries on the OECD Convention (OECD 1998), payments 'which, in some countries, are made to induce public officials to perform their functions, such as issuing licenses or permits'. Yet the commentaries on the OECD Convention recognise such payments as a serious problem and underline that this 'corrosive phenomenon' should be addressed by such means as support for programmes of good governance. See the commentaries on the OECD Convention: www.oecd.org/document/1/0,2340,en_2649_34859_2048129_1_1_1_37447,00.html, accessed 8 March 2004.

(Clark 2002).[27] In this case, criticism may be justified that RSPP and similar organisations support the prevailing close relations between the authority and the economic elite (Tsirel' 2003). Yet concerning anti-corruption efforts, besides the NGO community, the corporate sector is engaged in pushing legal reform and keeping international actors informed about domestic facts on an issue of common concern.

RSPP has also developed a 'Charter of Corporate Business Ethics'[28] and lobbied the so-called 'integrity pacts'. The latter are designed to bring corporations, SMEs and NGOs together in order to create better conditions for transparent and fair competition. An example of such pacts is the 'no-bribery pledge', where corporations competing in privatisation acts commit themselves not to take or give any bribes, while officials in the committee promise to carry out transparent procedures.[29] As mentioned above, co-operation emerging with NGOs for the development of codes of good conduct and management education in SMEs is promising progress in the area of good governance 'on the ground'.

For RSPP and other leading corporations, there are various incentives to engage in anti-corruption measures. Transparent business relations may attract investors and step up the economy. But they may also disturb the current political system, which relies heavily on informal rules. It is therefore hardly surprising that lobbyism for transparency by non-governmental actors is currently rather conceived as *coup d'état* on the part of the government.

18.4 Conclusions: towards linking transnational and domestic advocacy

Throughout the last decade, we can observe a trend towards transnational anti-corruption advocacy with a striking emphasis on involving civil society as one of the main advocacy forces. However, there is a stark contrast between the discourse framed by the international community and the domestic reality in post-communist Russia. That the success of reaching international agreements is now frequently attributed to the determination of NGOs on the international stage is certainly one of the most encouraging lessons learned from successful advocacy in the spheres of protecting human rights and the environment. There is reason to trust in NGOs as potential advocates in counteracting corruption—but can these organisations also be potent advocates in contemporary Russia?

When studying anti-corruption advocacy, reaching into a post-communist country, we are confronted with the analytical difficulty that both corruption and the domestic

27 Meanwhile, the previous RSPP online portal (www.rsppr.ru) has been abandoned and a new one established (www.rsppr.biz). So far in Russian language only, the latter is still of limited use for the wider international business community.
28 For the full text version, see www.rspp.ru/articles?fid=131&aid=499 (in Russian).
29 For more information and examples, see Center for Business Ethics and Corporate Governance at www.cfbe.ru and www.ethicsrussia.org.

context of transformation are complex issues involving all levels and sectors of society. In these respects, conventional theories, developed with a view to human rights and environmental advocacy, are in need of further elaboration. International relations approaches are confined to an analysis of changing state behaviour due to international lobbyism and, regarding post-communist contexts, tend to overestimate the potential of NGOs as primary advocacy forces while neglecting the processes of business-sector formation and increasing state authoritarianism.

Evidence from contemporary Russia demonstrates how actual processes do not correspond to conventional theoretical assumptions. With a current trend towards re-centralising governmental control on flows of information and the organisation of the emerging NGO community, fundamental prerequisites for effective transnational mobilisation and networking in any advocacy realm remain matters of sovereign state policy. Regarding the local level, the case of the Russian South illustrates that bottom-up initiatives by local NGOs to counteract corruption are often blocked by unwillingness of municipal authorities, which are in turn subject to top-down intervention. Apart from that, the economic dimension, as well as locally embedded NGO–business sector collaboration, is insufficiently accounted for in transnational mobilisation research and practice.

Future studies on transnational advocacy networks have to take domestic context conditions more seriously and relate micro-level interactions to macro-level patterns in convincing ways. Concerning the question of why some NGO communities organise for common goals easily and effectively whereas others seem unable to mobilise, we propose a closer focus on interpersonal networks involving different members of the macro networks, in order to understand whether related aspects might facilitate or block organisation (Granovetter 1973). In addition, conflicts between advocacy dynamics and long-standing social norms in post-communist contexts, where democratic traditions are lacking and corruption is entrenched, can be better understood by integrating insights from transformation approaches. Transfer of international anti-corruption norms to the domestic level has not taken place because corruption is systemic, but at the same time not the only problem of the system. Corruption cannot be removed from everyday reality, while the emergence of an NGO sector is taking place within an operational environment that is in crucial respects different from that in advanced democracies. Transformation involves a diversity of aspects in governmental, business and civil-society sectors, and corrupt as well as informal relations therein must be addressed by pursuing an integrative approach—by both scholars and practitioners dealing with this puzzle.

References

ACN (2003) 'Anti-Corruption Network for Transition Economies', www.anticorruptionnet.org/index-txt.html, accessed 8 March 2004.

Appel, H. (2002) 'Corruption and the Collapse of the Czech Transition Miracle', *East European Politics and Societies* 15.3: 528-53.

Black, B.S., and A.S. Tarassova (2003) 'Institutional Reform in Transition: A Case Study of Russia, *Supreme Court Economic Review* 10: 211-78

Bode, T. (2002) 'Das Auftreten der NGOs spiegelt nur das Versagen der offiziellen Politik', *Transit* 24 (Winter 2002/2003): 125-39.

Bondarenko, M., and A. Serenko (2004a) 'Polpred ystal ot politiki: Viktor Kazantsev ublekcia "tschistoi" ekonomikoi', *Hezavisimaia gazeta* 23 (3136) Edition, ng.ru/regions/2004-02-06/4_kazancev.html.

—— and —— (2004b) 'V preddverii otstavki Kazantsev bankrotil predpriiatiia', *Hezavisimaia gazeta* 48 (3163) Edition, ng.ru/regions/2004-03-11/1_kazantsev.html, accessed 10 February 2004.

Bondarenko, S. (ed.) (2001) *Mezhdunarodno-prakticheskaia konferentsiia 'Bor'ba s korruptsiei na Iuge Rossii kak sistemnaia problema: Prepiatstbiia i strategii'* (Rostov-on-Don, Russia: Westminster Foundation for Democracy/Centre for Applied Researches into Intellectual Property).

—— (2002) *Korrumpirovannye Obshchestva* (Rostov-on-Don, Russia: Westminster Foundation for Democracy/Centre for Applied Research on Intellectual Property).

Brysk, A. (1993) 'From Above and Below: Social Movements, the International System, and Human Rights in Argentina', *Comparative Political Studies* 26.3: 259-85.

Carothers, T. (1999/2000) 'Civil Society', *Foreign Policy* 117 (Winter 1999/2000): 18-29.

Carroll, T.F. (1992) *Intermediary NGOs: The Supporting Link in Grassroots Development* (West Hartford, CT: Kumarian Press).

Clark, T. (2002) 'RSPP to Fund Pro-Russia PR Campaign', *Moscow Times*, Moscow, 12 September 2002: 7.

CoE (Council of the European Union) (1997) *Convention on the Fight against Corruption involving Officials of the European Communities or Officials of Member States of the European Union*, europa. eu.int/scadplus/printversion/en/lvb/l33027.htm.

Dawisha, K., and B. Parrot (eds.) (1997) *Politics, Power and the Struggle for Democracy in South-East Europe* (Cambridge, UK: Cambridge University Press).

EBRD (European Bank for Reconstruction and Development) (2002) *Strategy for the Russian Federation*.

EC (European Commission) (2000) 'Council Regulation (EC, EURATOM) No 9/2000 of 29 December 1999 concerning the provision of assistance to the partner States in Eastern Europe and Central Asia', europa.eu.int/comm/external_relations/ceeca/tacis/reg99_00.pdf, accessed 10 February 2004.

—— (2001) 'Russia: Country Strategy Paper 2002–2006, and National Indicative Programme 2002–2003', europa.eu.int/comm/external_relations/russia/esp/index.htm, accessed 10 February 2004.

Eigen, P. (2003) *Das Netz der Korruption: Wie eine weltweite Bewegung gegen Bestechung kämpft* (Frankfurt/New York: Campus Verlag).

Elshorst, H. (2003) 'NGOs als Hoffnungsträger bei Versagen von Staat und Markt im globalisierten Umfeld—am Beispiel der Bekämpfung der internationalen Korruption', in M. Birgit (ed.), *Globale öffentliche Güter—für menschliche Sicherheit und Frieden* (Berlin: BWV Berliner Wissenschafts-Verlag GmbH): 185-202.

Finnemore, M., and K. Sikkink (1998) 'International Norm Dynamics and Political Change', *International Organisation* 52.4: 887-917.

Galtung, F. (2000) 'A Global Network to Curb Corruption: The Experience of Transparency International', in A.M. Florini (ed.), *The Third Force: The Rise of Transnational Civil Society* (Washington, DC: Carnegie Endowment for International Peace): 17-47.

Glynn, P., S.J. Kobrin and M. Naim (1997) 'The Globalization of Corruption', in K.A. Elliott (ed.), *Corruption and the Global Economy* (Washington, DC: Institute for International Economics).

Granovetter, M.S. (1973) 'The Strength of Weak Ties', *American Journal of Sociology* 78.6: 1,360-80.

Grugel, J. (2002) *Democratization: A Critical Introduction* (Basingstoke, UK/New York: Palgrave).

Haerpfer, C.W. (2002) *Democracy and Enlargement in Post-Communist Europe: The Democratisation of the General Public in Fifteen Central and Eastern European Countries, 1991–1998* (London/New York: Routledge).

Hellman, J.S., G. Jones and D. Kaufmann (2002) 'Far From Home: Do Foreign Investors Import Higher Standards of Governance in Transition Economies?', www.worldbank.org/wbi/governance/pdf/farfromhome.pdf, accessed 8 March 2004.

Henderson, S.L. (2002) 'Selling Civil Society: Western Aid and the Nongovernmental Organization Sector in Russia', *Comparative Political Studies* 35.2: 139-67.

—— (2003) *Building Democracy in Contemporary Russia: Western Support for Grassroots Organisations* (Ithaca, NY/London: Cornell University Press).

Hessel, M., and K. Murphy (2000) *Stealing the State, and Everything Else: A Survey of Corruption in the Postcommunist World* (Berlin: Transparency International).

Höhmann, H.-H. (ed.) (2002) *Wirtschaft und Kultur im Transformationsprozess. Wirkungen, Interdependenzen, Konflikte* (Bremen: Edition Temmen).

INDEM (Information for Democracy) (1998) *Russia vs Corruption: Who Wins?* (Moscow: INDEM Foundation).

—— (2001) *Diagnostics of Corruption in Russia: Sociological Analysis* (Moscow: INDEM Foundation).

Johnston, M. (1997) *What can be Done about Entrenched Corruption?* (International Bank for Reconstruction and Development/World Bank).

JRL (Johnson's Russia List) (2003) 'Transcript of Putin's State of the Nation Address (BBC Monitoring 16 May 2003),' *JRL* 7186; www.cdi.org.

Kachiani, K., and M. Kriutshkov (2004) ' "Oborotni v galstukach" Malyi I srednii biznes ottshaialsia borot'sia c korruptsiei', *Novye Izvestiia*, www.newizv.ru/news/?id_news=5527&date=2004-03-30.

Kaufmann, D. (1997) 'Corruption: The Facts', *Foreign Policy*, Summer 1997: 114-31.

Keck, M.E., and K. Sikkink (1998a) *Activists beyond Borders: Advocacy Networks in International Politics* (Ithaca, NY/London: Cornell University Press).

—— and —— (1998b) 'Transnational Advocacy Networks in the Movement Society', in D.S. Meyer and S. Tarrow (eds.), *The Social Movement Society: Contentious Politics for a New Century* (Oxford: Rowman & Littlefield): 217-38.

Kopecký, P., and C. Mudde (eds.) (2003) *Uncivil Society? Contentious Politics in Post-Communist Europe* (London/New York: Routledge).

Lízal, L., and E. Kocenda (2001) 'State of Corruption in Transition: Case of the Czech Republic', *Emerging Markets Review* 2: 137-59.

Marschall, M. (2002) *Legitimacy and Effectiveness: Civil Society Organizations' Role in Good Governance* (Baden, Germany: Transparency International).

Medetsky, A. (2003) 'Creation of Anti-Corruption Council Seen as Liberal Win', *The St Petersburg Times*, 923 Edition, www.sptimes.ru/archive/times/923/news/n_11061.htm.

Meier, C. (2003) *Deutsch-Russische Beziehungen auf dem Prüfstand: Der Petersburger Dialog 2001–2003* (Berlin: Stiftung Wissenschaft und Politik/Deutsches Institut fur Internationale Politik und Sicherheit).

Mendelson, S.E. (2002) 'Conclusion: The Power and Limits of Transnational Democracy Networks in Postcommunist Societies', in S.E. Mendelson and J.K. Glenn (eds.), *The Power and Limits of NGOs: A Critical Look at Building Democracy in Eastern Europe and Eurasia* (New York/Chichester, UK: Columbia University Press): 232-51.

—— and J.K. Glenn (eds.) (2002) *The Power and Limits of NGOs: A Critical Look at Building Democracy in Eastern Europe and Eurasia* (New York/Chichester, UK: Columbia University Press).

Miller, W.L., A.B. Grodeland and T.Y. Koshechkina (2001) *A Culture of Corruption? Coping with Government in Post-Communist Europe* (Budapest/New York: Central University Press).

Naim, M. (1995) 'The Corruption Eruption', *The Brown Journal of World Affairs* 2.2 (Summer 1995): 245-61.

Oates, S., and S. White (2003) 'Politics and the Media in Postcommunist Russia', *Politics* 23.1: 31-37.

OECD (Organisation for Economic Co-operation and Development) (1998) *Convention on Combating Bribery of Foreign Public Officials in International Business Transactions* (Paris: OECD).

—— (2003a) *Anti-Corruption Action Plan for Armenia, Azerbaijan, Georgia, the Russian Federation, Tajikistan and Ukraine. Preamble*, www.oecd.org/dataoecd/60/59/12593443.pdf.

—— (2003b) *Co-operating with the Private Sector and Civil Society in the Fight against Corruption*, www.oecd.org/EN/about_further_page/0,,EN-about_further_page-89-3-no-no—0-no-no-1,00.html, accessed 10 February 2004.

Pieth, M. (1997) 'International Co-operation to Combat Corruption', in K.A. Elliot (ed.), *Corruption and the Global Economy* (Washington, DC: Institute for International Economics): 119-31.

Pope, Y. (2000) *Confronting Corruption: The Elements of a National Integrity System* (Berlin/London: Transparency International).

Risse, T. (2000) 'The Power of Norms versus the Norms of Power: Transnational Civil Society and Human Rights', in A.M. Florini (ed.), *The Third Force: The Rise of Transnational Civil Society* (Washington, DC: Carnegie Endowment for International Peace): 177-209.

—— and S.C. Ropp (1999) 'International Human Rights Norms and Domestic Change: Conclusions', in T. Risse, S.C. Ropp and K. Sikkink (eds.), *The Power of Human Rights: International Norms and Domestic Change* (Cambridge, UK: Cambridge University Press): 234-78.

—— and K. Sikkink (1999) 'The Socialization of International Human Rights Norms into Domestic Practices: Introduction', in T. Risse, S.C. Ropp and K. Sikkink (eds.), *The Power of Human Rights: International Norms and Domestic Change* (Cambridge, UK: Cambridge University Press): 1-38.

——, S.C. Ropp and K. Sikkink (eds.) (1999) *The Power of Human Rights: International Norms and Domestic Change* (Cambridge, UK: Cambridge University Press).

Rose, R., and N. Munro (2002) *Elections without Order: Russia's Challenge to Vladimir Putin* (Cambridge, UK: Cambridge University Press).

Rosenau, J.N. (2000) 'Governance in a Globalizing World', in D. Held and A. McGrew (eds.), *The Global Transformations Reader: An Introduction to the Globalizations Debate* (Cambridge, UK: Polity Press): 181-93.

RSF (Reporters Sans Frontières) (2002) 'Russia: Annual Report 2002', www.rsf.fr.

—— (2003) 'Russia: Annual Report 2003', www.rsf.fr.

Sakwa, R. (2004) *Putin: Russia's Choice* (London/New York: Routledge).

Serenko, A., and A. Schapovalov (2004) 'Liudei Kazantsaeva prosiat "VON". Novy polpred v YOFO natschal "zatschistku" svoeve apparata', *Hezavisimaia gazesta* 53 (3168) Edition, ng.ru/regions/2004-03-18/4_ykovlev.html.

Shevtsova, L.F. (2003) *Putin's Russia* (Washington, DC: Carnegie Endowment for International Peace).

Shlapentokh, V. (2001) 'Putin's First Year in Office: The New Regime's Uniqueness in Russian History', *Communist and Post-Communist Studies* 34: 371-99.

—— (2003) 'Wealth versus Political Power: The Russian Case', *JRL* 7438; www.cdi.org.

The Associated Press (2003) 'OSCE Frets about Media Freedom', *Moscow Times*, www.moscowtimes.ru/stories/2003/09/17/013.html.

Theobald, R. (2003) 'Conclusion: Prospects for Reform in a Globalised Economy', in A. Doig and R. Theobald (eds.) *Corruption and Democratisation* (London: Frank Cass): 149-59.

Thomas, D.C. (2001) *The Helsinki Effect: International Norms, Human Rights, and the Demise of Communism* (Princeton, NJ: Princeton University).

TI (Transparency International) (2002a) 'Corruption Fighters' Tool Kit: Civil Society Experiences and Emerging Strategies', Transparency International, www.transparency.org/toolkits/index.html, accessed 8 March 2004.

—— (2002b) 'Facilitation Payments in the Legislation of Signatories to the OECD Anti-Bribery Convention', Transparency International (UK), admin.corisweb.org/files/Murray2002Facilitation_Payments1049984765.pdf.

—— (ed.) (2003) 'Global Corruption Report 2003. Special Focus: Access to Information', Transparency International, www.globalcorruptionreport.org, accessed 10 February 2004.

Tkatshuk, S. (2004) 'Prodazhny vse. Za technogennye katastrofy I terakty grazhdane dolzhny "blagodarit" korruptsionerov', *Novye Izvestiia*, www.newizv.ru/news/?n_id=5074&curdate=2004-03-05.

Tsirel', S. (2003) 'Kakie Sily Mogut Sozdat' Grazhdanskoe Obshchestvo v Roccii?' ('Which Forces can Build Civil Society in Russia?'), *NZ(1)*: www.eurozine.com/partner/nz/current-issue.html.

United Nations (2001) *Russian Capitalism and Money-Laundering* (New York: United Nations).

—— (2003) *United Nations Convention against Corruption*, www.unodc.org/pdf/crime/convention_corruption/signing/Convention-e.pdf, accessed 10 February 2004.

USAID (US Agency for International Development) (1999) *From Transition to Partnership: A Strategic Framework for USAID Programs in Europe and Eurasia* (United States Agency for International Development, Bureau for Europe and Eurasia, www1.worldbank.org/wbiep/decentralization/ciesin/PDABS123.pdf).

—— (2002) 'Russia', *NGO Sustainability Index*, USAID, 142-48; www.usaid.gov/locations/europe_eurasia/dem_gov/ngoindex/2002/russia.pdf.

White, S., R. Rose and I. McAllister (1996) *How Russia Votes* (New York: Seven Bridges Press).

Williams, R., and R. Theobald (eds.) (2000) *Corruption in the Developing World* 2 (Cheltenham, UK/Northampton, UK: Edward Elgar).

Wolf, T., and E. Gürgen (2002) 'Improving Governance and Fighting Corruption in the Baltic and CIS Countries: The Role of the IMF', in G.T. Abed and S. Gupta (eds.), *Governance, Corruption, and Economic Performance* (Washington, DC: International Monetary Fund): 538-64.

World Bank (2000) *Anticorruption in Transition: A Contribution to the Policy Debate* (Washington, DC: World Bank).

—— (2003) *Multi-pronged Strategies for Combating Corruption: Civil Society Participation*, www1.worldbank.org/publicsector/anticorrupt/civilsociety.htm.

Part 5
Multinational companies and their implications for the new governance structures, regulators and civil society

19

NGO–business collaborations and the law

SUSTAINABILITY, LIMITATIONS OF LAW, AND THE CHANGING RELATIONSHIP BETWEEN COMPANIES AND NGOS

*Kees Bastmeijer and Jonathan Verschuuren**

Tilburg University, the Netherlands

Relationships between governments, companies and NGOs are changing in the context of the promotion of sustainable development. With regard to various sustainability issues, governments seem to 'lose their grip' and the relationship between companies and NGOs appear to become more and more important. This is illustrated by the increase in collaboration projects—lately referred to as 'partnerships'—between companies and NGOs in the challenge to find solutions for the various sustainability issues.

This is a conceptual chapter addressing the role of company–NGO collaboration in relation to the role of national and international law in finding solutions for complex and transboundary sustainability issues. We seek to integrate a theoretical perspective with practice and focus on European and North American multinational companies. NGOs in the context of this chapter can be local, regional or worldwide organisations dealing with the various sustainability issues, such as human rights, environmental protection and labour conditions.[1] In Section 19.1, a general outline is presented of the changing relationships between government, companies and NGOs in addressing various policy issues. In Section 19.2, the role of traditional national and international law in addressing transboundary sustainability issues is discussed. The potential asset of company–NGO collaboration in relation to the different links in the 'regulatory chain' is discussed in Section 19.3. In the light of these discussions of company–NGO collaboration, the authors return to the role of national and international legislation in Section 19.4: can the government sit back and relax, or does it still have a role to play? In Section 19.5 our main conclusions are presented.

* The authors would like to thank Prof. P.C.M. van Seters, R.M.H. Maessen and E.R.R.M.C. van Rijckevorsel for their co-operation and valuable comments on an earlier draft of this chapter.

1 In this contribution, we specifically deal with NGOs. In the literature, the category of NGOs is regarded as an important category of civil society (Kaldor 2003).

19.1 Changing relations in the 'governance triangle'

In discussions on promoting sustainable development, the government, companies and NGOs (as representatives of the broader public) are often placed in a 'governance triangle'. At the national level as well as at the regional and global levels, the relations between these three 'sectors of society' are continuously changing. Although practice is much more complex, in various states in the Western hemisphere 'dialogue' becomes more common than **command and control**, and particularly in recent years various dialogues have resulted in concrete collaboration initiatives.

Under the well-known 'command-and-control' approach attention was focused on the relation between government and companies, and norm setting was primarily to be found in legislation. NGOs tried to influence the substance of legislation, primarily through their relationship with government. Relationships between NGOs and companies were generally characterised by 'confrontation' and 'keeping them at a distance'. Although under this command-and-control model there was some dialogue, collaboration initiatives were not common.

Since the 1980s, the 'command-and-control' model has often been criticised in the field of environmental policy as well as in other policy areas (Harrison 1999: 2):

> In recent years, governments throughout the world have expressed increasing dissatisfaction with so-called 'command-and-control' environmental regulation, which is widely criticized as economically inefficient, adversarial, and administratively cumbersome.

Generally speaking, this dissatisfaction particularly changed the relationship between government and business: the *own responsibility* of businesses has become one of the central issues in policy-making in many states, especially in Europe and North America, and more often norm setting is the result of intensive dialogues. Furthermore, the types of instruments to regulate companies' activities are becoming more diverse. Instruments, such as voluntary agreements, certification systems and various types of financial instruments, have become more important to support the effectiveness of existing legislation, or even to replace legislation. This process can be observed in various states (De Waard 2000), but also at the European and international levels. For example, within the EU the recent governance debate clearly indicates that the command-and-control approach is no longer considered to be the most promising path. Also in various EU policy fields, the changing view on the role of legislation as a governance instrument is clearly visible (European Commission 2001a). For example, in the field of environmental protection within the EU, for many years the institutions have been focused on adopting legislation; however, since the mid-1990s other policy instruments, such as voluntary agreements, certification and emissions trading have also received earnest attention.

This process of developing more efficient and more effective instruments based on the acknowledgement of the responsibility of business primarily changed the relationship between government and business. Generally speaking, in the 1990s the role of most NGOs was still limited to 'influencing the decision-makers' by confrontation or dialogue. This may be illustrated by the fact that, in the Netherlands up until 2000, more than 30 environmental covenants had been concluded between the Dutch central government and business; however, only once was an environmental NGO a contracting party to such an agreement.[2]

More recently, and partly parallel to the process described above, the types of relationships between governments and NGOs, and those between companies and NGOs, are also becoming more intensive. Confrontational actions by NGOs—for instance, legal actions, demonstrations, or accusations in the press—have certainly not disappeared, but they are more often involved in dialogues and collaboration initiatives. In the field of sustainable business, **partnership** appears to be the new magic word.

The term 'partnership' has been defined as 'a commitment by a corporation or a group of corporations to work with an organisation from a different economic sector (public or nonprofit)' (Googins and Rochlin 2000: 130, quoting Waddock). Googins and Rochlin have suggested that partnerships 'are, in fact, at very early stages of development, loosely arranged, largely unexamined, and exist only in very crude forms at the present' (2000: 131). Nevertheless, these authors also stress that 'cross-sector partnerships are essential mechanisms by which corporations and communities can maximize their goals' and that 'the challenge will be to move beyond the rhetoric of partnership and achieve a clear understanding of the potential of partnerships to be a vehicle of productive social change' (2000: 128, 143).

This development of changing relations between the government, companies and NGOs cannot be explained easily; most likely many factors influence this process. For instance, incidents concerning, for example, the offshore platform 'Brent Spar', oil pollution in Nigeria, and life-threatening labour conditions at the ship-dismantling sites in India increased the awareness of companies that NGOs may have a substantial influence on business reputation. Without doubt, these incidents have pushed the issue of stakeholder dialogue high on the agenda of the worldwide debate on sustainability and corporate social responsibility (CSR) (Svendsen 2003). However, in this CSR debate many authors and institutions have stressed that the importance of good relationships with stakeholders, including NGOs, goes far beyond the issue of reputation management. Sustainable development includes many extremely complex challenges and it is generally recognised that governments, companies and members of civil society heavily depend on each other in finding solutions. This is possibly the most important reason why 'partnership' is considered to be a promising CSR instrument: Wilson and Charlton state that 'it has been suggested that a partnership should seek to achieve an objective that no single organisation could achieve alone—an idea described by Huxham (1993) as "collaborative advantage" ' (Googins and Rochlin 2000: 131, quoting Wilson and Charlton).

This collaborative advantage may be of particular importance in relation to complex transboundary sustainability issues, such as the comprehensive protection of transboundary ecosystems and the improvement of transboundary food and production chains (Wijffels 2003). Limitations of national and international law to address these complex issues may enhance the changes in relationships and may in particular con-

---

2 In 1992–93, WWF-the Netherlands and IUCN were actively involved in the negotiations of a voluntary agreement on the import of sustainable tropical timber in the Netherlands. In June 1993, Dutch timber companies, various Dutch ministries, and WWF and IUCN became contracting parties to this agreement.

stitute an additional argument for companies and NGOs to intensify their relations, or even to start partnerships.

19.2 Limitations of traditional national and international law

19.2.1 National law

Transboundary sustainability issues are generally regarded as 'difficult to regulate' under national law. One of the difficulties relates to the issue of jurisdiction. Although, in the literature, many different definitions of the term 'jurisdiction' can be found (Malanczuk 1997: 109), most authors refer to this term when they speak about 'the lawful power to make and enforce rules' (Oxman 1987: 55). In international law, several principles have been developed which are used to determine whether a state has legislative jurisdiction ('powers to legislate in respect of the persons, property, or events in question' [Malanczuk 1997: 109]). The most important principles include: the territoriality principle, the principle of nationality, the protective principle, the universality principle and the passive nationality principle (Brownlie 1998; Molenaar 1998; Schachter 1991).

In the field of CSR, the limitations of state governments and national law are often linked with the sovereign territory of a state (Browne 2001):

> [The] partial process of globalisation has had a number of effects. It is weakening the traditional national structures of policy-making and limiting the power of national governments to control events in their own territory. The sense of authority over a particular geographic space has been diminished and in some cases lost. The word sovereignty has acquired an antique ring.

Although this general notion appears to be correct, stakeholders involved in the CSR discussion seem to conclude, too often and too easily, that no options exist in national law for regulating transboundary sustainability issues. For example, other principles—in particular, the nationality principle—may provide interesting options and it should be noted that the principles are not absolute. Their exact meaning and the use of the different principles depend on the legal system and some principles are subject to continuous development. In particular the territoriality principle has been broadened over the years (Orrego Vicuña 1988: 85). Furthermore, it is not clear whether 'the position is that the state is free to act unless it can be shown that a restrictive rule of treaty or customary law applies to it', or that a 'state is entitled to exercise its jurisdiction only in pursuance of a principle or rule of international law conferring that right' (Schachter 1991: 251; Molenaar 1998: 80); the *Lotus* case has been an important basis for the former opinion (Schachter 1991: 251). It has been stated that '[w]hatever the underlying conceptual approach, a state must be able to identify a sufficient nexus between itself and the object of its assertion of jurisdiction' (Oxman 1987: 55-56). This general requirement of a sufficient link is also emphasised by other scholars: 'It is well recognized in international law that a state cannot exercise legislative or enforcement jurisdiction unless there exists some linkage between the state and the event it acts upon' (Wolfrum 1986). Based on these thoughts, the options to regulate certain transboundary sustainability issues may be more comprehensive than is generally assumed.

Nonetheless, the possibilities for a national government to subject multinationals and international production chains to domestic legislation are not fully clear and may easily conflict with trade law and competition law as adopted within either the EU (Jans 2000: 263) or the WTO (Birnie and Boyle 2002: 707). Also the issue of supervision and enforcement raises important questions on the value of developing national law to address transboundary sustainability issues. Furthermore, even if the legal options to regulate transboundary sustainability issues through national law were fully clear and instruments existed for adequate supervision and enforcement, the question is whether the responsible national authorities have the political will to use these opportunities. Governments, at least in the Western hemisphere, are less willing to address social and environmental problems as a consequence of a growing call for deregulation (less detailed, simpler and more effective legislation) in many countries (European Commission 2001a; Mank 1998: 4). This is reflected by the following quotation from a recent keynote speech on CSR by the then Dutch State Secretary for Development Co-operation (Van Ardenne-Van der Hoeven 2003):

> Many societal organizations feel that the WTO and Western governments should enact binding laws and regulations. I would like to express my confidence in the strength of society. On the basis of this confidence, the government refuses to opt for the enactment of binding regulations.

19.2.2 International law

Particularly in view of the limitations of national law, international law at first glance seems to be the most suitable way to address global or transboundary sustainability issues. Certain limitations of national law may be addressed at the international level. For example, through amendments to international and European trade legislation, the national legislator may obtain more options for regulating particular issues in relation to products. International law may also constitute the legal basis or a stimulus for national governments to adopt domestic legislation that regulates activities that are conducted in other states or in areas beyond state jurisdiction. The Environmental Protocol to the Antarctic Treaty of 1991[3] is one of the examples. However, international law also has its weaknesses.

In the first place, international treaties are concluded between state governments, so some of the problems with state law mentioned above occur here as well. NGOs and transnational corporations do play a role in the process leading to an international agreement, but their formal position is not strong. NGOs may affect the outcome of international environmental law-making by using their political influence at conventions (Arts 1998: 304). A hybrid NGO such as IUCN even does preparatory work at inter-

---

3   The Protocol entered into force on 14 January 1998 and establishes a comprehensive system of obligations and prohibitions, addressing most types of activities in the region south of 60 degrees South latitude. For a detailed discussion, see Bastmeijer 2003.

national conventions, such as drafting proposals (Birnie and Boyle 2002: 68).[4] Formally, however, only states can adopt binding international law. Recently, Ellen Hey showed that traditional international law is not well suited to address issues of concern to the international community as a whole which directly involve individuals, and groups: such as NGOs, indigenous peoples or transnational corporations (Hey 2003: 5):

> Given the inter-state nature of the traditional international legal system and its focus on the shared interests of states, efforts to develop legal relationships involving entities other than states and that seek to address community interests entail the introduction of systemic change into the existing international legal system. In other words, the inter-state nature of the current international legal system entails that that system is ill-equipped to translate social relationships that are arising as a result of globalization into legal relationships.

Another limitation of international law is the fact that, in today's world, it is becoming increasingly difficult to get the international community to agree to specific legally binding rules, given the political, cultural, religious and developmental diversity of contemporary international society. Treaties—although a more useful medium than national legislation to address global sustainability issues—either do not enter into force, or apply to only a limited number of states. In particular in relation to transboundary sustainability issues, this is a severe handicap that may seriously limit the effectiveness of the international agreement concerned. For instance, even a relatively successful international law programme such as the 1985 Vienna Convention for the Protection of the Ozone Layer experiences difficulties such as a reluctance among developing countries, especially the world's largest producers of CFCs, China and India, to agree to reducing ozone-depleting chemicals, as well as the reluctance by some developed countries, especially the US, to finance protective measures in developing countries or to transfer Western technologies to these countries.

Also, transboundary sustainability issues may be difficult to address through international agreements if not all states involved decide to become contracting parties. For example, it will be difficult to limit the adverse effects for the environment and people caused by multinationals if not all the states that host the individual plants of a multinational corporation, or the states where the actual problems occur, are willing to join (Birnie and Boyle 2002: 24-25). Another example is provided by the Antarctic Treaty System: the 30 contracting parties to the Protocol on Environmental Protection to the Antarctic Treaty 'commit themselves to the comprehensive protection of the Antarctic environment' (see Article 2),[5] but legally they have no instruments to prevent governments of other states from initiating, for instance, mining activities in Antarctica (Bastmeijer 2003).

Implementation, as well as monitoring and enforcement, is another weakness of traditional international environmental law. Implementation and enforcement must be carried out by national authorities (Bush 1991: 34):

---

4   The IUCN (World Conservation Union) has a hybrid character because it is a federative membership organisation with not only 758 NGO members, but also with state and government agency memberships.

5   The text of the Protocol is available at www.ats.org.ar/docarch.htm.

> Many, if not most treaties, do not specify how the parties to it are to give effect
> to it under their domestic administrative procedures and legal system. It is
> the end result that matters: that each party ensures that a breach does not
> occur within its area of responsibility.

Usually, the implementation and enforcement efforts of the parties are subject to
review by intergovernmental commissions and meetings of treaty parties. These international institutional arrangements, however, are often found to be disappointingly
inadequate: they are no more than the expression of their members' willingness or
unwillingness to act (Birnie and Boyle 2002: 181). Only recently, things seem to be
changing somewhat for the better with the adoption of a strict enforcement mechanism
under the Kyoto Protocol.[6]

Finally, international law traditionally has limited possibilities for addressing disputes concerning the implementation of treaties. In regular international law, there are
usually either special tribunals, such as the International Tribunal for the Law of the
Sea (ITLOS) or the International Court of Justice that can be addressed. However, these
institutions are only competent to resolve disputes between states in so far as the states
concerned explicitly accepted the jurisdiction of the institutions. Other interested parties, such as NGOs or business corporations, let alone interested citizens, cannot address
these institutions. The establishment of an international environmental court, although proposed by many (Hey 2000), still seems to be a distant illusion.

The limitations of international law discussed above are not absolute. In recent years,
many initiatives have been taken to find solutions and to improve the effectiveness of
international environmental agreements. For example, David Freestone mentions various instruments that are applied to improve the implementation process at the domestic level, such as capacity building, financial support and the use of other non-binding
instruments (Freestone 1999). However, at the same time it should be noted that the
recognition of the complexity of sustainability issues has grown: attention is more and
more focused on the protection of entire ecosystems and improving the sustainability
of complete production chains (Wijffels 2003). Although there are examples of international environmental agreements that are based on these more comprehensive
approaches (Redgwell 1999),[7] it is clear that the difficulties discussed above may constitute serious blockades against establishing effective international environmental
agreements on these issues.

19.3 Company–NGO collaboration

From a governance perspective, the above limitations of traditional national and international law make the emergence of multi-stakeholder approaches all the more interesting. Multi-stakeholder approaches can be seen as an alternative way to steer multi-

---

6 Decided upon during COP7, Marrakesh, November 2001; see unfccc.int.
7 For example, Redgwell states that the 1980 Convention on the Conservation of Antarctic Marine
   Living Resources (CCAMLR) is 'a path-breaking example of the ecosystem approach to resource
   conservation and management'.

national corporations towards a more sustainable way of doing business. Multi-nationals can be 'self-disciplined' through collaborate approaches, either in international business organisations or in bilateral or multilateral initiatives involving NGOs. The latter type of self-regulation has the advantage that NGOs offer a countervailing power to mighty transnational business corporations. In the (sharp) words of Falk: 'There is nothing in the history of business operations to suggest that the long-term public good can be safely entrusted to those whose priority is short-term profits' (Falk 1996: 17).

From the perspective of transnational corporations, co-operative action can be used to legitimise their actions at a time when government approval alone is no longer considered to be sufficient for demonstrating adequate sustainable performance (Grolin 1998: 220). Also, NGOs can provide corporations with social, ecological, scientific and legal expertise, and they can help corporations build social networks with other stakeholders (Stafford *et al.* 2000: 123).

As shown above, since the 1990s multi-stakeholder approaches have begun to emerge in international sustainability policies. Transnational corporations and NGOs, with or without the involvement of governments, together are trying to find ways to tackle social and environmental problems. Many of these collaborative activities involve legal or semi-legal activities.

Let us now focus on one of the types of multi-stakeholder approaches, that is to say the partnerships already mentioned in Section 19.1. In partnerships, multinationals and NGOs together (a) set new standards, and (b) implement them. They (c) monitor and enforce both existing international law and these new standards without government or state intervention. They sometimes even arrange for (d) arbitration or other ways of dispute settlement. Traditionally, all of these elements of the 'regulatory chain' have been considered to belong to the domain of national or international state authorities. Below we will elaborate on these four elements of the regulatory chain, using the perhaps best-known examples of business–NGO collaboration projects, the Marine Stewardship Council (MSC) and the Forest Stewardship Council (FSC), as illustrations.[8]

19.3.1 Norm setting

Sustainability standards can be set within industry or business organisations alone (Roht-Arriaza 1995), and in business–NGO collaboration projects. As stated above, the latter is preferred because of its greater legitimacy. Important examples in the field of environmental policy of such norms are those that are the basis of the FSC and the MSC.

The FSC, founded in 1993 by environmental groups and the timber industry, is basically a certification system. Products from and traceable to certified forests are entitled to carry the FSC logo. Companies seeking to use this logo must receive certification of a 'chain of custody' from primary production through to retail sale: every wood product, therefore, must always be traceable to a particular certified forest. The certification system is based on 'principles' and 'criteria' intended to clarify the application of these principles. These principles and criteria set norms on how to sustainably manage forests and forest operations (Meidinger 2000: 130). One of the principles, for instance,

---

8   The MSC has its headquarters in London (see www.msc.org), and the FSC in Bonn (see www.fsc.org).

states that biological diversity is to be conserved, as well as its associated values, water resources, soils, and unique and fragile ecosystems and landscapes, and by so doing, maintain the ecological functions and the integrity of the forest (principle 6). This principle has been elaborated in several criteria. For instance, one criterion states that rare, threatened and endangered species and their habitats (e.g. nesting and feeding areas) must be protected, that conservation zones and protection areas must be established, appropriate to the scale and intensity of forest management and the uniqueness of the affected resources, and that inappropriate hunting, fishing, trapping and collecting must be controlled. Establishing the FSC was a reaction to the failure of governments to reach agreements, for example, on the introduction of a government-run certification system, within the International Tropical Timber Organization (ITTO) (Meidinger 2000: 131). To date, there is no binding international law regarding the protection of tropical forests.[9] The FSC rapidly grew into an organisation with more than 500 members including, representatives of environmental and social groups, the timber trade and the forestry profession, indigenous peoples' organisations, community forestry groups and forest product certification organisations from around the world. Government organisations are denied membership.

The MSC, modelled on the FSC, was founded in 1997 by Unilever, one of the largest buyers of fish, and the WWF to ensure the long-term viability of the global fish populations. The system was to introduce incentives for all stakeholders to work toward the goal of sustainable fisheries (Constance and Bonanno 2000: 130). Again, principles and criteria constitute the basis for an accreditation and certification system (such as the, internationally endorsed, precautionary principle). The MSC now has links to more than 100 major seafood processors, traders and retailers from more than 20 countries around the world. The difference with the FSC, however, is that, in this case, a large body of binding international law exists: for instance, the UN Convention on the Law of the Seas (UNCLOS). UNCLOS gives rules on fisheries and the protection of the living resources of the high seas, some of which have been worked out in the recent 'Agreement for the Implementation of the Provisions of the United Nations Convention on the Law of the Sea relating to the Conservation and Management of Straddling Fish Stocks and Highly Migratory Fish Stocks'.[10]

19.3.2 Implementation

Implementation of the norms that have been agreed upon seems to be less of a problem as far as multi-stakeholder approaches are concerned than the implementation of traditional international law. Taking the FSC as an example, the organisation evaluates, using fixed procedures and standards, which certification bodies are able to provide certification. In this accreditation process, it is decided which organisations are allowed to carry out the certification scheme and evaluate forests. The (regular) certi-

---

9 Only 'soft law', such as the 'Authoritative Statement of Forest Principles', adopted during the 1992 UN Conference on Environment and Development in Rio de Janeiro. This document not only has a very weak legal status, but its meagre content also received much criticism (NGOs have called the statement a 'chainsaw charter').

10 This agreement entered into force on 11 December 2001. All UNCLOS documents are available at the UNCLOS secretariat website, www.un.org/Depts/los.

fication organisations, therefore, implement the FSC scheme. At the same time, the NGO members of the FSC are actively trying to build demand for FSC products (by advertising, by establishing groups of retailers and product dealers committed to FSC products, and by persuading retailers to carry FSC products).

Multi-stakeholder agreements can also stimulate the implementation of traditional international environmental law. For instance, one of the principles of MSC states that fisheries management systems should respect local, national and international laws and standards.

19.3.3 Monitoring and enforcement

As stated above, the monitoring and enforcement of international environmental law is usually regarded as problematic, to put it mildly. Because of the inherent weakness of the public enforcement, NGOs traditionally played an important role in monitoring and enforcing international law, either in collaboration with governments through special monitoring organisations such as TRAFFIC, initiated by the WWF and IUCN to monitor the Convention on International Trade in Endangered Species (Braithwaite and Drahos 2000: 574), or by exposing illegal conduct or even confiscating illegal fishing gear on the high seas (Greenpeace 2000). The European Commission has recognised this role of NGOs and is looking for methods to further facilitate its development. In its 6th Environmental Action Programme, the Commission states that 'NGOs have an important role to play . . . in monitoring the implementation of legislation' (European Commission 2001b: 62).

Monitoring and enforcing multi-stakeholder agreements such as the FSC and the MSC is a logical part of the certification process. Not only is the work of the certifier peer-reviewed before a certificate is actually issued, but the certificate is also subject to the minimum requirement of annual monitoring by the certifiers. Certifiers have the right to conduct irregularly timed, short-notice inspections. This is stated in contractual agreements between the certification body and the recipient company. In the case of non-compliance, additional conditions can be included in these agreements or the certificate can be withdrawn.[11]

Also with regard to other transboundary sustainability issues, supervision and enforcement may constitute an important element of NGO–company collaboration. For example, multinationals may collaborate with labour unions, environmental NGOs or other NGOs in developing countries to check whether the various actors in the supply chain respect the company's sustainability policy. Recently, various 'incidents' in the media illustrate the desirability of such types of collaboration. For example, in its report 'Labour Conditions of IKEA's Supply Chain', the Dutch foundation SOMO concluded that various suppliers in India, Bulgaria and Vietnam 'violated' IKEA's code of conduct, 'IKEA Way of Purchasing Home Furnishing Products' (SOMO 2003). According to a press release of 24 September 2003, the Dutch labour union FNV—which had requested SOMO to conduct the research—argued that local and international labour

---

11   See, for instance, the MSC Certification Methodology; the latest version of the methodology can be requested at fisheries@msc.org.

unions should be involved in the process of implementing and monitoring codes of conduct.[12]

19.3.4 Dispute resolution

Resolving disputes concerning the implementation of norms set in multi-stakeholder approaches has long been neglected. Several of the NGO–multinational corporation arrangements did provide for objection procedures, but a full dispute resolution arrangement usually is missing. However, things are changing rapidly. For instance, the FSC now has a newly established Dispute Resolution Committee and an 'Interim Dispute Resolution Protocol'.[13]

19.4 The changing role of national and international law

From a legal point of view, the growing importance of multistakeholder approaches sheds a new light on the role of traditional law. This leads to a series of interesting questions that have to be dealt with in the near future, such as: what role, then, remains for government regulation? In our view, the changing relationships do not so much reduce the role of legislation, as change this role.

First of all, if the government is convinced of the value of a more intensive relationship and collaboration between companies and NGOs, legislation may be used to support this development. For example, legislation may provide for obligations to increase transparency and to improve access to information. As Halina Ward states:

> Mandatory legislation on various aspects of business transparency is emerging around the world. It can form part of company law, environmental regulation, or tailored legislation for institutional investors or on social and environmental reporting (Ward 2003: iii).

Generally, it is thought that government regulation has to leave as much room as possible for multi-stakeholder approaches and should aim to increase the institutional competence of the transnational corporation rather than aim to emphasise fixed rules, violations and fines. In the words of Selznick, responsive regulation tries to bring about the maximum feasible self-regulation (Selznick 1994: 401). However, it must be acknowledged that national and international state law will always impose some limitations on NGO–multinational collaborations. For instance, NGO–multinational collaborations may, depending on the type chosen and the parties involved, lead to a cartel, thus restricting competition. This is not allowed under European and WTO law (Vedder 2002).

---

12   Published at the Dutch CSR Platform's website, www.mvo-platform.nl/pers/persbericht_24sept_ ikea.html.
13   Available at the FSC website, www.fsc.org/keepout/en/content_areas/39/1/files/1_4_3_Interim_ dispute_resolution_protocol.pdf.

Secondly, a role for traditional government regulation may be to codify the norms that have been agreed on by companies and NGOs. There may be various reasons why this is desirable or even necessary:

a. To prevent free-rider behaviour. The level of ambition and the possibilities with regard to promoting sustainability differ from company to company, and the discussion and policy-making should not only focus on those companies that have shown commitment; it may be necessary to impose the negotiated norms on others as well. In this scenario, company–NGO collaboration influences national and international law by clearing the road for agreements on global, often complex, environmental issues. An example may be found at the national level in the Netherlands, where the Bill on Sustainably Produced Wood has been based on the FSC.[14]

b. To ensure governmental supervision and enforcement. In particular, if company–NGO collaboration does not include a system of supervision and enforcement, the government may wish to codify the crucial norms in legislation to ensure government supervision and enforcement. For example, on the basis of a detailed study of an incident in the United States concerning StarLink corn—a genetically modified variety of corn—Rebecca Bratspies concludes:

> StarLink provides a chilling example of how badly an oversight system built solely upon voluntary compliance can fail . . . These failures undermine the basic assumption underlying compliance schemes based on co-operation and self-policing—a belief that public and private interests converge in environmental stewardship (Bratspies 2003: 631).

c. To protect the interests of third parties that may be affected without them being actively involved in the partnership (Verschuuren 2000: 20-21).

The above reasons for codification do not necessarily result in the establishment of two completely overlapping regimes (e.g. a partnership and government legislation). The result may well be that activities of companies are subjected to a combination of obligations and prohibitions in (international or national) legislation on the one hand and 'obligations and prohibitions' laid down in (international or national) agreements or codes of conduct on the other hand. For this phenomenon, the EU White Paper on European Governance introduces the term 'co-regulation', that is to say combining legislative and regulatory action with actions taken by the actors concerned, drawing on their practical expertise, but within the framework of (general) EU legislation (European Commission 2001a: 21).

14 Parl. Doc. I, 2000–2001, 23 982 and 26 998, No. 173a, 9.

19.5 Conclusions

In this chapter, we sketched the possible consequences of the changing relationships between the government, companies and NGOs in addressing various transboundary sustainability issues for national and international law. The reasons for dialogue and collaboration with NGOs go beyond the issue of 'reputation management'. We showed that, in particular with regard to transboundary sustainability issues, the limitations of national and international law might further stimulate active relationships between companies and NGOs. Although we think that these limitations are often presented as too absolute, it is clear that the issues are too complex to be solved by government regulation alone. We have shown that the relationships between companies and NGOs may play an important role in respect of all elements of the regulatory chain: norm setting, implementation, monitoring and enforcement, and dispute resolution. In some cases, NGOs and companies may decide to start partnerships: the influence of NGOs in such partnerships is essential. Partnerships such as FSC and MSC differ from 'self-regulation' by businesses alone. Research into self-regulation in the field of the environment in the US shows that self-regulation projects should involve public-interest groups (Steinzor 1998: 201). Co-operation with NGOs enhances corporate legitimacy. One could argue that, in these cases, there is no self-regulation, because the 'self' indicates the enterprise while, in the case of multi-stakeholder approaches, stakeholders together make rules and regulations. Therefore, these collaborations are sometimes described as *civil regulation*, as opposed to self-regulation (Bendell 2000: 245). In other cases, NGOs may decide to keep a distance in order not to complicate their watchdog role. An interesting question for further research would be whether and how NGOs can keep this watchdog role within partnerships with companies.

Let us, by way of concluding, turn once again to the three positions in the governance triangle. From the perspective of *governments*, they have to find a way to match state law with multi-stakeholder approaches. In our view, the changing relationships do not so much reduce the role of legislation as change this role. First of all, if the government is convinced of the value of a more intensive relation and collaboration between companies and NGOs, legislation may be used to support this development. Second, a role for traditional government regulation may be to codify the norms that have been agreed on by companies and NGOs: for example, to prevent free-rider behaviour and to ensure government supervision and enforcement if necessary. The ultimate goal of the ideal relationship between national and international law and multi-stakeholder approaches should be to legitimately, effectively and efficiently address global sustainability issues: that is to say, issues that cannot be resolved by national or international law alone.

From the perspective of *business corporations*, it may be clear that the expectations of society go beyond the adoption of codes of conduct and 'partnerships'. The importance of adequate implementation and enforcement of the self-regulation systems and partnerships is widely acknowledged, and various international and national NGOs show that they are successful in their 'watchdog role'. Furthermore, companies will not have to deal with 'just' the NGOs. Government regulation will always remain a factor in regulating the 'ecological behaviour' of enterprises. A recent study by Thornton and others shows that corporate environmental management, market incentives and pressure by local communities or environmentalists are the chief determinants of variations in firm-level environmental performance (Thornton *et al.* 2003). However, Kagan *et al.* (2002) also state that the larger improvements in corporate environmental controls have been associated with tightening regulatory requirements and intensifying political pressures.

From the perspective of NGOs, it may equally be clear that they are burdened with a heavy task. Governments may be pleased with the development that the relationship between companies and NGOs is becoming more intensive and may even use this development as an argument to play a less dominant role in finding solutions for transboundary sustainability issues. But are the NGOs sufficiently equipped? Peter Newell and Wyn Grant state: 'The shift towards self-regulation and voluntary codes may [. . .] thrust NGOs, however inadequately resourced or trained to perform the task, into a watchdog capacity' (Newell and Grant 2000: 228).

If the developments discussed in Section 19.3 continue, multinational corporations and NGOs may have to perform tasks that are usually performed by large bureaucratic governmental organisations, staffed with thousands of civil servants. Many NGOs will not have sufficient financial capacity and personnel to play this role. Parallel to its legislative role discussed above, the government should consider this problem as well. Once it is clear that the role of states is reduced in favour of a more active role of NGOs and multinational corporations, it seems almost inevitable that in the future governments will offer NGOs financial and practical assistance.

References

Arts, B. (1998) *The Political Influence of Global NGOs: Case Studies on the Climate and Biodiversity Conventions* (Nijmegen, Netherlands: International Books).

Bastmeijer, C.J. (2003) *The Antarctic Environmental Protocol and its Domestic Legal Implementation* Vol. 65 (International Environmental Law and Policy Series; The Hague: Kluwer Law).

Bendell, J. (2000) 'Civil Regulation. A New Form of Democratic Governance for the Global Economy?', in J. Bendell (ed.), *Terms for Endearment: Business, NGOs and Sustainable Development* (Sheffield, UK: Greenleaf Publishing): 239-54.

Birnie, P.W., and A.E. Boyle (2002) *International Law and the Environment* (Oxford, UK: Oxford University Press, 2nd edn).

Braithwaite, J., and P. Drahos (2000) *Global Business Regulation* (Cambridge, UK: Cambridge University Press).

Bratspies, R.M. (2003) 'Myths of Voluntary Compliance: Lessons from the StarLink Corn Fiasco', Social Science Research Network Electronic Paper Collection, Michigan State University, papers.ssrn.com/sol3/papers.cfm?abstract_id=421700, January 2004.

Browne, J. (2001) 'Governance and Responsibility. The Relationship between Companies and NGOs: A Progress Report', Judge Institute, 29 March 2001, www.ragm.com/archpub/ragm/032901judge_institute.html, January 2004.

Brownlie, I. (1998) *Principles of Public International Law* (Oxford, UK: Clarendon Press, 5th edn).

Bush, W.M. (1991) *Antarctica and International Law: A Collection of Inter-State and National Documents* (New York: Oceana Publications).

Constance, D., and A. Bonanno (2000) 'Regulating the Global Fisheries: The World Wildlife Fund, Unilever, and the Marine Stewardship Council', *Agriculture and Human Values* 17.2: 125-39.

De Waard, B. (2000) *Negotiated Decision-Making* (The Hague: Boom Juridische uitgevers).

European Commission (2001a) 'White Paper on European Governance' (COM[2001]428 final), europa.eu.int/comm/governance/index_en.htm, January 2004.

—— (2001b) '6th Environmental Action Programme 2001–2010. Environment 2010: Our Future, Our Choice' (COM[2001]31), europa.eu.int/comm/environment, January 2004.

Falk, R. (1996) 'Environmental Protection in an Era of Globalization', Yearbook of International Environmental Law 6 (Oxford, UK: Oxford University Press): 3-25.

Freestone, D. (1999) 'The Challenge of Implementation: Some Concluding Notes', in A. Boyle and D. Freestone (eds.), International Law and Sustainable Development: Past Achievements and Future Challenges (Oxford, UK: Oxford University Press): 359-64.

Googins, B.K., and S.A. Rochlin (2000) 'Creating the Partnership Society: Understanding the Rhetoric and Reality of Cross-sectoral Partnerships', Business and Society Review 105.1: 127-44.

Greenpeace (2000) 'Greenpeace confiscates illegal fishing gear on the high seas', press release, 8 May 2000, available at archive.greenpeace.org/pressreleases oceans/2000may8.html.

Grolin, J. (1998) 'Corporate Legitimacy in Risk Society: The Case of Brent Spar', Business Strategy and the Environment 7: 213-22.

Harrison, K. (1999) 'Voluntarism and Environmental Governance', University of British Columbia, Canada, www2.arts.ubc.ca/cresp/khvolun.pdf, January 2004.

Hey, E. (2000) Reflections on an International Environmental Court (The Hague: Kluwer Law International).

—— (2003) Teaching International Law (The Hague: Kluwer Law International).

Jans, J.H. (2000) European Environmental Law (Groningen, Netherlands: Europa Law Publishing, 2nd edn).

Kagan, R.A., N. Gunningham and D. Thornton (2002) 'Explaining Corporate Environmental Performance: How Does Regulation Matter?', UC Berkeley Public Law and Legal Theory Research Paper Series, Paper No. 78, 2002, available at the Social Science Research Network Electronic Library, papers.ssrn.com/sol3/papers.cfm?abstract_id=299239, accessed October 2003.

Kaldor, M. (2003) Global Civil Society (Cambridge, UK: Polity Press).

Malanczuk, P. (1997) Akehurst's Modern Introduction to International Law (London: Routledge, 7th edn).

Mank, B.C. (1998) 'The Environmental Protection Agency's Project XL and Other Regulatory Reform Initiatives: The Need for Legislative Authorization', Ecology Law Quarterly 25.1: 1-88.

Meidinger, E.E. (2000) ' "Private" Environmental Regulation, Human Rights, and Community', Buffalo Environmental Law Journal, 1999–2000: 123-237.

Molenaar, E.J. (1998) Coastal State Jurisdiction over Vessel-Source Pollution (The Hague: Kluwer Law International).

Newell, P., and W. Grant (2000) 'Environmental NGOs and EU Environmental Law', Yearbook of European Environmental Law I (Oxford, UK: Oxford University Press): 225-52.

Orrego Vicuña, F. (1988) Antarctic Mineral Exploitation: The Emerging Legal Framework (Cambridge, UK: Cambridge University Press).

Oxman, B.H. (1987) 'Jurisdiction of States', in R. Bernhardt (ed.), Encyclopedia of Public International Law (Max Planck Institute for Comparative Public Law and International Law; Amsterdam: Elsevier [1997]): 55-60.

Redgwell, C. (1999) 'Protection of Ecosystems under International Law: Lessons from Antarctica', in A. Boyle and D. Freestone (eds.), International Law and Sustainable Development: Past Achievements and Future Challenges (Oxford, UK: Oxford University Press): 205-24.

Roht-Arriaza, N. (1995) 'Private Voluntary Standard-Setting, the International Organization for Standardization, and International Environmental Lawmaking', Yearbook of International Environmental Law 6 (Oxford, UK: Oxford University Press): 107-63.

Schachter, O. (1991) International Law in Theory and Practice (Dordrecht, Netherlands: Kluwer Academic Publishers).

Selznick, P. (1994) 'Self-Regulation and the Theory of Institutions', in G. Teubner, L. Farmer and D. Murphy (eds.), Environmental Law and Ecological Responsibility: The Concept and Practice of Ecological Self-organization (New York: John Wiley): 395-402.

SOMO (2003) 'Labour Conditions of IKEA's Supply Chain: Case Studies in India, Bulgaria and Vietnam', www.somo.nl/html/paginas/pdf/IKEA_eindrapport_2003_NL.pdf, January 2004.

Stafford, E.R., M.J. Polonsky and C.L. Hartman (2000) 'Environmental NGO–Business Collaboration and Strategic Bridging: A Case Analysis of the Greenpeace–Foron Alliance', *Business Strategy and the Environment* 9: 122-35.

Steinzor, R.I. (1998) 'Reinventing Environmental Regulation: The Dangerous Journey from Command to Self-Control', *Harvard Environmental Law Review* 22.1: 103-202.

Svendsen, A. (2003) 'Co-Creative Engagement at the Edge of Chaos in North America', keynote speech at the Conference *Managing on the Edge*, Nijmegen, the Netherlands, 25 September 2003.

Thornton, D., R.A. Kagan and N. Gunningham (2003) 'Sources of Corporate Environmental Performance', *California Management Review* 46.1: 127-41.

Van Ardenne-van der Hoeven, A.M.A. (2003) 'Corporate Social Responsibility', Keynote Speech Netherlands State Secretary for Development Co-operation, 17 January 2003 (in Dutch).

Van Gestel, R.A.J. (2000) *Zelfregulering, milieuzorg en bedrijven, naar een eigen verantwoordelijkheid binnen kaders* (The Hague: Boom Juridische uitgevers).

Vedder, H. (2002) *Competition Law, Environmental Policy and Producer Responsibility* (Groningen, Netherlands: Europa Law Publishing).

Verschuuren, J.M. (2000) 'EC Environmental Law and Self-regulation in the Member States: In Search of a Legislative Framework', *Yearbook of European Environmental Law* I (Oxford, UK: Oxford University Press): 103-21.

Ward, H. (2003) *Legal Issues in Corporate Citizenship* (London: Globalt Ansvar/IIED 2003; www.iied.org).

Wolfrum, R. (1986) 'Means of Ensuring Compliance with an Antarctic Mineral Resources Regime', in R. Wolfrum (ed.), *Antarctic Challenge II* (Proceedings of an Interdisciplinary Symposium, 17–21 September 1985; Berlin: Duncker & Humbolt): 177-90.

Wijffels, H. (2003) 'Managing on the Edge: A Perspective from the Netherlands', keynote speech at the Conference *Managing on the Edge*, Nijmegen, the Netherlands, 25 September 2003.

20
Strategic options for multinational corporate programmes in international corporate social responsibility

Bryane Michael

University of Oxford, UK

International corporate responsibility (ICR) has been seen as a boon for international development.[1] Especially given recent trends toward globalisation, the value of ICR in international development spans the business literature (Bendell 2000; Hopkins 1998; Schwartz and Gibb 1999) and the development literature (Fox *et al.* 2002). Inspired by many of these deliberations, the World Bank (2002, 2003) has held a number of e-conferences about using corporate responsibility programmes for public–private partnerships to help provide social services and reduce policy risks. According to these works, ICR offers a gambit of benefits from promoting higher incomes, achieving a fairer redistribution of national and international income, fostering greater political stability, increasing tax revenue for states, and raising participation in the political process by non-governmental organisations.

Yet, assuming that these purported benefits do arise from ICR activities, ICR must be managed given the corporation's strategic environment. Multinational enterprises contribute to changing economic relations that affect the welfare of many—and the nature of this change is addressed in Sections 20.1 and 20.2. In Sections 20.3 and 20.4 I will discuss MNE strategy more specifically, looking at the interaction with international government and international NGO strategy. Section 20.5 will provide a concrete model of this interaction while Section 20.6 will present a basic model for MNEs engaging in ICR. The final section will present conclusions. In order to make this chapter accessible to a wider audience, most of my arguments will be drawn from the popular develop-

---

1 Throughout this chapter, I use 'international corporate responsibility' to refer to corporate social responsibility practised at the international level. Thus I will at times refer to corporate social responsibility when discussing principles that can be applied at either the national or international levels. 'International corporate responsibility' may be used interchangeably with 'international corporate social responsibility'.

ment literature rather than the more specialised strategy literature from management (O'Rourke 2003; Newell 2001; Leal *et al.* 2003). In the attempt to provide managers with a basic background on some of the issues and present a couple of useful models, I have not provided comprehensive literature surveys or a complete discussion of many of these topics which can be found elsewhere.

20.1 Strategy space for MNEs

The concept of international corporate responsibility is not new, but has been discussed in relation to the international political economy for some time—and more recently in reference to globalisation. In both international business and international development discussions, globalisation—defined as increased amount of economic, political and social interaction across physical space—necessitates more international corporate responsibility due either to increased economic *convergence, divergence or ambivalence*. Table 20.1 shows a 'representative author(s)' attached to each position, some authors extolling the benefits of such globalisation while others chastising the harms of globalisation. While this list is not meant to be comprehensive, authors can, in general, be categorised by whether they argue at the enterprise level, system level or world level.[2]

Authors who claim that MNEs are promoting global economic convergence often point to the increased use of information technologies attendant with the 'rise of the network society' (Castells 1996), and social relations that promote the 'new production of knowledge' (Gibbons *et al.* 1994)—all forces militating for more ICR. Authors who address MNE-specific factors for economic convergence usually point to either global economies of scale (Dunning 1992), the rise of global brands and marketing (Levitt 1983), or the need to seek out new markets (Ohmae 1990; Doz *et al.* 2001). More generally, authors arguing for economic convergence note that within the past 30 years, incomes per capital around the world (even in the poorest countries) have risen in absolute terms and that multinational enterprises (MNEs) have represented a larger share of this global economy with some MNEs, such as General Electric or Ford, holding more resources than 80% of the countries in the world today (Cohn 2000).[3] Many of these large international corporations are US companies by origin and their expansion has been seen as a form of US 'hegemonic' commercial expansion (Gilpin 1987). Other authors such as Berger and Dore (1996), and Hall and Soskice (2001), are less sure that global capital will reflect American capitalism, but will instead differentiate between Europe, Asia and North America. Convergence in this case refers to the con-

---

2 The literature on MNEs in international is long and the taxonomy I provide differs from others which focus on classifying MNE theories according to market power, Peoples and Sugden 2000; internationalisation, Hennart 2000; eclectic, Tolentino 2001; resource-based approaches, Kay 2000; and developmental approaches, Ozawa and Castello 2001.

3 Throughout this chapter, I use the term 'multinational enterprise' to refer to corporations that operate internationally. There are a number of different labels for these entities such as 'multinational corporation' (MNC) and 'transnational corporation' (TNC), whose differences I will overlook in this chapter for analytical simplicity.

	Economic convergence	Economic divergence	Ambivalent
Enterprise-level logic	MNEs bring economic growth and innovation (Ohmae 1990)	Outsourcing requires exploitation (Klein 2000)	MNEs organise for competitive advantage (Bartlett and Ghoshal 2001; Hedlund 1994)
Systemic logic	MNEs represent US hegemony (Gilpin 1987)	No real globalisation; regions reign (Hirst and Thompson 1996)	MNEs represent networks in global governance (Braithwaite and Drahos 2000)
	Regions will integrate into a system—even if it is 'divergent' (Berger and Dore 1996; Hall and Soskice 2001)*	State as executive committee of the bourgeoisie (Pilger 2002)	Variety of MNEs (Stopford 1998)
World-level logic	Globalisation is the next stage of economic evolution—for better or worse (Friedman 2000; Greider 2001)	MNEs foster natural differentiation in the 'world system' (Strange 1997)	MNEs are another layer in multi-layered governance (Held et al. 1999)
Policy implication	Common rules of the game (liberalisation, harmonisation)	Restrained competition	Decentralised enforcement

* This classification may appear idiosyncratic as these authors apparently argue for the divergence of capitalist systems based on functional specialisation. However, on reflection, these authors argue for a functionalist conception (some would call it a 'functionalist fallacy') of the global economy—each region specialising in its own 'business system' and each system serving to form a global capitalism.

TABLE 20.1 Examples of authors discussing MNE involvement in the international economy

vergence toward a functionally integrated yet differentiated world marketplace (much like differentiated organs make up the physical body). If regionalisation, or the retreat of the state, is occurring, it is a temporary phenomenon on the road towards global markets and global forms of governance—for the better (Friedman 2000) or for the worse (Greider 1998).

If multinational corporate operations are causing economic convergence, ICR is necessary to ensure such convergence is welfare-enhancing and morally acceptable. If the world is converging at levels that 'revive forms of human exploitation that characterised industry one hundred years ago', then policy must work to prevent such exploitation by MNEs (Greider 1998). But if MNEs help provide salaries to the poor-but-talented and can influence governments in developing countries to accept certain policies, the MNE-led economic convergence should be encouraged—some often-cited examples being increased transparency of East Asian monetary and fiscal policy, and the eventual end of apartheid in South Africa. If MNEs, independently of government, provide the most efficient ICR programmes, then liberationalisation of business activity should be pursued. If not, then harmonisation of ICR would probably be the best policy response, yet the terms of such harmonisation would be open for negotiation (Jacobs 1994). Both the UN Global Compact and the OECD Guidelines for Multinational Enterprises have been seen to be attempts at such 'negotiated' harmonisation.

If multinational corporate operations are promoting national and international economic divergence (rather than convergence), especially due to worker exploitation or inefficient redistribution of income (by MNEs using transfer pricing to avoid tax payments), such divergences are worrying—and should be remedied through ICR. At the firm level, authors claiming that MNEs promote economic divergence point to global outsourcing strategies which offer low salaries to workers in developing countries (Collinson 2001; Klein 2000).[4] Authors who argue for economic divergence agree that income levels have been rising, yet so have income disparities—with poorer countries having less than 10% of the income per capita levels as the rich countries. Many commentators (over)emphasise the fact that the large multinational enterprise can trace its history back to the days of colonialism in the rapacious East India Company. A more recent putative testament to the continuing self-interest of the international firm is the case of Exxon using its bargaining power to the point of contributing to the death of Ken Saro-Wiwa (Klein 2000). If such MNEs are not pursuing their own rapacious ends, they are seen—according to the nationalist arguments of International Political Economy—to be pursuing the 'neo-imperialist' ends of their nation-states, whom in turn assist their companies in competing internationally (Strange and Stopford 1991; Pilger 2002). They also reject the notion of economic globalisation, pointing to low levels of trade relative to the pre-World War One era and claim that economic forces militate for regionalisation rather than globalisation (Hirst and Graham 2001). At the extreme, these forces contribute to a 'world system' which completes the historical march toward exploitative capitalism (Strange 1997)!

If multinational corporate operations are causing economic divergence, ICR is necessary to restrain deleterious economic competition, redress wrongs committed by MNEs and promote an ethic of fair trade. Rather than ICR setting 'rules of the game' for international business, ICR in the case of economic divergence, efficiently redistributes income that powerful market actors have taken from less powerful ones.[5] If countries could agree internationally on a set of ICR policies, harmonisation would be the best policy. In some ways, the international conventions of the OECD on bribery, the ILO on labour laws, and the UN on human rights represent important attempts at harmonisation which impact directly or indirectly on corporate responsibility. If countries cannot agree on a set of ICR policies, then policed enforcement of 'progressive' country ICR policies would probably be the best policy response. In practice, many developing countries already apply the law of the MNE country of origin to the MNE's operations (though not frequently enough).

Finally, there is a third school which argues against convergence or divergence, and instead notes the changing or 'ambivalent' power of MNEs in the world economy. Some commentators note that the MNE itself is changing from a centralised, hierarchical organisation to a decentralised, or 'network-based', one (Bartlett and Ghoshal 2001;

---

4   These outsourcing strategies have led to work on 'fair trade' or 'ethical trade' (Blowfield 1999). For more information, see the Ethical Trading Initiative (www.ethicaltrade.org.uk).

5   The case of such redistribution in promoting the stability of the system has been made by Acemoglu and Robinson (2000) and Benabou and Ok (2001), among others.

Hedlund 1994). Accordingly, large MNEs are not single consolidated entities and hegemonic organisations, but can often represent alliances or networks based on similar business interests. Given the sometimes-relative autonomy of local branches, viewing the MNE as a single entity can be misleading. At a systemic level, these MNEs may focus clusters of groups with international organisations or other international enterprises that concentrate economic and political power (Braithwaite and Drahos 2000). If these groups were able to exercise significant political power, such a trend would represent a multi-layered governance structure ' "re-engineering" the power, functions and authority of national governments' (Held *et al.* 1999: 8). In such a multi-layered governance structure, the MNE is one actor among many—able to use its economic power and its involvement in international organisations, but also constrained by international treaties and by action taken by 'international civil society'.[6]

Such a non-homogeneous—and probably most accurate view—of the international political economy poses difficulties for ICR regulation. Given both the positive and negative aspects of MNE operations, 'one size fits all' regulation is clearly inappropriate as harmonisation, liberalisation, policed enforcement and mutual recognition would over-regulate in certain cases and under-regulate in others. Regulation must occur at the decentralised level—often on a case-by-case level. As such, the best regulatory option would be to promote enforcement of ICR by courts or by the PR generated by NGOs. Such 'self-enforcing' arrangements would rely on hurt parties enforcing ICR infringements wherever they occur—assuming such hurt parties are able and willing to pursue enforcement (Bull 1987; Brousseau and Glachant 2002).[7]

While this discussion has focused mostly on the MNE, most writers note there are three main actors involved in the international economy—international governmental organisations, international business organisations, and the third (or civil-society) sector. In such a stylised 'tripartite model', government sets standards and regulates business. Business complies with such regulation.[8] The third sector, mostly NGOs—but also academics, local community activists, trade union representations and consumer groups—criticise regulation and questionable business practices. I have discussed in Michael 2003 the role of these actors at the local level. Now I will discuss the role of *international* public institutions, *international* private sector and *international* civil society. I will not cover all the topics but only salient issues that, I think, should enter into the debate on MNE CSR.

6   A number of international policy-making structures are increasingly accepting large MNEs as members, including the UN (in its Global Compact) and the World Economic Forum.

7   Other proposals of contractual-type arrangements include Hopkin's (2003) 'planetary bargain' which relies on voluntary co-operation between parties rather than enforcement stemming from conflict.

8   Business Partners for Development (2002) advocate the role of 'tri-sector partnerships'.

20.2 Strategic options for international government and the World Bank

International governmental organisations—defined as international organisations whose members consist of nation-states such as the United Nations, the OECD or the World Bank—are increasingly working on ICR issues. Such organisations can provide ICR 'public goods' which promote commerce such as harmonised international regulation (Berger and Dore 1996).[9] These organisations can also provide 'missing goods' (such as ICR programmes), which have not been supplied by poorly functioning national governments. The UN's Global Compact purportedly represents one example of such ICR activity at the international level. The Global Compact asks companies to voluntarily sign on to a set of nine CSR principles encompassing human rights, environment and labour.[10] The OECD has its Guidelines for Multinational Enterprises supposedly representing another international initiative which—unlike private initiatives such as the Caux Principles, the Global Sullivan Principles and the Keidanren Charter or standards such as the Global Reporting Initiative (GRI) guidelines, the Social Accountability 8000 (SA 8000) standard, and the AccountAbility 1000—provides an explicit role for governmental involvement.

Unlike the UN and OECD (which are political organisations representing the interests of their member countries), as an international financial institution, the World Bank especially could play an important role given its involvement in the international economy through its procurements and participation in international bond markets. A number of proposals have been mooted for World Bank participation in ICR (World Bank 2003). The World Bank's possible involvement in CSR activities can be portrayed along a continuum from lowest to highest as shown in Table 20.2.[11]

	LOWEST					HIGHEST
Level	Information dissemination	Advocacy	Watch-dogging	Consulting	Debt and equity participation	Conditionality
Probable commit-ment	High	High	Medium	Medium	Low	Medium

TABLE 20.2 **Levels of World Bank involvement in CSR**

Source: adapted from discussions held during the World Bank's e-conference on Public Policy and Corporate Social Responsibility

9   See Bell 2002 for more on the role of governments, and National Policy Association 2003 for an overview of national governmental initiatives.

10 See www.unglobalcompact.org for more. For a civil-society criticism, see www.globalpolicy. org/reform/2001/0308fel.htm, accessed 13 October 2004.

11 The reader may ask why the World Bank should be assuming the role of promoting ICR and how it relates to its charter. The Bank has already undertaken this role just like its leadership role in other issues not specifically defined by its charter—such as tackling corruption or promoting free markets.

The World Bank acting as a 'clearinghouse' of corporate social responsibility materials represents the lowest level of Bank involvement in ICR. Such a clearinghouse could consist of databases of cases, best practice, contact databases and analysis. Just as the Bank currently acts as a clearinghouse for information on investment, economic statistics and studies in a wide range of development issues, it could also provide information—perhaps through channels such as its Development Gateway.[12] The Bank clearly has the mandate to collect such information and is already doing so. Given its explicit focus on development, there would probably be little 'crowding out' of business and NGO activity.[13] As the Bank has already engaged in a large programme of information dissemination through its World Bank Institute, such information will probably continue for the foreseeable future.

The second level of commitment is represented by the Bank acting as advocate, not only with firms but also with governments. Rather than simply collecting other people's information, it would generate its own research and field results illustrating the potential benefits and harms of ICR. The Bank has precedents of acting as an advocate of policies—from promoting free markets to reducing corruption. The Bank is currently acting as advocate, claiming in its publications—albeit conference reports—that ICR promotes international development.[14] Yet the Bank's advocacy of other topics has been widely criticised; its competence in corporate social responsibility could be questioned given its relatively recent involvement in the subject, and its involvement in CSR could represent a form of 'mandate creep' (Einhorn 2001).

A third level of World Bank commitment to corporate responsibility could comprise the Bank acting as a watchdog—assessing company regulation and auditing. In this view, state failure provides a mandate for the Bank. Such assessment could comprise company evaluations based on a star system (such as those done by Moody's or Oxford Analytica's e-standards) and could be based on a version of a triple-bottom-line reporting or using some weighted average of responsibility indicators.[15] The envisioned effects range from 'naming and shaming' to providing clear benchmarks for fund managers to alter international investment decisions (thus punishing inadequate corporate responsibility). The benefits for such a proposal would be the establishment of a potentially impartial assessment of companies by an international organisation. However, by rating companies, the Bank would be 'crowding out' private actors currently involved in assessment (which would be much more lucrative than simply providing documents). More important, such a practice would also represent a shift in Bank policy away from working with governments and more toward working with the private sector—a practice that has questionable status in its Articles of Agreement.

The fourth level of World Bank commitment would include providing consulting services to firms in developing countries. In this view, the Bank would send consultants and experts to member countries to assist them with developing and implementing ICR

---

12   See www.developmentgateway.org for more.
13   Such 'crowding out' would depend on complementarities versus competition between corporate responsibility information providers. A number of large research institutions provide information on social responsibility such as Eldis, Business for Social Responsibility, CSR Wire and others.
14   See www.worldbank.org/wbi/corpgov/csr/r_pubs.html for more, accessed 13 October 2004.
15   One example of such an index includes the Business in the Community Index (www.bitc.org.uk/docs/CR_Index_Execsummary.pdf, accessed 13 October 2004).

programmes and business strategies, which pass some test of corporate responsibility. Just as with the other activities proposed, there is a precedent for the Bank engaging directly into company affairs—as the IFC participates in investment deals and sometimes becomes directly or indirectly involved in large (usually public) companies whose reform enters as a condition for structural adjustment or other lending. However, such a proposal would undoubtedly meet with resistance for the reasons cited above (the Bank's advocacy of other topics being widely criticised, its competence in corporate social responsibility questioned and its involvement in CSR representing 'mandate creep').[16] World Bank involvement in private-sector consulting (in the guise of public–private partnerships) would also call into question its mandate and raise broader questions about the advantages of it advising to the private sector. Worse, such proposals may amount to an attempt to (re)assert government authority over business through an intergovernmental organisation (Braithwaite and Drahos 2000). If World Bank advice goes against national law or custom, it could even reflect an encroachment of national sovereignty.

A fifth level of commitment could see the World Bank engaged in consulting and taking equity or debt positions in the companies it advises—thus providing financial returns and providing incentives for good advice. In an extended version of this proposal for such public–private partnerships, the returns could be reinvested similarly to a micro-finance scheme. Again, there are (loose) precedents for the Bank engaging in this type of activity, as its work in micro-credit shows, as does the taking of promises of repayments (which themselves constitute assets). However, besides all the other harms mentioned in the consulting-only scenario, this proposal would encourage business as well as government to become financially committed to the World Bank and possibly encourage soft budget constraints in borrowing enterprises. More importantly, the line between the World Bank as a public entity and the global consulting companies as private entities would become blurrier—putting the legitimacy of the Bank as a representative and government-accountable organisation into question.[17]

Lastly, and most controversially, the Bank could tie country lending to national implementation and compliance with ICR programmes. In this view, compliance with mutually agreed ICR planks would enter as another set of conditions in structural adjustment and project lending. The advantages for such a proposal are the increased incentive for borrowing-country governments and business to adhere to ICR covenants. Bank withdrawal of finance due to corruption may be seen as a precedent for such a policy, as can the sometimes detailed negotiations over public enterprise reform. However, besides the possible dangers attendant with the other proposals, ICR provisions in

16   A number of studies find that Bank lending and technical assistance as been inefficient or 'hegemonic': Mosley *et al.* 1995; Caufield 1996.

17   There are clearly links between ICR standards developed at an international level with those applying in the host governments. Future work may explore the relationships between hypernorms (or universal obligations or standards that supersede all others) and community norms. This chapter does not put forward an ICR agenda, but simply provides tools for strategic analysis by the Bank, MNEs and INGOs.

conditionality could shift a large amount of economic and political power into the World Bank—a position that would be widely opposed.[18]

20.3 Strategic options for international MNEs

Most advocates of MNE-led ICR follow a contingency theory view of the firm (Woodward 1965; Lawrence and Lorsch 1967), which sees the firm as simply responding to its stakeholders. International business—namely MNEs—may use ICR to respond to their customers, financiers and employees (Hopkins 1998; Schwartz and Gibb 1999). In product markets, customers want responsible behaviour as shown by the rising popularity of The Body Shop. Financiers want responsible behaviour as shown by 'responsible indices' such as the FTSE4Good. Employees and potential management candidates show concern about their employer's responsibility as demonstrated by the number of employee-led corporate responsibility programmes and hesitation to join an employer widely known for questionable business practices.[19]

One area that differentiates the MNE for the standard nationally based enterprise—and which adds a special dimension to ICR—is its reliance on international outsourcing and particularly the extraction of some valuable resource. On the one hand, such outsourcing arrangements may represent the need to lower transactions costs by pulling all production within the boundaries of the firm or may represent the normal extension of product cycles (Dunning 1992). On the other hand, such outsourcing arrangements may also represent an insidious attempt to pay for expensive branding strategies through cost savings in the production process by hiring sweatshop workers and by using MNE size-derived bargaining power to reduce terms of trade of raw materials, labour and capital—as illustrated by the Nike case (Klein 2000).

International outsourcing arrangements relate to social responsibility because the terms of trade of such arrangements affect the company's rate of return (and thus the rate of return of its stakeholders) and the returns to the host government. The rate of return to host governments then determines its ability to finance health, education and a host of other services. Figure 20.1 shows the relative distribution of income between the firm and the host government.[20] In the hypothetical division of resources between MNE and host government, resource exploitation generates returns and harms (such as pollution generated in obtaining the resources, populations that are resettled and environmental damage). Of these resources and harms, the MNE and the host government

18   As the referee for this chapter rightly notes, 'one might envisage that the World Bank and the IFC could make adherence to some sort of international standards part and parcel of corporations involved in development schemes that it is financing, but it is hard to see how a general watchdog, policeman, etc. role could be allied to its charter. Like corporations themselves, the World Bank must also be accountable to its constituents when engaging in various activities.' I personally agree but other views exist.

19   For a perspective on responsibilities for labour standards, see Polaski 2003 or Wells-Dang 2002.

20   Fig. 20.1 represents a simple portrayal of the relative distribution of income between the two parties. In a more formal chapter, I would present algebraically the relative division of income and define optimal conditions.

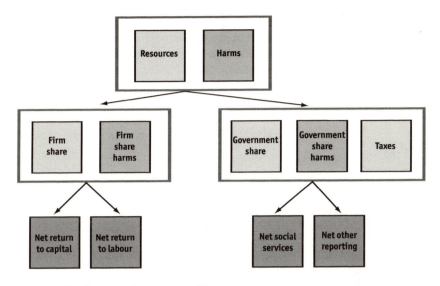

FIGURE 20.1 Distribution of returns and harms

receive a share. In the case of mining, often the MNE obtains the resources and the government is left to finance programmes ameliorating harms arising from reallocated populations, increased needs for social services and environmental damage. In the long run, resources are used to provide returns to owners of MNE capital and its workers, while, in the host country, returns are used to finance social services and other budgetary and non-budgetary spending (some of which could be welfare-decreasing such as military spending or resources siphoned off in corruption). Most would agree that leaving too few resources to the host government is irresponsible—yet it is difficult to draw the exact line.[21]

International oil company involvement in oil exploitation in Nigeria provides an example of some of these issues. Nigeria in 2002 earned US$17 billion in oil revenue—being one of the middle-ranking OPEC exporters (Middle East Economic Survey 2002). Yet the extraction of much Nigerian oil is undertaken by MNEs such as Shell, Chevron, Mobil, Elf and Agip.[22] Negative impacts include environmental damage (such as oil spills and gas flares) in the Niger Delta region.[23] Even the distribution of resources within the government should be a concern for the MNE, as corruption in Nigeria shows (Lewis 1996). In order to both increase returns to government and reduce harms, the Nigerian government has required the establishment of Community Liaison Offices

---

21 Several reports address the responsibilities of MNEs in natural resource management including International Institute for Environment and Development 2002, or Warner *et al.* 2003.

22 While it is currently difficult to estimate the returns to oil extraction, initiatives such as 'publish what you pay' should assist in both bringing returns toward market levels for business and ensuring that government proceeds do not get squandered.

23 For more on human rights violations tied to oil exploitation in Nigeria, see Manby 1999.

within the large oil-producing MNEs—acting as an intermediary between the MNE and the host community (World Bank 2003).

In order to redress the damage committed, many MNEs invest in social programmes targeted at the host country. For example, British Petroleum invested a total of US$108 million in social programmes in 2001 (World Bank 2003). Most of these tend to be small projects. Of the business consultancies working with local NGOs, most work by helping them to improve their 'operational performance'—such as AT Kearney's work with the Indian NGO Deepalaya, or McKinsey & Company's work with Ashoka Innovators for the Public (World Bank 2003). While all work is pro bono, these consultancies gain knowledge of a rapidly expanding 'third sector'. IBM, in addition to giving funds, also donates its technology and encourages its 90,000 employees to be active in the community. In the case of Shell, over 1,500 company employees and volunteers work with health and welfare organisations. Such relationships can be portrayed as in Figure 20.2, which shows funds flowing to NGOs which then provide services. Yet two points can be made. First, if MNEs offered better terms of trade to host governments, governments could provide these services themselves (assuming they are willing and able). Second, such arrangements support a burgeoning third sector which contributes demand to MNEs' goods and services. At the worst, ICR programmes may themselves become business 'products' offered to customers, financiers and employees (Michael 2003).

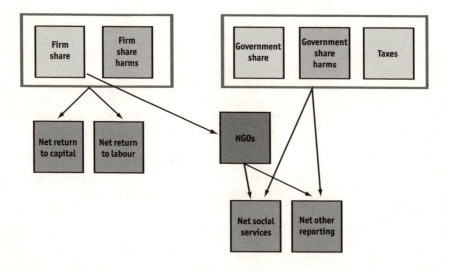

FIGURE 20.2 MNEs providing social services

Rather than establish small funds to support social investment, MNEs can change their project structures to address many of these issues. Rather than design projects that are socially responsible in the first place, MNEs design irresponsible projects then 'net out' the harms through socially responsible investment. Rather than engaging in such 'palliative' investment, MNEs can do several things to minimise harms arising from their principal business activities. First, global stakeholder boards, or advisory boards, could be established—bringing in a wider range of stakeholders from consumers to environmentalists in the boardroom, truly establishing public–private partnerships. Smaller affiliate boards could also be established for local filials of the parent company. Second, given the large-scale externalities generated by MNEs, greater use of triple-bottom-line reporting could be used at both the global and local levels.[24]

20.4 Strategic options for international NGOs

International NGOs—such as the International Business Leaders' Forum, Global Reporting Initiative, Social Accountability International and CSR-Europe—are increasingly becoming active in ICR.[25] International NGOs provide an important ballast against the power of international governmental organisations and MNEs, most vividly illustrated by the Seattle protests (Cockburn and St Claire 2000).[26] They have also done much to raise awareness about the need for ICR. Yet, as demonstrated above at the national level, NGOs can work with business or can act as a watchdog against corporate abuse. Some of the options for international NGOs are presented in Table 20.3, which shows possible interactions with international business and international governmental organisations (such as the World Bank).[27]

	Co-operation	Conflict
International government	Work on international codes	Monitor actions of IFIs
International business	Participate in social projects	Monitor actions of MNEs

TABLE 20.3 Strategic options for international NGOs

International NGOs have a role to play in working with international governmental organisations on ICR codes. The Global Compact was designed with the wide co-operation of a number of NGOs—both working on issues related to ICR and not. In many cases, these NGOs take a leading role in monitoring actions and objecting if these

24 MNEs are already positively predisposed to triple-bottom-line reporting, as a 2002 survey conducted by PricewaterhouseCoopers shows that roughly two-thirds of European MNEs and 41% of US MNEs are considering such initiatives (see www.srimedia.com/artman/publish/article_169.shtml, accessed 13 October 2004).

25 Kingsnorth 2003 views non-organised individuals and community groups as key representatives of international civil society. I will not discuss the role of such 'spontaneous' groups on the grounds that strategic planning cannot be undertaken for such decentralised, non-organised groups.

26 See Florini 2000 and O'Brien *et al.* 2000 for more on international civil-society organisations. Civil-society action against the OECD's Multilateral Investment Agreement represents another supposed example of 'third-sector' activity against excessive MNE power.

27 A coherent examination of the role of NGOs in ICR is beyond the scope of this chapter which does not seek to problematise the role of NGOs in ICR, but rather to provide strategic options. Future work may fruitfully look at these problems and references to the literature have been given.

actions are seen to harm the NGOs' stakeholders. While such participation has been well regarded, there are a number of dangers. First, international governments may involve international NGOs simply to promote their own social legitimacy. By showing that they are partnering with international NGOs, international organisations may portray their programmes as broadly representative and endorsed by a wide range of interests. Second, international NGOs do not need to take account of the wider welfare beyond their own stakeholders. Environmental NGOs could be willing to negotiate away labour standards to focus more attention on environmental issues. Whereas government is supposed to consider the welfare of all its citizens, NGOs may not. Third, international NGOs may be co-opted in order to obtain consulting or project contracts. Given the increased willingness of international government organisations to work in NGOs of all kinds, the potential of collusion exists.

International NGOs also have a role to play in working with international business. Often international NGOs—such as Pro-Natura—work much more closely with international business than with international government.[28] In general, NGOs have been very successful in the past ten years in raising awareness about international business and many of the voluntary CSR codes that have been adopted by MNCs in recent years have significant input from international NGOs. However, there are a number of dangers. First, international NGOs may be co-opted by international business (which may have final overt or tacit editorial power over the NGOs' findings). Second, international NGO action may simply represent another type of business competition. Many international NGOs offer ICR 'products' and provide fee-based or membership-based services. The advocacy of such organisations might try to maximise their revenues rather than social welfare. Indeed, many international NGOs gain recognition, political power and revenue from conference participation and publication as well as having only a tenuous relationship with the civil society they supposedly represent (Keane 2000). Third, international NGOs are not required to look out for the big picture and are generally unaccountable. A vivid example is Greenpeace's ill-advised campaign to force Royal Dutch/Shell to raise an old oil platform from burial in the north Atlantic—incorrectly arguing that such a burial would harm the ecosystem more than a land burial (World Bank 2003).

Given the range of options outlined above, which strategic course should each international actor pursue? Should the World Bank become more involved if NGOs become conflictive rather than co-operative? Should international business finance social projects if the World Bank refuses to do so? Given the range of possible strategic interactions, a model is required to bring out the issues clearly.

20.5 A simple model of MNE CSR in the three sectors

While many of the speeches and the writings about ICR discuss these trends and look at the role of international business, international government and international NGOs, there is no concrete model offered to illustrate their interaction and make predictions.

28   Gereffi *et al.* 2002 discuss the fine line between NGOs and business.

In order to explicitly model the changing ICR relations, a very *basic model* will be employed to present the issues.

In this simple model (based on the famous Cournot model from economics), each actor must decide how much ICR activity to provide.[29] As mentioned in the last section, the World Bank can become fully committed to ICR and assume most of the ICR work by engaging in consulting and ICR-related conditionality. International business can become heavily involved through extensive donations of staff time and financial contributions to ICR programmes (as well as moderating demands for natural resource remuneration). International NGOs can become involved through extensive co-operation in ICR programmes. Realistically, though, each actor knows it cannot cover the entire range of ICR activities and so must 'share' ICR activity—working in public–private partnership.

The logic behind such sharing might be as follows. International government knows that international business will find it in its interest to self-regulate to some extent, and thus will leave some ICR activity to firms.[30] Firms know that governments will want to engage in some regulation, and thus will not seek full self-regulation. International NGOs know that both business and government cannot be relied on to promote the socially optimal level of ICR and thus will claim a field of activity for themselves. At first glance, as each actor pursues its ICR activity without centralised co-ordination, one would expect *over-provision* of ICR activity. Yet, even though each actor tries to cover a certain proportion of ICR activity, overall there is *under-provision* of ICR activities due to their strategic interaction. Simply put, each actor overestimates the amount of ICR activity to be provided by other actors and so under-provides its own share of ICR activity due to lack of public–private partnership. Interestingly, if an actor, such as international government, takes a leadership role to promote such partnership, then such under-provision may not occur. Such a model goes a long way toward explaining the current level and distribution of ICR activity today.

In order to motivate the model, assume current business operations produce a fixed level of social harm requiring a fixed level of ICR activity. To provide such ICR activity, government engages in a share of ICR activities and so does non-government.[31] While in the last section, government, business and NGOs were discussed, in this model only government and non-government are discussed to simplify the model. There are two rules in deciding the level of activity. First, government must decide *at the same time* as non-government the level of ICR activity it will provide. Second, it does not pay for either government or non-government to engage fully in ICR because of falling productivity (diminishing returns) to ICR activity. In other words, large programmes are expensive to run and many programmes are difficult to co-ordinate. Such an assumption is realistic given the current speed with which all sectors are engaging in ICR activity.

One simple solution to this 'game' is shown in Figure 20.3, where government decides to engage in half the ICR activity and non-government will then engage in half

---

29   For readers interested in better understanding the Cournot model, see Foulton 1997.
30   OECD 2001 finds that government has provided for extensive self-regulation by business.
31   As before, a rigorous explanation would use algebra which has been removed here for readability.

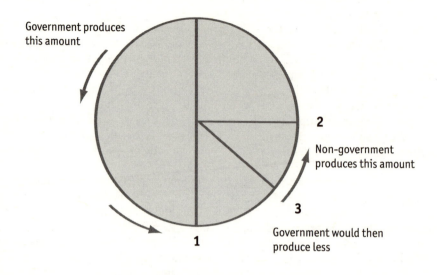

FIGURE 20.3 Action and reaction of each actor

of that.[32] If non-government could expect government to provide half of the ICR activity, then it would fill in only half of the remaining activity to be done as shown by point 3. Government would also reduce the amount of ICR activity it provides to half of what it thinks the residual demand will be and so on. A public–private 'partnership' in this is under-provisioned due to strategic interaction.

These strategies can be shown using a simple diagram as shown in Figure 20.4. The diagram represents all ICR activity as a 'pie'. The reader may be tempted to conclude that government should engage in ICR—thus filling the 'pie'. At that point, the government engages in all ICR and non-government engages in none. However, when non-government provides no ICR, it is in the interest of the government only to provide half. Therefore, as non-government has the possibility of stepping in to provide more ICR activities, the government has the incentive to provide less. As shown in the figure, the equilibrium level (where there is no incentive for change) is that each actor provides only one-third of the total ICR activity. According to this simple model, insufficient ICR is provided due to a lack of leadership governing the public–private partnership. Insufficient ICR is not due to apathy or ignorance, but is due to strategic interaction.

32 This discussion takes advantage of the fact that, in the teaching model, Cournot oligopolists have constant elasticity of demand curves, making the optimal production quantity half the market. For simplicity, I have set a 'rule of thumb' for each actor to produce half the market (replicating the optimising behaviour of actors under these special demand curves). Alternatively, I could have argued that each actor has social demand curves, social marginal revenue curves and found the optimum. However, such an argumentation strategy would only confound the main intuitions behind the discussion.

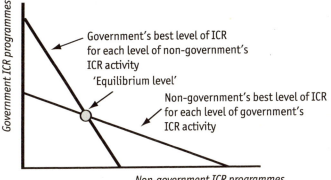

FIGURE 20.4 ICR actions and reactions

While I do not have space to discuss the issues fully here, I should note that, if government and non-government have different costs (for example, non-government is more cost-efficient at providing ICR), then non-government will have a larger market share. If there are more than two actors, then the amount of ICR activity increases as each actor becomes uncertain about the response of other actors. The main implication of these two points is that how ICR markets are designed vitally determines how much ICR activity is provided. When ways are found of lowering the cost of ICR or increasing the number of actors involved, then more ICR will be provided.

20.6 A simple model of MNE CSR within itself

Even if the overall business and policy environment dictates the overall level of the MNE's ICR activity, the firm still must exercise strategic choice over the distribution of ICR within its business activities. According to Utting (2000), an increasing number of companies have claimed to have moved from eclectic to holistic approaches to ICR. Yet explanations for such change, beyond the simple 'spread of ideas' or management fashion, have been lacking.[33] Moreover, a yardstick for determining whether such changes are optimal needs to be established.

Barelett and Ghoshal's (1989) model of international strategy can be used to help determine the type of ICR project to pursue—and the ideal degree of public–private partnership. In their model, the firm must decide on project structure depending on the firm's economies of scale in production and the specificity of local demand. According

33 Collective adoption of such practices may represent the formation of an 'epistemic community' or 'institutional isomorphism' (Fligstein 2001). Yet, even if such a widely adopted change in ICR strategy is occurring due to such isomorphism, there is no guarantee that such adoption is optimal.

to this adaptation of their model, the MNE must choose its ICR product structure based on the type of ICR product it is delivering. Following the (over)simple 2 × 2 matrices popular in the management literature, the MNE can choose its ICR activity depending on its economies of scale in ICR products and the homogeneity of local ICR demands. Clearly economies of scale are achievable in some activities but not in others (Table 20.4 assumed diminishing returns—or negative economies of scale—which may not be the case with all ICR projects). Some local needs are also much more obvious, such as oil damage to the Niger Delta region. The strategic options are shown in Table 20.4.[34]

Economics of scale *Specificity of needs*	**High**	**Low**
High	Centralised structure (Nike, The Body Shop)	Federated structure (IBM)
Low	Network structure (ABB)	Decentralised structure (Ahold)

TABLE 20.4 Matching knowledge to objectives

If there are economies of scale and demand is also standard, then the MNE should pursue a centralised, standardised ICR programme. Operating regulations and product standards and regulation can be applied across the MNE and can generally benefit all stakeholders. Some examples include Nike's reconsideration of its supply-chain relationships, Starbuck's consideration of fair-trade coffee and many MNEs' policies encouraging employees to engage in community work. Other MNEs such as The Body Shop design their whole product around the notion of social (environmental) responsibility. The work done by international governments represents work on ICR activities which display economies of scale and are not particularly locally focused. Given such standardisation, there is a role for government and NGO involvement, if regulation is seen as simply the 'standardised contract' (Hart 1995). In history, regulation has often followed contracts that business found in their interest to repeatedly implement and many of these contracts could be based on notions of social responsibility.

If there are economies of scale but locally based demand, a network structure can be employed to deliver ICR programmes. Community-based investment represents one example of such ICR work. Such investment exhibits economies of scale because more funds contribute to globally better outcomes (such projects are often by financed on a multi-country basis), yet each country programme is tailored to meet differing and specific needs. Investments in local community health and education programmes—such as Cola-Cola's investments in HIV work in Africa or AstraZeneca's donations of medicines—are salient examples. ABB's sustainability networks also provide another example of such a network structure (Harila and Petrini 2003).

---

34 In the company descriptions that follow, I do not give a moral value to the programmes or claim they are successful. In most cases, I was not able to investigate the veracity of the claims made by the companies featured in this section. Further work will be done along these lines.

If there are low economies of scale and non-homogenous demand, then a federated structure can be employed. Unlike a network structure where ICR initiatives can be devised centrally and then adapted at the local level, low economies of scale and non-homogeneous demand mean that each locality designs and executes its own projects. IBM represents an example of such a network structure as each local branch is able to pursue its own ICR policy. Policy can encourage firms to respond to specific country circumstances but cannot proscribe rules of behaviour. IBM follows a decentralised approach to ICR where in Argentina, Austria, Britain and the US, the company has helped to equip job training centres for unemployed young people, while in Peru, equipment, software, training and cash have been combined to help the better monitoring and control of diarrhoea. Each country where the company has significant business interests—such as Brazil, France, Germany, Japan, UK and USA—develops its own community involvement strategy, approved and actively supported by local senior executives.

Finally, if there are low economies of scale and homogeneous local demand, then a decentralised structure of ICR delivery must be used. Unlike the federated structure where there is some affinity between programmes (even if they are conceived and executed independently), in a decentralised structure, projects may be very different. Such a strategy may be represented by corporate headquarters purposely not having strategy but rather letting each country unit decide on its own projects. Ahold (the food provider) is an example of such a decentralised ICR provider—letting its network of companies provide their own ICR according to their own estimations of local demand.[35] Given the costs of such delivery, there is a role for government and NGOs to help provide the public goods needed to deliver these ICR programmes—not just for MNEs but also for local corporations.

Such a matrix has a number of limitations. Each MNE will have specific circumstances which requires a different competitive reaction. Companies may also pursue a number of strategies simultaneously—having both global projects and locally focused projects. Also if other actors—such as government—are involved, complementarities may override the lack of economies of scale in ICR provision. While theory is simple, real cases are complex. The point of the matrix is not to reduce reality into simple categories, but provide simple descriptions to help managers choose the best types of programmes given business environment circumstances.

20.7 Conclusions

Increasing engagement in ICR programmes represents an important step in increasing the accountability of business and promoting public–private partnership. However, most ICR programmes are poorly managed due to a lack of strategic thinking about ICR. This chapter has found that the overall direction of ICR activity depends vitally on the direction of globalisation and whether MNEs are causing economic convergence, diver-

---

35   For more information, see www.ahold.com/_media/pdf/csr2002.pdf, accessed 15 August 2005.

gence or whether these effects are ambiguous. International government, and especially the World Bank, has a role to play but this role is—and should be—circumscribed by the actions of other actors. International business supports a range of local programmes, yet lacks a wider vision of ICR funding and fails to see how its relations with government constrain its options at the local level. International NGOs can be important allies, but also not. Looking at the interaction of these three actors, they might tend to under-provide ICR activity due to the strategic nature of their interaction. And these actors may fail to balance economies of scale in ICR provision with local needs. This chapter has attempted to present several concrete models allowing both academics and practitioners to evaluate and promote ICR in the MNE.

References

Acemoglu, D., and J. Robinson (2000) 'Why Did the West Extend the Franchise? Democracy, Inequality, and Growth in Historical Perspective', *Quarterly Journal of Economics* 115 (November 2000): 1,167-99.

Bartlett, C., and S. Ghoshal (2001) *Managing across Borders: The Transnational Solution* (Boston, MA: Harvard Business School Press).

Bell, D. (2002) 'The Role of Government in Advancing Corporate Sustainability', www.worldbank.org/wbi/corpgov/csr/econferences/publicpolicy/pdf/The_Role_of_Government.pdf.

Bendell, J. (ed.) (2000) *Terms for Endearment: Business, NGOs and Sustainable Development* (Sheffield, UK: Greenleaf Publishing).

Berger, S., and R. Dore (1996) *National Diversity and Global Capitalism* (Ithaca, NY: Cornell University Press).

Benabou, R., and E. Ok (2001) 'Social Mobility and the Demand for Redistribution: The POUM Hypothesis', *Quarterly Journal of Economics* 116.2 : 447-87.

Blowfield, M. (1999) 'Ethical Trade: A Review of Developments and Issues', *Third World Quarterly* 20.4: 1-28 (www.nri.org/NRET/3wqart.pdf, accessed 13 October 2004).

Braithwaite, J., and P. Drahos (2000) *Global Business Regulation* (Cambridge, UK: Cambridge University Press).

Brousseau, E., and J.-M. Glachant (2002) *The Economics of Contracts: Theories and Applications* (New York: Cambridge University Press).

Bull, C. (1987) 'The Existence of Self-enforcing Implicit Contracts', *Quarterly Journal of Economics* 102.1: 147-59.

Business Partners for Development (2002) 'Results and Recommendations for Developing Country Governments in Putting Partnering to Work', www.worldbank.org/wbi/corpgov/csr/econferences/publicpolicy/pdf/bmo3of5.pdf, accessed 13 October 2004.

Castells, M. (1996) *The Rise of the Network Society. The Information Age: Economy, Society and Culture* (Oxford, UK: Blackwell).

Caufield, C. (1996) *Masters of Illusion: The World Bank and the Poverty of Nations* (New York: Henry Holt).

Cockburn, A., and J. St Claire (2000) *Five Days that Shook the World: Seattle and Beyond* (London: Verso).

Cohn, T. (2000) *Global Political Economy: Theory and Practice* (New York: Longman).

Doz, Y., J. Santos and P. Williamson (2001) *From Global to Metanational: How Companies Win in the Knowledge Economy* (Boston, MA: Harvard Business School Publishing).

Dunning, J. (1992) *Multinational Enterprises and the Global Economy* (London: Addison Wesley).

Einhorn, J. (2001) 'The World Bank's Mission Creep', *Foreign Affairs* 80.5 (September/October 2001): 22-35.

Fligstein, N. (2001) *The Architecture of Markets: An Economic Sociology of Capitalist Societies* (Princeton, NJ: Princeton University Press).

Florini, A. (2000) *The Third Force: The Rise of Transnational Civil Society* (Washington, DC: Carnegie Endowment for International Peace).

Fox, T., H. Ward and B. Howard (2002) *Public Sector Roles in Strengthening Corporate Social Responsibility: A Baseline Study* (Washington, DC: World Bank).

Friedman, T. (2000) *The Lexus and the Olive Tree: Understanding Globalization* (New York: Anchor Books).

Fulton, M. (1997) 'A Graphic Analysis of the Cournot Nash and Stackelberg Models', *Journal of Economic Education* 28.1: 48-57.

Gereffi, G., R. Garcia-Johnson and E. Sasser (2001) 'The NGO–Industrial Complex', *Foreign Policy* 125 (July/August 2001): 56-66.

Gibbons, M., C. Limoges, H. Nowotny, S. Schwartzman, P. Scott and M. Trow (1994) *The New Production of Knowledge* (London: Sage).

Gilpin, R. (1987) *The Political Economy of International Relations* (Princeton, NJ: Princeton University Publications).

Greider, W. (1997) *One World, Ready or Not: The Manic Logic of Global Capitalism* (New York: Simon & Schuster).

Hall, P., and D. Soskice (2001) *Varieties of Capitalism: The Institutional Foundations of Comparative Advantage* (New York: Oxford University Press).

Harila, H., and K. Petrini (2003) 'Incorporating Corporate Social Responsibility', epubl.luth.se/1404-5508/2003/064/LTU-SHU-EX-03064-SE.pdf, accessed 13 October 2004.

Hart, O. (1995) *Firms, Contracts and Financial Structure* (Oxford, UK: Oxford University Press).

Hedlund, G. (1994) 'A Model of Knowledge Management and the N-Form Corporation', *Strategic Management Journal* 15 (Summer 1994): 73-90.

Held, D., A. McGrew, D. Goldblatt and J. Perraton (1999) *Global Transformations: Politics, Economics and Culture* (Cambridge, UK: Polity Press).

Hennart, J.-F. (2000) 'Transaction Costs Theory and the Multinational Enterprise', in C.N. Pitelis and R. Sugden (eds.), *The Nature of the Transnational Firm* (New York: Routledge).

Hirst, P., and G. Thompson (1996) *Globalization in Question* (Cambridge, UK: Polity Press).

Hopkins M. (1998) *The Planetary Bargain: Corporate Social Responsibility Comes of Age* (Basingstoke, UK: Macmillan).

International Institute for Environment and Development (2002) *Breaking New Ground: Mining, Minerals, and Sustainable Development* (London, UK: Earthscan Publications).

Jacobs, S. (1994) *Regulatory Cooperation for an Interdependent World* (Paris: OECD Publications).

Kay, N. (2000) 'The Resource-Based Approach to Multinational Enterprise', in C.N. Pitelis and R. Sugden, *The Nature of the Transnational Firm* (New York: Routledge).

Keane, J. (2000) *Global Civil Society?* (Cambridge, UK: Cambridge University Press).

Kingsnorth, P. (2003) *One No, Many Yeses: A Journey to the Heart of the Global Resistance Movement* (London, UK: Free Press).

Klein, N. (2000) *No Logo: Taking Aim at the Brand Bullies* (Toronto: Vintage Canada Edition).

Korten, D. (1995) *When Corporations Rule the World* (New York: Kumarian Press).

Leal, G., M. Fa and J. Pasola (2003) 'Using Environmental Management Systems to Increase Firms' Competitiveness', *Corporate Social Responsibility and Environmental Management* 10.2 (June 2003): 101-10.

Levitt, T. (1983) 'The Globalization of Markets', *Harvard Business Review* 61 (May/June 1983): 92-102.

Lewis, P. (1996) 'From Prebendalism to Predation: The Political Economy of Decline in Nigeria', *The Journal of Modern African Studies* 34.1: 79-103.

Manby, B. (1999) *The Price of Oil: Corporate Responsibility and Human Rights Violations in Nigeria's Oil Producing Communities* (London: Human Rights Watch).

Michael, B. (2003) 'Corporate Social Responsibility in International Development: An Overview and Critique', *Journal of Corporate Social Responsibility and Environmental Responsibility* 10.3: 115-28

Middle East Economic Survey (2002) 'OPEC's Export Revenue Falls 21% in 2001, Says EIA', *Middle East Economic Survey* 45.27 (8 July 2002).

Mosley, P., J. Harrigan and J. Toye (1995) *Aid and Power: The World Bank and Policy-Based Lending* (London: Routledge).

National Policy Association (2003) 'Why A Role for Government?', www.multinationalguidelines.org/csr/why_a_role_for_the_government.htm, accessed 22 May 2003.

Newell, P. (2001) 'Managing Multinationals: The Governance of Investment for the Environment', *Journal of International Development* 13.7 (October 2001): 907-19.

O'Brien, R., A. Goetz, J. Scholte and M. Williams (2000) *Contesting Global Governance: Multilateral and Global Social Movements* (Cambridge, UK: Cambridge University Press).

O'Rourke, A. (2003) 'A New Politics of Engagement: Shareholder Activism for Corporate Social Responsibility', *Business Strategy and the Environment* 12.4 (July/August): 227-39.

OECD (Organisation for Economic Co-operation and Development) (2001) 'Public Policy and Voluntary Initiatives: What Roles have Governments Played?' (OECD Working Paper on International Investment no. 2001/4; OECD: Paris, February 2001).

Ohmae, K. (1990) *The Borderless World* (London: William Collins).

Ozawa, T., and S. Castello (2001) 'Toward an "International Business" Paradigm of Endogenous Growth: Multinationals and Governments as Co-endogenisers', *International Journal of the Economics of Business* 8.2: 211-28.

Peoples, J., and R. Sugden (2000) 'Divide and Rule by Transnational Corporations', in C.N. Pitelis and R. Sugden (eds.), *The Nature of the Transnational Firm* (New York: Routledge).

Pilger, J. (2002) *The New Rulers of the World* (London: Verso Books).

Polaski, S. (2003) 'Trade and Labor Standards: A Strategy for Developing Countries', www.worldbank.org/wbi/corpgov/csr/econferences/publicpolicy/pdf/Polaski.pdf, accessed 13 October 2004.

Schwartz, P., and B. Gibb (1999) *When Good Companies Do Bad Things: Responsibility and Risk in an Age of Globalization* (New York: Wiley).

Stiglitz, J. (2002) *Globalization and its Discontents* (New York: W.W. Norton).

Stopford, J. (1998) 'Multinational Corporations', *Foreign Policy* 113 (Winter 1998): 12-24.

Strange, S. (1997) 'The Future of Global Capitalism; or, Will Divergence Persist Forever?', in C. Crouch and W. Streeck (eds.), *Political Economy of Modern Capitalism* (London: Sage): 182-92.

—— and J. Stopford (1991) *Rival States, Rival Firms* (Cambridge, UK: Cambridge University Press).

Tolentino, P. (2001) 'From a Theory to a Paradigm: Examining the Eclectic Paradigm as a Framework in International Economics', *International Journal of the Economics of Business* 8.2: 191-209.

Utting, P. (2000) *Business Responsibility for Sustainable Development*, UNRISD Occasional Paper 2.

Warner, M., G. Larralde and R. Sullivan (2003) 'Oil Production and Long-Term Regional Development, Partnerships for Managing Social Issues in the Extractive Industries', www.worldbank.org/wbi/corpgov/csr/econferences/publicpolicy/pdf/casanare_exec_summ.pdf, accessed 13 October 2004.

Wells-Dang, A. (2002) 'Linking Textiles to Labor Standards: Prospects for Cambodia and Vietnam', *Foreign Policy in Focus*, June 2002; www.fpif.org.

Woodward, J. (1965) *Industrial Organization* (Oxford, UK: Oxford University Press).

World Bank (2002) 'Corporate Social Responsibility and Sustainable Competitiveness', www.worldbank.org/wbi/corpgov/csr/index.html, accessed 13 October 2004.

—— (2003) 'Public Policy and Corporate Social Responsibility—World Bank Institute and Private Sector Development Vice Presidency E-Conference', www.worldbank.org/wbi/corpgov/csr/econferences/publicpolicy/readings.html, accessed 13 October 2004.

21
Concluding remarks on emerging governance structures and practices
THE STATE, THE MARKET AND THE VOICE OF CIVIL SOCIETY

Istemi Demirag, John Barry and Iqbal Khadaroo
Queen's University Belfast, UK

This book has been concerned, on a global basis, with the relationships between the state, the market and civil society in the development of corporate social responsibility, accountability and sustainable development. The book seeks to unmask the power vested in each discreet sector and illustrates through theoretical and empirical case studies how power has been regulated and exploited to gain advantage. It also shows how the interdependent, contingent and dynamic interchange between the state, corporations and civil society is integral to the development of corporate social responsibility and accountability processes (Demirag 1995).

The book is multidisciplinary and focuses on the political, social, economic, technological, legal and organisational shaping of corporate social responsibility, accountability and ethical practices. This approach is vital in order to calibrate more effectively the dynamic and interdependent concepts of responsibility, accountability and governance (Demirag 1998; Demirag and Solomon 2003). Social corporate responsibility and sustainable development cannot be adequately understood within the confines of a single perspective (Demirag *et al.* 2004).

Globalisation and the corresponding changing role and structure of governance in corporations underpin the rationale for the book. It is responsive to the calls from regulators and civil society that corporations have a significant role to play in: meeting the increasing demands of stakeholders, better corporate social responsibility, accountability and governance (Clark and Demirag 2002).

The book has five main parts. In the first part, emerging governance structures, networks and associated risk management issues have been examined within a conceptual framework. In Part 2, corporate social responsibility and stakeholder relations have been explored and critiqued. Part 3 has provided empirical studies on the emerging patterns of governance structures for corporate social responsibility, sustainable development and networking. The implications of these new structures for governance, accountability and ethics have been examined in Part 4. Part 5 has highlighted the implications of multinational operations for new governance structures, regulators and civil society, and indicated the limitations of criminal law enforcement.

Far from a monolithic form, multinational corporations are governed by a multitude of social actors in pursuit of their own self-interest, often with conflicting interests and motives. Yet corporations struggle to provide economic, social and political harmony and often are successful in providing economic and social benefits. Some writers have suggested that there may be a strong relationship between accountability, responsibility and governance, and the roles of corporations in providing the necessary input for social order and corporate responsibility. However, whether, and if so, to what extent, regulation can play an important role in changing the behaviour of corporations has been problematic. The mode of regulating—by the state or by self-regulation—is also a complex issue (Demirag et al. 2004).

In an attempt to explore and critique the presumed relationship between the development of corporate social responsibility and the governance structures and accountability we have used the state, the market and the community framework throughout this book.[1]

In Chapter 16, Demirag and O'Brien, in their study of US regulation, indicate that Streeck et al. (1985) argue that a model for 'social order' can be best described by conflicts, incompatibilities and mutual complementarities between three ordering principals. The key actors identified by their respective and guiding principles by Streeck and Schmitter are: spontaneous solidarity (the community); dispersed competition (the market); and hierarchical control (the state or the bureaucracy). A state of equilibrium is reached in a society when certain key actors with restricted passions or interests are allowed to co-operate and conflict with each other according to certain patterns or rules, with beneficial results for most, if not all, of their members (Demirag 1995). Demirag and O'Brien posit that the SS framework does not provide a robust theoretical underpinning for understanding the recent changes in the US financial regulation. However, they point out that the model helps them to identify key actors and principals behind the conflicting and conflating imperatives between economic, social and political governance in the regulation of financial markets in the United States. Moreover, it identifies the motives of other 'private governance' interests in the constant battle for 'better' and 'more effective' regulation of the financial markets. The private-interest government relationships identified in the case studies also help us to explain the distortions in the markets occasioned by recent financial malfeasance and misfeasance in the United States.

In an ideal case, equilibrium in terms of corporate social responsibility, accountability, sustainable development and ethical behaviour is required in order to have a well-functioning society. In this equilibrium, not only the state and the corporations would have a major say, but civil society would also be involved and influence the decisions of corporations. In practice, however, while groups and organisations in civil society have become more critical in many respects of corporations and businesses, especially multinational corporations, the equilibrium point has not been reached in Western democ-

---

1 For the implications of the state, the market and the community framework of Streeck and Schmitter model 1985 on accounting profession, see Demirag 1995.

racies. There has, however, been a notable trend in terms of the strategy and rationale of (some) of these 'watchdogs' towards more partnership approaches based on positive (but still critical) engagement with corporations, trying to work with corporations rather than criticising them from the outside as it were (see, for example, Byerly, Chapter 7). What is also discernable is that, while the state and its agencies are often the focus of civil-society action, as the agency or mechanism to better regulate and control or manage corporations, there is also an interesting development in terms of direct civil society–corporate partnerships and dialogue above, beyond and outside the state.

Turcotte and Gendron also stress this point in Chapter 3 and conclude that involving civil society in deliberate processes to define the common good is a long-standing political tradition and it is fraught with difficulties. These should, however, be seen as challenges and opportunities to revisit, construct and revise our conception of the common good within an ongoing process of social production. For example, within the global justice–anti-globalisation movement (while there is still a sizeable section of this movement comprised of, *inter alia*, anti-capitalist, environmental, trades union, indigenous peoples, development and third world, and women's advocacy groups), there is a growing recognition for a more positive agenda that does not simply reject trade and the globalisation of 'fair not free trade' (Monbiot 2003). Equally, connections are being made between these 'reformist' elements and other groups who have long advocated the strategy of working with rather than against corporations (Porritt 2001).

David Korten (2000) suggests that what is required is a 'post-corporate' world, which is typified by a discernible shift towards a more 'transformatory' strategy where the aim is to change or reform (through political pressure, consumer boycotts, regulation, etc.) corporations. In the latter case, the aim is to make corporations work for society rather than vice versa. In support of this view, in Chapter 11, Munkelien, Goyer and Fratczak argue that one of the major issues in corporate social responsibility is 'triple-bottom-line reporting' where governmental regulation and legislation meets voluntary actions by corporations. They report, however, that this process is uneven, even within Scandinavian countries where the role of governmental bodies and corporate practices in relation to the development of CSR varies. However, they conclude that the corporate sector throughout Scandinavia clearly indicates its preference for a stronger involvement from governments, not necessarily in terms of more regulation but more support and dialogue.

In many respects, the debate about the appropriate assessment of corporations within the CSR and 'landscape of sustainable development'—that is to say, whether they are seen as a part of the problem or part of the solution in terms of the structural, institutional framework of achieving sustainable development—is similar to the debate within critical green or progressive civil-society debates about the place of the state within the vision for and achievement of a sustainable society and economy. Increasingly, it is the case that the state (while never innocent in terms of the underlying causes or drivers of unsustainable development), is viewed as part of the solution by civil-society groups and interests, hence, in reference to the green–global justice movement, the recent theoretical and practical political and strategic debates around the 'greening of the state' (Barry and Eckersley 2005; Dryzek *et al.* 2002; Barry 2003).

Indeed, as indicated above in the Scandinavian countries, it is important to stress the point that the 'reformist' agenda of civil-society groups and organisations working with corporations to improve their triple bottom line and make them better 'corporate citizens' through the norms, procedures, and accountability and transparency mechanisms of 'corporate social responsibility', cannot be understood without linking it directly to a 'reformist' approach by these civil-society groups and interests to the state (for example, see Munkelien *et al.*, Chapter 11). Hence the 'greening' of the corporation (through CSR and 'triple-bottom-line' operating procedures and aims) goes hand in hand with the 'greening' of the state.

In Chapter 4 Lüth, Schäfers and Helmchen, referring to McIntosh *et al.* 1998, argue that regulation is a two-way process. Companies are not only affected by regulation; they also have responsibility to effect proper regulation themselves. They identify three different levels of regulation: institutional, industry and corporate. The authors give relevant examples of each type and state that companies require competence and credibility to match the rising expectations and their perceived lack of legitimacy as a policy-maker. This requires better understanding of the workings and politics of multi-level, multi-interest regulatory frameworks. They point out the classical free-rider problem and indicate that companies will only implement a regulatory framework if the benefits derived from regulation outweigh the advantages of deregulation. There are of course variations in the extent of government regulations and the corresponding level of development of corporate social responsibility practices across the different types of corporate governance systems. The extent of regulation is important here, as Clark and Demirag (2002) argue in the case of the radical deregulation of the energy markets in California: the state was left powerless to deal with greedy demands of giant corporations, such as Enron, for higher profits.

Samaha in Chapter 17 also argues that globalisation has created an environment in which public-sector governance in the United States has undergone radical change in its administration and decision-making. She also identifies the California Energy Crisis of 2000–2001 as a good example of the consequences of the deregulation of the systems. The deregulation resulted in California energy prices jumping to 40% of the pre-deregulation levels—precisely the opposite effect that had been expected with the introduction of the deregulation of the energy sector. However, the design of opening the California energy system followed an approach known as 'shock therapy' with many unknown variables at many levels. For example, while the energy generation was competitive, its transmission was regulated with competitive wholesale and retail markets.

In Chapter 15, Šević outlines three models of corporate governance: the European model, Anglo-American model and a modified stakeholder model (Demirag *et al.* 2000). Šević regards the latter model as a model of the future, together with private production of rules of corporate governance and delegation of government regulatory and legislative powers to professional bodies. Bleischwitz, Andersen and Latsch in Chapter 10 argue that, especially in the Anglo-American model of governance, markets often fail to contribute sustainability improvements in areas concerning the provision of 'public goods'. They point out the problematic nature of 'public goods' and posit that learning processes can change actors' interests and preferences leading to new markets for sustainability. Bleischwitz *et al.* suggest that management of sustainability mandates co-evolution between market and state, through a learning process, where both private and public actors are in a permanent search for both market and policy developments and improvements.

While there are a variety of reasons against reformist strategies, the lack of credible alternatives, and the failure of anti-state, anti-capitalist and anti-corporate strategies, loom large. Here what is interesting to note is that the discourse of the anti-globalisation and global justice movement has evolved to the extent that it does not simply and simplistically equate the *market organisation* of the economy with *corporate organisation* of the economy. In other words, there is a growing recognition that the failures of corporations do not amount to conclusive evidence that the market system should, therefore, be rejected. This leads to calls by civil-society groups for the greater regulation of corporations, the transformation of corporations themselves to include social, environmental and human rights concerns alongside their profit-making economic rationale and the fiduciary duty of corporate executive officers and boards, as well as arguments against untrammelled corporate economic activity in certain sectors.

While anti-globalisation protesters rightly proclaim that 'another world is possible', the question of strategy, tactics and the combining of theoretical critique with *realpolitik* awareness of the contemporary configuration of ideological and practical political resistance, have to be answered and addressed head-on. Thus, reformist approaches to the state and the market (corporations), within those movements critical of current economic and political structures, are also solutions-focused in a way abstract ideological or normative critiques have never been. While of course not true of all elements of this critical civil-society position, it is nevertheless the case that many critical voices within civil society concerned with the environmentally and socially irresponsible behaviour of states and corporations, are no longer satisfied with the older (Marxist-based) view that everything will be sorted out and better 'after the revolution'. Radical reformist movements want to work with the grain of the economy and society and demonstrate to people here and now that 'another world is possible'.

Perhaps the example *par excellence* of the 'reformist' aim of making corporations work for society is the concept of 'sustainable development', which has become a key feature of the 'common ground' for corporate actors and interests, civil-society groups, and states and regulators. Bleischwitz *et al.*, in Chapter 10, argue that the governance of sustainable development goes well beyond traditional, state-centred policy-making. They argue that markets and governments in their attempt to regulate are not successful in encouraging sustainable development. What is required is the development of networks capable of harnessing collective learning processes in order to find long-term solutions. They conclude that, in the case of developing wind turbines by the Swedish, German and Dutch industries, new knowledge is based on the absorption of societal views, where the main function of the governments has been to facilitate learning processes that depart from the traditional world-view associated by a reliance on welfare economics. As Jacobs (1999) has pointed out, the fact that diverse groups can 'buy into' and articulate their concerns within the discourse of sustainable development makes it a powerful tool for change. He argues that the very fact that business and corporate interests and actors now speak the language of sustainable development is a strategic advantage to the environmental movement. Concluding his discussion of the pros and cons of sustainable development, and sensitive to the charge that the radical aims of greens are being watered down by being 'co-opted' by powerful state and business elites, he states,

> The 'discourse coalition' of sustainable development may therefore be having
> exactly the opposite effect to that worrying the ultra-greens. Far from co-opt-

ing the environmental movement into a conservative government and business programme of non-reform, it may be allowing the articulation and dissemination of a radical world-view under the shelter of government and business approval (1999: 44-45).

In other words, the fact that the concept of 'sustainable development' as a meta-policy objective has been integrated into the 'everyday landscape and language' of business and state decision-making means that radical policy goals can be pursued. Jacobs's point, and one not lost on more astute elements of the global justice and green movements, is that the concept of sustainable development contains commitments not just to the 'triple bottom line' (conventionally understood as social, economic and environmental objectives), but also commitments to human rights, democracy, participation, social justice and equity, intergenerational concern, social inclusion, women's rights and equality, and good governance, among others. When one looks at the 'originating' sources of sustainable development at the international level (usually thought of as the Brundtland Commission's report on Environment and Development or the Rio 'Earth Summit' in 1992), it is clear that 'sustainable development' is conceptualised not simply as a 'technical adjustment' to 'business as usual' in terms of how corporations, the economy, civil society and the state interact, but it is centrally about a different type of society and therefore a different set of arrangements between the state, civil society and the market, both nationally and globally.

Of course this can (and is) contested by those who seek to reduce the radical and transformative goals and implications of sustainable development to a couple of minor 'side constraints' or 'qualifiers' to current patterns of trade, business practices and regulatory regimes. However, it is also the case that these 'reactionary' (as opposed to radical or positive) interpretations of sustainable development are often based on the uncertain grounds of deliberately excluding the full range of concerns of sustainable development—something that is readily exploited by civil society and state and regulatory interests, and decision-makers. In other words, it sometimes appears as if corporations, business (and indeed state) interests do not fully appreciate the radical potentials of sustainable development and that in signing up to the concept of sustainable development they are signing up to a new view of who they are, what they do and how they relate to social, environmental and political concerns in a manner previously unthinkable—the common ground that sustainable development opens up within which a variety of stakeholders, interests and groups can meet and use a common language to discuss solutions to a common problem, and in the process experiment with new forms of governance between state, civil society and market actors and institutions, develop new norms, regimes and multi-learning processes. At the very least the collaborative, stakeholder and partnership approach at the heart of sustainable development can provide the opportunity for trust and some degree of mutual understanding to emerge between groups and organisations with different and perhaps (initially) mutually exclusive interests and agendas. As Dempsey argues in Chapter 9, this form of shared understanding could reduce the barriers to effective cross-sector engagement and, framed by the wider societal context, create a potential nexus around which sustainable relationships that are both economically and socially viable can develop.

This is particularly the case if we explore the 'ecological modernisation' interpretation of sustainable development. The advantage of adopting an ecological modernisation approach, from an environmentalist point of view, is that 'environmentalist interest in pollution control and conservation of material resources can be attached to the economic imperative via the idea of ecological modernisation. Demands to protect the intrinsic value of natural systems cannot make this link' (Dryzek *et al.* 2003: 161). Making the business case for sustainable development means that 'ecological questions are linked to questions of global social justice and the radicalisation of democracy' (Doherty 2002: 217). Equally important point here is the capacity of transnational enforcement mechanisms. Bastmeijer and Verschuuren in Chapter 19 consider the possible consequences for national and international law of the changing relationships between governments, companies and the NGOs in addressing the transboundary sustainability issues. They posit that the limitations of national and international law might encourage active relationships between companies and NGOs. This may result in governments accepting multi-stakeholder concerns, companies recognising the need for government regulation on ecological behaviour as well as the dealing with NGOs, and NGOs taking over new functions that were previously performed by large bureaucratic governmental organisations. More recently, however, NGOs are involved in dialogues with governments and there have been fewer confrontations with governments. This may have also helped to bring forward the issue of stakeholder dialogue and corporate social responsibility (CSR) high on the agenda of the multinational companies. Globalisation has also had some effect on the limiting of the governments to control events in their own territory as CSR issues spread over a number of jurisdictions. Referring to Browne (2001) and Hey (2003), the authors conclude that the current international legal system is not well equipped to translate the emerging social relationships.

Michael, in Chapter 20, explains some of the new roles that would have to be adopted by multinational companies in this dynamic global political and economic environment.

Here an interesting issue to observe and research are the impacts of the Aarhus Convention on state, corporate and civil-society relations. The Aarhus Convention is a UN convention and its official title, 'Convention on Access to Information, Public Participation in Decision-making and Access to Justice in Environmental Matters', indicates its salience and significance for relations between state, corporate and civil-society actors. Indeed, much of the preamble of the convention fits well with much of the network and stakeholder-partnership approach articulated in various chapters of this volume. The preamble of the convention states that:

> The Aarhus Convention is a new kind of environmental agreement. It links environmental rights and human rights. It acknowledges that we owe an obligation to future generations. It establishes that sustainable development can be achieved only through the involvement of all stakeholders. It links government accountability and environmental protection. It focuses on interactions between the public and public authorities in a democratic context and it is forging a new process for public participation in the negotiation and implementation of international agreements. The subject of the Aarhus Convention goes to the heart of the relationship between people and governments. The Convention is not only an environmental agreement, it is also a Convention about government accountability, transparency and responsiveness (United Nations Economic Commission for Europe 1998).

While primarily aimed at enhancing and empowering civil-society interests *vis-à-vis* state interests in environmental matters, it is clear that such 'enabling' politico-legal frameworks do provide opportunities for new models of partnerships, alliances and organisational linkages and networks for corporate–civil society relations.[2]

Carter (2001) points to the central critical policy aim of transforming or eroding the 'traditional' environmental policy paradigm that emerged in the 1970s. This traditional approach is reactive, piecemeal, tactical, with a preference for 'end-of-pipe' solutions, and judges environmental issues on a case-by-case basis (UK policy style being perhaps the classical example of this), and is also characterised by viewing and maintaining the environment as a discrete policy area—as seen in the setting-up of separate environmental ministries across Europe in the 1970s. Carter points out that the reason for this environmental policy logic is related to the structural power of dominant producer groups (business and farmers mainly) and the state's dependence on and openness to the influence of these groups. He suggests that the alternative environmental policy paradigms offered by greens need to 'connect' with and be attractive to or necessary for policy (state and corporate) elites. Accordingly, for Carter, paradigm change is also dependent on a process of social learning by government and business policy elites (and wider society). The success of the alternative paradigms of sustainable development and ecological modernisation will depend on their capacity to win the hearts and minds of policy elites and to persuade them that their interests are compatible with a sustainable society (2001: 192).

A key aspect of the claim made for the adoption of an explicitly 'ecological modernisation' strategy for sustainable development concerns the role of the state in terms of its 'enabling', co-ordinating and supporting role, in terms of encouraging technological innovation and greater economic and ecologically efficient use of resources and energy. This shift from a 'providing' or 'welfare' state to an 'enabling' state is of course consistent with arguments about the shift in state policy away from 'government' to 'governance' and the 'rolling back' of the state such that in economy, environment and social policy areas, the modern state 'steers rather than rows'.

In the case of ecological modernisation, the argument is that the state, through subsidies and research and development provides assistance for renewable energy, or investment in fuel cell technology, to forms of environmental regulation, setting emissions standards, environmental taxes and other regulatory mechanisms: 'Regulation can be used to drive the process of industrial innovation with environmental and economic gains realised as a result' (Murphy 2001). Indeed, much of the 'modernisation' aspect of ecological modernisation rests on the central emphasis on innovation, both technologically as well on production processes and management and distribution systems.[3] Smart production systems, 'doing more with less', applying novel scientific breakthroughs (for example, in renewable energy, biotechnology and information and communication technology, such as nanotechnology) and developing and utilising 'clean' technologies, are all hallmarks of the modern, dynamic, forward-looking, solu-

---

2   It is interesting to note that some of the most interesting examples of new collaborative corporate–state–civil society action are in the environmental and sustainable development area. As well as the Aarhus Convention at the supra-state level, there is also the sub-state example of Local Agenda 21 sustainable development plans which have been developed in partnership between local government and local stakeholders (business, voluntary groups, churches, NGOs, etc.).

3   'Innovation is central to ecological modernisation of production because it is through innovation and change that environmental concerns can begin to be integrated into production' (Murphy 2001: 9).

tions-focused character of ecological modernisation. While the state 'enables' and supports innovation, it is left to the private sector to develop, test and market these new ecologically efficient innovations and production methods.

Meyer in Chapter 2 argues that multi-actor policy networks include public authorities (government, political parties) as well as private actors (commercial organisations, non-profit organisations, interest groups). Meyer points out that the collective ability of corporate actors to produce common goods is simultaneously restrained and challenged by egoistic behaviour and measures. He indicates that networks are primarily structural modes to solve these co-ordination problems. The modes, in turn, have four defining characteristics: trust in the reliability of each member to act in a co-operative way; durability and continuous interaction between same actors; strategic dependency to avoid egoistic behaviour; and a degree of institutionalisation necessary to establish rules to stabilise the bargaining process.

Of course what is less clear in these arrangements is the role and voice of civil society in this state–corporate partnership, but civil-society involvement is not ruled out in ecological modernisation (Barry 2003), and increasingly the involvement and participation of various stakeholders and interest groups in economic and policy decision-making is both increasingly legally required and desirable in terms of corporate-business 'best practice'. However, having a voice or participating in stakeholder processes does not mean that one's voice is heard or that one's participation makes a difference in terms of the eventual decision or outcome. If corporate social responsibility and the emerging 'partnership' and 'network' models of relations between state, market and civil-society interests and groups (discussed in this volume) is to have real meaning, legitimacy and longevity, a greater sense of rough equality needs to be built into and recognised by all participants. In Chapter 9 Dempsey, for example, points out that governments need to ensure that corporations who are acting in line with voluntary and mandatory requirements relating to corporate governance and social responsibility issues are not penalised by prescriptive regulations primarily aimed at those with poor records on accountability and ethical behaviour. In turn governments must also act in a more socially responsible manner towards accountability and disclosure standards. Referring to the British government's 'Conversation with the People' initiative (2003), Dempsey argues that these initiatives disproportionately enable the stakeholders to set the agenda and go much further than merely inviting public comment on policy decisions.

From the perspective of civil society, 'voice' without equality will quickly lead to accusations of tokenism, and may undermine trust and partnership. Thus 'voice' without equality can lead to 'exit' and the undermining of participants' commitment and loyalty to the arrangement (Hirschmann 1970). The challenge these new models and networks of state, market and civil society face is to recognise that equality must now be built into their preconditions alongside participation.

References

Barry, J. (2003) 'Ecological Modernisation', in J. Proops and E. Page (eds.), *Environmental Thought* (Cheltenham, UK: Edward Elgar).

—— and R. Eckersley (eds.) (2005) *The State and the Global Ecological Crisis* (Cambridge, MA: MIT Press).

Browne, J. (2001) Governance and Responsibility. The Relationship between Companies and NGOs: A Progress Report, Judge Institute, 29 March 2001, www.ragm.com/hottopics/2001/032901judge_institute.pdf, January 2004.

Carter, N. (2001) *The Politics of the Environment: Ideas, Activism, Policy* (Cambridge, UK: Cambridge University Press).

Clark, W., and I. Demirag (2002) 'Enron: The Failure of Corporate Governance', *Journal of Corporate Citizenship* 8 (Winter 2002): 105-22.

Demirag, I. (1995) 'Social Order of the Accounting Profession in Turkey: The State, the Market and the Community', in C. Balim, E. Kalaycioglu, C. Karatas, G. Winrow and F. Yasamee (eds.), *Turkey: Political, Social and Economic Challenges in the 1990s* (Leiden, Netherlands: Brill): 256-75.

—— (1998) *Corporate Governance, Accountability and Pressures to Perform: An International Study* (Studies in Managerial and Financial Accounting, 8; Greenwich, CT: JAI Press).

—— and J. Solomon (2003) 'Developments in International Corporate Governance and the Impact of Recent Events', *Corporate Governance: An International Review* 11.1: 1-7.

——, S. Sudarsanam and M. Wright (2000) 'Corporate Governance: Overview and Research Design', *British Accounting Review* 32 (December 2000): 341-54.

——, M. Dubnick and I. Khadaroo (2004) 'Exploring the Relationship between Accountability and Performance in the UK's Private Finance Initiative (PFI)', paper presented at the *Corporate Governance Conference*, 20–21 September, Institute of Governance, Public Policy and Social Research, Queen's University Belfast.

Doherty, B. (2002) *Ideas and Actions in the Green Movement* (London: Routledge).

Dryzek, J.S., D. Downes, C. Hunold and D. Schlosberg (2003) *Green States and Social Movements: Environmentalism in the US, Britain, Germany and Norway* (Oxford, UK: Oxford University Press).

Hey, E. (2003) *Teaching International Law* (The Hague: Kluwer Law International).

Hirschmann, A.O. (1970) *Exit, Voice and Loyalty: Responses to Decline in Firms, Organisations and States* (Cambridge, MA: Harvard University Press).

Jacobs, M. (1999) 'Sustainable Development as a Contested Concept', in A. Dobson (ed.), *Fairness and Futurity: Essays on Environmental Sustainability and Social Justice* (Oxford, UK: Oxford University Press), 21-45.

Korten, D. (2000) *The Post-Corporate World: Life after Capitalism* (San Francisco: Kumarian Press).

McIntosh, M, D. Leipziger, K. Jones and G. Coleman (1998) *Corporate Citizenship: Successful Strategies for Responsible Companies* (London: Financial Times Professional).

Monbiot, G. (2003) *The Age of Consent: A Manifesto for a New World Order* (London: Flamingo).

Murphy, J. (2001) *Ecological Modernisation: The Environment and the Transformation of Society* (Research Paper No. 20; Oxford, UK: Oxford Centre for Environment, Ethics and Society).

Porritt, J. (2000) 'Does Working with Business Compromise the Environmentalist?', *The Ecologist* 169 (22 August 2000).

Schmitter, P., and W. Streeck (1985) 'Community, Market, State and Associations?', in W. Streeck and P. Schmitter (eds.), *Private Interest Government* (London: Sage).

United Nations Economic Commission on Europe (1998) 'The Aarhus Convention on Access to Information, Public Participation in Decision-making and Access to Justice in Environmental Matters', www.unece.org/env/pp, 23 June 2004.

Abbreviations

3R	reduce, re-use and recycle
ABB	Asea Brown Boveri
ACCA	Association of Chartered Certified Accountants (UK)
ALI	American Law Institute
ARET	Accelerated Reduction/Elimination of Toxics
ASB	Accounting Standards Board (UK)
ATA	Air Transport Association
BA	British Airways
BOOT	build, own, operate and transfer
BOT	build, operate and transfer
CAA	Civil Aviation Authority
CalPERS	California Public Employees' Retirement System
CAS	complex adaptive system
CCAMLR	Commission for the Conservation of Antarctic Marine Living Resources
CD	compact disc
CEO	chief executive officer
CERES	Coalition for Environmentally Responsible Economies
CET	Centre for Environmental Technology (FIRJAN)
CFC	chlorofluorocarbon
CFO	chief financial officer
CMA	Chemical Manufacturers Association
CoE	Council of the European Union
CONANP	Comisión Nacional de Áreas Naturales Protegidas (National Commission of Natural Protected Areas, Mexico)
CPI	corruption perception index (TI)
CPUC	California Public Utilities Commission
CSC	Corporate Steering Committee (Carris Companies)
CSR	corporate social responsibility
DBFO	design, build, finance and operate
DETR	Department of the Environment, Transport and the Regions (UK)
DSM	demand-side management
EBM	Ecosystem-Based Management
EBRD	European Bank for Reconstruction and Development
EEP	Environmental Exchange Program (FIRJAN)
EIDHR	European Initiative for Democracy and Human Rights
EMS	environmental management system
EOB	Electricity Oversight Board
EPA	Environmental Protection Agency

ESOP	Employee Stock Ownership Plan
ESOP	employee stock ownership plan
EU	European Union
EVA	environmental value added
FAA	Federal Aviation Administration (us)
FEEMA	Fundação Estadual de Engenharia do Meio Ambiente (State Environmental Agency of Rio de Janeiro State)
FERC	Federal Energy Regulatory Commission (us)
FIRJAN	Federação das Indústrias do Estado do Rio de Janeiro (Federation of Industries of Rio de Janeiro State)
FNV	Federatie Nederlandse Vakbeweging (Dutch labour union)
FRS	Financial Reporting Standard (ASB)
FSC	Forest Stewardship Council
FT	*Financial Times*
FTSE	*Financial Times* Stock Exchange
GAAP	generally accepted accounting principles
GAP	Global Accountability Project (One World Trust)
GDP	gross domestic product
GRI	Global Reporting Initiative
HIV	human immunodeficiency virus
HR	human resources
HRIA	human rights impact assessment
HSE	health, safety and environment
ICR	international corporate responsibility
IfB	Initiative für Beschäftigung (Initiative for Employment, Germany)
IFOK	Institut für Organisationskommunikation (Institute for Organisational Communication, Germany)
IGO	intergovernmental organisation
ILO	International Labour Organisation
IMF	International Monetary Fund
INDEM	Information for Democracy (Russia)
INGO	international NGO
IOU	investor-owned utility
ISO	International Organisation for Standardisation
ISO	Independent System Operator
IT	information technology
ITLOS	International Tribunal for the Law of the Sea
ITN	invitation to negotiate
ITTO	International Tropical Timber Organisation
IUCN	The World Conservation Union (formerly the International Union for the Conservation of Nature)
LTP	*Long Term Plan* (Carris Companies)
LTPSC	*Long Term Plan* Steering Committee (Carris Companies)
MCP	multi-stakeholder collaborative process
MCU	Media Communications Unit (UK)
MLB	Major League Baseball (us)
MNC	multinational corporation
MNE	multinational enterprise

MORI	Market Opinion Research International
MSC	Marine Stewardship Council
MVA	market value added
MW	megawatt
NAFTA	North American Free Trade Agreement
NAO	National Audit Office (UK)
NATS	National Air Traffic Service (UK)
NCEO	National Center for Employee Ownership (US)
NFL	National Football League (US)
NGO	non-governmental organisation
NHO	Næringslivets Hovedorganisasjon (Confederation of Norwegian Business and Industry)
NHS	National Health Service (UK)
NIF	National Infrastructure Forum (UK)
NPM	New Public Management
NYSE	New York Stock Exchange
OA	Ownership Associates
OBC	outline business case
OECD	Organisation for Economic Co-operation and Development
OPEC	Organisation of Petroleum Exporting Countries
OSCE	Organisation for Security and Co-operation in Europe
OSHA	Occupational Safety and Health Administration (US)
P/E	price/earnings
PA	Protected Area
PC	Parks Canada Agency
PELC	Political and Economic Link
PFI	Private Finance Initiative
PIT	public interest test
PPP	public–private partnership
PR	public relations
PROFEPA	Procuraduría Federal de Protección al Ambiente (Federal Environmental Attorney, Mexico)
PSC	public-sector comparator
PUC	Public Utility Commission
PwC	PricewaterhouseCoopers
PX	power exchange
R&D	research and development
RBV	resource-based view
RNNO	Rada vlády pro nestátní neziskové organizace (Government Council for the Non-Profit Sector, Czech Republic)
RSPP	Union of Industrialists and Entrepreneurs (Russia)
RTO	Regional Transmission Organisation
SEC	Securities and Exchange Commission (US)
SEMARNAT	Secretaría del Medio Ambiente y Recursos Naturales (Ministry of Environment and Natural Resources, Mexico)
SHW	safe hazardous waste
SME	small or medium-sized enterprise
SPC	special-purpose company

SRI	socially responsible investment
SS	Streeck and Schmitter (1985) framework
TCC	The Copenhagen Centre
TI	Transparency International
TNC	transnational corporation
UN	United Nations
UNCLOS	UN Convention on the Law of the Seas
UNEP	United Nations Environment Programme
VFM	value for money
VP	vice president
WAC	Water Advisory Committee (Canada)
WBCSD	World Business Council for Sustainable Development
WCPA	World Commission on Protected Areas
WEM	Waste Exchange Market (FIRJAN)
WTO	World Trade Organisation
WWII	World War II
Y2K	Year 200 (Millennium Bug)

About the contributors

Kristian Snorre Andersen is a student of political science at the Institute for Political Science at Aarhus University (Denmark). He is writing his thesis in co-operation with the Sustainable Production and Consumption Department at the Wuppertal Institute (Germany).

Craig E. Armstrong is a doctoral student in management at the University of Texas at San Antonio. His research interests include inter-organisational relations, entrepreneurship, corporate governance, corporate social and environmental performance, and emergent forms of organising.
carmstrong@utsa.edu

John Barry is Deputy Director, Institute of Governance, Public Policy and Social Research, Queen's University Belfast, Northern Ireland.
j.barry@qub.ac.uk

Kees Bastmeijer has a PhD on the legal protection of Antarctica, from Tilburg University, where he is now an Associate Professor of Environmental Law. Issues that receive his special interest include the role of law in promoting corporate social responsibility. Between 1989 and 1999, Dr Bastmeijer worked for the Dutch environmental ministry.
c.j.bastmeijer@uvt.nl

Stephanie Bertels is a PhD student majoring in strategy and sustainable development and a research associate of the TransCanada International Institute for Resource Industries and Sustainability Studies (TC-IRIS) at the Haskayne School of Business, University of Calgary, Canada. Her dissertation explores the processes needed to build and maintain resilient inter-organisational collaboration. Prior to joining TC-IRIS, Stephanie worked as an environmental engineer and completed a master's degree from Stanford University in petroleum (environmental) engineering and a bachelor's in geological (environmental) engineering from Queen's University, Canada.
stephanie.bertels@haskayne.ucalgary.ca

An independent researcher, **Cecile G. Betit**, PhD, East Wallingford, Vermont, has studied the transition to employee ownership and governance at the Carris Companies since 1996.
cgbetit@vermontel.net

Raimund Bleischwitz, PhD and habilitation in Economics, is Co-director of the Research Group 'Material Flows and Resource Management' at the Wuppertal Institute (Germany). He also holds the 'Toyota Chair for Industry and Sustainability' at the College of Europe in Bruges (Belgium). He held previous positions within the Max Planck Project Group on the Law of Common Goods in Bonn, the Institute for European Environmental Policy and the German Bundestag.
rbleischwitz@coleurop.be

Sergey Bondarenko is Director of the Centre of Applied Research on Intellectual Property and author of the book *Korrumpirovannye Obshchestva* (*Corrupted Societies*), published by Westminster Foundation, 2002. He has written more than 50 sociological contributions on problems of corruption and social aspects of telecommunication networks, including five monographs and textbooks (in Russian).
rcs@jeo.ru

Robin T. Byerly is an Associate Professor of Management at Appalachian State University in Boone, North Carolina, USA. She has published in several academic journals and presented at numerous conferences. Specific research and teaching interests are in the areas of corporate social responsibility and citizenship, business and the environment, ethics in healthcare management and business portfolio strategy.
byerlyrt@appstate.edu

Istemi Demirag is Professor of Accounting at Queen's University Belfast where he acted as the Director of Accounting Research Group from 2000–2004. He has been the Chairman of the British Accounting Association's Special Interest Group on Corporate Governance since 1998 and a member of the British Accounting Association's executive group. His research interests include corporate governance, accountability, short-termism, and value for money in the public sector. He has authored, co-authored and co-edited a number of books including, *Financial Management for International Business* (McGraw-Hill, 1994), *Corporate Governance, Accountability and Pressures to Perform: An International Study* (first published in 1988 by JAI Press, and later by Elsevier). He has been a guest editor and co-editor of a number of major peer-reviewed international journals, including *The Journal of Corporate Citizenship*, *British Accounting Review*, *Corporate Governance: An International Review* and *The European Journal of Finance*.
i.demirag@qub.ac.uk

At the time of writing, **Alison L. Dempsey** BA Hon., LLB, LLM was Director, Programs and Project Development at the Chumir Foundation for Ethics, Calgary, Canada. She has worked in England and Canada with multinational companies seeking to achieve business success while sustaining positive relationships with shareholders, stakeholders and the wider community in increasingly complex domestic and international markets. Alison is now pursuing her PhD in Law focusing on the complex intersection between law, ethics and public policy in the oversight and regulation of business.
ald65@rogers.com

Melvin J. Dubnick is from Rutgers University, Newark, and is visiting professor and senior fellow at the Institute of Governance, Public Policy and Social Research, Queen's University Belfast, Northern Ireland.
dubnickmj@yahoo.com

Angeles Mendoza Durán, PhD Candidate at the Faculty of Environmental Design, University of Calgary, Canada, received her BSc in Biology and MsSc in Ecology and Environmental Sciences (1997) from the Universidad Nacional Autónoma de Mexico (UNAM). She worked at UNAM as research assistant at the Laboratory of Ecology and Conservation of Wildlife (Institute of Ecology) and professor of Hydrology and Conservation of Natural Resources (Geography).
angeles@angelesmendoza.com

Izabela Fratczak is currently working on her master's thesis on Corporate Social Responsibility. She is completing a double degree from the Technical University of Lodz (Poland) as well as at the Turku Polytechnic (Finland). During summer 2003 she worked in DNV Research, on the project 'CSR and Global Variations'.
izabelafratczak@o2.pl

Corinne Gendron is a professor in the Department of Organisation and Human Resource Management, and holds the Chair of Social Responsibility and Sustainable Development in the School of Management Sciences at UQÀM (Université du Québec à Montréal). She teaches in the fields of corporate social responsibility, environmental management and sustainable development. Currently she is directing several research projects on emerging socioeconomic movements around fair trade and new modes of regulation in an era of globalisation. Gendron has published several works, including *La gestion environnementale et ISO 14001*, with Presses de l'Université de Montréal.

corinne.gendron@uqam.ca

Pia Rudolfsson Goyer is a lawyer presently working on her doctoral thesis on business and human rights at the University of Oslo, Centre for Human Rights. Her work experience is primarily from the Ministry of Foreign Affairs of Sweden. She has been involved in several projects concerning corporations and human rights at the Centre since she became employed there in 1997.

p.e.v.r.goyer@nchr.uio.no

Political scientist by training, **Constanze J. Helmchen** holds a graduate degree from the Government Department of the London School of Economics and Political Science. She has worked in the fields of conflict management, commercial consulting and development co-operation for consulting firms, independent think-tanks and governmental agencies for the last five years. In 2002, she joined IFOK's Global Governance, Sustainability and Corporate Responsibility Unit as Project Manager, with special focus on international projects.

c_helmchen@yahoo.com

M. Iqbal Khadaroo is a lecturer at the School of Management and Economics, Queen's University Belfast, Northern Ireland.

i.khadaroo@qub.ac.uk

Michael Latsch holds degrees in Economics and Business Administration and was formerly teaching assistant at the 'Toyota Chair for Industry and Sustainability' at the College of Europe in Bruges (Belgium). He also specialises in environmental economics and the economic analysis of sustainable development. He is currently in D6 Industry of the European Commission.

michael.latsch@cec.eu.int

Having studied Theology at Göttingen, Oxford and Heidelberg, **Arved Lüth** began his consulting career in 1995. Since then he has worked with IFOK, where he is head of the Global Governance, Sustainability and Corporate Responsibility Unit, and has advised many German blue-chip companies as well as governments, business associations and local authorities in sustainability and CSR issues.

arved.lueth@ifok.de

Dr **Wolfgang Meyer** is a sociologist, senior scientist and project co-ordinator of 'Labour Market and Environmental Evaluation' department at the Centre for Evaluation (CEval), Saarland University. He is also the executive editor of *Zeitschrift für Evaluation* (ZfEv) and chair of the working group 'Evaluation of Environmental Policy' for the German Evaluation Society (DeGEval). His areas of research include: environmental sociology, evaluation methods and labour market research.

w.meyer@mx.uni-saarland.de

Bryane Michael is currently conducting research and teaching Economics and Management at Oxford. He worked at the World Bank and the OECD. His research focuses on government reform, organisational strategy, and institutional design, methods of project management in the post-industrial era, NGO management and macroeconomics and microeconomics.

bryane.michael@linacre.oxford.ac.uk

Eli Bleie Munkelien has worked in DNV Research on CSR since 2001. She is involved in and has been active in initiating an EU project on Sustainability in the oil and gas sector, as well as a new project in co-operation with ETI in Norway looking at the use of reporting as a driver for implementing CSR strategies.

Eli.Bleie.Munkelien@dnv.com

Justin O'Brien is a Senior Research Fellow at the Institute of Governance, Public Policy and Social Research at Queen's University, Belfast. His research interests focus on the political determinants of corporate governance design, with particular reference to the American financial markets. Dr O'Brien was the Academic Director of 'Governing the Corporation', a major international colloquium held at the Institute of Governance in September 2004. A former investigative journalist and television executive, he now runs the corporate governance programme at the Institute.

j.obrien@qub.ac.uk

José Antônio Puppim de Oliveira is associate professor at the Brazilian School of Public and Business Administration (EBAPE), Getulio Vargas Foundation (FGV), Rio de Janeiro, Brazil. He has a PhD in Planning from the Massachusetts Institute of Technology (MIT, USA), an MS in Regional and Environmental Planning from the University of Hokkaido, Japan, and a BS in Electronic Systems Engineering from the Instituto Tecnológico de Aeronáutica (ITA) in Brazil. He has had professional and academic experience in Brazil, Argentina, Ecuador, the US, Spain, Angola and Japan. He has published in the areas of planning; sustainable development; corporate social responsibility; environmental management and policy, both in his native Brazil and worldwide.

puppim@fgv.br

Kevin Quigley is a PhD candidate at the Institute of Governance, Public Policy and Social Research, an inter-disciplinary research centre at Queen's University Belfast.

k.quigley@qub.ac.uk.

Kimberly Samaha has worked in leadership roles within the deregulating US energy market for the past 15 years. A majority of her work was within the highly volatile climate of the California energy market. Kimberly currently lives in Paris, France, where she heads an organisational consulting company, AMP, serving multinationals in the energy sector. She is also concurrently working on a PhD in human and organisational development at Fielding University in Santa Barbara, California.

kimberlysamaha@yahoo.com

Stefan Schäfers studies Economics at the Catholic University of Eichstätt and the École Supérieure de Commerce in Nice with a focus on International Business Administration and has a PhD in International Business Ethics. He has several years' experience working as an independent consultant with both companies and political organisations. In 2003 he joined IFOK as a consultant.

schaefers@ifok.de

Diana Schmidt studied Geography and Anthropology in Cologne, Germany, and Vancouver, Canada (1995–2002). She worked as a junior research associate at the Max Planck Institute for the Study of Societies in Cologne (2000–2002) and has been conducting PhD research on anti-corruption since 2002, including extensive field research in various parts of Russia.

d.schmidt@qub.ac.uk

Željko Šević is the Professor of Accounting, Finance and Public Policy in the University of Greenwich Business School, where he also serves as the Director of Research, Outreach and European Affairs. Professor Šević's current research interests are in the public (sector) reform in Japan and Vietnam (ongoing projects), and accounting reform in the public sector with the particular emphasis on the use of management accounting in public-sector restructuring and the design of effective and efficient financial/fiscal information systems.

Z.Sevic@gre.ac.uk

Dixon Thompson is Professor of Environmental Science in the Faculty of Environmental Design and Adjunct Professor in the Haskayne School of Business. He teaches courses at the graduate level in environmental management, sustainable development, water management and product and technology assessment. He recently published *Tools for Environmental Management: A Practical Introduction and Guide* with New Society Publishers.

dixont@telus.net

Marie-France Turcotte is a professor at the University of Quebec at Montreal (UQÀM)'s Business School, and is the main researcher at the Chair on Social Responsibility and Sustainable Development (CSRDD, www.ceh.uqwam.ca). She is undertaking research on topics such as multi-stakeholder collaborations, corporate social responsibility, sustainable development, social and ethical investment, fair trade, social and environmental certification schemes, and socioeconomic movements.

turcotte.marie-france@uqam.ca

Jonathan Verschuuren is a full professor of International and European Environmental Law at the Centre for Legislative Studies, Tilburg University (the Netherlands). His research is mainly aimed at the role environmental legislation has in society. Professor Verschuuren has published several books and more than 200 articles in (international) law journals, contributions to edited works and conference papers.

j.m.verschuuren@uvt.nl

Harrie Vredenburg is Professor and Suncor Energy Chair in Competitive Strategy and Sustainable Development and Director of the TransCanada International Institute for Resource Industries and Sustainability Studies (TC-IRIS). He is Academic Chair for the MSc programme in sustainable energy development for Latin America and the Caribbean, at the Haskayne School of Business, University of Calgary, Canada.

harrie.vredenburg@haskayne.ucalgary.ca

Index